TOWARD A
MORE PERFECT
PSYCHOLOGY

TOWARD A MORE PERFECT PSYCHOLOGY

Improving Trust, Accuracy, and Transparency in Research

Edited by

Matthew C. Makel and **Jonathan A. Plucker**

AMERICAN PSYCHOLOGICAL ASSOCIATION
WASHINGTON, DC

Published by
American Psychological Association
750 First Street, NE
Washington, DC 20002
www.apa.org

To order
APA Order Department
P.O. Box 92984
Washington, DC 20090-2984
Tel: (800) 374-2721; Direct: (202) 336-5510
Fax: (202) 336-5502; TDD/TTY: (202) 336-6123
Online: www.apa.org/pubs/books
E-mail: order@apa.org

In the U.K., Europe, Africa, and the Middle East, copies may be ordered from
American Psychological Association
3 Henrietta Street
Covent Garden, London
WC2E 8LU England

Typeset in Goudy by Circle Graphics, Inc., Columbia, MD

Printer: Edwards Brothers, Inc., Lillington, NC
Cover Designer: Beth Schlenoff Design, Bethesda, MD

The opinions and statements published are the responsibility of the authors, and such opinions and statements do not necessarily represent the policies of the American Psychological Association.

Library of Congress Cataloging-in-Publication Data

Names: Makel, Matthew C., editor. | Plucker, Jonathan A., 1969- editor.
Title: Toward a more perfect psychology : improving trust, accuracy, and
  transparency in research / edited by Matthew C. Makel and Jonathan Plucker.
Description: First Edition. | Washington, DC : American Psychological
  Association, [2017] | Includes bibliographical references and index.
Identifiers: LCCN 2016048756 | ISBN 9781433827549 | ISBN 1433827549
Subjects: LCSH: Psychology—Research. | Psychology—Research—Methodology.
Classification: LCC BF76.5 .T69 2017 | DDC 150.72—dc23 LC record available at https://
  lccn.loc.gov/2016048756

British Library Cataloguing-in-Publication Data
A CIP record is available from the British Library.

Printed in the United States of America
First Edition

http://dx.doi.org/10.1037/0000033-000

This is for my parents, Linda and Martin,
who taught me right from wrong.
—*Matthew C. Makel*

For my uncles, Jim, Greg, and Tim, who were willing role models
and helped me learn that the only job worth doing
is a job well done.
—*Jonathan A. Plucker*

CONTENTS

CONTRIBUTORS

Megan J. Austin, MA, University of Notre Dame, South Bend, IN
Mark Berends, PhD, University of Notre Dame, South Bend, IN
Brian M. D'Onofrio, PhD, Indiana University, Bloomington
Samuel H. Field, PhD, FHI 360, Durham, NC
Howard Gardner, PhD, Harvard University, Cambridge, MA
Isabel Gauthier, PhD, Vanderbilt University, Nashville, TN
Thomas L. Good, PhD, University of Arizona, Tucson
William P. Hetrick, PhD, Indiana University, Bloomington
Alyson L. Lavigne, PhD, Roosevelt University, Chicago, IL
Alison Ledgerwood, PhD, University of California, Davis
Matthew C. Makel, PhD, Duke University, Durham, NC
Matthew T. McBee, PhD, East Tennessee State University, Johnson City
Terri D. Pigott, PhD, Loyola University Chicago, Chicago, IL
Jonathan A. Plucker, PhD, Johns Hopkins University, Baltimore, MD
Joshua R. Polanin, PhD, Development Services Group, Inc., Bethesda, MD
Jennifer J. Richler, PhD, Vanderbilt University, Nashville, TN
Stefan Schmidt, PhD, Medical Center, University of Freiburg,
      Freiburg, Germany
Amy Lynne Shelton, PhD, Johns Hopkins University, Baltimore, MD

Paul J. Silvia, PhD, University of North Carolina at Greensboro, Greensboro
Benjamin K. Smith, PhD, University of Mary Washington, Fredericksburg, VA
Jeffrey K. Smith, PhD, University of Otago, Otago, Dunedin, New Zealand
Lisa F. Smith, EdD, University of Otago, Otago, Dunedin, New Zealand
Courtney K. Soderberg, PhD, Center for Open Science, Charlottesville, VA
Jehan Sparks, PhD, University of California, Davis
Jeffrey C. Valentine, PhD, University of Louisville, Louisville, KY
Oshin Vartanian, PhD, University of Toronto, Toronto, Ontario, Canada
Richard J. Viken, PhD, Indiana University, Bloomington
Jelte M. Wicherts, PhD, University of Tilburg, Tilburg, the Netherlands
Ryan T. Williams, PhD, American Institutes for Research, Chicago, IL

TOWARD A
MORE PERFECT
PSYCHOLOGY

INTRODUCTION:
WHY IS THIS BOOK NECESSARY?

MATTHEW C. MAKEL AND JONATHAN A. PLUCKER

The preamble to the U.S. Constitution contains the phrase "in Order to form a more perfect Union." This sentiment acknowledges that perfection could likely not be obtained (and perhaps not even wholly understood). We approach this book from much the same mind-set; we do not know what a perfect psychological science looks like, but we believe that scholars should and can strive to reach this goal. Our path to this book started in 2007, when one of us (Jonathan A. Plucker) dropped a page from a magazine on the other's desk and said, "We need to think about stuff like this." The page was a summary of some new findings showing that, in marketing research, studies were rarely replicated and, when they were, the replicating studies often failed to confirm the original findings (Evanschitzky, Baumgarth, Hubbard, & Armstrong, 2007). And with that quick drop-in, a whole new world was opened to us.

http://dx.doi.org/10.1037/0000033-001
Toward a More Perfect Psychology: Improving Trust, Accuracy, and Transparency in Research, M. C. Makel and J. A. Plucker (Editors)

The idea of needing to assess and improve the quality (not to mention the public image) of research was certainly not new to us. At the time, the federal Institute of Education Sciences had recently been created in response to perceptions of low research quality in education research. We initially focused our attention on gifted education and talent development research because it often relies on either general education findings or research conducted with small (and often idiosyncratic) samples of gifted students. As such, professionals in the field are often unsure whether and when research findings found in one context for one group of students can be generalized to other contexts and other groups of students. Our concerns fell quite nicely into two categories: issues pertaining to (a) direct versus (b) conceptual replications (see Schmidt, 2009, and Chapter 14, this volume).

The more we dug, the more we found that many others were also worried about issues of replicability and generalizability. One article that garnered perhaps the most attention had the provocative title "Why Most Published Research Findings Are False" (Ioannidis, 2005). This spurred us on, and we eventually learned that in attempts to replicate findings in medical research, researchers succeeded in replicating only six of 53 (11%) highly cited cancer trial studies (Begley & Ellis, 2012).

With such damaging findings coming from fields typically associated with higher levels of methodological rigor than the social sciences, our focus soon moved to psychology, and we began our first large-scale examination of replication in the social sciences, specifically within psychological research (Makel, Plucker, & Hegarty, 2012). Bem (2011)[1] published a controversial study on the existence of *psi* (e.g., telepathy) that served as a focal point for much ensuing conversation. However, the topic was only the tip of the controversy; its methods also spurred strong and immediate negative reaction (see, e.g., Sutton, 2012; Wagenmakers, Wetzels, Borsboom, & van der Maas, 2011). Bem's provocative article certainly did not invent concerns about the psychology research process; indeed, they had been around for decades (e.g., Bakan, 1966; Cohen, 1994; Lykken, 1968; Rosenthal, 1966, 1979). However, we believe that the publicity the article received helped blaze the path for many of the new movements in psychology and the social sciences.

---

[1]In the interest of full disclosure, we should share that one of us (Matthew C. Makel) took a class from Bem while earning a master's degree. Bem was a wonderful teacher. In his class and his writing, Bem told the story of how he was brought into psi research as an outsider who could help the field with its methodological rigor. He was impressed with their methods and helped publish findings in a top psychology journal (Bem & Honorton, 1994, but cf. Hyman, 1994) because he knew how to navigate the publication process. In perhaps an unintentional irony, taking advantage of this expertise in how the publication system worked helped catalyze the current revolution in assessing research quality.

Nothing is new under the sun (e.g., Makel & Plucker, 2014). In 1984, Furchtgott made the following lament:

> It would seem that after more than 30 years the [American Psychological Association] Publication Committee or an ad hoc committee should examine the publication policy pertaining to replications. Not only will this have an impact on investigations that are undertaken, but it will reduce the space devoted to the repetitious pleas to replicate experiments. (p. 1316)

In that spirit, with this book we hope to take a few steps backward (and perhaps one or two to the side) so that the field may accelerate its forward momentum, not just on replication but also on other relevant issues. At its foundational level, the heart of science is that its methods allow for others to believe its results. This foundation is served by trust, accuracy, and transparency. It is only with all three that science succeeds. Without one, the others are weakened.

We also seek to introduce readers to the many proposals that are being developed to help strengthen the field's research. It is our hope that this book will help researchers not just as they develop their own research ideas, question, methods, and analyses but also as they evaluate and respond to the research of others.

ORGANIZATION OF THE BOOK

To develop and discuss these concepts (and a great deal more) in more detail, we have organized this book into five sections to help highlight the different perspectives researchers take throughout the research process as well as their careers.

Part I has the central theme of asking what individual researchers can do to increase research quality while focusing on different steps of the research process. Chapter 1, by Oshin Vartanian, discusses three factors that increase the probability that scientists will pursue important phenomena and processes: the researcher's (a) choice of theory, (b) pursuit of cumulative science, and (c) explicit focus on problem finding. These processes often occur (although not often enough) before data collection, at the idea generation stage. Chapter 2, by Alison Ledgerwood, Courtney K. Soderberg, and Jehan Sparks, covers how to design a study to maximize its informational value. In Chapter 3, Matthew T. McBee and Samuel H. Field focus on methodological issues pertaining to confirmatory study design and data analysis techniques. The goal is to make sure that researchers remain focused on results that matter.

The remaining chapters in Part I broaden the scope to discuss how practices conducted for individual studies influence the larger research community. Chapter 4, by Terri D. Pigott, Ryan T. Williams, and Jeffrey C. Valentine, examines selective outcome reporting. Research studies are not portfolios where researchers can manipulate post hoc what they asked, what they analyzed, and what they found. As the chapter authors discuss, when such manipulation happens researchers paint an inaccurate portrait of what has been evaluated, what works, and what should be done. Alyson L. Lavigne and Thomas L. Good conclude Part I with Chapter 5, in which they explain how citations serve as a researcher's intellectual footprint. They focus in particular on who is cited, why, and what it means to be cited (or not).

Whereas Part I focuses on different aspects of the research process, Part II provides perspectives on different roles researchers take as part of the research process (i.e., peer reviewers, disseminators of research to the public, and disseminators of research to other researchers). In their careers, researchers often have responsibilities beyond merely conducting research, including connecting research to practice, reviewing the research of others, and disseminating research. Part II begins with Chapter 6, by Jennifer L. Richler and Isabel Gauthier. Drawing on their considerable editorial experience, these authors provide advice to authors, peer reviewers, and editors about all stages of the paper submission process. In Chapter 7, Howard Gardner discusses how one should communicate research to the public in ways outside of typical academic publishing. Chapter 8, by Jonathan A. Plucker and Paul J. Silvia, addresses how to disseminate one's research in ways that maximize its influence on the field. Together, the chapters in Part II help readers understand what can be done with academic research and contextualize how others will apply, consume, and share research results.

The chapters in Part III provide some views from the field regarding research quality. The authors in this section offer examples of how different subfields can have unique strengths and struggles with producing rigorous research results. Chapter 9, by Mark Berends and Megan J. Austin, discusses forming positive relationships with practitioners to improve research quality while enhancing the likelihood that research findings will be implemented by practitioners. Amy Lynne Shelton, author of Chapter 10, addresses research in cognitive neuroscience. She highlights the importance of maintaining methodological rigor while harnessing technological sophistication to answer relevant questions. In Chapter 11, Brian M. D'Onofrio, Richard J. Viken, and William P. Hetrick focus on the importance of grounding clinical psychology in scientific epistemology, taking advantage of the methods and knowledge in related fields and integrating research with clinical practice in order to make both as reproducible as possible. Finally, Chapter 12, which we coauthored, introduces readers to some potential ethical pitfalls they may experience in careers as professional researchers.

Part IV of the book focuses on three central components of reproducibility of research: (a) open data, (b) replication, and (c) meta-analysis. In Chapter 13, Jelte M. Wicherts addresses data reanalysis and open data, two emerging practices that help provide a form of "sunshine law" that allows others to verify specific results, thus increasing the accuracy and trust of social science results. Another method of accomplishing this that has garnered growing attention is replication, covered in Chapter 14 by Stefan Schmidt. Purposefully repeating the same methods of a previous researchers or systematically modifying small components of previous research have long been desired but only recently have begun to be perceived more positively within psychology research community. Chapter 15, by Ryan T. Williams, Joshua R. Polanin, and Terri D. Pigott, focuses on meta-analysis and reproducibility. Systematic reviews and meta-analyses have long served as a ballast of the field by removing the idiosyncratic blips that are often associated with individual studies. Together, the chapters of Part IV cover field-wide practices whose prevalence can help make psychology a stronger, more rigorous science.

A book about research quality and reproducibility certainly should not rely on a single perspective of "what it all means." Therefore, the final section, Part V, consists of two synthesis chapters: one by Jeffrey K. Smith, Lisa F. Smith, and Benjamin K. Smith (Chapter 16), and one coauthored by us (Chapter 17). Only with time will we know which trends will evolve into common practice and which will turn out to be fads. However, instead of simply throwing our hands into the air and waiting, each team of authors assesses which of the discussed practices will most help the field produce more accurate, trustworthy, and reproducible results.

In our invitations to the chapter authors we explained that our goal for this book was to help researchers improve the quality of their own work as well as that of colleagues. Our perspective is largely based on our own studies of replication in the social sciences, but we expanded the focus to address research quality in the social sciences in general. We told authors that our broad vision of each chapter would be to introduce the reader to many of these events and issues and to discuss how the field is (and should be) responding. Our priority with this book is to share the evolving ideas of how to create a field that yields trustworthy, reproducible, and accurate research findings to a broad audience of social scientists as well to future researchers so that their training includes new practices of quality research methods, not just the status quo approaches.

The ideas presented in this volume will not perfect science. Solutions to one set of problems can often create new, unintended consequences. With the creation of processes like meta-analysis, multilevel modeling, and regression discontinuity, our statistical and methodological sophistication has grown tremendously in the past 50 years. Also, with the flood of new movements seeking to improve how science is conducted (e.g., open data, preregistration), we expect that researchers 50 years from now will be conducting even better science we are today.

From this perspective, we are cautiously optimistic. As is often recommended in recovery programs, psychology has begun to admit it has a problem, and a great many psychologists have been working diligently to develop ways to minimize, remove, work around, and avoid many of the problems that plague the field. We hope books like this one help accelerate the field's path toward increasing scientific quality and rigor and thus a more perfect psychology.

REFERENCES

Bakan, D. (1966). The test of significance in psychological research. *Psychological Bulletin, 66*, 423–437. http://dx.doi.org/10.1037/h0020412

Begley, C. G., & Ellis, L. M. (2012, March 29). Drug development: Raise standards for preclinical cancer research. *Nature, 483*, 531–533. http://dx.doi.org/10.1038/483531a

Bem, D. J. (2011). Feeling the future: Experimental evidence for anomalous retroactive influences on cognition and affect. *Journal of Personality and Social Psychology, 100*, 407–425. http://dx.doi.org/10.1037/a0021524

Bem, D. J., & Honorton, C. (1994). Does psi exist? Replicable evidence for an anomalous process of information transfer. *Psychological Bulletin, 175*, 4–18.

Cohen, J. (1994). The Earth is round ($p < .05$). *American Psychologist, 49*, 997–1003. http://dx.doi.org/10.1037/0003-066X.49.12.997

Evanschitzky, H., Baumgarth, C., Hubbard, R., & Armstrong, J. S. (2007). Replication research's disturbing trend. *Journal of Business Research, 60*, 411–415. http://dx.doi.org/10.1016/j.jbusres.2006.12.003

Furchtgott, E. (1984). Replicate, again and again. *American Psychologist, 39*, 1315–1316. http://dx.doi.org/10.1037/0003-066X.39.11.1315.b

Hyman, R. (1994). Anomaly or artifact? Comments on Bem and Honorton. *Psychological Bulletin, 115*, 19–24. http://dx.doi.org/10.1037/0033-2909.115.1.19

Ioannidis, J. P. A. (2005). Why most published research findings are false. *PLOS Medicine, 2*(8), e124. http://dx.doi.org/10.1371/journal.pmed.0020124

Lykken, D. T. (1968). Statistical significance in psychological research. *Psychological Bulletin, 70*, 151–159. http://dx.doi.org/10.1037/h0026141

Makel, M. C., & Plucker, J. A. (2014). Facts are more important than novelty: Replication in the education sciences. *Educational Researcher, 43*, 304–316. http://dx.doi.org/10.3102/0013189X14545513

Makel, M. C., Plucker, J. A., & Hegarty, B. (2012). Replications in psychology research: How often do they really occur? *Perspectives on Psychological Science, 7*, 537–542. http://dx.doi.org/10.1177/1745691612460688

Sutton, J. (Ed.). (2012). Replication: Psychology's house of cards? [Special issue]. *The Psychologist, 25*(5).

Rosenthal, R. (1966). *Experimenter effects in behavioral research.* East Norwalk, CT: Appleton-Century-Crofts.

Rosenthal, R. (1979). The file drawer problem and tolerance for null results. *Psychological Bulletin, 86,* 638–641. http://dx.doi.org/10.1037/0033-2909.86.3.638

Schmidt, S. (2009). Shall we really do it again? The powerful concept of replication is neglected in the social sciences. *Review of General Psychology, 13,* 90–100.

Wagenmakers, E. J., Wetzels, R., Borsboom, D., & van der Maas, H. (2011). Why psychologists must change the way they analyze their data: The case of psi: Comment on Bem (2011). *Journal of Personality and Social Psychology, 100,* 426–432. http://dx.doi.org/10.1037/a0022790

I

THE RESEARCH PROCESS

1

THE CONTRIBUTIONS OF THEORY CHOICE, CUMULATIVE SCIENCE, AND PROBLEM FINDING TO SCIENTIFIC INNOVATION AND RESEARCH QUALITY

OSHIN VARTANIAN

KEY POINTS

- Scientific innovation is facilitated to the extent that scholars have access to high-quality theories—defined as theories that are accurate, consistent, broad in scope, simple (i.e., parsimonious), and fruitful of new research. In this sense, theory choice is an important factor for conducting good science.
- Research quality will benefit not only from the evaluation of knowledge but also from an increased understanding of the factors that lead to its discovery.
- *Cumulative science*—defined as science wherein later advances are built on earlier advances—is advantageous to both scientific innovation as well as research quality.
- Choosing good theories can contribute to the emergence of cumulative science.

http://dx.doi.org/10.1037/0000033-002
Toward a More Perfect Psychology: Improving Trust, Accuracy, and Transparency in Research, M. C. Makel and J. A. Plucker (Editors)

- If predictions derived from a theory disagree with experimental data, then it is necessary to discard the theory in search of a better theory.
- Researchers must improve the ways in which they collect, analyze, and interpret data to achieve a proper mechanism for theory falsification in psychology.
- Greater emphasis should be placed on the role of successful problem finding in science because doing so can increase the probability of focusing on phenomena that are sufficiently important to warrant study.
- The literature on the scientific study of creativity contains a wealth of information for promoting successful problem finding strategies.

There has been recent widespread concern in psychology over issues related to research quality (Makel, 2014). This has led to a reexamination of the norms and standards that govern data collection and analysis as well as the procedures in place to establish the veracity of our inferences. In essence, this represents a concern about the evaluation of our discipline's evidential base. Although the present concern about the evaluation of evidence is clearly justified, it has inadvertently overshadowed concerns over what is an equally important issue, namely how choices are made about which phenomena warrant study and the processes that lead to idea generation. In this chapter I make the case that research quality in psychology will benefit to the extent that we reexamine not only how we evaluate the quality of empirical evidence but also how we facilitate innovation within our discipline.

For readers familiar with epistemology, my argument will ring familiar. It touches on a classic distinction between the *context of discovery* versus the *context of justification* in the philosophy of science (see Reichenbach, 1938). Although philosophers of science have distinguished among several variants of this distinction (Hoyningen-Huene, 1987), according to the standard formulation discovery and justification are temporally distinct processes (Mowry, 1985). To be specific, in the beginning there is a discovery, which typically includes the emergence of a novel hypothesis, theory, model, classification, or problem representation (Hoyningen-Huene, 2006). Henceforth follows justification, which involves an evaluation of that which has been discovered. To Karl Popper (1934/1959), the distinction between discovery and justification was crystal clear:

> The questions of justification or validity are of the following kind. Can a statement be justified? And if so, how? Is it testable? Is it logically dependent on certain other statements? Or does it perhaps contradict them?

In order that a statement may be logically examined in this way, it must already have been presented to us. Someone must have formulated it, and submitted it to logical examination. . . . I shall distinguish sharply between the process of conceiving a new idea, and the methods and results of examining it logically. (p. 31)

Over the years, various thinkers have proposed variants of the discovery–justification distinction (Hoyningen-Huene, 1987). For example, some have argued that the process has three parts: In the first part a new idea is generated; in the second part the plausibility of the idea is considered or pursued (e.g., through comparison with alternative ideas); and in the third step the idea is put to critical testing and, if successful, it is accepted. Still others have suggested a four-step process consisting of (a) generation, (b) pursuit, (c) test, and (d) decision (Goldman, 1983; see also Wallas, 1926).

However, aside from noting a strong demarcation between the contexts of discovery and justification, some philosophers have also argued that because of the "irrational" nature of idea generation, the context of discovery by definition falls outside of the purview of logical analysis. Here again, Popper's (1934/1959) verse is clearest:

My view of the matter, for what it is worth, is that there is no such thing as a logical method of having new ideas. . . . My view may be expressed by saying that every discovery contains "an irrational element," or "a creative intuition" . . . In a similar way Einstein speaks of the "search for those highly universal laws . . . from which a picture of the world can be obtained by pure deduction." There is no logical path, he says, "leading to these . . . laws. They can only be reached by intuition, based upon something like an intellectual love (Einfühlung) of the objects of experience." (p. 32)

In other words, they believed that although there can be a logic for evaluating ideas, there can be no such a thing as a logic of scientific discovery (Gillies, 1993; see also Carnap, 1950/1963).

Perhaps the quintessential example of the aforementioned temporal and logical discovery–justification distinction is illustrated by the classic account of the discovery of benzene. As the story goes, after a long but unsuccessful search for devising the structure of the benzene molecule, one evening in 1865 the solution sprang to August Kekulé's mind as he was dozing in front of the fireplace; specifically, he envisioned arrays of atoms dancing in a snakelike fashion. Suddenly, one of the heads seized hold of its tail, forming a circular structure that formed the basis for the hexagonal ring that underlies benzene's molecular structure. It is perhaps not surprising that, when construed this way, it would indeed appear that there is no logic to scientific discovery.

However, despite the "blind" processes that govern idea generation (Campbell, 1960), scientists have nevertheless maintained logical control over the evaluation of those ideas:

> Scientific objectivity is safeguarded by the principle that while hypotheses and theories may be freely invented and *proposed* in science, they can be *accepted* into the body of scientific knowledge only if they pass critical scrutiny, which includes in particular the checking of suitable test implications by careful observation or experiment. (Hempel, 1966, p. 16)

According to this view, we can exert logical quality control in science by means of the manner in which we test and evaluate the products of idea generation (but not idea generation itself).

In the latter half of the 20th century this rigid demarcation between contexts of discovery and justification fell into disfavor among many philosophers of science (see Feigl, 1970). There were many reasons for this reconsideration. First and foremost, the discovery–justification distinction is not unidimensional but instead consists of a set of "intermingled distinctions" (Hoyningen-Huene, 2006). Worse yet, in most cases the specific version of the discovery–justification distinction is not made explicit by the writer. This makes it difficult to conceptualize this distinction clearly on the basis of a single relevant dimension. To understand discovery, one's focus would be on the factual and historical processes that led to the genesis of an idea, whereas to understand justification one's focus would switch to the methods and procedures involved in the evaluation or testing of the generated idea. According to yet another version, the analysis of discovery involves an *empirical* enterprise, whereas the analysis of justification is primarily a *logical* enterprise. Thus, because many variants of this distinction exist, any clear discussion of it necessitates that one indicate explicitly which version is under consideration.

Second, and chiefly driven by historical analyses of how science is actually practiced, it has become clear that it is typically very difficult to assign specific developments in science to the discovery or justification categories exclusively. For example, Hoyningen-Huene (2006) considered a case in which an established empirical law is subsequently subjected to higher degrees of quantitative accuracy because of the developments of new methods of measurement. How should one classify these new advancements? On the one hand, one could argue that the quantitative refinements constitute the discovery of an altogether new version of the law. On the other hand, one could argue that quantitative refinements involve the continued justification of the original law. This example is germane because, as most scientists can attest, laws and other formulations are malleable historical entities that undergo developmental changes in their utility. As a result, rather than maintaining a rigid demarcation between the contexts of discovery and justification, current thinking reflects a more flexible interplay between these two modes of scientific thought. This means scientists are perceived to transition smoothly between discovery and justification and that the movement can be bidirectional in the sense that evaluative exercises that probe the quality of one's evidence can reveal new gaps in knowledge and prompt discoveries.

HOW TO PROMOTE SCIENTIFIC INNOVATION AND RESEARCH QUALITY

The preceding discussion suggests that, strictly speaking, discovery cannot be an exclusively rational process. Nevertheless, it is possible to foster preconditions and encourage scientific practices that will increase the probability that scientists will pursue important phenomena and processes. I believe that there are three factors that can have a bearing on this probability: (a) theory choice; (b) the pursuit of cumulative science; and (c) an explicit focus on a set of controllable factors that are known to promote creative problem solving, in particular problem finding. I will argue that a focus by working scientists on these three factors will likely lead to greater scientific innovation and research quality in the discipline of psychology.[1]

FROM PARADIGMS TO GOOD THEORIES

According to Kuhn (1962/1970), science occurs within *paradigms*, a term he defined in two senses. According to the first sense, a paradigm is "an entire constellation of beliefs, values, techniques and so on shared by the members of a given community" (p. 175). As such, paradigms represent systems of rules and standards for scientific practice shared by the practitioners of a scientific discipline. Kuhn also noted that within a given paradigm scientists engage in what he referred to as *normal science*, defined as "research firmly based on one or more past scientific achievements, achievements that some particular scientific community acknowledges for a time as supplying the foundation for its further practice" (p. 10). Periods of paradigmatic normal science were contrasted with scientific revolutions, during which an old

---

[1]Although because of my training most of my examples will necessarily be drawn from the literatures on creativity and empirical aesthetics, the ideas are meant to apply more broadly to psychological science.

paradigm was replaced by a new paradigm that showed greater promise in solving outstanding problems in the field.

The practice of normal science provides the underpinning for the second sense in which a paradigm is defined; specifically, Kuhn argued that the predominant activity of scientists working within any given paradigm is working on puzzles. In turn, successful puzzle solutions become the templates that replace explicit rules as the basis for determining the solution of the remaining puzzles within that paradigm. Paradigms are instrumental in facilitating coherent traditions of scientific practice because they facilitate the emergence of solution templates.

The notion of paradigm naturally evokes the notion of theory. Although theories have been defined in numerous ways, I adopt a general definition of a *theory* as a system of statements (i.e., axioms) used to explain a group of phenomena. Theories typically emerge as novel insights that explain regularities in a (large) group of observations:

> Theories are usually introduced when previous study of a class of phenomena has revealed a system of uniformities that can be expressed in the form of empirical laws. Theories then seek to explain those regularities and, generally, to afford a deeper and more accurate understanding of the phenomena in question. (Hempel, 1966, p. 70)

Scientists working within any given paradigm might nevertheless deal with theories of varying flavor within it. For example, a research paradigm that governs much of contemporary research in the domains of reasoning, judgment, and social cognition involves the postulation of two systems that govern thinking. This dual-process approach postulates one system that underlies fast, automatic, and unconscious thinking (i.e., System 1) and another system that underlies slow, deliberative, and conscious thinking (i.e., System 2; Evans, 2008). How a human thinks and behaves is perceived to be a function of how these two systems interact in the course of processing the mind's content. However, there is tremendous heterogeneity in terms of the specifics of the theories that fall under the generic dual-process banner. For example, in his extensive review of that literature Evans (2008) noted no fewer than 14 different theoretical versions of this general approach (e.g., Epstein, 1994; Schneider & Shiffrin, 1977; Sloman, 1996). In other words, scientists working under the dual-process paradigm could be conducting research based on theories that vary in important ways in their specifics. Here we can pose an important question: Are there any features that can help researchers choose good theories over bad theories within any given paradigm? Many influential thinkers have argued that such distinguishing features do indeed exist, and below I review some criteria that have been proposed for choosing good theories.

CHOOSING GOOD THEORIES

Kuhn (1977) proposed five (nonexhaustive) criteria for choosing theories. The first is *accuracy*, by which he meant that predictions derived from the theory must converge with the results of known experiments and observations. The second feature is *consistency*, both internal and external. Internal consistency implies consistency among the components within the theory itself, whereas external consistency implies consistency with other accepted theories and aspects of nature that fall outside its direct purview. Third, a theory should have *broad scope*, meaning that its consequences should extend far beyond the particular phenomena or observations that it was initially designed to explain. Fourth, it should be *simple*, meaning that it should bring order to and unify ideas that were hitherto isolated and perhaps even contradictory (i.e., parsimony). Fifth, a theory should "be fruitful of new research findings" by disclosing new phenomena.[2]

CUMULATIVE SCIENCE

In what he humorously referred to as the "toothbrush problem," Mischel (2005, 2008) has noted psychologists' well-known tendency to treat other people's theories like used toothbrushes and therefore to stray away from them as much as possible. In contrast, mature sciences frequently involve the fine-tuning of theories that increase their explanatory power to account for more phenomena than the original theory was intended to address. By so doing they lead to the emergence of *cumulative science*: a science wherein later advances are built on earlier advances (Bird, 2013). Cumulative science typifies mature sciences wherein theories frequently undergo fine-tuning to increase their explanatory power (see Mischel, 2005, 2008). The upshot of a cumulative science is greater conceptual integration over time, thereby allowing more widespread tests of the veracity of its concepts.

It is interesting that choosing good theories can contribute to the likelihood of having a cumulative science. For example, a broad scope can contribute to the emergence of cumulative science because it ensures that an existing theory has a greater likelihood of explaining phenomena and observations beyond what it was initially designed to explain. As such, rather than being replaced, its scope can be expanded over time. The same is true for

---

[2]Key aspects of Kuhn's criteria for good theories are shared by other philosophers of science (e.g., Hempel, 1966; Laudan, 1990). Thus, it appears that generally agreed-on criteria do exist for the selection of good theories in science.

simplicity: In accordance with Occam's razor, it is preferable to have a single unifying theory that can organize a large body of knowledge rather than a complicated edifice of theories that can explain the same body of knowledge. This too contributes to the development of a cumulative science because it increases the likelihood that simple (i.e., parsimonious) ideas will evolve or be incorporated into theories of larger scope rather than be discarded for new ones. For example, Martindale's (1995) connectionist theory incorporated Mednick's (1962) associative theory, Kris's (1952) psychoanalytic theory, and Mendelsohn's (1976) defocused attention theory into a unified neural network theory of creativity. This is because the axioms of connectionism were able to account for the predictions derived from all three theories successfully. Finally, a theory that breeds new ideas is particularly beneficial for a cumulative science because the scientists working within that theoretical framework will have conceptually related novel puzzles to work on, instead of pursuing other potentially unrelated avenues of research.

USING GOOD THEORIES

Armed with knowledge about what makes a good theory, a practicing scientist can decide whether the theory on which one is working qualifies as a good choice. This consideration of which theory to choose is important for three reasons. First, because of the overarching nature of paradigms, practicing scientists typically do not have the luxury of choosing the specific paradigm under which they will conduct their work. For example, in the heyday of the behaviorist and cognitive paradigms the dominant currents of research likely determined the paradigmatic work deemed socially acceptable. Whereas within the behaviorist paradigm it was not acceptable to study mental states, within the cognitive paradigm this restriction was lifted. In contrast, within any given paradigm there is relatively more flexibility in choosing the specific theory on which one opts to focus, and here agency can be exercised in the choice of better theories. For example, contemporary neuroscientists studying emotion might adhere to theories in which there exists a finite set of basic, discrete emotions (Ekman, 1999) or to theories that advocate the existence of a single "core affect" construct (Barrett, Mesquita, Ochsner, & Gross, 2007). Although these divergent positions are theoretically important, research motivated by either theory can still flourish under the same paradigm that currently guides scientific practice within the discipline of emotion neuroscience. This means that Kuhn's (1977) five criteria described above can be applied to selecting which theory to focus on.

Second, better theories are more likely to lead to cumulative science. As Mischel (2005) noted, "a cumulative science can flourish if many small but solidly data-based theories become integrated into . . . stronger, broader, multi-level ones." The emergence of cumulative science will be particularly beneficial for external consistency because in the unfolding of the accumulation process predictions and axioms derived from any given theory can be cross-referenced vis-à-vis other accepted theories. This will make the survival of theories that can explain only isolated phenomena less likely.

Third, theories that are more likely to promote novel findings are particularly useful for innovation in science. Certain features of a theory promote novel findings. The first is the extent to which a theory can help isolate what the specific gaps in knowledge are, which in turn can propel researchers to generate creative solutions to them. For example, according to Martindale's (1999) theory, creativity is associated with variability in the focus of attention rather than a permanent state of focused or defocused attention. In the earlier phases of problem solving when the problem space is relatively ill defined and ambiguity is high, creativity is associated with a widening of the focus of attention. This defocused state enables a creative person to consider more bits of information in the search for the building blocks of a solution. In turn, in the later phases of problem solving, when the problem space is relatively well defined and ambiguity is low, creativity is associated with a narrowing of the focus of attention. This focused state enables a creative person to work exclusively on more fruitful ideas as they are refined and completed into bona fide solutions. Indeed, there is empirical evidence to show that creative people are more variable in their focus of attention than less creative people in relation to task ambiguity (e.g., Dorfman, Martindale, Gassimova, & Vartanian, 2008; Vartanian, Martindale, & Kwiatkowski, 2007). However, to date it remains unclear how the switching between these two modes of attention is precisely regulated. Martindale argued that this adjustment is automatic or reactive rather than involving self-control and that this bottom-up process is sensitive to the granularity or ambiguity of the problem space. In contrast, however, there are also data to suggest that this flexibility could be regulated by top-down processes in the service of strategy change (Haider, Frensch, & Joram, 2005). The discovery of the nexus of this regulatory mechanism remains an important goal in this research area. In this sense Martindale's theory promotes further research by pinpointing a specific gap in knowledge that must be addressed by researchers in the area.

A second feature about a theory that can generate novelty is the extent to which its core features can be incorporated into other domains and tested under new conditions. For example, in Mednick's (1962) now-classic article, he drew heavily from Locke (1690) and Bain (1855) to propose an associationist theory of creativity, according to which "any condition or state of the organism which will tend to bring the requisite associative elements into ideational contiguity will increase the probability and speed of a creative solution" (p. 221). In turn, Mednick and Mednick (1967) devised the Remote Associates Test (RAT) to quantify individual differences in associative and combinatorial ability. Each item on the RAT presents subjects with a triplet of words (e.g., *chamber, staff, box*), in response to which the subject must generate a fourth word that is common to all three words (i.e., *music*). According to Mednick's theory, solving RAT problems will be facilitated to the extent that more distant nodes are activated in relation to each word.

Although the RAT was originally introduced to measure an associative hierarchy (i.e., gradient) as a creative mechanism, more recently the theory and the test have been adopted by cognitive neuroscientists to study the neural processes that underlie insight in the brain (Kounios & Beeman, 2009). As a result of the insertion of the RAT into the neuroscience literature on insight, the concept of an associative hierarchy (i.e., gradient) is forced to carry more theoretical weight than before because predictions derived from it must now work in the context of insight as well as creativity. As a result, the evidence base in relation to creativity and insight is more interconnected. It is important to note that it is not just the test but also the underlying theory that has crossed over into a new domain.

DISCARDING BAD THEORIES

My focus in this chapter has thus far been on good theories. Of course, bad theories also exist. How do we identify and discard them? On the surface, this would appear to be a question with a straightforward answer: In the words of Richard Feynman regarding any scientific law, "If it disagrees with experiment, it's wrong" (http://www.presentationzen.com/presentationzen/2014/04/richard-feynman-on-the-scientific-method-in-1-minute.html). In other words, if predictions derived from a theory disagree with observation, then one would have to abandon the theory in search of another theory. In reality, however, this state of affairs is difficult to achieve because scientific hypotheses (derived from theories) are typically tested not in isolation but instead against a set of largely implicit background assumptions (i.e., auxiliary assumptions). As a result, in cases when experimental data disagree with a hypothesis, instead of discarding the theory a scientist might instead opt to revise any of a number of the background assumptions to bring the data in line with the hypothesis. In essence, this means that "crucial experiments" in which data can unambiguously disconfirm a theory might be difficult to conduct (see Harding, 1976).

Within psychology, our inability to identify and discard bad theories has led to the proliferation of *undead theories*, defined in the singular as follows:

> a theory that continues in use, having resisted attempts at falsification, ignored disconfirmatory data, negated failed replications through the dubious use of meta-analysis or having simply maintained itself in a fluid state with shifting implicit assumptions such that falsification is not possible. (Ferguson & Heene, 2012, p. 559)

This state of affairs must be rectified by working to eliminate the influence of a number of organizational and individual factors that have been identified as contributing to this problem, including publication bias, an aversion to publishing null results, questionable research practices, and ideologically driven science (for a detailed list see Ferguson, San Miguel, Garza, & Jerabeck, 2012). We must improve the ways in which we collect, analyze, and interpret data to achieve a proper mechanism for theory falsification in psychology.

BEYOND GOOD THEORIES: PROBLEM FINDING

Having explored factors that distinguish good theories from poor theories, and discussed the features of good theories that promote research quality and innovation in science, I would now like to focus on factors that promote good problem finding, which is an important hallmark of creative excellence in science (Runco, 1994). When choosing a problem for study, how can we know that we have stumbled upon a problem that is more likely to yield a creative solution? This question brings us head to head with a key question in creativity research: To what extent are creative ideas the result of inside-the-box versus outside-the-box thinking?

Process Versus Content

Researchers traditionally have tried to distinguish creative solutions from noncreative solutions by virtue of differences in the cognitive processes and structures that lead to the generation of creative ideas (Finke, Ward, & Smith, 1992). This focus has led to numerous research findings that have distinguished cognitive processes that lead to the generation of creative ideas from cognitive processes that lead to the generation of noncreative ideas. Relatively less attention has been paid to variation in the contents of the mind that can undergo ordinary thought processes in the service of creative idea generation. It is interesting that, despite his interest in the role of the organization of semantic memory (i.e., associative networks) as an engine for creativity, Mednick (1962) was quick to highlight the role of the contents of memory (i.e., associative elements) in creativity:

> It should be clear that an individual without the requisite elements in his response repertoire will not be able to combine them so as to arrive at a creative solution. An architect who does not know of the existence of a new material can hardly be expected to use it creatively. (p. 222)

It is now generally well established that people who exhibit levels of exceptional creativity in various domains appear to have spent a considerable amount of time for the acquisition of expertise in those domains—typically referred to as the "10-year rule" (Gardner, 1983; see also Simonton, 1994). The most common explanation of this phenomenon is that a considerable amount of time is necessary to encode the key associative elements of a domain, which in turn enable one to better see gaps in the knowledge and possible ways to overcome them (i.e., problem finding). Related to this factor is that some fields (e.g., music) necessitate the acquisition of instrumental and procedural mastery, which also requires time.

An important issue related to the 10-year rule is the positive correlation frequently observed between quantity (i.e., idea fluency) and quality (e.g., originality) in idea generation. This relationship was formally captured by Simonton's (1997) *equal-odds rule*, according to which "the relationship between the number of hits (i.e., creative successes) and the total number of works produced in a given time period is positive, linear, stochastic, and stable" (p. 73). The equal-odds rule is supported by several lines of independent evidence. For example, fluency has been shown to be correlated positively ($r = .73$) with expert ratings of the creativity of responses (Jung et al., 2015). In addition, fluency accounts for the majority of variance in performance in tests of divergent thinking (Plucker & Renzulli, 1999). In this sense, longer engagement in a field should also give an individual a greater opportunity to display productivity and, in turn, creativity. For example, Simonton (1997) examined the relationship between career age (as opposed to chronological age) and achievement by generating curves that predicted annual productivity rates as a function of career age. The 10-year rule was observed among scientists, meaning that it took approximately 10 years to display productivity or quality peaks from the time of initial contribution to the field. Among artists this gap was, interestingly enough, approximately 20 years. The upshot of the equal-odds rule is that time investment in a field has benefits for creativity, and there is reason to believe that it can contribute positively to the acquisition of domain-specific knowledge necessary for the exhibition of creativity.[3]

---

[3]We know that greatness is achieved via the contribution of many factors, including motivation and creative thinking skills (Amabile & Mueller, 2008).

Lumping Versus Splitting

A second method for determining whether one is working on a good problem involves whether the solution brought about by that problem is likely to lead to more elegant versus splintered ideas. Here I borrow terminology from the literature on language classification, according to which thinkers can be categorized as either *lumpers* or *splitters* (Vartanian & Locher, 2010). Lumpers focus on commonalities between concepts, facilitating the emergence of overarching patterns. Splitters, in contrast, focus on divergences between concepts, facilitating the emergence of complexity. Many fields in science have historically been dominated by the pursuit of universal laws that govern our interactions with nature. Empirical studies of the arts and creativity are no exception (e.g., Locher, 2003; Martindale, 1990; McManus, Cheema, & Stoker, 1993). For example, according to fluency theory, positive aesthetic experiences are driven by processing ease (Reber, Schwarz, & Winkielman, 2004; Reber, Winkielman, & Schwarz, 1998).

This single axiom can explain a very wide range of phenomena in the domain of aesthetics (e.g., mere exposure, prototypicality) using a single mechanism. Another such example was provided by Martindale (2001), who used a single postulate from neural network theory to account for an astonishing 60 well-known effects in empirical aesthetics. From this perspective, discoveries that can elegantly explain the greatest number of phenomena based on the fewest number of principles and axioms are deemed to constitute the most important contributions to a given field. In turn, one can use this principle as a yardstick for problem selection: In the long run, it is better to select phenomena and processes for study that hold the promise of contributing to the discovery of elegant, universal laws. In turn, such laws can contribute to the cumulative growth of knowledge in the field through the integration of findings based on a minimum number of common axioms (but see Bullot & Reber, 2013).

High-Risk Investment

Sternberg and Lubart's investment theory of creativity (see Sternberg, 2012) suggests a third approach for facilitating the discovery of potentially important phenomena and processes. According to this theory, creative people are adept at pursuing ideas that have growth potential but happen to be unknown or out of favor within the field. They develop and nurture unpopular ideas and make an impact in the field by bringing those ideas into the fold. In this sense, they "buy low and sell high in the realm of ideas" (Sternberg, 2012, p. 5). A useful feature of this approach to problem finding is that it can infuse a field with novel approaches to understanding concepts within its own domain. In turn, within the context of a self-correcting science, the veracity of these newly introduced or popularized ideas can be tested to determine the extent to which they contribute to the accumulation of knowledge within the dominant paradigm. In cases where there is a discord between such an idea and a paradigm, a shift in the latter might be necessary (Kuhn, 1962/1970)—perhaps the ultimate indicator of an important idea. It is important to note, however, that this practice of high-risk investment can have detrimental consequences for one's career because the field might initially actively resist the entry of the novel idea into the domain (Czikszentmihalyi, 1988). Here the personality factors (e.g., motivation, ego strength) necessary to push the idea forward become key drivers for overcoming systemic barriers to idea propagation (Amabile & Mueller, 2008).

Closing the Loop: From Good Problems to Good Theories

In this section I have discussed three controllable factors that can be implemented in a scientist's search for better problems. In turn, focusing on better problems can incrementally improve our understanding of an important process or phenomenon, leading to the development of more refined models of how nature operates. I will use an example to illustrate this point. One of the most historically reliable findings in the neuropsychology literature has involved the lateralization of linguistic processing to the left hemisphere and, to a lesser extent, the lateralization of visuospatial processing to the right hemisphere. However, for a long time the precise factor that determines the involvement of each hemisphere in linguistic versus visuospatial processing, as well as how this lateralized allocation is regulated, had remained unknown.

Tackling this important problem would help provide important insights into the nature of hemispheric specialization of cognitive processes (McIntosh & Lobaugh, 2003). In an ingenious experiment, Stephan et al. (2003) were able to demonstrate that it is not the nature of the stimulus, but instead what must be done with the stimulus (i.e., the task), that determines which hemisphere is engaged in processing the input. To be specific, they found that identifying the location of a letter within a word activated the right hemisphere rather than the left hemisphere, demonstrating that the mere presentation of a linguistic stimulus (e.g., a word) is not sufficient for the automatic engagement of the left hemisphere; instead, the nature of the task (i.e., visuospatial localization) is the critical factor. In addition, the researchers were able to show that it was variation in the strength of the lateralized functional coupling between the anterior cingulate cortex and either hemisphere that regulated which hemisphere was switched on. This finding provided a cognitive control mechanism for task-dependent hemispheric lateralization. Stephan et al.'s study demonstrated how focus on an important problem in a particular domain can strengthen our theories. Recall that theories typically emerge when the study of a problem or set of problems reveals regularities in nature. The novel explanations tend to offer "a deeper and more accurate understanding of the phenomena in question" (Hempel, 1966, p. 70).

CONCLUSION

In this chapter I have argued that one can improve research quality and innovation in science by paying attention to the selection of good theories; pursuing a cumulative science; and fostering controllable factors that benefit creativity, such as problem finding. Following Mischel (2005, 2008), who identified the establishment of robust and replicable effects about important phenomena and processes as a key requirement of good science, we can make psychological science more cumulative by emphasizing the critical role of general theory building and by improving our methods for the identification of important phenomena and processes for study. In the absence of these two features our science will be a fragmented collection of observations about trivial effects. It is important to note, however, that although replication is critical for improving research quality, in the long run its contribution is meaningful only if the effects being replicated are themselves nontrivial.

RECOMMENDED READING

Ferguson, C. J., & Heene, M. (2012). A vast graveyard of undead theories: Publication bias and psychological science's aversion to the null. *Perspectives on Psychological Science, 7*, 555–561.

Gillies, D. (1993). *Philosophy of science in the twentieth century.* Cambridge, MA: Blackwell.

Hoyningen-Huene, P. (2006). Context of discovery versus context of justification and Thomas Kuhn. In J. Schickore & F. Steinle (Eds.), *Revisiting discovery and justification* (pp. 119–131). New York, NY: Springer.

Laudan, L. (1977). *Progress and its problems: Towards a theory of scientific growth.* Berkeley: University of California Press.

Runco, M. A. (Ed.). (1994). *Problem finding, problem solving, and creativity.* Norwood, NJ: Greenwood Press.

Simonton, D. K. (1997). Creative productivity: A predictive and explanatory model of career trajectories and landmarks. *Psychological Review, 104*, 66–89.

REFERENCES

Amabile, T. M., & Mueller, J. S. (2008). Studying creativity, its processes, and its antecedents: An exploration of the componential theory of creativity. In J. Zhou & C. E. Shalley (Eds.), *Handbook of organizational creativity* (pp. 33–64). Mahwah, NJ: Erlbaum.

Bain, A. (1855). *The senses and the intellect.* London, England: Parker. http://dx.doi.org/10.1037/12115-000

Barrett, L. F., Mesquita, B., Ochsner, K. N., & Gross, J. J. (2007). The experience of emotion. *Annual Review of Psychology, 58,* 373–403. http://dx.doi.org/10.1146/annurev.psych.58.110405.085709

Bird, A. (2013). Thomas Kuhn. In E. N. Zalta (Ed.), *The Stanford encyclopedia of philosophy.* Retrieved from http://plato.stanford.edu/archives/fall2013/entries/thomas-kuhn/

Bullot, N. J., & Reber, R. (2013). The artful mind meets art history: Toward a psychohistorical framework for the science of art appreciation. *Behavioral and Brain Sciences, 36,* 123–137. http://dx.doi.org/10.1017/S0140525X12000489

Campbell, D. T. (1960). Blind variation and selective retention in creative thought as in other knowledge processes. *Psychological Review, 67,* 380–400. http://dx.doi.org/10.1037/h0040373

Carnap, R. (1963). *Logical foundations of probability* (2nd ed.). Chicago, IL: University of Chicago Press. (Original work published 1950)

Czikszentmihalyi, M. (1988). Society, culture, and person: A systems view of creativity. In R. J. Sternberg & J. Davidson (Eds.), *The nature of creativity* (pp. 47–61). New York, NY: Cambridge University Press.

Dorfman, L., Martindale, C., Gassimova, V., & Vartanian, O. (2008). Creativity and speed of information processing: A double dissociation involving elementary versus inhibitory cognitive tasks. *Personality and Individual Differences, 44,* 1382–1390. http://dx.doi.org/10.1016/j.paid.2007.12.006

Ekman, P. (1999). Basic emotions. In T. Dalgleish & M. Power (Eds.), *Handbook of cognition and emotion* (pp. 45–60). New York, NY: Wiley.

Epstein, S. (1994). Integration of the cognitive and the psychodynamic unconscious. *American Psychologist, 49,* 709–724. http://dx.doi.org/10.1037/0003-066X.49.8.709

Evans, J. St. B. T. (2008). Dual-processing accounts of reasoning, judgment, and social cognition. *Annual Review of Psychology, 59,* 255–278. http://dx.doi.org/10.1146/annurev.psych.59.103006.093629

Feigl, H. (1970). The "orthodox" view of theories: Remarks in defense as well as critique. In M. Radner & S. Winokur (Eds.), *Minnesota studies of the philosophies of science: Vol. 4. Analyses of theories and methods of physics and psychology* (pp. 3–16). Minneapolis: University of Minnesota Press.

Ferguson, C. J., & Heene, M. (2012). A vast graveyard of undead theories: Publication bias and psychological science's aversion to the null. *Perspectives on Psychological Science, 7,* 555–561. http://dx.doi.org/10.1177/1745691612459059

Ferguson, C. J., San Miguel, C., Garza, A., & Jerabeck, J. M. (2012). A longitudinal test of video game violence influences on dating and aggression: A 3-year longitudinal study of adolescents. *Journal of Psychiatric Research, 46*, 141–146. http://dx.doi.org/10.1016/j.jpsychires.2011.10.014

Finke, R. A., Ward, T. B., & Smith, S. M. (1992). *Creative cognition: Theory, research, and applications.* Cambridge, MA: MIT Press.

Gardner, H. (1983). *Frames of mind: The theory of multiple intelligences.* New York, NY: Basic Books.

Gillies, D. (1993). *Philosophy of science in the twentieth century.* Cambridge, MA: Blackwell.

Goldman, A. I. (1983). Epistemology and the theory of problem solving. *Synthese, 55*, 21–48. http://dx.doi.org/10.1007/BF00485372

Haider, H., Frensch, P. A., & Joram, D. (2005). Are strategy shifts caused by data-driven processes or by voluntary processes? *Consciousness and Cognition, 14*, 495–519. http://dx.doi.org/10.1016/j.concog.2004.12.002

Harding, S. G. (Ed.). (1976). *Can theories be refuted? Essays on the Duhem–Quine thesis.* Dordrecht, the Netherlands: D. Reidel. http://dx.doi.org/10.1007/978-94-010-1863-0

Hempel, C. G. (1966). *Philosophy of natural science.* Englewood Cliffs, NJ: Prentice Hall.

Hoyningen-Huene, P. (1987). Context of discovery and context of justification. *Studies in History and Philosophy of Science, 18*, 501–515. http://dx.doi.org/10.1016/0039-3681(87)90005-7

Hoyningen-Huene, P. (2006). Context of discovery versus context of justification and Thomas Kuhn. In J. Schickore & F. Steinle (Eds.), *Revisiting discovery and justification* (pp. 119–131). New York, NY: Springer. http://dx.doi.org/10.1007/1-4020-4251-5_8

Jung, R. E., Wertz, C. J., Meadows, C. A., Ryman, S. G., Vakhtin, A. A., & Flores, R. A. (2015). Quantity yields quality when it comes to creativity: A brain and behavioral test of the equal-odds rule. *Frontiers in Psychology, 6*, 864. Advance online publication. http://dx.doi.org/10.3389/fpsyg.2015.00864

Kounios, J., & Beeman, M. (2009). The aha! moment: The cognitive neuroscience of insight. *Current Directions in Psychological Science, 18*, 210–216. http://dx.doi.org/10.1111/j.1467-8721.2009.01638.x

Kris, E. (1952). *Psychoanalytic explorations in art.* New York, NY: International Universities Press.

Kuhn, T. S. (1970). *The structure of scientific revolutions* (2nd ed., enlarged). Chicago, IL: University of Chicago Press. (Original work published 1962)

Kuhn, T. S. (1977). Objectivity, value judgment, and theory choice. In *The essential tension: Selected studies in the scientific tradition and change* (pp. 320–339). Chicago, IL: University of Chicago Press.

Laudan, L. (1990). *Science and relativism: Some key controversies in the philosophy of science.* Chicago, IL: University of Chicago Press.

Locher, P. J. (2003). An empirical investigation of the visual rightness theory of picture perception. *Acta Psychologica, 114,* 147–164. http://dx.doi.org/10.1016/j.actpsy.2003.07.001

Locke, J. (1690). *Essays concerning the human understanding.* London, England: Printed for Tho. Basset and sold by Edw. Mory. http://dx.doi.org/10.1093/oseo/instance.00018020

Makel, M. C. (2014). The empirical march: Making science better at self-correction. *Psychology of Aesthetics, Creativity, and the Arts, 8,* 2–7. http://dx.doi.org/10.1037/a0035803

Martindale, C. (1990). *The clockwork muse: The predictability of artistic change.* New York, NY: Basic Books.

Martindale, C. (1995). Creativity and connectionism. In S. Smith, T. Ward, & R. Finke (Eds.), *The creative cognition approach* (pp. 249–268). Cambridge, MA: MIT Press.

Martindale, C. (1999). Biological bases of creativity. In R. J. Sternberg (Ed.), *Handbook of creativity* (pp. 137–152). New York, NY: Cambridge University Press.

Martindale, C. (2001). How does the brain compute aesthetic experience? *The General Psychologist, 36,* 25–35.

McIntosh, A. R., & Lobaugh, N. J. (2003). When is a word not a word? *Science, 301,* 322–323. http://dx.doi.org/10.1126/science.1087853

McManus, I. C., Cheema, B., & Stoker, J. (1993). The aesthetics of composition: A study of Mondrian. *Empirical Studies of the Arts, 11,* 83–94. http://dx.doi.org/10.2190/HXR4-VU9A-P5D9-BPQQ

Mednick, S. A. (1962). The associative basis of the creative process. *Psychological Review, 69,* 220–232. http://dx.doi.org/10.1037/h0048850

Mednick, S. A., & Mednick, M. T. (1967). *Examiner's manual: Remote Associates Test.* Boston, MA: Houghton Mifflin.

Mendelsohn, G. A. (1976). Associative and attentional processes in creative performance. *Journal of Personality, 44,* 341–369. http://dx.doi.org/10.1111/j.1467-6494.1976.tb00127.x

Mischel, W. (2005, December). The toothbrush problem. *APS Observer, 21*(11). Retrieved from http://www.psychologicalscience.org/index.php/publications/observer/2008/december-08/the-toothbrush-problem.html

Mischel, W. (2008, March). Alternative futures for our science. *APS Observer, 18*(3). Retrieved from http://www.psychologicalscience.org/index.php/publications/observer/2005/march-05/alternative-futures-for-our-science.html

Mowry, B. (1985). From Galen's theory to William Harvey's theory: A case study in the rationality of scientific theory change. *Studies in History and Philosophy of Science, 16,* 49–82. http://dx.doi.org/10.1016/0039-3681(85)90007-X

Plucker, J. A., & Renzulli, J. S. (1999). Psychometric approaches to the study of human creativity. In R. J. Sternberg (Ed.), *Handbook of creativity* (pp. 35–61). New York, NY: Cambridge University Press.

Popper, K. R. (1959). *The logic of scientific discovery* (6th ed., rev.). London, England: Hutchinson. (Original work published 1934)

Reber, R., Schwarz, N., & Winkielman, P. (2004). Processing fluency and aesthetic pleasure: Is beauty in the perceiver's processing experience? *Personality and Social Psychology Review, 8,* 364–382. http://dx.doi.org/10.1207/s15327957pspr0804_3

Reber, R., Winkielman, P., & Schwarz, N. (1998). Effects of perceptual fluency on affective judgments. *Psychological Science, 9,* 45–48. http://dx.doi.org/10.1111/1467-9280.00008

Reichenbach, H. (1938). *Experience and prediction: An analysis of the foundations and the structure of knowledge.* Chicago, IL: University of Chicago Press. http://dx.doi.org/10.1037/11656-000

Runco, M. A. (Ed.). (1994). *Problem finding, problem solving, and creativity.* Norwood, NJ: Greenwood Press.

Schneider, W., & Shiffrin, R. M. (1977). Controlled and automatic human information processing: 1. Detection, search, and attention. *Psychological Review, 84,* 1–66. http://dx.doi.org/10.1037/0033-295X.84.1.1

Simonton, D. K. (1994). *Greatness: Who makes history and why.* New York, NY: Guilford Press.

Simonton, D. K. (1997). Creative productivity: A predictive and explanatory model of career trajectories and landmarks. *Psychological Review, 104,* 66–89. http://dx.doi.org/10.1037/0033-295X.104.1.66

Sloman, S. A. (1996). The empirical case for two systems of reasoning. *Psychological Bulletin, 119,* 3–22. http://dx.doi.org/10.1037/0033-2909.119.1.3

Stephan, K. E., Marshall, J. C., Friston, K. J., Rowe, J. B., Ritzl, A., Zilles, K., & Fink, G. R. (2003, July 18). Lateralized cognitive processes and lateralized task control in the human brain. *Science, 301,* 384–386. http://dx.doi.org/10.1126/science.1086025

Sternberg, R. J. (2012). The assessment of creativity: An investment-based approach. *Creativity Research Journal, 24,* 3–12. http://dx.doi.org/10.1080/10400419.2012.652925

Vartanian, O., & Locher, P. (2010). Colin Martindale (1943–2008). *American Psychologist, 65,* 925. http://dx.doi.org/10.1037/a0021189

Vartanian, O., Martindale, C., & Kwiatkowski, J. (2007). Creative potential, attention, and speed of information processing. *Personality and Individual Differences, 34,* 1370–1380.

Wallas, G. (1926). *The art of thought.* New York: Harcourt, Brace & World.

2

DESIGNING A STUDY TO MAXIMIZE INFORMATIONAL VALUE

ALISON LEDGERWOOD, COURTNEY K. SODERBERG, AND JEHAN SPARKS

KEY POINTS

Use this chapter to guide your methodological decisions before you start collecting or analyzing your data, in order to maximize what you can learn from your results. The toolbox of cutting-edge strategies provided here will enable you to

- understand the importance of statistical power, boost it when needed, and consider strategies for confronting real-world challenges to running highly powered studies;
- consider both the benefits and drawbacks of using online samples;
- distinguish between exploratory and confirmatory analyses so that you can learn as much as possible from your data; and
- plan programs of research that include direct, systematic, and/or conceptual replications.

http://dx.doi.org/10.1037/0000033-003
Toward a More Perfect Psychology: Improving Trust, Accuracy, and Transparency in Research, M. C. Makel and J. A. Plucker (Editors)

Recent years have witnessed a broad movement to improve methods and practices across scientific disciplines (e.g., Begley & Ellis, 2012; Button et al., 2013; Ledgerwood, 2014, 2016; McNutt, 2014; Nosek, Spies, & Motyl, 2012; Nyhan, 2015). In response to a renewed focus on how to maximize the knowledge we get from the work that we do, researchers have developed an impressive toolkit of new and newly rediscovered methodological and statistical practices. In this chapter, we draw on the cutting-edge literature on this topic to highlight a number of crucial decisions many social scientists face when designing a study that influence how informative the results can be. In other words, this chapter is the one to consult before you begin to conduct a study or analyze a preexisting data set. The decisions you make at such critical phases of the research process can have a dramatic impact on how much you learn from your eventual results.

THE CRITICAL IMPORTANCE OF POWER

One key set of decisions you will need to make at this early stage of the research process centers on the issue of statistical power. Adequately powering your study is crucial for maximizing the informational value of your eventual results, for reasons relating to both Type I error (the likelihood of erroneously detecting an effect in your study when no true effect exists) and Type II error (the likelihood of failing to detect a true effect).

Researchers often think about the issue of power as an issue of avoiding Type II errors: You want high power because it increases the likelihood that you will detect an effect if the effect is there. This way of thinking about power leads to the idea that it is desirable to have high power but that low power is only a problem if you do not see an effect. Researchers who think about power in this way might (understandably but erroneously) conclude that if they run an underpowered study and detect an effect, it constitutes especially trustworthy and impressive evidence for an effect ("I found it even with low power working against me!").

However, the fact is that low power also undermines our ability to trust effects when we do see them, in that reducing power reduces the *positive predictive value* (PPV) of a significant finding (see Button et al., 2013). PPV is the probability that a statistically significant result reflects a true positive (a real effect in the population). The PPV of your own findings would be the proportion of all of your significant results that are true positives—in other words, the likelihood that any given significant effect you detect is real. As the power of your study decreases, the number of true positives in your personal pool of significant results decreases. Meanwhile, though, if your Type

I error rate is constant, the number of false positives in your personal pool stays constant. The dwindling number of true positives means that the probability of any one of your significant results being true goes down. In addition, when power drops below 50%, effect sizes start to become dramatically overestimated, and when power drops below 10%, they can be in the wrong direction (leading you to conclude, e.g., that your manipulation increases your dependent variable when in fact the opposite is true; see Gelman & Carlin, 2014). Thus, low power reduces your ability to trust your results not only when you fail to see a significant effect but also when you do see one.

Another way to think about the issue of low power is that underpowered studies tend to produce "bouncier" effect size estimates (see Figure 2.1 for an illustration). In other words, the estimates produced by underpowered research will tend to fluctuate more wildly from one study to the next or from one subjective researcher decision to the next (e.g., decisions about whether to exclude outliers or drop an item from a scale), compared with the

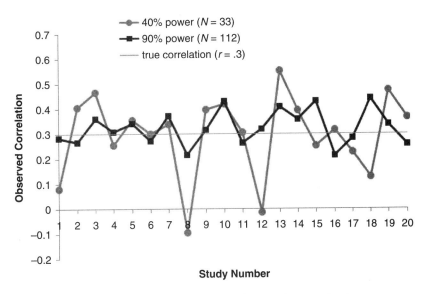

Figure 2.1. Underpowered studies tend to produce estimates that bounce more wildly from one study to the next, compared with more highly powered studies. Here we see illustrative results from a simple simulation in which a researcher runs 20 underpowered studies (powered at 40% to detect a medium-sized effect of $r = .30$) or 20 highly powered studies (powered at 90% to detect the medium-sized effect). Notice that the estimates produced by the underpowered studies (gray line) fluctuate widely around the true population correlation of .30, whereas the estimates produced by the highly powered studies (black line) cluster more tightly near the true population parameter.

more precise and stable estimates provided by highly powered studies (see Cumming, 2012; Ioannidis, 2008; and Schönbrodt & Perugini, 2013). This makes it harder to glean useful information from your results and can lead to problems later on when you or other researchers try to replicate your findings (Maxwell, 2004). Taken together, these issues point to the critical importance of estimating power when planning a study, so that you can not only boost power when needed but also acknowledge the uncertainty inherent in underpowered studies when high power cannot be achieved.

Effect Size Estimation

The potentially tricky part of any power calculation is estimating the effect size of interest. There are multiple ways to construct this estimate. Perhaps the most obvious is to look to the prior literature for similar studies or meta-analyses that provide an estimate of the expected effect size (or that enable you to put limits on the range of plausible effect sizes; see Gelman & Carlin, 2014). However, such estimates are not always available; for instance, some researchers are often interested in studying new effects that have not already been well documented. Moreover, publication bias can lead these estimates to be inflated when publication decisions were based on the presence or size of the effect of interest (e.g., in cases where publication decisions are determined by the presence of a single significant effect).[1]

One option in such cases is to identify the smallest effect size of interest and use that effect size in your power calculations—to say, in essence, that you care about the effect only if it is larger than size X. Indeed, this practice of defining a smallest effect size of interest is what many researchers do implicitly when they decide, without conducting a power analysis, to conduct a study with a particular sample size. For instance, if you decide that a particular research question is worth the resources it would take to conduct a two-group study with 100 participants, you are in effect deciding that you are interested in the effect only if it is greater than $d = 0.57$ (the effect size that can be detected with 80% power in a study this size). If you decide instead that your research question is worth 200 participants, you are in effect deciding that you are interested in the effect if it is greater than $d = 0.40$. A power analysis in this context simply makes the implicit decision an explicit one, allowing you to consider whether it is worth conducting the study (and perhaps it is not, if you realize you only have enough power to detect a giant

---

[1]Note that it is extremely difficult to adjust for publication bias accurately in meta-analysis. If it is likely that a given literature has been influenced by publication bias, meta-analysis may be more helpful for providing a range of plausible estimates that result from assuming different kinds of publication bias, rather than a single estimate that purports to provide the "real" effect size (see McShane, Böckenholt, & Hansen, 2016).

effect), whether you want to spend more resources, and how confident you can be in your conclusions.

Another option is to conduct a pilot study to provide an initial estimate of the effect size, which you could then use to inform the power calculation for your main study. This approach seems promising in theory, but it is worthwhile to consider several issues that may limit its usefulness in practice. First, the size of the pilot study must be large enough to provide a relatively precise estimate of the effect size—after all, a wildly inaccurate effect size estimate based on a small sample is not much help for planning your study. How large is large enough? Schönbrodt and Perugini (2013) suggested that researchers consider when a sample size will be large enough that effect size estimates reach a "corridor of stability" around the true population effect size. In other words, as the sample size increases, effect sizes go from bouncing wildly around the true population effect size to moving within a narrower and narrower corridor; as the corridor narrows, one can be more and more confident that the effect size estimate from any particular study is fairly accurate.

On the basis of their simulation, Schönbrodt and Perugini (2013) provided sample sizes typically required to reach a very narrow or moderately narrow corridor of stability around bivariate correlations ranging from quite small to very large (see Table 1 of Schönbrodt & Perugini, p. 611; see also Kelley & Maxwell, 2003, for a related discussion of precision in the more complex context of multiple regression). We can use their table to get a sense of the sample size required to get a fairly stable estimate of small, medium, or large correlations. For instance, they recommended that a reasonable heuristic for personality psychologists—who could plausibly expect to be studying an effect size somewhere in the ballpark of $r = .21$ (Richard, Bond, & Stokes-Zoota, 2003)—would be to aim for a sample size of at least 250. A slightly wider (i.e., less precise) but arguably still reasonable corridor of stability for researchers studying effect sizes around this order of magnitude would require sample sizes of approximately 100 ($n = 50$ per condition in a two-group experiment). In many cases, such sample sizes would require a considerable investment of resources before even beginning to conduct the main study of interest.

One might hope, then, that the resources devoted to a pilot study could also be incorporated into the main study, and this hope is what gave rise to the idea of an *internal pilot study*, or the idea that researchers could start collecting data to estimate an unknown effect size and then use this estimate to decide on an ultimate total sample size for that same study, in what has been termed an *adaptive design* (see, e.g., Lakens & Evers, 2014, and Wittes & Brittain, 1990). However, research has shown that reestimating a final sample size on the basis of the size of a treatment effect (e.g., a mean difference between conditions) can substantially inflate Type I error rates, and there is controversy about the best way to correct for this problem (e.g., Gordon Lan,

Soo, Siu, & Wang, 2005; Proschan & Hunsberger, 1995). For now, then, we recommend using one the strategies suggested above, or sequential analyses (described in more detail below).

Calculating Power

Once you have an effect size estimate in hand, you can conduct a classic power analysis to estimate the required sample size to achieve your desired level of power (often 80%) with your desired Type I error level (usually .05; Cohen, 1988; Ellis, 2010). One popular (and free) program that calculates power for many types of frequently used designs is G*Power (see http://www. gpower.hhu.de/en.html). However, it is important to note that such power analyses can be overly optimistic, for at least two reasons. First, when an effect size estimate comes from the prior literature on a topic, publication bias can cause that estimate to be too high (and the resulting sample size calculation to be too low to provide adequate power). To safeguard against the bias introduced by inflated effect size estimates, Perugini, Gallucci, and Costantini (2014) recommended that researchers conduct a *safeguard power analysis*, which constructs a confidence interval around the effect size estimate taken from previous research and uses the lower bound of this confidence interval in the power calculation.[2]

A second reason why classic power analyses can be overly optimistic is that they fail to take into account effect size heterogeneity; that is, the possibility that the size of an effect can vary across settings, samples, and operationalization of variables (McShane & Böckenholt, 2014). For instance, the effect of an SAT preparation course on SAT scores might be larger when the course is taught in a quiet room where students can concentrate versus a loud setting with many distractions. Classic power formulas ignore this possibility (they assume that heterogeneity is 0) and can therefore lead researchers to run underpowered studies, especially when effect sizes are small to medium. To address this problem and help researchers account for heterogeneity when planning studies, McShane and Böckenholt (2014) provided a new tool for calculating power that accounts for effect size heterogeneity and allows researchers to explore the potential consequences of heterogeneity when planning their sample sizes.[3]

Of course, these different strategies for calculating power will produce different estimates of the sample size necessary for your study. Which is right? Given that both publication bias and effect size heterogeneity characterize many areas of research, it is likely that the sample size suggested by a classic

---

[2]See p. 3 of their supplementary materials for the R code to run a safeguard power analysis (http://journals. sagepub.com/doi/suppl/10.1177/1745691614528519/suppl_file/10.1177_1745691614528519_ SuppData.pdf).
[3]See https://blakemcshane.shinyapps.io/hetsampsize for a tutorial and instructions.

power analysis will lead you to run an underpowered study. Getting a sense of the sample sizes recommended by these updated techniques can give you useful information about how well powered your study is likely to be, allowing you to make informed choices about where to devote your resources and how much to trust your eventual findings.

Confronting Real-World Challenges to Running Highly Powered Studies

It is one thing to know you need a sample size of 250 to shed light on your research question and another to actually get that sample. Depending on your institutional resources (e.g., whether you have a large subject pool and/or funds to pay participants), the type of research you conduct (e.g., survey studies vs. intensive laboratory procedures), and the type of participants you need (e.g., adults vs. children, individuals vs. couples), obtaining large samples can be very challenging. The solution is not to ignore power considerations or conduct only easy studies but instead to confront the power challenge head on, get creative whenever possible, and—when necessary— acknowledge the limitations that arise when ideals are constrained by reality.

Large samples are one route to high power, but they are not the only one (see Asendorpf et al., 2013, and Ellis, 2010). Understanding some of the other factors that affect power can provide you with a toolbox of different strategies for conducting well-powered research. For instance, when feasible, within-subject (vs. between-subjects) designs can dramatically boost the power of an experiment (see Greenwald, 1976, for a deeper consideration of the benefits and drawbacks of within-subject designs). Likewise, researchers would do well to invest in reliable measures of their constructs. Power drops as measurement error increases—indeed, although a scale reliability of $\alpha = .70$ is often described as "adequate," such low levels of reliability can lead to substantially underpowered studies, especially when one is examining small effects (Ledgerwood & Shrout, 2011; see Stanley & Spence, 2014, for a vivid illustration of how measurement error can produce results that fluctuate wildly). Conversely, identifying or constructing and validating highly reliable measures can give your study a much-needed power boost.[4]

---

[4]Researchers often attempt to address measurement error at the analysis phase; for instance, latent variables are often used because they protect against the bias produced by measurement error (in that they help ensure that the estimates produced across studies will accurately center on the true population parameter). However, latent variables are even more adversely affected by measurement error than are observed variables when it comes to power. To address this issue, Ledgerwood and Shrout (2011) offered a two-step approach to testing mediation models using both latent and observed variables that maximizes both accuracy and power when unreliability is unavoidable. Still, careful planning at the design phase of a study to minimize measurement error can allow you to avoid accuracy–power trade-offs altogether and provides the best route to making your later analyses as informative as possible.

In experimental designs, the careful choice of a covariate can boost power by soaking up some of the noise in your dependent variable. For instance, a researcher interested in whether stressful (vs. relaxing) situations make people less likely to behave cooperatively could reduce some of the unexplained variance in her dependent variable of cooperative behavior by measuring individual differences in the general predisposition to be cooperative and using this variable as a covariate in her analyses. Note, however, that using covariates can lead you astray in experimental designs[5] if the covariate changes the pattern of condition means rather than simply reducing error variance or you attempt analyses with and without the covariate and report only those that reach significance (e.g., Simmons, Nelson, & Simonsohn, 2011). You can check the first by running your analysis with and without the covariate and comparing the means and error terms; you can avoid the second by selecting and recording your intended analysis plan ahead of time (see the section Distinguishing Between Exploratory and Confirmatory Research later in this chapter).

Yet another power-boosting strategy worth considering is the option of aggregating several small, underpowered studies in a small-scale meta-analysis that can provide reliable results. Researchers limited by the number of participants they can recruit in a particular time frame (e.g., an academic semester or year) or in a particular setting (e.g., a political rally) might choose to run two or more separate, small studies testing the same effect that, when aggregated, achieve adequate power. Researchers who face resource constraints in terms of their access to participants or research funds can initiate a multi-laboratory collaboration in which two or more research teams conduct a study using identical protocols. The results of such study sets can then be pooled across settings or laboratories using meta-analytic techniques to provide greater power than any one study alone (see Braver, Thoemmes, & Rosenthal, 2014, for more on small-scale meta-analyses and relevant R code[6]). Alternatively, you can start a community-augmented meta-analysis (see Tsuji, Bergmann, & Cristia, 2014) that provides a simple way for any researcher who conducts a similar study to add their data to a continually updating online meta-analysis.

Whereas some research contexts make it challenging to attain adequate power, others make it easy—for instance, researchers who work with very large data sets can often run highly powered analyses with ease. Note that when power is very high, effect size estimation becomes much more informative than significance testing because even tiny correlations can reach significance in very large samples; it is important in such cases to think carefully about

---

[5]In correlational designs, on the other hand, failing to include an important covariate can lead to omitted-variable bias (Kennedy, 2003).
[6]This is also available at http://www.human.cornell.edu/hd/qml/software.cfm.

effect sizes (and what effect sizes are meaningful) rather than focusing solely on whether an effect can be detected (see, e.g., Gignac & Szodorai, 2016; Hill, Bloom, Black, & Lipsey, 2008; Valentine & Cooper, 2003).

Sequential Analyses

Ensuring adequate power can also be challenging when you are conducting initial studies in new lines of research for which you have very little information about the likely size of an effect. If you guess too high when estimating your effect size, your study could be woefully underpowered; if you guess too low, you could waste substantial resources when a smaller sample would have been sufficient to detect significance. In such cases, sequential analyses can provide a valuable tool that allows you to adequately power your study to detect a potentially small effect size but to stop early and conserve resources if the effect turns out to be larger than anticipated (Lakens & Evers, 2014; Proschan, Lan, & Wittes, 2006).

In a sequential design, you choose ahead of time both a planned total sample size as well as the number of points throughout data collection at which you will conduct interim analyses on your data. At each interim analysis point that you choose you will have the option of stopping data collection early if the p value for the planned analysis falls below a planned criterion point. Whereas unplanned optional stopping inflates Type I error (Sagarin, Ambler, & Lee, 2014), planned optional stopping in a sequential analysis holds Type I error constant by portioning out the total desired alpha level (often .05) across the interim and final analyses.

To calculate the criterion for each interim analysis, you can use the GroupSeq package in R, which includes a graphical user interface for those who are unfamiliar with the R programming language (a step-by-step guide to using GroupSeq can be found at https://osf.io/qtufw/). This package will also calculate all the adjustments to p values, effect sizes, and confidence intervals necessary to account for the fact that sequential analysis was used (Lakens, 2014).

There are a few different options for setting the criterion at each interim analysis point (DeMets & Lan, 1995). Some, such as the O'Brien–Fleming method, require researchers to choose the number of interim analyses they will conduct ahead of time and to make them equally spaced. For instance, if you plan a study with a target final sample size of 300 participants and want to conduct two interim analyses, you would have to conduct those analyses after collecting data from 100 participants and then after collecting data from 200 participants. Other methods, which include different types of spending functions, allow more flexibility: You must decide a priori the upper bound on the sample size and the type of spending function you will use, but you do not have to choose the number of interim analyses ahead of time or keep them equally spaced.[7] The R package can compute the appropriate statistics for a few different types of spending functions and for both equally and nonequally spaced interim analyses, allowing you flexibility in choosing which approach works best for you.

Although sequential designs can provide a valuable tool for balancing between the goals of boosting power and conserving resources, it is important to also acknowledge their downsides. In particular, the effect sizes obtained from sequential analyses will tend to be inflated because early interim analyses are conducted on relatively small samples and, as we saw above, small samples produce widely fluctuating estimates. Early interim analyses are therefore more likely to hit significance when a fluctuating estimate is too large, and so sequential analyses tend to overestimate effect sizes; moreover, the earlier the study is stopped, the greater the inflation will be (Zhang et al., 2012). Thus, sequential analyses are best suited for studies in which researchers are mainly interested in testing whether an effect exists rather than determining a stable estimate of the effect size itself (Lakens, 2014). Researchers interested in estimating effect sizes should use larger samples and/or use meta-analytic techniques to gain more stable, precise estimates.

ONLINE SAMPLES

As researchers have begun to pay more attention to power and the importance of adequate sample sizes, recruiting online samples has become increasingly popular. Multiple platforms now enable data collection from online participants, including Project Implicit, Amazon's Mechanical Turk (MTurk), Prolific Academic, CrowdFlower, Microworkers, and others (see, e.g., Chandler, Mueller, & Paolacci, 2014; Peer, Samat, Brandimarte, & Acquisti, 2015).

There are both benefits and drawbacks to online participant pools. One obvious benefit is that many of the platforms mentioned above allow social scientists to recruit large convenience samples quickly and at a relatively low cost. One obvious drawback is that researchers are limited to study procedures that can be effectively implemented online, and many aspects of the testing environment (e.g., distractions, multitasking) are not under the researcher's control.

---

[7]You may need an initial guess of the planned total sample size and the spacing of interim analyses to run the power calculations for the design, but the actual number and spacing of the analyses in the final study can deviate from the initial specifications without significantly influencing the Type I error rate, as long as the spacing of the analyses is independent of the results at any given interim analyses (see DeMets & Lan, 1995).

Other costs and benefits are perhaps less obvious. For instance, MTurk's large participant pool may allow for a more diverse sample than the typical college student sample (Buhrmester, Kwang, & Gosling, 2011; DeSoto, 2016), which could help researchers address the potential generalizability concerns that come with an exclusive reliance on undergraduate samples (Sears, 1986). Moreover, evidence suggests that MTurk data quality is high (Buhrmester et al., 2011; Crump, McDonnell, & Gureckis, 2013; Peer et al., 2015) but also potentially variable (Paolacci & Chandler, 2014). MTurk participants appear to be both extrinsically and intrinsically motivated to take surveys (e.g., Paolacci, Chandler, & Ipeirotis, 2010), and research on attention checks suggests that MTurk substantially outperforms other crowd-sourcing websites and performs equally well as community samples (Peer et al., 2015). In comparison with student samples, the evidence has been more mixed, with different studies showing that MTurkers are less attentive (Goodman, Cryder, & Cheema, 2013), equally attentive (Paolacci et al., 2010), and more attentive (Hauser & Schwarz, 2015). The latest consensus appears to be that MTurkers tend to pay better attention than college students (Hauser & Schwarz, 2015; Klein et al., 2014). This newer evidence suggests that student samples often involve participants with low intrinsic motivation to pay attention to instructions (i.e., they participate only to fulfill a course requirement) and little time to learn the norms of survey participation. In contrast, the high intrinsic motivation and nonnaïveté of the MTurk population may provide the right mix of incentives to pay attention, and the attention gap between student samples and MTurk samples may widen as MTurkers become increasingly familiar with survey participation (Hauser & Schwarz, 2015). In addition, MTurk data appear to be at least as reliable (in terms of both measurement reliability and replicability) as data from laboratory experiments; however, that reliability varies across different platforms (e.g., CrowdFlower and MicroWorkers may be less reliable than MTurk; see Buhrmester et al., 2011; Peer et al., 2015).

On the other hand, online participant pools may have hidden drawbacks. Participant attrition can differ dramatically across conditions, leading to erroneous conclusions if researchers do not take steps to minimize, check, and transparently report attrition rates (see Zhou & Fishbach, 2016, for concrete recommendations). Recent research has also highlighted the small size of the total population of MTurk participants: A typical laboratory can access a pool of approximately 7,300 MTurkers at a given point in time, and this pool is largely shared with the many other researchers in the world running studies on MTurk at the same time (DeSoto, 2016; Stewart et al., 2015). Moreover, turnover is fairly slow: It takes about 7 months for half of this participant pool to leave and be replaced by new participants (Stewart et al., 2015). Whereas familiarity with survey participation in general may have benefits, as noted above, nonnaïveté with respect to particular paradigms and hypotheses may be costly. Many MTurkers are "professional survey-takers" who complete multiple related studies (Chandler et al., 2014; Peer et al., 2015), and they may use the Internet to find answers to survey questions (Goodman et al., 2013). Although there are some methods to mitigate these problems,[8] they may still produce inaccurate effect size estimates and could limit both internal and external validity (Berinsky et al., 2012; Chandler, Paolacci, Peer, Mueller, & Ratliff, 2015).

In addition, although online convenience samples can improve your ability to generalize your findings when they offer greater diversity than a typical college student sample, they can be far from representative; for instance, an MTurk sample is unlikely to enable researchers to generalize across cultures (e.g., Henrich, Heine, & Norenzayan, 2010). Moreover, using online samples can constrain generalizability to the extent that they impose methodological constraints on your research (e.g., requiring the use of hypothetical scenarios rather than in-person interactions in the laboratory; see Eastwick, Hunt, & Neff, 2013).

Overall, then, online participant pools offer a promising tool for enabling researchers to improve power by collecting larger samples, and yet they are not a panacea. The choice to use them should be a considered and careful one, and the push for greater power should not cause us to lose sight of their very real limitations. Online platforms such as MTurk may be particularly well suited for simple and infrequently used paradigms (rather than complex or commonly used ones). In the meantime, we should ask questions about the generalizability of conclusions that rely exclusively on data collected from online participant pools and/or hypothetical rather than live scenarios in the same way that we ask questions about the reliability of underpowered research.

Our ability to learn useful information from research conducted with online participant pools also depends on the extent to which researchers can work together to maintain these limited and shared resources. For instance, a single researcher's choice to use deception in an MTurk study may have ramifications for how those participants respond in future studies (see Hertwig & Ortmann, 2008; Jamison, Karlan, & Schechter, 2008): An MTurk worker deceived about an ostensible interaction with another participant in one study may be suspicious of the existence of a real interaction partner in a subsequent study. Researchers may want to consider strategies for minimizing deception in at least some of these shared participant pools (Bardsley, 2000).

---

[8]For example, researchers can ask questions about prior experience with tasks and set a priori exclusion criteria to eliminate participants with certain levels of experience.

Likewise, researchers interested in promoting the importance of highly powered studies should consider the practical tools that will help push research practices in this direction, including strategies to increase both the size of online participant pools and the capabilities of online platforms to support different types of methods and paradigms. More broadly, scholars in the social sciences would do well to design platforms for online data collection that align researcher incentives to maximize individual self-interest (i.e., to recruit a large sample as quickly as possible for the lowest cost) with the goal of preserving a high-quality shared participant pool for future use.

DISTINGUISHING BETWEEN EXPLORATORY AND CONFIRMATORY RESEARCH

When planning a study, it is important to think about whether you would like any of your eventual analyses to be confirmatory—that is, set and recorded ahead of time—rather than more exploratory and flexible in nature. Sometimes you may want to conduct purely exploratory research. The goal in such cases is to use a bottom-up approach to learn about the patterns suggested by a particular data set, in order to generate new hypotheses and/or inform future studies. Exploratory analyses can be data dependent (i.e., researchers can tailor their analytic approach to the particular nuances of the data to help capture potentially interesting patterns). For example, an exploratory approach to a correlation table might reveal a suggestive pattern in which one variable positively (and perhaps nonsignificantly) predicts several items that could plausibly tap a common construct; a researcher might then fruitfully collapse those related items into a single measure and discover a stronger relation between the predictor and the new aggregate measure (Ghiselli, Campbell, & Zedeck, 1981). In exploratory analyses, then, the point is to learn from suggestive patterns in the data rather than to use inferential statistics for the purpose of testing particular a priori hypotheses and drawing strong conclusions.

Purely exploratory research can be enormously generative, especially in the first phases of a research program when venturing into new scientific territory. Often, however, researchers are interested in conducting research that has a confirmatory component (frequently in addition to an exploratory component). If you are interested in being able to attach a high level of confidence to a particular finding (e.g., you want to be able to conclude that your experimental manipulation influenced your key dependent measure of interest or that two groups differ in their level of a particular attribute), it is important to set and record the analysis plan that you will use to test this particular finding ahead of time.

Recording Your Analysis Before Examining a Data Set

There are two simple reasons why it is important for researchers to record their analysis plan before looking at a given data set. First, the number of different ways that you look for a result changes your Type I error rate (i.e., the likelihood that you see a result in your data that is actually just chance fluctuation). For instance, if you test a single correlation with an alpha set at .05, you have a 5% chance of erroneously concluding that there is a relation between those two variables when there is none. Of course, if you test 10 different correlations, your chance of erroneously detecting a relation between at least one pair of variables increases substantially. Perhaps less intuitive is that testing an effect in multiple ways (e.g., before and after excluding a subset of participants from the analysis, using any one of several potential outcome measures) increases your Type I error rate as well (see Gelman & Loken, 2014; Kaplan & Irvin, 2015; MacCallum, Roznowski, & Necowitz, 1992; Sagarin et al., 2014; Simmons et al., 2011). Thus, to be able to interpret a small p value (e.g., $p < .05$) as strong evidence for your effect you need to know that you have not unintentionally inflated your Type I error rate by testing your effect in multiple ways. Alternatively, you can in some cases account for data-dependent flexibility by adjusting your p value (as in the case of optional stopping [see Sagarin et al., 2014] or post hoc adjustments for multiple comparisons [see Welkowitz, Cohen, & Lea, 2012]). Either way, the goal is to be able to take a statistical result at face value in terms of the strength of evidence it provides for a particular finding: If you do not know what your Type I error rate is, you cannot get a good sense of how strong the evidence is for a given conclusion (de Groot, 2014).

Second, because scientists are human, and because the human mind tends to be biased in how it processes and remembers information—especially when we are motivated to reach a particular conclusion—we cannot rely on our own minds to accurately remember what our original analysis plan was (Chaiken & Ledgerwood, 2012; Kunda, 1990; Nosek, Spies, & Motyl, 2012). In other words, once you see a significant correlation in your table of correlations, or once you notice that your effect is significant when you analyze the data one way but not the other, your human mind is quite capable of convincing you that this was the one test you intended to run all along. Recording your plan ahead of time enables you to circumvent human bias—you can know for sure which analyses you planned and which were data dependent, so that you can accurately distinguish between confirmatory and exploratory findings.

Confirmatory findings are useful because they allow you to have a high level of confidence in a particular observed relation between operational variables in your study. For instance, if you plan to test the effect of being in a high (vs. low) stress situation on a measure of creativity in a (well-powered) study and you find a significant result, you can conclude with a reasonable level of confidence that your manipulation affected your measure. In other words, confirmatory research allows you to place a high degree of trust in the relations you observe between the particular manipulations and/or measures in your study; you can trust that the result you see is likely to be truly there, instead of an artifact of chance.

Confirmatory research is therefore an important complement to exploratory research because it allows researchers to infer with confidence the presence of a specific relation between operational variables. On the other hand, exploratory research can help bolster confidence in the meaning of that specific relation (Finkel, Eastwick, & Reis, 2015). For instance, a significant effect of a stress manipulation on a creativity measure does not guarantee that these operational variables are accurately tapping their intended constructs. If exploratory analyses were to reveal that stress also influences a host of other cognitive outcomes that (like creativity) require cognitive resources, you might begin to suspect that the initial result you observed was part of a broader story about stress and cognitive resources, not creativity per se. Such exploratory analyses can be especially important when working with large data sets or when conducting independent conceptual replications is difficult or costly (see Finkel et al., 2015). A preanalysis plan should never prevent researchers from conducting additional exploratory analyses—the point is simply to clearly and transparently label such additional analyses as exploratory instead of as specified ahead of time (Casey, Glennerster, & Miguel, 2012; Chambers, Feredoes, Muthukumraswamy, & Etchells, 2014; de Groot, 2014; Humphreys, Sanchez de la Sierra, & van der Windt, 2013).

Setting Plans for Confirmatory Research

There are a variety of ways to set and record a preanalysis plan for confirmatory research, ranging from very basic to very detailed and from private to public. For instance, a research team might develop a set of core features (e.g., planned total sample size, planned exclusion criteria, any planned confirmatory statistical tests) that they always record for themselves before conducting a study, so that they can easily distinguish between exploratory and confirmatory findings later when conducting their analyses. Another research team might prefer to publicly preregister a detailed preanalysis plan for each study, using an independent registry (e.g., http://www.socialscience registry.org, http://www.openscienc:framework.org, http://www.egap.org/ design-registration).[9] The most useful format and content of a preanalysis

---

[9]Note that public preregistration has the added benefit of helping to address the file drawer problem (Rosenthal, 1979; Simes, 1986).

TABLE 2.1
Common Content for a Preanalysis Plan

Consider specifying	Example
Planned sample size	Target total: $N = 200$
Inclusion and exclusion criteria	Participants must respond correctly to attention-check item
Variable construction	Predictor: Group identification (average of 10-item measure)
	DV: Willingness to pay for identity-related products (average of dollar amounts indicated for each of the five products presented)
Primary versus secondary outcome measures	Primary outcome measure: Willingness to pay DV
	Secondary measure: Liking for products (average of liking ratings for each of the five products)
Any planned covariates	Annual household income measure
Planned statistical tests involving specific operational variables	Linear regression (regressive willingness to pay on group identification with income as a covariate)
Any planned follow-up or subgroup analyses	N/A

Note. DV = dependent variable; N/A = not applicable.

plan is likely to vary across research teams and projects, depending on the type of research, the complexity of the analyses, and the norms of a given field (see Casey et al., 2012, for an excellent example of how to grapple with the nuances and trade-offs involved in choosing the timing and level of detail for various elements in a preanalysis plan). If you are new to confirmatory plans, consider starting with something basic that you feel comfortable with (something is better than nothing) and building from there. Your main goal is to ensure that you will be able to accurately distinguish between exploratory and confirmatory analyses and conclusions and that any decisions you make for your confirmatory analyses are independent of the data themselves. Common examples of content that a researcher might specify in a preanalysis plan are listed in Table 2.1 (see also Glennerster & Takavarasha, 2013).

Of course, it is difficult to anticipate every possible complication that can arise in the research process, and there will be times when you need to alter a preanalysis plan after recording it.[10] For instance, you might plan to conduct a linear regression only to realize on seeing the data that the pattern

---

[10]There are also research contexts in which preanalysis plans are simply not feasible. In such cases, a more complete analysis of the data that explicitly takes into account all possible comparisons may be the best way forward (Gelman & Loken, 2014; see Steegen, Tuerlinckx, Gelman, & Vanpaemel, 2016, for concrete recommendations).

is curvilinear. In such cases, the preanalysis plan should never prevent you from performing the more statistically appropriate test; instead, you should transparently record the change to the preanalysis plan and note the rationale. More broadly, it is always important, regardless of whether you are conducting exploratory or confirmatory analyses, to test your statistical assumptions and to actually look at your data. Are your measures skewed? Could your results be misleading because of an extreme outlier, a failed manipulation, the presence of an unexpected moderator, an unanticipated ceiling effect, or a measure with limited variability? The point of a preanalysis plan is not to constrain your data analysis to the rote and unconsidered implementation of a fixed analysis script—the point is to clearly distinguish between what you planned ahead of time and what you chose to do after looking at your data.

PLANNING PROGRAMMATIC RESEARCH: DIRECT, SYSTEMATIC, AND CONCEPTUAL REPLICATION

No matter how carefully you plan your study to maximize its informational value, at the end of the day it is still a single study—a data point that can usefully contribute to a cumulative understanding of a phenomenon rather than providing a definitive, stand-alone conclusion (see Braver et al., 2014; Cumming, 2012; Ledgerwood & Sherman, 2012). You want that data point to be as informative as possible, but you may also want to accumulate multiple data points that can together provide a more substantial contribution to a given topic area. When considering how best to assemble a package of studies, it is useful to consider how direct, systematic, and conceptual replication could each contribute to your cumulative understanding of a research question (see also Chapter 14, this volume).

Direct replications (also called *close* or *exact* replications) aim to repeat the procedures used in a prior study as closely as possible (Fabrigar & Wegener, 2016; Hendrick, 1991; Schmidt, 2009). Direct replications serve to increase confidence in an observed relationship between particular operational variables (i.e., the specific manipulations and/or measures used in a previous study). For instance, if exploratory analyses in an initial study provide evidence suggestive of a particular pattern of results, a direct replication would provide an opportunity to confirm that pattern in an independent data set. If you wish to increase your confidence in a particular finding (e.g., you observed an interesting effect of your manipulation on your primary outcome measure, but only after an unanticipated change to your preanalysis plan), direct replication is often a useful next step.

Systematic replications aim to vary presumably incidental aspects of the context in which a finding was initially obtained, in order to test the critical assumption that those details are in fact irrelevant to the finding (Kantowitz, Roediger, & Elmes, 2014). Systematic replications help increase confidence in the generalizability of an observed relation between particular operational variables. For instance, upon noting an interesting correlation in an initial study, a survey researcher might want to systematically replicate it in a second study that varies the order of the survey questions, to rule out the possibility that the initial results might be specific to a particular question order (Schwarz, 1999). An experimental researcher might want to systematically replicate the effect of a manipulation on a particular measure in a second study using different stimuli, to test whether the initial results were specific to a particular stimulus set (Roediger, 2012; see also Westfall, Judd, & Kenny, 2015). Systematic replications help scientists combat confirmation bias in their research process by pushing them to explicitly consider and test whether variables presumed irrelevant for producing an effect might be relevant. Systematic replications encourage the question "What *shouldn't* be important for producing this effect?" rather than only "What *should* be important?" Systematic replication is therefore often a useful intermediate step between direct and conceptual replication.

Conceptual replications aim to vary the particular operationalizations of a given theoretical construct (i.e., the manipulations and/or measures used in a particular study), in order to test whether different operationalizations of the same theoretical construct will produce the same effect. Conceptual replications serve to increase confidence in the meaning of a particular result. If multiple possible operationalizations of the same theoretical variable produce the same pattern of findings, you can be more confident that the results reflect something about the theoretical construct rather than the particular operationalization used to assess it (Brewer & Crano, 2014; Cook & Campbell, 1979). Conceptual replications are therefore useful when you are confident about the presence of a particular pattern of results between operational variables but you want to know if they are really tapping the intended theoretical concepts. If your theoretical predictions hold up across a range of operationalizations, then you can be more confident that you are learning about the underlying concepts and theory rather than a specific instance of an effect (Crandall & Sherman, 2016; Fabrigar & Wegener, 2016).

In general, when conducting replications it is important to appreciate how widely results can fluctuate from one study to the next because of chance, especially with small samples and imperfect measures, and to adopt a cumulative approach that aggregates across studies rather than counting each one in isolation as a "success" or "failure" (see Braver et al., 2014; Eastwick, Neff, Finkel, Luchies, & Hunt, 2014; Fabrigar & Wegener, 2016; Stanley & Spence, 2014). For instance, suppose you conduct a confirmatory analysis of a particular effect in three independent data sets and find a significant result in one case and a nonsignificant result in the other two. The best approach to understanding these data would be a meta-analytic one that aggregates across the three findings to provide a cumulative understanding of the effect (rather than concluding that one study "worked" and the other two "failed to replicate"; see also Gelman & Stern, 2006).

It is also important to recognize that the goals served by conducting an independent direct, systematic, or conceptual replication can be served in other ways as well, and the best tool for pursuing a given goal is likely to vary across different research contexts. For instance, the goal of attaining high confidence in a given relation between operational variables can be served by conducting a series of smaller, tightly controlled experiments or by conducting one very large and well-powered study in the first place. The goal to increase confidence in the generalizability of a given relation between operational variables can be served by conducting a series of systematic replication studies that vary in the stimulus set used, or by including a larger set of stimuli in the original study and treating stimuli as a random factor in the design (Judd, Westfall, & Kenny, 2012). And the goal to increase confidence in the meaning of a particular result can be served by conducting conceptual replications, or by conducting additional analyses in a large data set that help provide converging evidence for an effect across a range of measures, boosting confidence in convergent and divergent validity (Finkel et al., 2015). Choose the tools that work best for addressing your particular goals in your own particular research context.

CONCLUSION

The decisions you make when planning a study or a series of studies have important implications for how much you learn from your results. How can you ensure adequate power? Who will comprise your sample? How will you distinguish between exploratory and confirmatory findings? What tools will best enable you to have a high level of confidence in your results, and what kind of confidence is most important to you at this stage of the research process? A careful consideration of these questions will help maximize the information you learn from the work that you do.

RECOMMENDED READING

Braver, S. L., Thoemmes, F. J., & Rosenthal, R. (2014). Continuously cumulating meta-analysis and replicability. *Perspectives on Psychological Science, 9*, 333–342.

Button, K. S., Ioannidis, J. P., Mokrysz, C., Nosek, B. A., Flint, J., Robinson, E. S., & Munafò, M. R. (2013). Power failure: Why small sample size undermines the reliability of neuroscience. *Nature Reviews Neuroscience, 14,* 365–376.

Fabrigar, L. R., & Wegener, D. T. (2016). Conceptualizing and evaluating the replication of research results. *Journal of Experimental Social Psychology, 66,* 68–80. http://dx.doi.org/10.1016/j.jesp.2015.07.009

Gelman, A., & Loken, E. (2014). The statistical crisis in science. *American Scientist, 102,* 460–465.

Schönbrodt, F. D., & Perugini, M. (2013). At what sample size do correlations stabilize? *Journal of Research in Personality, 4,* 609–612.

REFERENCES

Asendorpf, J. B., Conner, M., De Fruyt, F., De Houwer, J., Denissen, J. J., Fiedler, K., . . . Wicherts, J. M. (2013). Recommendations for increasing replicability in psychology. *European Journal of Personality, 27,* 108–119. http://dx.doi.org/10.1002/per.1919

Bardsley, N. (2000). Control without deception: Individual behaviour in free-riding experiments revisited. *Experimental Economics, 3,* 215–240. http://dx.doi.org/10.1023/A:1011420500828

Begley, C. G., & Ellis, L. M. (2012). Drug development: Raise standards for preclinical cancer research. *Nature, 483,* 531–533. http://dx.doi.org/10.1038/483531a

Berinsky, A. J., Huber, G. A., & Lenz, G. S. (2012). Evaluating online labor markets for experimental research: Amazon.com's Mechanical Turk. *Political Analysis, 20,* 351–368.

Braver, S. L., Thoemmes, F. J., & Rosenthal, R. (2014). Continuously cumulating meta-analysis and replicability. *Perspectives on Psychological Science, 9,* 333–342. http://dx.doi.org/10.1177/1745691614529796

Brewer, M. B., & Crano, W. D. (2014). Research design and issues of validity. In H. T. Reis & C. Judd (Eds.), *Handbook of research methods in social and personality psychology* (2nd ed., pp. 11–26). New York, NY: Cambridge University Press.

Buhrmester, M., Kwang, T., & Gosling, S. D. (2011). Amazon's Mechanical Turk: A new source of inexpensive, yet high-quality, data? *Perspectives on Psychological Science, 6,* 3–5. http://dx.doi.org/10.1177/1745691610393980

Button, K. S., Ioannidis, J. P., Mokrysz, C., Nosek, B. A., Flint, J., Robinson, E. S., & Munafò, M. R. (2013). Power failure: Why small sample size undermines the reliability of neuroscience. *Nature Reviews Neuroscience, 14,* 365–376. http://dx.doi.org/10.1038/nrn3475

Casey, K., Glennerster, R., & Miguel, E. (2012). Reshaping institutions: Evidence on aid impacts using a pre-analysis plan. Report No. W17012, National Bureau of Economic Research, Cambridge, MA. http://dx.doi.org/10.3386/w17012

Chaiken, S., & Ledgerwood, A. (2012). A theory of heuristic and systematic information processing. In P. A. M. van Lange, A. W. Kruglanski, & E. T. Higgins (Eds.), *Handbook of theories of social psychology* (pp. 246–266). Thousand Oaks, CA: Sage. http://dx.doi.org/10.4135/9781446249215.n13

Chambers, C. D., Feredoes, E., Muthukumaraswamy, S. D., & Etchells, P. J. (2014). Instead of "playing the game" it is time to change the rules: Registered reports at *AIMS Neuroscience* and beyond. *AIMS Neuroscience, 1,* 4–17.

Chandler, J., Mueller, P., & Paolacci, G. (2014). Nonnaïveté among Amazon Mechanical Turk workers: Consequences and solutions for behavioral researchers. *Behavior Research Methods, 46,* 112–130. http://dx.doi.org/10.3758/s13428-013-0365-7

Chandler, J., Paolacci, G., Peer, E., Mueller, P., & Ratliff, K. A. (2015). Using nonnaive participants can reduce effect sizes. *Psychological Science, 26,* 1131–1139. http://dx.doi.org/10.1177/0956797615585115

Cohen, J. (1988). *Statistical power analysis for the behavioral sciences* (2nd ed.). Hillsdale, NJ: Erlbaum.

Cook, T. D., & Campbell, D. T. (1979). *Quasi-experimentation: Design and analysis for field settings.* New York, NY: Rand McNally.

Crandall, C., & Sherman, J. (2016). On the scientific superiority of conceptual replications for scientific progress. *Journal of Experimental Social Psychology, 66,* 93–99. http://dx.doi.org/10.1016/j.jesp.2015.10.002

Crump, M. J., McDonnell, J. V., & Gureckis, T. M. (2013). Evaluating Amazon's Mechanical Turk as a tool for experimental behavioral research. *PLOS ONE, 8,* e57410. http://dx.doi.org/10.1371/journal.pone.0057410

Cumming, G. (2012). *Understanding the new statistics: Effect sizes, confidence intervals, and meta-analysis.* New York, NY: Routledge.

de Groot, A. D. (2014). The meaning of "significance" for different types of research [translated and annotated by E.-J. Wagenmakers, D. Borsboom, J. Verhagen, R. Kievit, M. Bakker, A. Cramer, . . . H. L. J. van der Maas]. *Acta Psychologica, 148,* 188–194. (Original work published 1956) http://dx.doi.org/10.1016/j.actpsy.2014.02.001

DeMets, D. L., & Lan, K. K. G. (1995). The alpha spending function approach to interim data analyses. In P. Thall (Ed.), *Recent advances in clinical trial design and analysis* (pp. 1–27). Boston, MA: Kluwer Academic. http://dx.doi.org/10.1007/978-1-4615-2009-2_1

DeSoto, A. (2016, March). Under the hood of Mechanical Turk. *APS Observer, 29*(3). Retrieved from https://www.psychologicalscience.org/publications/observer/2016/march-16/under-the-hood-of-mechanical-turk.html

Eastwick, P. W., Hunt, L. L., & Neff, L. A. (2013). External validity, why art thou externally valid? Recent studies of attraction provide three theoretical answers. *Social & Personality Psychology Compass, 7,* 275–288. http://dx.doi.org/10.1111/spc3.12026

Eastwick, P. W., Neff, L. A., Finkel, E. J., Luchies, L. B., & Hunt, L. L. (2014). Is a meta-analysis a foundation, or just another brick? Comment on Meltzer, McNulty, Jackson, and Karney (2014). *Journal of Personality and Social Psychology*, *106*, 429–434. http://dx.doi.org/10.1037/a0034767

Ellis, P. D. (2010). *The essential guide to effect sizes: Statistical power, meta-analysis, and the interpretation of research results*. New York, NY: Cambridge University Press. http://dx.doi.org/10.1017/CBO9780511761676

Fabrigar, L. R., & Wegener, D. T. (2016). Conceptualizing and evaluating the replication of research results. *Journal of Experimental Social Psychology*, *66*, 68–80. http://dx.doi.org/10.1016/j.jesp.2015.07.009

Finkel, E. J., Eastwick, P. W., & Reis, H. T. (2015). Best research practices in psychology: Illustrating epistemological and pragmatic considerations with the case of relationship science. *Journal of Personality and Social Psychology*, *108*, 275–297. http://dx.doi.org/10.1037/pspi0000007

Gelman, A., & Carlin, J. (2014). Beyond power calculations: Assessing Type S (sign) and Type M (magnitude) errors. *Perspectives on Psychological Science*, *9*, 641–651. http://dx.doi.org/10.1177/1745691614551642

Gelman, A., & Loken, E. (2014). The statistical crisis in science. *American Scientist*, *102*, 460–465. http://dx.doi.org/10.1511/2014.111.460

Gelman, A., & Stern, H. (2006). The difference between "significant" and "not significant" is not itself statistically significant. *The American Statistician*, *60*, 328–331. http://dx.doi.org/10.1198/000313006X152649

Ghiselli, E. E., Campbell, J. P., & Zedeck, S. (1981). *Measurement theory for the behavioral sciences: Origin and evolution*. New York, NY: W. H. Freeman.

Gignac, G. E., & Szodorai, E. (2016). Effect size guidelines for individual differences researchers. *Personality and Individual Differences*, *102*, 74–78.

Glennerster, R., & Takavarasha, K. (2013). *Running randomized evaluations: A practical guide*. Princeton, NJ: Princeton University Press.

Goodman, J. K., Cryder, C. E., & Cheema, A. (2013). Data collection in a flat world: The strengths and weaknesses of Mechanical Turk samples. *Journal of Behavioral Decision Making*, *26*, 213–224. http://dx.doi.org/10.1002/bdm.1753

Gordon Lan, K. K., Soo, Y., Siu, C., & Wang, M. (2005). The use of weighted Z-tests in medical research. *Journal of Biopharmaceutical Statistics*, *15*, 625–639. http://dx.doi.org/10.1081/BIP-200062284

Greenwald, A. G. (1976). Within-subjects designs: To use or not to use? *Psychological Bulletin*, *83*, 314–320. http://dx.doi.org/10.1037/0033-2909.83.2.314

Hauser, D. J., & Schwarz, N. (2015). Elaborative thinking increases the impact of physical weight on importance judgments. *Social Cognition*, *33*, 120–132. http://dx.doi.org/10.1521/soco.2015.33.2.120

Hendrick, C. (1991). Replications, strict replications, and conceptual replications: Are they important? In J. W. Neuliep (Ed.), *Replication research in the social sciences* (pp. 41–49). Newbury Park, CA: Sage.

Henrich, J., Heine, S. J., & Norenzayan, A. (2010). The weirdest people in the world? *Behavioral and Brain Sciences*, *33*, 61–83. http://dx.doi.org/10.1017/S0140525X0999152X

Hertwig, R., & Ortmann, A. (2008). Deception in experiments: Revisiting the arguments in its defense. *Ethics & Behavior*, *18*, 59–92. http://dx.doi.org/10.1080/10508420701712990

Hill, C. J., Bloom, H. S., Black, A. R., & Lipsey, M. W. (2008). Empirical benchmarks for interpreting effect sizes in research. *Child Development Perspectives*, *2*, 172–177. http://dx.doi.org/10.1111/j.1750-8606.2008.00061.x

Humphreys, M., Sanchez de la Sierra, R., & van der Windt, P. (2013). Fishing, commitment, and communication: A proposal for comprehensive nonbinding research registration. *Political Analysis*, *21*, 1–20. http://dx.doi.org/10.1093/pan/mps021

Ioannidis, J. P. (2008). Why most discovered true associations are inflated. *Epidemiology*, *19*, 640–648. http://dx.doi.org/10.1097/EDE.0b013e31818131e7

Jamison, J., Karlan, D., & Schechter, L. (2008). To deceive or not to deceive: The effect of deception on behavior in future laboratory experiments. *Journal of Economic Behavior & Organization*, *68*, 477–488. http://dx.doi.org/10.1016/j.jebo.2008.09.002

Judd, C. M., Westfall, J., & Kenny, D. A. (2012). Treating stimuli as a random factor in social psychology: A new and comprehensive solution to a pervasive but largely ignored problem. *Journal of Personality and Social Psychology*, *103*, 54–69. http://dx.doi.org/10.1037/a0028347

Kantowitz, B., Roediger, H., III, & Elmes, D. (2014). *Experimental psychology*. Stamford, CT: Cengage Learning.

Kaplan, R. M., & Irvin, V. L. (2015). Likelihood of null effects of large NHLBI clinical trials has increased over time. *PLOS ONE*, *10*, e0132382. http://dx.doi.org/10.1371/journal.pone.0132382

Kelley, K., & Maxwell, S. E. (2003). Sample size for multiple regression: Obtaining regression coefficients that are accurate, not simply significant. *Psychological Methods*, *8*, 305–321. http://dx.doi.org/10.1037/1082-989X.8.3.305

Kennedy, P. (2003). *A guide to econometrics*. Cambridge, MA: MIT Press.

Klein, R. A., Ratliff, K. A., Vianello, M., Adams, R. B., Jr., Bahník, Š., Bernstein, M. J., . . . Nosek, B. A. (2014). Investigating variation in replicability. *Social Psychology*, *45*, 142–152. http://dx.doi.org/10.1027/1864-9335/a000178

Kunda, Z. (1990). The case for motivated reasoning. *Psychological Bulletin*, *108*, 480–498. http://dx.doi.org/10.1037/0033-2909.108.3.480

Lakens, D. (2014). Performing high-powered studies efficiently with sequential analyses. *European Journal of Social Psychology*, *44*, 701–710. http://dx.doi.org/10.1002/ejsp.2023

Lakens, D., & Evers, E. R. (2014). Sailing from the seas of chaos into the corridor of stability: Practical recommendations to increase the informational value of studies. *Perspectives on Psychological Science, 9*, 278–292. http://dx.doi.org/10.1177/1745691614528520

Ledgerwood, A. (2014). Introduction to the special section on advancing our methods and practices. *Perspectives on Psychological Science, 9*, 275–277. http://dx.doi.org/10.1177/1745691614529448

Ledgerwood, A. (2016). Introduction to the special section on improving research practices: Thinking deeply across the research cycle. *Perspectives on Psychological Science, 11*, 661–663. http://dx.doi.org/10.1177/1745691616662441

Ledgerwood, A., & Sherman, J. W. (2012). Short, sweet, and problematic? The rise of the short report in psychological science. *Perspectives on Psychological Science, 7*, 60–66. http://dx.doi.org/10.1177/1745691611427304

Ledgerwood, A., & Shrout, P. E. (2011). The trade-off between accuracy and precision in latent variable models of mediation processes. *Journal of Personality and Social Psychology, 101*, 1174–1188. http://dx.doi.org/10.1037/a0024776

MacCallum, R. C., Roznowski, M., & Necowitz, L. B. (1992). Model modifications in covariance structure analysis: The problem of capitalization on chance. *Psychological Bulletin, 111*, 490–504. http://dx.doi.org/10.1037/0033-2909.111.3.490

Maxwell, S. E. (2004). The persistence of underpowered studies in psychological research: Causes, consequences, and remedies. *Psychological Methods, 9*, 147–163. http://dx.doi.org/10.1037/1082-989X.9.2.147

McNutt, M. (2014, January 17). Reproducibility. *Science, 343*, 229. http://dx.doi.org/10.1126/science.1250475

McShane, B. B., & Böckenholt, U. (2014). You cannot step into the same river twice: When power analyses are optimistic. *Perspectives on Psychological Science, 9*, 612–625. http://dx.doi.org/10.1177/1745691614548513

McShane, B. B., Böckenholt, U., & Hansen, K. T. (2016). Adjusting for publication bias in meta-analysis: An evaluation of selection methods and some cautionary notes. *Perspectives on Psychological Science, 11*, 730–749. http://dx.doi.org/10.1177/1745691616662243

Nosek, B. A., Spies, J. R., & Motyl, M. (2012). Scientific utopia II: Restructuring incentives and practices to promote truth over publishability. *Perspectives on Psychological Science, 7*, 615–631. http://dx.doi.org/10.1177/1745691612459058

Nyhan, B. (2015). Increasing the credibility of political science research: A proposal for journal reforms. *Political Science & Politics, 48*, 78–83. http://dx.doi.org/10.1017/S1049096515000463

Paolacci, G., & Chandler, J. (2014). Inside the Turk: Understanding Mechanical Turk as a participant pool. *Current Directions in Psychological Science, 23*, 184–188. http://dx.doi.org/10.1177/0963721414531598

Paolacci, G., Chandler, J., & Ipeirotis, P. G. (2010). Running experiments on Amazon Mechanical Turk. *Judgment and Decision Making, 5*, 411–419.

Peer, E., Samat, S., Brandimarte, L., & Acquisti, A. (2015). *Beyond the Turk: An empirical comparison of alternative platforms for crowdsourcing online behavioral research.*

SSRN. Retrieved from https://papers.ssrn.com/sol3/papers.cfm?abstract_id=2594183. http://dx.doi.org/10.2139/ssrn.2594183

Perugini, M., Gallucci, M., & Costantini, G. (2014). Safeguard power as a protection against imprecise power estimates. *Perspectives on Psychological Science, 9,* 319–332. http://dx.doi.org/10.1177/1745691614528519

Proschan, M. A., & Hunsberger, S. A. (1995). Designed extension of studies based on conditional power. *Biometrics, 51,* 1315–1324. http://dx.doi.org/10.2307/2533262

Proschan, M. A., Lan, K. G., & Wittes, J. T. (2006). *Statistical monitoring of clinical trials: A unified approach.* New York, NY: Springer.

Richard, F. D., Bond, C. F., Jr., & Stokes-Zoota, J. J. (2003). One hundred years of social psychology quantitatively described. *Review of General Psychology, 7,* 331–363. http://dx.doi.org/10.1037/1089-2680.7.4.331

Roediger, H. L., III (2012, February). Psychology's woes and a partial cure: The value of replication. *APS Observer, 25*(9). Retrieved from http://www.psychological science.org/publications/observer/2012/february-12/psychologys-woes-and-a-partial-cure-the-value-of-replication.html

Rosenthal, R. (1979). The "file drawer problem" and tolerance for null results. *Psychological Bulletin, 86,* 638–641. http://dx.doi.org/10.1037/0033-2909.86.3.638

Sagarin, B. J., Ambler, J. K., & Lee, E. M. (2014). An ethical approach to peeking at data. *Perspectives on Psychological Science, 9,* 293–304. http://dx.doi.org/10.1177/1745691614528214

Schmidt, S. (2009). Shall we really do it again? The powerful concept of replication is neglected in the social sciences. *Review of General Psychology, 13,* 90–100. http://dx.doi.org/10.1037/a0015108

Schönbrodt, F. D., & Perugini, M. (2013). At what sample size do correlations stabilize? *Journal of Research in Personality, 47,* 609–612. http://dx.doi.org/10.1016/j.jrp.2013.05.009

Schwarz, N. (1999). Self-reports: How the questions shape the answers. *American Psychologist, 54,* 93–105. http://dx.doi.org/10.1037/0003-066X.54.2.93

Sears, D. O. (1986). College sophomores in the laboratory: Influences of a narrow data base on social psychology's view of human nature. *Journal of Personality and Social Psychology, 51,* 515–530. http://dx.doi.org/10.1037/0022-3514.51.3.515

Simes, R. J. (1986). An improved Bonferroni procedure for multiple tests of significance. *Biometrika, 73,* 751–754. http://dx.doi.org/10.1093/biomet/73.3.751

Simmons, J. P., Nelson, L. D., & Simonsohn, U. (2011). False-positive psychology: Undisclosed flexibility in data collection and analysis allows presenting anything as significant. *Psychological Science, 22,* 1359–1366. http://dx.doi.org/10.1177/0956797611417632

Stanley, D. J., & Spence, J. R. (2014). Expectations for replications: Are yours realistic? *Perspectives on Psychological Science, 9,* 305–318. http://dx.doi.org/10.1177/1745691614528518

Steegen, S., Tuerlinckx, F., Gelman, A., & Vanpaemel, W. (2016). Increasing transparency through a multiverse analysis. *Perspectives on Psychological Science, 11,* 702–712. http://dx.doi.org/10.1177/1745691616658637

Stewart, N., Ungemach, C., Harris, A. J., Bartels, D. M., Newell, B. R., Paolacci, G., & Chandler, J. (2015). The average laboratory samples a population of 7,300 Amazon Mechanical Turk workers. *Judgment and Decision Making, 10,* 479–491.

Tsuji, S., Bergmann, C., & Cristia, A. (2014). Community-augmented meta-analyses: Toward cumulative data assessment. *Perspectives on Psychological Science, 9,* 661–665. http://dx.doi.org/10.1177/1745691614552498

Valentine, J. C., & Cooper, H. (2003). *Effect size substantive interpretation guidelines: Issues in the interpretation of effect sizes.* Washington, DC: What Works Clearinghouse.

Welkowitz, J., Cohen, B. H., & Lea, R. B. (2012). *Introductory statistics for the behavioral sciences.* New York, NY: Wiley.

Westfall, J., Judd, C. M., & Kenny, D. A. (2015). Replicating studies in which samples of participants respond to samples of stimuli. *Perspectives on Psychological Science, 10,* 390–399. http://dx.doi.org/10.1177/1745691614564879

Wittes, J., & Brittain, E. (1990). The role of internal pilot studies in increasing the efficiency of clinical trials. *Statistics in Medicine, 9,* 65–71. http://dx.doi.org/10.1002/sim.4780090113

Zhang, J. J., Blumenthal, G. M., He, K., Tang, S., Cortazar, P., & Sridhara, R. (2012). Overestimation of the effect size in group sequential trials. *Clinical Cancer Research, 18,* 4872–4876. http://dx.doi.org/10.1158/1078-0432.CCR-11-3118

Zhou, H., & Fishbach, A. (2016). The pitfall of experimenting on the web: How unattended selective attrition leads to surprising (yet false) research conclusions. *Journal of Personality and Social Psychology.* Advance online publication. http://dx.doi.org/10.1037/pspa0000056

3

CONFIRMATORY STUDY DESIGN, DATA ANALYSIS, AND RESULTS THAT MATTER

MATTHEW T. McBEE AND SAMUEL H. FIELD

KEY POINTS

- The rigor of a study is determined by its ability to persuade skeptics.
- Researchers should distinguish more clearly between exploratory, data-driven, hypothesis-generating research and confirmatory, theory-driven, hypothesis-testing research.
- Rigorously designed and executed confirmatory studies propel scientific progress by resolving theoretical disagreements.
- Any time a study design or analysis plan is leveraged on the data, the study becomes exploratory—even when the intent was to run a confirmatory study.
- The usual ways of summarizing statistical evidence (p values and confidence intervals) should be reserved for fully confirmatory studies. Descriptive statistics provide adequate summaries of exploratory studies.

http://dx.doi.org/10.1037/0000033-004

Toward a More Perfect Psychology: Improving Trust, Accuracy, and Transparency in Research, M. C. Makel and J. A. Plucker (Editors)

- Researchers should generate and disclose directed acyclic graphs in order to justify their decisions to control (or not control) specific variables in the analysis.
- Propensity score matching is a powerful and robust alternative to linear regression as a means of controlling for potential confounders.
- The evidentiary value of a study depends on both technical and procedural rigor.

Empirical research serves two ends in science. One kind of research is oriented toward hypothesis generation; another is oriented toward hypothesis testing. These two modes of research are often referred to as *exploratory* and *confirmatory*, respectively. Whereas the role of hypothesis-generating research is to generate discoveries or insights that may stimulate theory generation or refinement—in other words, expanding the range of potential explanations of phenomena—the goal of hypothesis-testing research is to select between competing theories. One function of confirmatory research is to settle theoretical arguments in a field; another is to provide highly trustworthy observations that serve to constrain theory development.

These two types of research are more different than is commonly appreciated. A psychometric analog seems appropriate: quality in exploratory, hypothesis-generating research emphasizes *sensitivity*, whereas quality in confirmatory, hypothesis-testing research emphasizes *specificity*. Of course, both sensitivity and specificity are important to both types of research, but they do differ in prioritization. Exploratory research is about openness, novelty, casting a wide net in the search of new phenomena, discovering previously unknown associations between variables, or the data-assisted construction of mathematical or statistical models (e.g., the process of exploratory factor analysis or model building guided by modification indices in structural equation modeling). Confirmatory research is about making a theoretically motivated observation as precisely and reliably as possible.

From a design and analysis point of view, everything about a confirmatory study must be prespecified a priori, before collecting (or at least examining) the data (Wagenmakers, Wetzels, Borsboom, van der Maas, & Kievit, 2012). The role of statistical analysis in confirmatory research is to arbitrate the fate of the research hypothesis (often via its foil, the null hypothesis). We speculate that the vast majority of statistical training offered in graduate programs in psychology implicitly assumes that the researcher in engaged in confirmatory work. The whole language of statistical analysis, the "test statistic" and "p value," for example, is based on the idea that the researcher is testing an a priori hypothesis.

Contrast this with exploratory research, in which everything from the type of analysis conducted to the specification of statistical models is leveraged on the data. It would be impossible to prespecify much about the intended analysis before examining the data because everything, or nearly everything, depends on the data. One might end up exploring gender differences or correlations between sets of variables, or even examining a large set of variables as potential mediators or moderators of effects. In such situations the purpose of statistical analysis is to provide a succinct description of the data and the potential effects they contain. Statistical models are not being used to test hypotheses because there are none. Instead, statistical models are used to provide a journalistic account of the patterns contained in a data set. In the exploratory world, the role of statistical analysis is quite similar to the role of the telescope in astronomy or the microscope in biology: It simply renders the invisible visible.

Although exploratory research and confirmatory research are both valuable and necessary facilitators of scientific progress in the social sciences, the credibility of results could be improved if researchers increased their emphasis on conducting confirmatory research (Wagenmakers et al., 2012). As statistical consultants and teachers of statistics and research methods, we encounter a great deal of concern from students and applied researchers about performing the wrong statistics. In the ever-expanding menu of methods and models for analyzing data, a great deal of concern is placed on choosing the "correct" statistical model. Although choosing the wrong statistical model is a problem (and one that is, perhaps, likely to be noted by reviewers), there are more fundamental errors. Unless a researcher has followed a very specific, prespecified analysis plan, as one must in a rigorous confirmatory study, the standard error (and the resulting p value or confidence interval [CI]) does not have the meaning that we would like it to have. Using confirmatory statistical techniques in a nonconfirmatory setting is one example of what we call "doing statistics wrong." Ultimately, we believe that doing statistics wrong, rather than doing the wrong statistics, is a much more widespread and damaging error.

RIGOR EMERGES FROM A RIGOROUS PROCESS

We think of *rigor* as the persuasiveness of a study. The results of rigorous studies are able to change the thinking of intellectually honest skeptics. Rigor is not simply the result of the high-level design parameters that are emphasized in research methods courses; instead, rigor is about the entire research process. It may be tempting to think, for example, that randomized designs should always be considered more rigorous than quasi-experiments, but these macro design details tell only part of the story. Randomized designs may be exposed to fewer "threats to validity" (Campbell & Stanley, 1963), but they can still be poorly motivated, improperly executed, or otherwise compromised. Science fiction writer David Gerrold is fond of a particular analogy about integrity. Integrity, he wrote, "[is] like a balloon. It doesn't matter how good the rubber is; the air still goes out the hole" (Gerrold, 1984, p. 269). The same notion applies to rigor.

Imagine, for example, two studies operating at the extremes of the rigor spectrum. The first study takes place after extensive discussion among key researchers and theorists involved in multiple research teams. The research team includes a mixture of strong believers and strong skeptics of the phenomenon to be investigated; therefore, this study could be described as an "adversarial collaboration" (Kahneman & Klein, 2009). This group reaches a consensus on the design, sampling (including a minimum sample size), instrumentation, and measurement, and data analysis. These decisions are made in a transparent way, with substantial effort devoted to the anticipation of possible flaws. The details of statistical power, missing data, potential confounding variables, and statistical assumptions are discussed to the satisfaction of all. The code for running the statistical analysis is written and publicly disseminated in advance of the data collection. The proposal is submitted to a journal as a registered report. The journal's peer reviewers and editors note additional weaknesses in the study and request revisions to the proposal. After three rounds of review, the peer reviewers are satisfied, and the paper is offered an in-principle acceptance. The research plan is publicly preregistered. The data are then collected in a transparent, collaborative way. Raw data, materials, and analysis scripts are made publicly available. The in-principle acceptance of the registered report means that the journal has committed to publishing the results regardless of how they turn out.

The second study is done by researchers in a single laboratory without any outside consultation. The researchers intend to use a randomized design but learn during data analysis that the subjects did not always comply with their assigned treatment, and a substantial number of subjects were lost to attrition. Although the initial plan was to analyze the data by means of a set of t tests, the compliance issue convinced the project statistician to switch to a linear regression model using a continuous measure of compliance, with treatment as the focal variable. Because exposure to the treatment is no longer controlled by the randomization, the researchers include covariates in the hopes of controlling for key confounding variables. The theory motivating the study does not identify these confounders, and most of them were not measured during data collection, so the researchers examine correlations to determine which covariates to include in the model. The initial data analysis does not yield a statistically significant main effect of exposure to treatment.

After some discussion, the group decides to test for moderation of the treatment effect within gender and race groups. This reveals a small but statistically significant effect of exposure to treatment in one combination of race and gender.

The resulting paper is submitted to a journal, where it is eventually accepted for publication after a few rounds of review. As per the norm, the published paper provides minimal detail about the true process that gave rise to the findings. The paper's introduction and literature review are rewritten (perhaps at the reviewers' insistence) to focus on theories predicting differential response to treatment across sociological groups, providing readers with the distinct impression that the researchers set out to test for moderated treatment effects when in fact these findings emerged from a post hoc statistical fishing expedition. Naturally, this study's findings are extremely unlikely to be replicated in future studies. Instead of contributing to the body of science, this paper merely adds to the scientific tragedy of the commons in which individual researchers win (by having another publication to add to their curriculum vitae), but the scientific integrity of the field's literature loses.

It would be difficult for someone displeased with the outcome of the first study—in particular, someone who was involved in the study design—to make a credible argument that that outcome resulted from poor design or inappropriate data analysis. For those people, such criticisms would be correctly perceived to be irrationally motivated reasoning and post hoc goalpost-moving and would be discounted and ignored by the larger professional community. It would be quite easy to dismiss the findings from the second study as essentially devoid of evidential support if the actual process that led to the findings was honestly reported. Unfortunately, the current paradigm—and, in some cases, demands for reasons of space—makes it all too easy to omit critical details of how the study was actually conducted. When this information is not disseminated, research consumers have no basis on which to judge the true procedural rigor of a paper and, therefore, its evidentiary value.

The lack of a consensus on what constitutes proper research practice outside of a strictly confirmatory framework means that it is improper to cast aspersions on individual researchers. The training that most psychologists receive regarding research methods and data analysis is largely specific to confirmatory studies. The American Psychological Association's (2010) *Publication Manual* does not describe reporting standards, necessary disclosures, or guidelines for exploratory research. As Simmons, Nelson, and Simonsohn (2012) wrote, "We cannot 'trust' our colleagues to run and report their studies 'properly' if there is no shared understanding of what 'properly' is. There is no shared understanding of what 'properly' is" (p. 5). The blame rests with our entire discipline, which has resisted the development of reporting standards, mandatory disclosures, and appropriate training experiences for exploratory studies (or "failed" confirmatory studies that become exploratory).

REPORTING p VALUES (AND CONFIDENCE INTERVALS) IS A PRIVILEGE, NOT A RIGHT

We regard the reporting of p values and standard errors as belonging exclusively to a purely confirmatory research program (Wagenmakers et al., 2012). When conditions—such as the application of exploratory data analysis techniques—render the computation of uncertainty in the estimates impossible, then the solution is to not provide those estimates. Providing no estimate of uncertainty is superior to providing an incorrect estimate. Reporting p values and standard errors is not a right; it should be a privilege that is earned by successfully running a confirmatory study. In the case of exploratory studies, researchers could report estimated effect sizes, discuss the implications of findings with respect to theories, and point out interesting occurrences that may merit more research, but they should not be free to provide misleading estimates of uncertainty.[1] Although this will reduce the degree of perceived strength of evidence provided by the study, a reasonable organizational model of science would value such contributions. However, they should rightly be viewed as far less rigorous (less able to settle arguments) than their confirmatory counterparts. This is no denigration of exploratory research because the goal of such research is not to persuade.

Yes, this means that scientists, reviewers, and journal editors would have to relinquish their irrational attachment to p values as the arbiter of interestingness, importance, and scientific value. Given that this naive interpretation of the p value has been thoroughly debunked by many critics (e.g., Cohen, 1994; Cumming, 2012, 2014), it is amazing that p values have continued to enjoy their undeserved centrality. We do not dispute that p values can make a scientific contribution as a safeguard against confirmation bias (White, 2012), but these values must have some grounding in reality in order to be useful, and this can occur only in the context of successfully executed confirmatory research. Implementing this advice would require some changes in our field's publication norms. As it is, most journals would probably desk-reject a submission in which the authors refused to provide standard errors or

---

[1]This would be inclusive of a situation in which a reviewer or journal editor suggests additional, unplanned analyses after seeing the results of the study. Researchers may comply with these requests, but they should be viewed as exploratory, and no p values or CIs should be reported for these tests. Under a registered report model, reviewers would be free to alter the design or proposed analyses without jeopardizing the confirmatory nature of the study because these suggestions would be made prior to data collection.

p values. However, recent editorials issued by some journal editors abolishing or otherwise limiting the role of *p* values suggests that this may be changing (cf. McBee & Matthews, 2014; Trafimow & Marks, 2015). In confirmatory research, the presentation of *p* values is justified, but their meaning becomes much clearer in the context of a preregistered analysis plan. After all, *p* values do indeed provide error control, but their ability to do this is completely determined by the researcher's intentions. Like many others, we are keenly interested in Bayes factors as alternative and in some ways superior measures of evidence.

CONFIRMATORY RESEARCH IS DIFFICULT

For most of us, in particular when we are not being very clear about whether we are doing exploratory work or confirmatory work, the usual data analysis procedure consists of multiple iterations over many possible analyses. Even when researchers intend to conduct confirmatory research, common practices yield situations in which decision are made on the basis of data—often in the guise of assumption checks or uncertain model specification. Even a small departure from a fully confirmatory approach can render *p* values misleading. In this condition they simply do not represent what they are intended to measure: the probability of obtaining a test statistic that is unlikely to have been observed under the null hypothesis.

Consider, for example, the practice of model building in regression models. The best way to build a regression model is by using a theoretical model that identifies confounders, mediators, moderators, and so on. However, applied researchers often examine correlation coefficients between potential predictor variables and the outcome in order to identify covariates to be included in the model. (For the record, we consider this to be a terrible idea, but it is nonetheless common.) If one of these covariates is a confounder, then the decision of whether or not to include it can strongly affect the model results for the focal parameter. In this case, however, the decision on whether or not to include this confounding variable as a control variable in the model is dictated by a correlation coefficient, which is itself susceptible to sampling variation. In thinking about the fictional set of identical repeated studies that gives rise to the idea of the sampling distribution and its descendants (including the standard error, CI, and *p* value), it is clear that the covariate would be included in the model when the estimated correlation fluctuates away from 0 (and is therefore "strong") but would not be included when it fluctuates toward 0. Because the estimated effect of the focal predictor strongly depends on whether or not this confounding variable is included in the model, in reality the sampling distribution of effect of the focal variable on the outcome would be far more unpredictable than the naïve analytical standard error would indicate.

Unfortunately, many of the standard procedures taught in applied statistics courses transform ostensible confirmatory analyses into exploratory analyses. Examples include testing for interactions between variables that are subsequently removed from the model if nonsignificant; in multilevel modeling, using measures of model fit (e.g., the Akaike information criterion) to determine whether to include a random slope; or using stepwise selection of variables in linear regression (cf. Thompson, 1995). What is a researcher to do? After all, how can one reasonably be expected to know, in advance of data collection, whether particular variables will have linear or curvilinear relationships with outcomes? How can one know if certain interactions will be present and therefore require representation in a statistical model? And how can one know whether certain variables are confounders? The issue of identifying and constraining the influence of confounders is discussed in the following section. There are methodological solutions to concerns about proper model specification and adherence to model assumptions. Like all good things, however, they come with a price. In this case, the price is statistical power.

When analyzing data, researchers often face a choice between a more efficient (meaning a smaller standard error and therefore narrower CIs and smaller p values) but assumption-laden approach and a less efficient, but more robust, method. By *robust*, we mean leveraged on fewer assumptions. One familiar example is the classic t test, which assumes equal population variances, versus Welch's t test, which makes no such assumption. If one is planning a completely confirmatory study it may be impossible to know in advance of data collection whether the population variances are likely to be equal. Therefore, researchers should plan on using Welch's t test from the outset (Lakens, 2015). In another example, imagine that a psychologist intends to examine the relationship between age and life satisfaction. The linear regression slope coefficient is based on the assumption that the association being described has a linear functional form. The usual approach might to use the data to determine whether this linear functional form is appropriate by fitting a succession of regression models. In the baseline model, the relationship between satisfaction and age is specified as linear. In the next model it is specified as quadratic, and in the next it is specified as cubic. The researcher's reported statistical model will be purged of all nonsignificant curvilinear components. For example, if the linear and quadratic components are statistically significant, but the cubic component is not, then the final model will include linear and quadratic components only. This method has its merits, but it suffers from the unfortunate side effect of converting the confirmatory situation to an exploratory one and "breaking" the standard error as a valid measure of uncertainty. The data can be used to test the assumption of linearity, but using data to inform the model specification makes the study exploratory.

The alternative, robust approach, which requires no foreknowledge of the proper functional form of the relationship between age and life satisfaction, is to break the continuous age predictor variable into a set of categorical variables, perhaps including late adolescence, early adulthood, middle adulthood, and so on. The researcher can then use the regression model to examine the relationship between these categorical variables and the satisfaction outcome. An F test of these age indicator variables provides a nonparametric test of the association between age and life satisfaction. This approach is robust in that it makes no assumptions about the shape of the relationship. The cost is that this approach is less efficient (meaning it has inferior statistical power) compared with approaches in which the correct functional form must be specified by the researcher. The researcher would need to collect data on a larger sample to achieve adequate power for this test as compared with the status quo. However, the payoff—the right to compute and disseminate accurate p values and CIs—is worthwhile. We note that this suggestion defies common statistical advice against categorizing continuous variables but believe that this procedure is worthwhile in that it allows the model to be prespecified without looking at the data. As an alternative, if the researcher is very certain that the relationship is linear, he or she may plan to fit a linear model. However, if the data suggest a nonlinear relationship, then the researcher must depart from the planned analysis to accommodate this feature of the data, rendering the study exploratory. This type of hedging trades statistical power for more confidence in the likelihood that one's confirmatory analysis plan will survive contact with the data.

Making and evaluating good a priori decisions about study design should be the hallmark of expertise that distinguishes experienced scholars from novices. It is another example of what we mean by "doing statistics right" as opposed to just "doing the right statistics." Expertise and experience bring an increased ability to anticipate, and to preemptively resolve, the problems that arise in research. When circumstances require changes to an intended confirmatory study that break its confirmatory nature, all it not lost. The results should be disseminated (sans p values and CIs, of course) along with a discussion of the conditions that led to the change in protocol or planned analysis. The strength of the evidence—the rigor, as we conceive it—provided by such a study has been reduced, but not eliminated. Skeptics are less likely to be persuaded by such evidence, it is true, but it still has value. A frank and honest description of the research process will allow readers to properly contextualize the study results and will inform other researchers about conditions they must consider in order to successfully execute the rigorous, confirmatory studies that can advance the field. The first several attempts to run a confirmatory study in a new area likely will fail because of unanticipated problems. Scientific progress is facilitated by an open discussion of these issues and collaborative effort in resolving them.

CAUSAL INFERENCE: IT'S WHAT IT'S ALL ABOUT

In the previous section we advocated for the necessity of researchers to adopt robust statistical analysis plans to hedge against the possibility of assumption violations. Planning from the outset to use these methods protects one from the possibility of being forced to abandon the plan because of information revealed by the data.

The next problem that must be considered is how to deal with the possibility of confounding. *Confounding* is what happens when the focal predictor and the outcome variable are themselves caused by a third variable. It is the reason that correlation is not the same as causality. Confounders can cause correlations between variables that are not, in reality, causally linked. The problem of confounding is not limited to explicitly correlational research: Ultimately, any parameter one might be interested in studying, including a mean difference between groups, regression slope, a ratio of variances, and so on, can always be expressed as a correlation coefficient (Cohen, 1988). No statistic describing relationships between groups or variables is immune from confounding. It is a fundamental problem.

We have noted an ad hoc quality to the process used by researchers to decide what variables should be controlled in a statistical analysis. A major improvement to normative data analysis practices could be achieved if researchers collectively relied on formalized techniques for identifying these variables in order to support valid inference of cause-and-effect relationships. It is beneficial to begin by admitting that only causal relationships are scientifically interesting (see Foster, 2010, and Widaman, Dogan, Stockdale, & Conger, 2010, for a discussion). Psychologists have adopted an unfortunate hand-waving attitude toward causal inference, often seeming to claim in discussion sections that, although a particular design does not allow unambiguous conclusions regarding causality to be reached, that was never the goal. This argument is silly and transparently false; we are scientists, not stamp collectors; of course we are interested in understanding the causes of phenomena! Incidental correlations between variables are interesting only because they signal the potential for causation. They are useful for motivating future research, but they rarely settle arguments. Only by understanding cause can one make accurate predictions, and only through accurate prediction can one demonstrate understanding. Studies unsupportive of causal inference cannot be deemed very rigorous.

Random assignment is a useful technique for reducing exposure to confounding variables, but random assignment can fail. Conditions can conspire to "break" randomization. For example, researchers might experience differential subject dropout in the treatment condition if that condition is unpleasant. Subjects may not comply with their assigned treatment. Although noncompliance may not be a serious concern in the typical laboratory study, when subjects are required to engage in activities outside of strict control by the researcher, some may choose not to actually do those activities, or they may do them less often.

For a study to accurately estimate the magnitude and direction of causal relationships, the influence of confounding variables must be constrained or removed. This can be done using a variety of methods. The most effective is randomization. Most of the other strategies involve identifying and measuring the confounders, which then can be controlled using a variety of methods, most commonly by including them as additional predictor variables in a statistical model such as linear regression. Alternative techniques, such as instrumental variables analysis, are underused in the social sciences (Bollen, 2012).

It is helpful to distinguish between the focal predictor and ancillary variables in an analysis. At a maximum, regression models can estimate only one causal effect in an unbiased way. The notion that regression models can support causal inference for multiple predictors through mutual adjustment has been called a *Table 2 fallacy* (Westreich & Greenland, 2013). The remaining ancillary variables in the analysis exist only to support the estimation of that single effect. In effect, the model can "tell the story" of one, and only one, variable. The remaining variables in the model play nothing more than a supporting role. These ancillary variables are often called *covariates* and they can have different roles. The role they play in the system of causal relations between variables in real life dictates how these variables should be handled in the analysis—in other words, whether the analyst should control for the variable in the analysis.

Identifying and managing the influence of these potential confounders is a major problem. No statistical procedure can definitively identify confounders or distinguish them from mediators. This territory can be navigated only by theory, consensus, and scientific insight. In other words, the identification and classification of these ancillary (or control) variables must be done on a theoretical basis; data are of little use. The researcher's theory about the (potentially) complex pattern of causal relationships between involved variables must ultimately be translated into a statistical model that includes a sufficient set of the confounders and none of the mediators or colliders. In the next section we describe a heuristic tool for expressing theories regarding the causal relationships between variables and recognizing their statistical implications in a planned analysis: directed acyclic graphs (DAGs; Pearl, 2009).

The Role of Directed Acyclic Graphs

DAGs are a graphical representation of the causal relationships among a set of variables. Unlike the familiar path diagrams or structural equation models, the arrows in a DAG do not denote a specific functional form of the causal relationship; otherwise, they are quite similar. In other words, the arrows in a DAG do not necessarily represent linear regression slopes; the relationships could be curvilinear. The DAG encodes the researcher's beliefs about the likely relationships between the variables that involve the focal predictor and the outcome.

DAGs make the implicit explicit. Researchers commonly make decisions about what variables to control in analysis in an ad hoc way. These decisions carry tremendous consequences for the findings, in particular when those findings are represented as causal relationships. When these decisions are based on the working theory of the nature of the causal linkages between variables in the system, this should be disclosed. The DAG is a convenient form for expressing this theory and justifying the researcher's choices regarding the variables to be controlled in the analysis (Foster & McCombs-Thornton, 2013).

The process of creating and using a DAG is simple; after all, the DAG is a figure. The researcher begins by sketching the focal predictor variables and the outcome variable. If these are thought to be causally connected, an arrow is drawn from the focal predictor to the outcome. Next, a comprehensive list of the other variables that might themselves cause the focal predictor or the outcome are added to the figure. Arrows are drawn to illustrate the theorized pattern of causation between these variables. The process of adding variables and causal relationships continues until the researcher is satisfied that the whole system of direct and indirect causal influences on the focal predictor and outcome variable has been represented, including those that have not or cannot be measured (e.g., genetic endowment). The rules of DAGs are applied to this figure to identify the set of variables that must be controlled in the analysis to achieve a valid estimate of the causal effect of the focal predictor on the outcome (Shrier & Platt, 2008). These rules are complicated, and introducing them is beyond the scope of this chapter. Applying these rules to the figure provides researchers with a list of ancillary variables whose influence must be constrained (perhaps via statistical control) in the analysis. It also reveals the variables that must not be controlled. Conditioning on these so-called collider variables, or their "downstream" descendants, can actually introduce endogenous selection bias, which is distinct from the more commonly emphasized omitted-variable bias that occurs when one fails to condition on a confounder (see Elwert & Winship, 2014). The set of variables whose influence must be constrained to achieve valid causal inference, whether using covariate adjustment, stratification, or matching, is called the *minimal adjustment set* (Shrier & Platt, 2008). A major appeal of DAGs is that they facilitate the identification of this adjustment set and provide a framework for communicating the rationale for controlling a specific set of variables.

Of course, a researcher's DAG may be wrong. If this happens, the minimal adjustment set used in the analysis is incorrect, and therefore the estimated relationship between the focal predictor and the outcome is not a valid estimate of the causal relationship between these variables. DAGs are not magical incantations; if the researcher had the deep knowledge of the phenomenon necessary to create a flawless DAG, he or she would probably not need to do the study at all. Instead, DAGs are tools for clarifying and communicating one's thinking in a rigorous way. The highest level of rigor regarding model specification occurs when many researchers working in a specific area reach a consensus regarding a DAG. In effect, this agreement largely disarms skeptics who wish to challenge a study result by arguing that key variables were not controlled (or were controlled inappropriately) in the analysis. The burden of specifying a competing DAG then falls on the skeptic. The two models described by the competing DAGs will likely differ in their testable implications, allowing future confirmatory work to gather the evidence necessary to arbitrate the disagreement. Contrast this thoughtful process with the typical, reflexive act of controlling for race and gender that one observes in many psychology studies. There is simply no comparison.

Because the DAG has such important implications for the validity of causal estimates that can be generated, it is paramount that it be transparently disclosed. Also, because the DAG will be a focus of criticism on the part of reviewers and skeptical readers, developing DAGs collaboratively with other research teams is one method of increasing the rigor of a study. Just as "Table 1" in most articles contains descriptive statistics, we believe that "Figure 1" should generally display the working DAG from which the researcher identified the confounders that were controlled in the analysis. In our view, building a consensus among a diverse group of content and technical experts around the role that ancillary or control variables will play in the analyses is a critical activity in the design of any study. An example DAG is provided in Figure 3.1.

For a more comprehensive introduction to the topic, we refer readers to Elwert (2013) and DAGitty (Textor, Hardt, & Knüppel, 2011), an online browser-based application for creating and interpreting DAGs. The DAGitty website (http://dagitty.net/) provides extensive and interactive learning resources. Using DAGitty, researchers can benefit from an automated identification of the variables composing the minimal adjustment set. All one needs to do is to generate the figure.

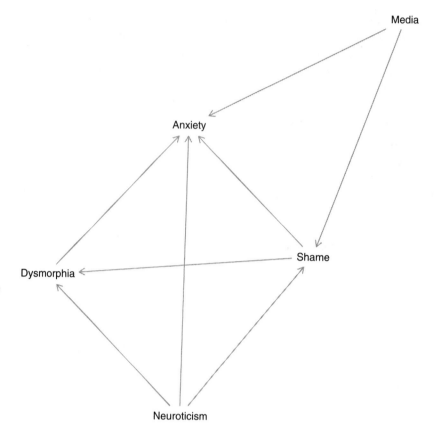

Figure 3.1. Example directed acyclic graph.

The Advantages of Propensity Score Matching

One shortcoming of DAGs is that they do not provide information on *how* the variables composing the minimal adjustment set should actually be used in the analyses. In other words, they do not address questions of whether interactions among the covariates and the focal predictor variable should be included in a regression model, the proper functional form for the relations between predictors and the outcome (e.g., linear? cubic?), or how to achieve balance or equivalence across levels of exposure on the multivariate distribution of measured covariates. They say nothing about whether the sample size is adequate—in particular with respect to the estimation of independent associations among variables that may be highly correlated. In short, difficult decisions remain even after identifying which variables must be included. These decisions, and the negative consequences of choosing poorly, can be largely obviated by moving beyond the typical linear modeling framework (i.e., regression) to propensity score matching.

We strongly advocate propensity score matching (PSM; Rubin, 2005) as an alternative, when possible, to linear regression as a means of removing the effects of confounding variables due to its vastly decreased exposure to assumptions. This is because it is typically safest in confirmatory work to select the most robust alternative to guard against the likelihood of the planned confirmatory study becoming an exploratory one. PSM is one way researchers can achieve this. We direct readers to Stuart's (2010) introduction for more information on PSM.

PSM provides a nonparametric means of controlling confounding variables as well as a means of estimating causal effects (Guo & Fraser, 2010; Rosenbaum & Rubin, 1983, 1984). The usual linear regression method of controlling for potential confounders suffers from two major problems when it comes to effectively constraining the influence of these variables. First, researchers must specify the functional form of each relationship with the outcome, which is typically unknown, inclusive of any interactions between variables. The default regression assumption is that all variables are linearly related to the outcome. If the confounder does not in fact have a linear relationship with the outcome, then the effect of the confounder is not adequately controlled, and the estimated effect of the focal variable will not represent its true causal effect on the outcome. One advantage of PSM is that no assumption is made regarding the functional form of these relationships, because PSM relies on matching rather than statistical adjustment. Therefore, it is impossible to be wrong about the functional form—something that is critical to get right when one is operating in a regression framework.

The second problem is that the regression solution can be reported in regions of sparse data. In such cases, the validity of inference is heavily leveraged on model assumptions. For example, a regression model may attempt to estimate the causal effect of college graduation on adult earnings by adjusting for background variables. The model will produce an estimated effect even if the graduates and nongraduates are completely dissimilar with respect to these background variables. In other words, identifying the earnings of a person who did not graduate college and who is similar to a college graduate with respect to background variables is computed by projecting the pattern of associations between background variables and earnings across a gulf of multivariate emptiness. Unlike regression, PSM techniques provide an easy method of limiting the inference to a "region of common support" (Stuart, 2010)—where treated and control cases are similar with respect to the minimal adjustment set of background variables that must be controlled, if one exists! This ensures that the estimated causal effects are minimally leveraged on assumptions.

PSM techniques have an additional and tremendously important advantage over multiple regression: Researchers are free to try multiple specifications for the PSM without jeopardizing the confirmatory nature of their study (Rubin, 2008). New techniques, such as boosted logistic regression, spare researchers from having to worry about optimally specifying the model for estimating the propensity scores (Westreich, Lessler, & Funk, 2010). Once the propensity scores have been satisfactorily estimated, various methods can be used for creating matched samples. At this stage, the only consensus needed among researchers involves the criteria for deciding whether covariates are adequately balanced across the levels of the exposure variable. When one considers what researchers must agree on in the specification of a regression model, it is easy to see the appeal of PSM in the design of a confirmatory study.

PROCEDURAL VERSUS TECHNICAL RIGOR

In the field of medicine, randomized controlled trials are typically considered to yield the highest level of evidence, with case-control studies, case series with no control, and expert opinion filling out the lower levels. The level of evidence is disclosed in abstracts and displayed in databases such as PubMed. This system acknowledges that although contributions can be made by studies that vary in rigor, studies with widely discrepant designs should not be considered equally persuasive. When the level of evidence is based exclusively on technical elements that may be present or absent in a particular study, we refer to this as the study's degree of *technical rigor*.

A parallel system for psychology might consider fully confirmatory, preregistered studies that rigorously support causal inference to be the highest level of evidence, whereas exploratory studies would be assigned a lower level of evidence. Such a system could distinguish between degrees of procedural rigor. Studies with ex ante hypotheses that relied on limited or no information from the data to inform model specification should be viewed as representing a higher level of evidence than studies reporting unanticipated or surprising findings from data that were not hypothesized in advance. However, we do not think that preregistration alone is sufficient. In addition to publishing the study protocol and statistical analysis plan before collecting any of the data used in hypothesis testing, researchers should be required to provide a statement about the level of evidentiary value their experiment is expected to generate. When researchers preregister their studies they are making an implicit claim about the study's evidentiary value—that it has crossed some threshold and is worth doing. Preregistration does not simply document the design decisions made in advance so that a researcher does not deviate from them; it should also constitute a statement to the field. Furthermore, a procedurally rigorous study will actively solicit input from researchers with diverse points of views and varying levels of expertise. We cannot expect our studies to be scientifically persuasive if we do not endeavor to solicit the input from the very people whose minds we seek to change or on whose expertise we depend. Reaching a broad consensus on every detail of a plan may be impossible. Although this should not stop a study from being carried out, it should have consequences with respect to its perceived level of evidentiary value.

CLOSING THOUGHTS

Nothing reveals ignorance more dramatically than when a carefully conducted experiment produces wildly implausible results. Did we measure the key outcome(s) or key exposure(s) correctly? Are the assumptions about the model specification inaccurate? Was the DAG unrealistic? It is natural to second-guess these key decisions about study design and model specification in the face of an unanticipated or nonsensical-seeming finding. After all, who can be expected to design and conduct a valid experiment or observation the first time he or she tries? Although such reactions to unexpected results from an initially confirmatory effort are commonplace, they stand in sharp contrast to physicist and Nobel laureate Isidor Isaac Rabi's own reaction when he learned about the discovery of the muon subatomic particle in 1936: "Who ordered that?" (http://www.thedailyblaa.com/2011/03/who-ordered-that-part-1.html). If we reform the way we do research, we can arrive in a place where unexpected findings will signal the arrival of new science, not merely another compromised study.

RECOMMENDED READING

Elwert, F. (2013). Graphical causal models. In S. L. Morgan (Ed.), *Handbook of causal analysis for social research* (pp. 245–274). New York, NY: Springer. http://dx.doi.org/10.1007/978-94-007-6094-3_13

Rubin, D. B. (2008). For objective causal inference, design trumps analysis. *The Annals of Applied Statistics, 2*, 808–840. http://dx.doi.org/10.1214/08-AOAS187

Stuart, E. A. (2010). Matching methods for causal inference: A review and a look forward. *Statistical Science, 25*, 1–21. http://dx.doi.org/10.1214/09-STS313

Wagenmakers, E. J., Wetzels, R., Borsboom, D., van der Maas, H. L., & Kievit, R. A. (2012). An agenda for purely confirmatory research. *Perspectives on Psychological Science, 7*, 632–638. http://dx.doi.org/10.1177/1745691612463078

REFERENCES

American Psychological Association. (2010). *Publication manual of the American Psychological Association* (6th ed.). Washington, DC: Author.

Bollen, K. A. (2012). Instrumental variables in sociology and the social sciences. *Annual Review of Sociology, 38*, 37–72. http://dx.doi.org/10.1146/annurev-soc-081309-150141

Campbell, D. T., & Stanley, J. C. (1963). *Experimental and quasi-experimental designs for research.* New York, NY: Wadsworth.

Cohen, J. (1988). *Statistical power analysis for the behavioral sciences* (2nd ed.). Mahwah, NJ: Erlbaum.

Cohen, J. (1994). The Earth is round (*p* < .05). *American Psychologist, 49*, 997–1003. http://dx.doi.org/10.1037/0003-066X.49.12.997

Cumming, G. (2012). *Understanding the new statistics: Effect sizes, confidence intervals, and meta-analysis.* New York, NY: Routledge.

Cumming, G. (2014). The new statistics: Why and how. *Psychological Science, 25*, 7–29. http://dx.doi.org/10.1177/0956797613504966

Elwert, F. (2013). Graphical causal models. In S. L. Morgan (Ed.), *Handbook of causal analysis for social research* (pp. 245–274). New York, NY: Springer. http://dx.doi.org/10.1007/978-94-007-6094-3_13

Elwert, F., & Winship, C. (2014). Endogenous selection bias: The problem of conditioning on a collider variable. *Annual Review of Sociology, 40*, 31–53. http://dx.doi.org/10.1146/annurev-soc-071913-043455

Foster, E. M. (2010). The *U*-shaped relationship between complexity and usefulness: A commentary. *Developmental Psychology, 46*, 1760–1766. http://dx.doi.org/10.1037/a0020180

Foster, E. M., & McCombs-Thornton, K. (2013). Child welfare and the challenge of causal inference. *Children and Youth Services Review, 35*, 1130–1142. http://dx.doi.org/10.1016/j.childyouth.2011.03.012

Gerrold, D. (1984). *The war against the Chtorr: Book 2. A day for damnation.* New York, NY: Spectra.

Guo, S., & Fraser, M. W. (2010). *Propensity score analysis: Statistical methods and applications.* Los Angeles, CA: Sage.

Kahneman, D., & Klein, G. (2009). Conditions for intuitive expertise: A failure to disagree. *American Psychologist, 64*, 515–526. http://dx.doi.org/10.1037/a0016755

Lakens, D. (2015, January 26). Always use Welch's *t*-test instead of Student's *t*-test [Blog post]. Retrieved from http://daniellakens.blogspot.com/2015/01/always-use-welchs-t-test-instead-of.html

McBee, M., & Matthews, M. S. (2014). Welcoming quality in non-significance and replication work, but moving beyond the *p*-value: Announcing new editorial policies for quantitative research in JOAA. *Journal of Advanced Academics, 25*, 73–87. http://dx.doi.org/10.1177/1932202X14532177

Pearl, J. (2009). *Causality: Models, reasoning and inference* (2nd ed.). New York, NY: Cambridge University Press. http://dx.doi.org/10.1017/CBO9780511803161

Rosenbaum, P. R., & Rubin, D. B. (1983). The central role of the propensity score in observational studies for causal effects. *Biometrika, 70*, 41–55. http://dx.doi.org/10.1093/biomet/70.1.41

Rosenbaum, P. R., & Rubin, D. B. (1984). Reducing bias in observational studies using subclassification on the propensity score. *Journal of the American Statistical Association, 79*, 516–524. http://dx.doi.org/10.1080/01621459.1984.10478078

Rubin, D. B. (2005). Causal inference using potential outcomes: Design, modeling, decisions. *Journal of the American Statistical Association, 100*, 322–331. http://dx.doi.org/10.1198/016214504000001880

Rubin, D. B. (2008). For objective causal inference, design trumps analysis. *The Annals of Applied Statistics, 2*, 808–840. http://dx.doi.org/10.1214/08-AOAS187

Shrier, I., & Platt, R. W. (2008). Reducing bias through directed acyclic graphs. *BMC Medical Research Methodology, 8*, 70–85. http://dx.doi.org/10.1186/1471-2288-8-70

Simmons, J. P., Nelson, L. D., & Simonsohn, U. (2012). A 21-word solution. *Dialogue, 26*(2), 4–7.

Stuart, E. A. (2010). Matching methods for causal inference: A review and a look forward. *Statistical Science, 25*, 1–21. http://dx.doi.org/10.1214/09-STS313

Textor, J., Hardt, J., & Knüppel, S. (2011). DAGitty: A graphical tool for analyzing causal diagrams. *Epidemiology, 22*, 745. http://dx.doi.org/10.1097/EDE.0b013e318225c2be

Thompson, B. (1995). Stepwise regression and stepwise discriminant analysis need not apply here: A guidelines editorial. *Educational and Psychological Measurement, 55*, 525–534. http://dx.doi.org/10.1177/0013164495055004001

Trafimow, D., & Marks, M. (2015). Editorial. *Basic and Applied Social Psychology, 37*, 1–2. http://dx.doi.org/10.1080/01973533.2015.1012991

Wagenmakers, E. J., Wetzels, R., Borsboom, D., van der Maas, H. L., & Kievit, R. A. (2012). An agenda for purely confirmatory research. *Perspectives on Psychological Science, 7*, 632–638. http://dx.doi.org/10.1177/1745691612463078

Westreich, D., & Greenland, S. (2013). The Table 2 fallacy: Presenting and interpreting confounder and modifier coefficients. *American Journal of Epidemiology, 177*, 292–298. http://dx.doi.org/10.1093/aje/kws412

Westreich, D., Lessler, J., & Funk, M. J. (2010). Propensity score estimation: Neural networks, support vector machines, decision trees (CART), and meta-classifiers as alternatives to logistic regression. *Journal of Clinical Epidemiology*, 63, 826–833. http://dx.doi.org/10.1016/j.jclinepi.2009.11.020

White, J. M. (2012, May 10). Criticism 1 of NHST: Good tools for individual researchers are not good tools for research communities [Blog post]. Retrieved from http://www.r-bloggers.com/criticism-1-of-nhst-good-tools-for-individual-researchers-are-not-good-tools-for-research-communities/

Widaman, K. F., Dogan, S. J., Stockdale, G. D., & Conger, R. D. (2010). Complexity, usefulness, and optimality: A response to Foster (2010). *Developmental Psychology*, 46, 1767–1770. http://dx.doi.org/10.1037/a0021293

4

SELECTIVE OUTCOME REPORTING AND RESEARCH QUALITY

TERRI D. PIGOTT, RYAN T. WILLIAMS, AND JEFFREY C. VALENTINE

KEY POINTS

- Outcome reporting bias—omitting information about outcomes collected in a study—is a well-documented phenomenon in medical and social science research.
- Outcome reporting bias is often related to the statistical significance of the results, whereby outcomes whose results do not reach statistical significance are more likely to be omitted from a research report.
- Outcome reporting bias can lead policymakers to incorrect decisions based on research and can thereby bias the results of systematic reviews.
- Researchers should provide full information about outcomes collected in a study, whether in the report itself, in a research appendix, or in an online repository.

http://dx.doi.org/10.1037/0000033-005
Toward a More Perfect Psychology: Improving Trust, Accuracy, and Transparency in Research, M. C. Makel and J. A. Plucker (Editors)

Scientific progress depends on thorough and transparent reporting on the underlying theory, methods, and results of research. Research transparency is important not only for replication but also for understanding the nuances of study findings. Social interventions aimed at improving the lives and health of individuals rarely have a uniform effect on all participants. To make informed decisions based on evidence, we need to be sure that the authors of research studies have fully reported on all measured outcomes.

One indicator of the quality of a research study is the *transparency* of reporting about the methods and analyses conducted. A critical component of complete reporting of methods and analysis strategies is the presentation of results from all measures collected in a study. *Outcome reporting bias* (ORB) occurs when researchers report their results selectively, omitting information about one or more measures that they gathered in a study. In this chapter we discuss the prevalence of selective outcome reporting and the potential bias that can result from incomplete reporting of outcomes. If we expect research knowledge to accumulate and to provide the basis for evidence-based practice, then we need to ensure that our study reporting is transparent and includes information on all evidence collected.

WHAT IS OUTCOME REPORTING BIAS?

Norris et al. (2013) described *selective outcome reporting* as providing incomplete information on a subset of the outcomes measured and analyzed in a study. For example, researchers investigating a new reading intervention will probably collect more than just a single measure of reading comprehension; they will likely also measure additional related outcomes, such as reading fluency, attitudes toward reading, and phonics knowledge.

Kirkham et al. (2010) outlined three ways that ORB can occur. The first type of selective reporting happens when a study report omits a measure that was collected. In the example given above, if the authors report attitudes toward reading and phonics knowledge but do not report reading fluency, this would be an example of ORB. Similarly, the research report might include only a subset of these measures, as when researchers publish results on an intervention in a number of different articles. For example, if our hypothetical reading researchers report on the intervention's effects on reading fluency and attitude toward reading in one article and discuss the intervention's influence on phonics knowledge in another, this is an example of ORB. The reason why this is an example of ORB is that readers of either article will not be aware of the unreported outcomes unless the authors take extreme care to mention all the outcomes collected in the original study.

A second way ORB occurs is through the selective reporting of specific outcomes. For example, a reader should suspect selective reporting if a study collected information on a comprehensive scale but reported results for only some of the subscales. This type of selective reporting might also happen when the outcome is measured several times, such as at baseline, immediate posttest, and follow-up. Omitting information about one or more of those time points signals selective reporting.

The third form of selective outcome reporting might occur when researchers omit details about outcomes. We often read reports in which the authors state there are no differences between experimental groups on some outcome ($p > .05$) but do not provide any summary statistics or other detailed information. This selective reporting most critically influences the use of the primary study in a subsequent research review, and it negatively affects anyone who wishes to understand the magnitude of the observed effect and its confidence interval.

PREVALENCE OF OUTCOME REPORTING BIAS

Research on selective outcome reporting grew out of investigations into *publication bias*, a term that refers to the fact that statistically significant results have a higher likelihood of being published than nonsignificant results. Publication bias was first identified by Sterling (1959) in his research on published studies in four major psychology journals. Of the articles that used statistical tests, 97% rejected the key null hypothesis, leading Sterling to conclude that experimental results are more likely to be published if the major statistical test rejects the null hypothesis. More recently, Tannock (1996) reviewed 32 reports of randomized clinical oncology trials. Tannock found that the number of statistical comparisons undertaken during the analysis of the trials was large and often exceeded the number reported. After Tannock's work, many researchers in medicine began to suspect selective reporting by noticing omissions from published articles (e.g., Hutton & Williamson, 2000; Streiner & Joffe, 1998).

Research on selective outcome reporting has developed more quickly in medicine than in the social sciences because of the stronger research norms that guide publishing protocols and registering clinical trials. In medicine, researchers identify the primary outcomes, which are the target of the intervention, and secondary outcomes, which may be influenced by a treatment but are not the key measure of the intervention's effectiveness. To examine publication bias in regard to primary outcomes, Dickersin, Min, and Meinert (1992) traced the publication progress of 737 studies submitted to two institutional review boards (IRBs) that serve Johns Hopkins health institutions. Of the studies that had complete analyses at the time Dickersin et al. interviewed authors, 81% of studies from the School of Medicine, and 66% of studies from the School of Hygiene and Public Health, had been published. They found evidence of an association between results reported to be significant and likelihood of publication. Using a similar framework, other research teams also found discrepancies in protocols (Hahn, Williamson, & Hutton, 2002) demonstrating that, compared to nonsignificant outcomes statistically significant outcomes had a higher odds of being fully reported (e.g., Chan, Hróbjartsson, Haahr, Gøtzsche, & Altman, 2004).

The finding that selective outcome reporting is related to statistical significance has been replicated in other countries (Chan, Krleža-Jerić, Schmid, & Altman, 2004) and through comparisons of publication protocol (Dwan et al., 2011; Fleming, Koletsi, Dwan, & Pandis, 2015; Mathieu, Boutron, Moher, Altman, & Ravaud, 2009; Vedula, Bero, Scherer, & Dickersin, 2009). Problems with selective outcome reporting in medicine have been uncovered chiefly by comparing protocols to published studies. This method for examining selective reporting is not available in many other areas of research, however, and thus the documentation of ORB in other scholarly fields has lagged behind medicine.

Professionals in the social sciences do not routinely use protocols and do not identify primary and secondary outcomes, but one can imagine problems similar to those identified by medical researchers. For example, imagine a study of an intervention aimed at alleviating symptoms of depression in which a brief measure of depression and a measure of stress levels were collected. The protocol submitted to an IRB might identify the intervention as one for depression, but when the study is published it may report only on the measures of stress. Changing the primary outcome from the planning stages to publication is an illustration of what Simmons, Nelson, and Simonsohn (2011) labeled *researcher flexibility*, a problem to which we return below.

Given that it is easy to imagine processes similar to those observed in medical studies operating in studies conducted in the social sciences, the challenge is in finding ways to investigate this suspicion empirically. A potential source of pre-research documentation (similar to a protocols) is IRB submissions. Documentation submitted to an IRB could help researchers investigate ORB. Cooper, Deneve, and Charlton (1997), for example, examined publication bias by surveying researchers with an approved IRB protocol to see what happened to the research (e.g., whether it was abandoned, published, completed but not published, etc.). However, IRB protocols are, in essence, prepared for nonexperts, and therefore they usually do not lay out in operational detail many of the methodological and statistical choices facing researchers, or even list all of the outcomes and how they will be measured.

Given that each institution's IRB is also subject to localized practices and policies, the nature and completeness of these protocols would likely differ too much across institutions to provide any meaningful comparisons from protocol to published work. In addition, obtaining the individual IRB protocols for social science research from any given institution may be difficult.

Social science researchers, however, use two systems that could serve as the basis for an analysis of ORB. First, grant proposals play a role similar to that of a protocol in that they describe (generally in highly operational terms) the methods and analytic strategies that will be used. Unfortunately, collecting these would likely be time consuming and require consent from researchers, funding agencies, and/or others. For example, Spybrook and Raudenbush (2009) examined the precision and technical accuracy of the first wave of randomized trials funded by the Institute of Education Sciences (IES). To obtain the proposals funded by IES, they wrote directly to the investigators and received 40 of 55 proposals. For the remaining 15 proposals, they filed a Freedom of Information Act request to IES in 2006. By 2009, they still had not received any of the 15 requested proposals.

The second system that could be used is the dissertation process. Dissertations are typically not approved on the basis of statistical significance. Most universities, furthermore, follow a process in which dissertation research is first proposed (and approved by a committee) and then carried out. Normative understandings of the dissertation process (e.g., that it is developmental) and a lack of length limitations generally lead to works that are reported in more detail than are typical journal articles. Although dissertation proposals are not available in the public domain, the dissertation itself usually presents a complete record of the methods and procedures that were actually used in the study, and a large percentage of dissertations are available via electronic databases (e.g., ProQuest Digital Dissertations) to which many university libraries subscribe, and, as such, are easily retrievable.

To examine selective reporting bias in educational research, Pigott, Valentine, Polanin, Williams, and Canada (2013) compared the dissertations conducted on K–12 educational interventions during 2001–2005 with their subsequent published versions. Of the 621 dissertations we identified, 79 dissertations with 1,599 different treatment outcomes had been published at the time of the search. On average, the published version included about half of the outcomes reported in the dissertation, with only 19 (24%) of the 79 published reports including all of the outcomes from the dissertation. Nonsignificant outcomes were about 1.30 times less likely to appear in the published version of the study than were statistically significant outcomes, a result similar to those found in medicine.

Other researchers have documented selective outcome reporting through surveys of researchers. John, Loewenstein, and Prelec (2012) anonymously surveyed more than 2,000 psychologists and found that 63% admitted to not reporting all dependent measures. Estimates were even higher in a condition that was incentivized to tell the truth. This finding is consistent with Chan and Altman's (2005) research, which included a retrospective analysis of published randomized trials and a follow-up survey of the trials' authors. When they combined data from the author surveys and the publications, Chan and Altman found that 75% (380/505) of trials did not fully report all their efficacy outcomes in the journal publication. Of the 308 trials that measured potential harms of a treatment, 64% did not fully report their harm outcomes.

Thus, although selective outcome reporting has not been studied as extensively in the social and behavioral sciences as in medicine, we have evidence for ORB from comparisons of dissertations and their published versions as well as from self-reports from research psychologists. Consistent with research in medicine, we also note that selective outcome reporting is related to the statistical significance of the results.

POTENTIAL REASONS FOR SELECTIVE OUTCOME REPORTING

When asked, authors give a number of rationales for why they omit outcomes from a published report. Chan and Altman (2005) surveyed authors about their decisions for excluding information from published studies. For efficacy outcomes, the most prevalent reasons for selectively reporting information were journal space restrictions (47%), lack of clinical importance (37%), and lack of statistical significance (24%). For harm outcomes, researchers reported that they omitted outcomes because of a lack of clinical importance (75%) or of statistical significance (50%). LeBel et al. (2013) found similar results in a survey of researchers with published articles in a set of psychology journals. Only 54.7% of respondents reported including all of their assessed measures in the journal article; their reasons for excluding these observations included a lack of statistical significance, psychometric problems with the measures, and editorial requests.

Trainor (2015) reexamined Pigott et al.'s (2013) original set of studies to code other potential correlates of the likelihood of an outcome to be published. Trainor found that outcomes with findings not consistent with the author's original hypothesis were 41% more likely to be omitted from the published report than findings that were consistent with hypotheses. This result provides support for Bakker and Wicherts's (2011) study of errors in reporting statistical results in psychology journals. In their sample of 281 studies, Bakker and Wicherts found that 15% contained at least one statistical conclusion that was incorrect and that most of those errors were in a direction congruent with the researchers' hypotheses. Rosenthal et al. (1964) reported that researchers who were more biased toward their hypothesis also made more, and larger, recording errors in favor of their hypothesis. In Trainor's work there was a relationship between the rate of selective outcome reporting and whether the author held an academic position, with a higher likelihood of omission for those holding academic jobs.

O'Boyle, Banks, and Gonzalez-Mulé (2014) conducted a similar study of the business management literature, comparing the ratio of supported to unsupported hypotheses from a dissertation to the subsequent publication. The ratio of supported to unsupported hypotheses more than doubled from the dissertation to the published version, indicating that researchers dropped statistically nonsignificant hypotheses when publishing the research. O'Boyle et al. documented that researchers added, dropped, or altered data and added or dropped hypotheses from dissertation to published article. They also found that a higher incidence of these questionable reporting practices were related to longer times between dissertation completion and publication and to a higher prestige ranking of the journal in which the study was published.

Another potential reason for selective outcome reporting may be related to a phenomenon Kerr (1998) called *HARKing*, or hypothesizing after results are known. Kerr defined HARKing as presenting a post hoc hypothesis that was informed by one's results in a research report as if it were an a priori hypothesis. To present a more coherent story about a given study, researchers might omit information about an outcome if the results for that outcome are not congruent with a priori hypotheses, as suggested by Bakker and Wicherts (2011). Ferguson and Heene (2012) went even further, to argue that the aversion to publishing any null result in psychology has led to a preponderance of theory-supported results and thus theories that cannot be falsified. Ferguson and Heene used the term *undead theory* to refer to theories that may continue in use because they can never be proven false.

Despite repeated calls for reducing the reliance of research on null hypothesis testing (Cumming, 2014; Ioannidis, 2005), publication bias and selective outcome reporting are both related to statistical significance, with researchers making decisions about what to publish, and what to include in submissions, on the basis of a statistically significant test. In addition, researchers may also be influenced by whether the results from a given outcome are congruent with their original hypotheses. In some cases, as noted by Kirkham et al. (2010) and Vedula et al. (2009), researchers may change their hypotheses to fit their results in a post hoc manner, making the report more consistent with their findings rather than their protocol. Trainor's (2015) work suggests that these practices may happen more frequently in educational research for those authors pursuing academic careers.

As John et al. (2012) pointed out, failing to report all dependent measures in a study could be appropriate if a researcher collects multiple measures of the same construct and the results using each measure are the same. However, readers of research cannot know whether outcomes are missing for reasons related to their statistical or clinical significance or whether the issue is simply journal restrictions. In any case, missing information from a primary study can affect not only the inferences made from the results but also the conclusions from any subsequent syntheses that use data from the study.

Bias obviously occurs with selective outcome reporting when the omitted information could change the direction of the inference from the results. Omitting the results about harmful outcomes, for example, provides decision makers with incomplete information and may lead to the implementation of interventions without knowing the full range of potential consequences. Even not reporting null results in an outcome could lead to faulty inferences about a phenomenon. As Vedula et al. (2009) discussed, the inaccurate reporting of the primary outcomes in the effectiveness of gabapentin for unapproved indications served to make the drug appear efficacious. As Vedula et al. wrote, "Once the data are known, the addition or subtraction of primary outcomes can lead to the presentation of chance findings as evidence of a drug's effectiveness" (p. 1969).

In studies of social and behavioral interventions, another potential problem is the reporting of negative or harmful outcomes. If researchers have a tendency to report only on statistically significant outcomes in a direction congruent with their a priori hypotheses, then many studies on social interventions could be missing information on harmful outcomes. Chan, Hróbjartsson, et al. (2004) found that harmful outcomes are more subject to selective reporting than primary outcomes in medical trial reports. This issue has yet to be examined in the social and behavioral sciences, but we imagine that similar results could be documented.

Biases from selective outcome reporting are compounded when studies with missing outcome data are used in subsequent research syntheses. For example, Hutton and Williamson (2000) examined the robustness of the results of a meta-analysis when the largest trial is missing a key outcome measure. They conducted a series of sensitivity analyses under differing assumptions about the true results of this trial and demonstrated that the conclusions of the original meta-analysis could easily be reversed. In addition, they examined the potential bias when selective reporting occurs on one of several measures of the same outcome. They found that even in cases where the correlation among the reported and omitted measure was greater than .95, bias can still substantially distort estimates of treatment effects and significance tests.

Not all investigators suggest that ORB can change meta-analytic conclusions. For example, Williamson and Gamble (2005) reanalyzed a set of published reviews that were suspected of selective ORB. In each case, they used missing data-imputation methods to compare the published results to those with imputed values for the missing outcomes. Although they did not change the findings of any the reviews examined, they cautioned that larger reviews with more missing data than in their examples could have substantial bias.

Kirkham et al. (2010) examined the potential impact of ORB on the results of 283 systematic reviews published in the Cochrane Library. These reviews included 2,562 trials that they coded for the possibility of ORB. Thirty-one percent (788 of 2,562) of the trials included a primary outcome of the review that was either partially reported or not reported. Of the 712 trial reports that were in English, 359 were coded as having a high risk of ORB. Kirkham et al. also conducted a sensitivity analysis of the results from 81 reviews in which there was a single meta-analysis of the review's primary outcome. Their sensitivity analysis shows that ORB can potentially influence the results of a systematic review, with the treatment effect estimate in 19 of 81 of these reviews (23%) being reduced by at least 20%.

The difficulties inherent in assessing the presence of ORB in the social sciences mean that almost no research exists to help quantify the extent to which it might affect results obtained in systematic reviews. However, the ease with which researchers such as John et al. (2012) and Simmons et al. (2011) have demonstrated how the flexibility afforded researchers in the social sciences can lead to faulty studies and unwarranted conclusions suggests that we should be concerned. Including studies with ORB and inaccurate conclusions can potentially bias a whole field of research. The question is, what can be done about it?

REMEDIES FOR OUTCOME REPORTING BIAS

Given the prevalence of ORB, strategies for its prevention should take place in the field in general, and at the level of the individual researcher, as Makel (2014) suggested. One strategy already in place in medicine is the requirement from some funding agencies to make research protocols publicly available. The National Institutes of Health (NIH) manages the website https://clinicaltrials.gov, where all NIH-funded trials, and most clinical drug trials, must be registered, as mandated by law. In addition, the International Committee of Medical Journal Editors (De Angelis et al., 2004) requires registration as a condition of publication. The member journals of the International Committee of Medical Journal Editors include the *Journal of the American Medical Association*, *The Lancet*, the *Annals of Internal Medicine*, and *The New England Journal of Medicine*. Researchers such as Dickersin and Rennie (2003) have repeatedly called for more complete registration of trials and, in particular, the protocols for those trials. However, not all medical researchers register their trials (Scherer, Sieving, Ervin, & Dickersin, 2012). The difficulties faced in medicine, where there are clear incentives and even legal requirements for registration (Weber, Merino, & Loder, 2015), do not provide much hope for a similar system working in the social and behavioral sciences.

Another strategy for preventing selective outcome reporting are reporting guidelines. The field of medicine has the CONSORT (Consolidated Standards of Reporting Trials) guidelines, a widely adopted set of standards for the reporting of clinical trials (Rennie, 2001). These standards include defining and reporting on prespecified primary and secondary outcomes and any changes to those outcomes. The SPIRIT (Standard Protocol Items: Recommendations for Interventional Trials) guidelines specifically address the reporting of protocols for trials (Chan et al., 2013).

An extension of CONSORT, called CONSORT–SPI (Consolidated Standards of Reporting Trials—Social and Psychological Interventions), is in development for the social and behavioral sciences (Montgomery et al., 2013). The American Psychological Association also has a set of guidelines for the reporting of primary studies and meta-analysis, called JARS (Journal Article Reporting Standards) and MARS (Meta-Analysis Reporting Standards; American Psychological Association Publications and Communications Board Working Group on Journal Article Reporting Standards, 2008). These guidelines pertain to various types of primary studies, including experimental and quasi-experimental studies. The existence of the reporting guidelines, however, does not guarantee that researchers will use the guidelines, or that journal editors will consistently apply the guidelines.

Simmons et al. (2011) also provided a series of suggestions for both reviewers and authors to increase the quality and transparency of the reporting of results. For researchers, one of the guidelines includes reporting all variables measured in the study. Simmons, Nelson, and Simonsohn (2012) provided a 21-word solution for reporting that encourages researchers to state the following: "We report how we determined our sample size, all data exclusions, if any, all manipulations, and all measures in the study." Simmons et al. (2012) pointed out that this statement provides readers confidence that the authors are committed to transparency around reporting issues. The inclusion of guidelines for reviewers highlights the fact that journals in the field of social sciences have been slow to adopt and apply existing reporting rules.

Space considerations remain another hindrance to fully reporting all outcomes. Paper journals have limited space, and thus some selective outcome reporting might be due to legitimate issues concerning that. However, journals are beginning to provide researchers online appendixes for storing more detailed information about a study that could include more complete reporting of all outcomes measured. Universities are also providing open, online repositories for their faculty to store preprints of journal articles as well as protocols and data associated with faculty research. In economics, several journals, such as *The American Economic Review*, require all authors to send their data, programs, and sufficient details to permit reproduction of their results (see the complete policy at https://www.aeaweb.org/journals/policies/data-availability-policy).

Journals could also facilitate and encourage full reporting of outcomes by providing space for data warehousing and by requiring that a well-documented database be submitted for online archiving before accepting a study, not unlike the agreement among medical journal editors to require a published protocol before accepting a study for publication. Well-documented data repositories only increase the accuracy and completeness of resulting meta-analyses. Even beyond the advantage of having the data available so that others can attempt to reproduce the results, the use of data warehousing could have additional benefits. For example, it would likely lead to increased use of individual participant data meta-analyses, whereby data from original studies are, when available, combined with study-level data in a single systematic research review (Cooper & Patall, 2009; Pigott, Williams, & Polanin, 2012; Valentine & Thompson, 2013).

In the social sciences a number of efforts are underway that encourage researchers to report more fully on all aspects of their study, including outcomes. The What Works Clearinghouse (http://ies.ed.gov/ncee/Wwc/; see Chapter 8, this volume, for a fuller discussion) provides space for a voluntary registry of ongoing and completed clinical trials for educational interventions but does not verify the accuracy of the information provided. There are four current registries for randomized and observational studies, although none require researchers to provide preanalysis plans or protocols. These include the (a) American Economic Association randomized controlled trial registry (https://www.socialscienceregistry.org), (b) Evidence in Governance and Politics registry (http://www.egap.org/content/registration), (c) International Initiative for Impact Evaluation's Registry of International Development Impact Evaluations (http://www.ridie.org/index.php), and (d) Open Science Framework (https://osf.io/). Ioannidis, Munafò, Fusar-Poli, Nosek, and David (2014) also discussed data repositories that are available but are used more widely in fields other than the social sciences. The Inter-University Consortium for Political and Social Research at the University of Michigan (https://www.icpsr.umich.edu/icpsrweb/deposit/index.jsp) archives raw data from social science research. The use of these registries and data depositories are currently voluntary, and there is no guarantee that the information provided contains all outcomes measured. This may be changing given that the NIH and the National Science Foundation both have policies for sharing data collected with funding from these institutions.

Another strategy for encouraging full disclosure of outcomes related to publishing research protocols is to move the field of social science research to conducting confirmatory rather than exploratory studies. Wagenmakers, Wetzels, Borsboom, van der Maas, and Kievit (2012) urged researchers to preregister their studies and commit to a statistical analysis strategy prior to collecting the data, to avoid HARKing and other questionable research practices. Preregistering methods sections of studies would force researchers to indicate what outcomes will be collected and how they all would be analyzed, thus avoiding selective outcome reporting. Makel (2014) provided strategies for how Wagenmakers et al.'s suggestions could be implemented, including moving the acceptance of a study to a point before the data are analyzed, thus preventing any analysis, reporting, or publishing decisions from being dependent on statistical significance.

Suggestions for Individual Researchers

Most researchers are committed to producing transparent and replicable research findings that contribute to the field. However, the pressures on early career researchers to publish as much as possible may lead to decisions that, in the long run, are detrimental to the field. How, then, can individual researchers avoid selective outcome reporting in their own work? One simple strategy is to follow reporting guidelines that exist in a researcher's field. For example, the JARS and MARS guidelines should be followed by individual researchers. In addition, Simmons et al.'s (2012) 21-word solution is a simple formula to ensure accurate and complete reporting.

Researchers also face the real constraints of journal article space. In these instances, individual researchers have a number of opportunities to ensure transparency. If a researcher needs to report on a large study in more than one research report, then he or she should be clear that not all outcomes are discussed and analyzed in any single article and should provide readers with a reference that contains the remaining information. If a journal cannot provide space in an online appendix for information on other outcomes not reported in an article, the researcher should, at the least, provide a contact address for readers and provide the results of those outcomes for interested readers.

Researchers who serve as reviewers can also ask questions about studies that do not include outcomes typical in a particular research area and should look for other signs that outcomes many not be fully reported in a study, in particular outcomes that might show a harmful or negative effect on participants. As reviewers, we need to be more tolerant and accepting of the messiness of typical research and be wary when a study's findings conform perfectly to all hypotheses.

Suggestions for Meta-Analysts

Researchers conducting systematic reviews and meta-analyses should be aware of the potential consequences of ORB for their results. Several methods are available for evaluating and adjusting for publication and ORB. Traditional methods to investigate publication bias focus on studying *funnel plots*: the graphical representation of effect sizes where the effect sizes are plotted on the y-axis and the effect sizes' standard error are plotted on the x-axis. Asymmetry in the plot may indicate potential publication bias. Duval and Tweedie (2000) and Egger, Smith, Schneider, and Minder (1997) each have created means to empirically investigate funnel plot asymmetry. Other methods for detecting and correcting for publication bias include sensitivity analysis using a priori weight functions (Vevea & Woods, 2005) and p-curve analysis (Simonsohn, Nelson, & Simmons, 2014).

Others have created model-based approaches for studying the effects of ORB. Copas, Dwan, Kirkham, and Williamson's (2014) model uses a likelihood-based approach for estimating the effect of ORB on the p values and standard errors of meta-analytic estimates. The technique provides a sensitivity analysis of the impact associated with ORB. Other methods for evaluating ORB and adjusting effect size estimates include selection models (Hedges & Vevea, 1996; Vevea & Hedges, 1995), which model the probability of observing effect size estimates in a meta-analysis as a function of their statistical significance and adjust mean effects and standard errors in the presences of ORB. However, it is important to note that adjusting meta-analytic estimates for ORB is not ideal. The methods described are often not sensitive, or they may impose additional statistical assumptions. Ongoing work highlighting the prevalence of ORB and opportunities to prevent it is needed.

CONCLUSION

What steps can we take to increase the quality of reporting of primary studies, and thus the completeness of syntheses using these studies? In an ideal world, all social science research would start with a highly operational, publicly available protocol that guides the research. This is a lofty goal, but perhaps we can start with the development of professional norms that hold researchers responsible for fully documenting the research methods and analytic choices, including reporting all outcomes they measure, as Simmons et al. (2011) suggested. Furthermore, we can continue to study the prevalence and magnitude of ORB by obtaining protocols of studies either from funding agencies or from local IRBs. As researchers, we need to apply pressure to those funding social science research to allow access to protocols in order to understand more fully the potential problems caused by selective outcome reporting.

With regard to ORB in particular, consistency in reporting of all outcomes measured in a study would not only improve our understanding of the full range of potential outcomes of an intervention but would also allow for a more complete picture of the state of a research area in a research synthesis. Without a full and transparent understanding of a research area, we could be pursuing research that is mostly false, as Ioannidis (2005) famously stated, or at least research that leads us down a wrong path. The scarcity of funding and support for research in the social and behavioral sciences requires us to be more careful with our resources, and thus we as researchers should be transparent and open about all of our research procedures and measures for the common good.

RECOMMENDED READING

Chan, A.-W., & Altman, D. G. (2005). Identifying outcome reporting bias in randomised trials on PubMed: review of publications and survey of authors. *British Medical Journal, 330*, 753. http://dx.doi.org/10.1136/bmj.38356.424606.8F

Cooper, H., Deneve, K., & Charlton, K. (1997). Finding the missing science: The fate of studies submitted for review by a human subjects committee. *Psychological Methods, 2*, 447–452.

John, L. K., Loewenstein, G., & Prelec, D. (2012). Measuring the prevalence of questionable research practices with incentives for truth telling. *Psychological Science, 23*, 524–532. http://dx.doi.org/10.1177/0956797611430953

Kirkham, J. J., Dwan, K. M., Altman, D. G., Gamble, C., Dodd, S., Smyth, R., & Williamson, P. R. (2010). The impact of outcome reporting bias in randomised controlled trials on a cohort of systematic reviews. *British Medical Journal, 340*, c365. http://dx.doi.org/10.1136/bmj.c365

Pigott, T. D., Valentine, J. C., Polanin, J. R., Williams, R. T., & Canada, D. D. (2013). Outcome-reporting bias in education research. *Educational Researcher, 42*, 424–432.

Vedula, S. S., Bero, L., Scherer, R. W., & Dickersin, K. (2009). Outcome reporting in industry-sponsored trials of gabapentin for off-label use. *The New England Journal of Medicine, 361*, 1963–71. http://dx.doi.org/10.1056/NEJMsa0906126

REFERENCES

American Psychological Association Publications and Communications Board Working Group on Journal Article Reporting Standards. (2008). Reporting standards for research in psychology: Why do we need them? What might they be? *American Psychologist, 63*, 839–851. http://dx.doi.org/10.1037/0003-066X.63.9.839

Bakker, M., & Wicherts, J. M. (2011). The (mis)reporting of statistical results in psychology journals. *Behavior Research Methods, 43*, 666–678. http://dx.doi.org/10.3758/s13428-011-0089-5

Chan, A.-W., & Altman, D. G. (2005). Identifying outcome reporting bias in randomised trials on PubMed: Review of publications and survey of authors. *British Medical Journal, 330*, 753. http://dx.doi.org/10.1136/bmj.38356.424606.8F

Chan, A.-W., Hróbjartsson, A., Haahr, M. T., Gøtzsche, P. C., & Altman, D. G. (2004). Empirical evidence for selective reporting of outcomes in randomized trials: Comparison of protocols to published articles. *JAMA, 291*, 2457–2465. http://dx.doi.org/10.1001/jama.291.20.2457

Chan, A.-W., Krleža-Jerić, K., Schmid, I., & Altman, D. G. (2004). Outcome reporting bias in randomized trials funded by the Canadian Institutes of Health Research. *Canadian Medical Association Journal, 171*, 735–740. http://dx.doi.org/10.1503/cmaj.1041086

Chan, A.-W., Tetzlaff, J. M., Altman, D. G., Laupacis, A., Gøtzsche, P. C., Krleža-Jerić, K., . . . Moher, D. (2013). SPIRIT 2013 statement: Defining standard protocol items for clinical trials. *Annals of Internal Medicine, 158*, 200–207. http://dx.doi.org/10.7326/0003-4819-158-3-201302050-00583

Cooper, H., Deneve, K., & Charlton, K. (1997). Finding the missing science: The fate of studies submitted for review by a human subjects committee. *Psychological Methods, 2*, 447–452. http://dx.doi.org/10.1037/1082-989X.2.4.447

Cooper, H., & Patall, E. A. (2009). The relative benefits of meta-analysis conducted with individual participant data versus aggregated data. *Psychological Methods, 14*, 165–176. http://dx.doi.org/10.1037/a0015565

Copas, J., Dwan, K., Kirkham, J., & Williamson, P. (2014). A model-based correction for outcome reporting bias in meta-analysis. *Biostatistics, 15*, 370–383. http://dx.doi.org/10.1093/biostatistics/kxt046

Cumming, G. (2014). The new statistics: Why and how. *Psychological Science, 25*, 7–29. http://dx.doi.org/10.1177/0956797613504966

De Angelis, C., Drazen, J. M., Frizelle, F. A., Haug, C., Hoey, J., Horton, R., . . . Van Der Weyden, M. B. (2004). Clinical trial registration: A statement from the International Committee of Medical Journal Editors. *The New England Journal of Medicine, 351*, 1250–1251. http://dx.doi.org/10.1056/NEJMe048225

Dickersin, K., Min, Y. I., & Meinert, C. L. (1992). Factors influencing publication of research results: Follow-up of applications submitted to two institutional review boards. *JAMA, 267*, 374–378. http://dx.doi.org/10.1001/jama.1992.03480030052036

Dickersin, K., & Rennie, D. (2003). Registering clinical trials. *JAMA, 290*, 516–523. http://dx.doi.org/10.1001/jama.290.4.516

Duval, S., & Tweedie, R. (2000). Trim and fill: A simple funnel-plot-based method of testing and adjusting for publication bias in meta-analysis. *Biometrics, 56*, 455–463. http://dx.doi.org/10.1111/j.0006-341X.2000.00455.x

Dwan, K., Altman, D. G., Cresswell, L., Blundell, M., Gamble, C. L., & Williamson, P. R. (2011). Comparison of protocols and registry entries to published reports for randomised controlled trials. *Cochrane Database of Systematic Reviews.* http://dx.doi.org/10.1002/14651858.MR000031.pub2

Egger, M., Smith, G. D., Schneider, M., & Minder, C. (1997). Bias in meta-analysis detected by a simple, graphical test. *British Medical Journal, 315,* 629–634. http://dx.doi.org/10.1136/bmj.315.7109.629

Ferguson, C. J., & Heene, M. (2012). A vast graveyard of undead theories: Publication bias and psychological science's aversion to the null. *Perspectives on Psychological Science, 7,* 555–561. http://dx.doi.org/10.1177/1745691612459059

Fleming, P. S., Koletsi, D., Dwan, K., & Pandis, N. (2015). Outcome discrepancies and selective reporting: Impacting the leading journals? *PLOS ONE, 10*(5), e0127495. http://dx.doi.org/10.1371/journal.pone.0127495

Hahn, S., Williamson, P. R., & Hutton, J. L. (2002). Investigation of within-study selective reporting in clinical research: Follow-up of applications submitted to a local research ethics committee. *Journal of Evaluation in Clinical Practice, 8,* 353–359. http://dx.doi.org/10.1046/j.1365-2753.2002.00314.x

Hedges, L. V., & Vevea, J. L. (1996). Estimating effect size under publication bias: Small sample properties and robustness of a random effects selection model. *Journal of Educational and Behavioral Statistics, 21,* 299–332. http://dx.doi.org/10.3102/10769986021004299

Hutton, J. L., & Williamson, P. R. (2000). Bias in meta-analysis due to outcome variable selection within studies. *Journal of the Royal Statistical Society: Series C. Applied Statistics, 49,* 359–370. http://dx.doi.org/10.1111/1467-9876.00197

Ioannidis, J. P. A. (2005). Why most published research findings are false. *PLOS Medicine, 2*(8), e124. http://dx.doi.org/10.1371/journal.pmed.0020124

Ioannidis, J. P. A., Munafò, M. R., Fusar-Poli, P., Nosek, B. A., & David, S. P. (2014). Publication and other reporting biases in cognitive sciences: detection, prevalence, and prevention. *Trends in Cognitive Sciences, 18,* 235–241. http://dx.doi.org/10.1016/j.tics.2014.02.010

John, L. K., Loewenstein, G., & Prelec, D. (2012). Measuring the prevalence of questionable research practices with incentives for truth telling. *Psychological Science, 23,* 524–532. http://dx.doi.org/10.1177/0956797611430953

Kerr, N. L. (1998). HARKing: Hypothesizing after the results are known. *Personality and Social Psychology Review, 2,* 196–217. http://dx.doi.org/10.1207/s15327957pspr0203_4

Kirkham, J. J., Dwan, K. M., Altman, D. G., Gamble, C., Dodd, S., Smyth, R., & Williamson, P. R. (2010). The impact of outcome reporting bias in randomised controlled trials on a cohort of systematic reviews. *British Medical Journal, 340,* c365. http://dx.doi.org/10.1136/bmj.c365

LeBel, E. P., Borsboom, D., Giner-Sorolla, R., Hasselman, F., Peters, K. R., Ratliff, K. A., & Smith, C. T. (2013). Grassroots support for reforming reporting standards in psychology. *Perspectives on Psychological Science, 8*, 424–432. http://dx.doi.org/10.1177/1745691613491437

Makel, M. C. (2014). The empirical march: Making science better at self-correction. *Psychology of Aesthetics, Creativity, and the Arts, 8*, 2–7. http://dx.doi.org/10.1037/a0035803

Mathieu, S., Boutron, I., Moher, D., Altman, D. G., & Ravaud, P. (2009). Comparison of registered and published primary outcomes in randomized controlled trials. *JAMA, 302*, 977–984. http://dx.doi.org/10.1001/jama.2009.1242

Montgomery, P., Grant, S., Hopewell, S., Macdonald, G., Moher, D., Michie, S., & Mayo-Wilson, E. (2013). Protocol for CONSORT-SPI: An extension for social and psychological interventions. *Implementation Science, 8*(1), 99. http://dx.doi.org/10.1186/1748-5908-8-99

Norris, S. L., Moher, D., Reeves, B. C., Shea, B., Loke, Y., Garner, S., . . . Wells, G. (2013). Issues relating to selective reporting when including non-randomized studies in systematic reviews on the effects of healthcare interventions. *Research Synthesis Methods, 4*, 36–47. http://dx.doi.org/10.1002/jrsm.1062

O'Boyle, E. H., Jr., Banks, G. C., & Gonzalez-Mulé, E. (2014). The chrysalis effect: How ugly initial results metamorphosize into beautiful articles. *Journal of Management.* Advance online publication. http://dx.doi.org/10.1177/0149206314527133

Pigott, T. D., Valentine, J. C., Polanin, J. R., Williams, R. T., & Canada, D. D. (2013). Outcome-reporting bias in education research. *Educational Researcher, 42*, 424–432. http://dx.doi.org/10.3102/0013189X13507104

Pigott, T., Williams, R., & Polanin, J. (2012). Combining individual participant and aggregated data in a meta-analysis with correlational studies. *Research Synthesis Methods, 3*, 257–268. http://dx.doi.org/10.1002/jrsm.1051

Rennie, D. (2001). CONSORT revised—Improving the reporting of randomized trials. *JAMA, 285*, 2006–2007. http://dx.doi.org/10.1001/jama.285.15.2006

Rosenthal, R., Friedman, C. J., Johnson, C. A., Fode, K., Schill, T., White, R. C., & Vikan, L. L. (1964). Variables affecting experimenter bias in a group situation. *Genetic Psychology Monographs, 70*, 271–296.

Scherer, R. W., Sieving, P. C., Ervin, A.-M., & Dickersin, K. (2012). Can we depend on investigators to identify and register randomized controlled trials? *PLOS ONE, 7*(9), e44183. http://dx.doi.org/10.1371/journal.pone.0044183

Simmons, J. P., Nelson, L. D., & Simonsohn, U. (2011). False-positive psychology: Undisclosed flexibility in data collection and analysis allows presenting anything as significant. *Psychological Science, 22*, 1359–1366. http://dx.doi.org/10.1177/0956797611417632

Simmons, J. P., Nelson, L. D., & Simonsohn, U. (2012). *A 21 word solution.* SSRN Scholarly Paper No. ID 2160588, Social Science Research Network, Rochester, NY. Retrieved from http://papers.ssrn.com/abstract=2160588

Simonsohn, U., Nelson, L. D., & Simmons, J. P. (2014). *p*-Curve and effect size: Correcting for publication bias using only significant results. *Perspectives on Psychological Science, 9*, 666–681. http://dx.doi.org/10.1177/1745691614553988

Spybrook, J., & Raudenbush, S. W. (2009). An examination of the precision and technical accuracy of the first wave of group-randomized trials funded by the Institute of Education Sciences. *Educational Evaluation and Policy Analysis, 31,* 298–318. http://dx.doi.org/10.3102/0162373709339524

Sterling, T. D. (1959). Publication decisions and their possible effects on inferences drawn from tests of significance—Or vice versa. *Journal of the American Statistical Association, 54,* 30–34.

Streiner, D. L., & Joffe, R. (1998). The adequacy of reporting randomized, controlled trials in the evaluation of antidepressants. *The Canadian Journal of Psychiatry, 43,* 1026–1030.

Tannock, I. F. (1996). False-positive results in clinical trials: Multiple significance tests and the problem of unreported comparisons. *Journal of the National Cancer Institute, 88,* 206–207. http://dx.doi.org/10.1093/jnci/88.3-4.206

Trainor, B. P. (2015). *Incomplete reporting: Addressing the problem of outcome-reporting bias in educational research* (Unpublished doctoral dissertation). Loyola University Chicago, IL.

Valentine, J. C., & Thompson, S. G. (2013). Issues relating to confounding and meta-analysis when including non-randomized studies in systematic reviews on the effects of interventions. *Research Synthesis Methods, 4,* 26–35. http://dx.doi.org/10.1002/jrsm.1064

Vedula, S. S., Bero, L., Scherer, R. W., & Dickersin, K. (2009). Outcome reporting in industry-sponsored trials of gabapentin for off-label use. *The New England Journal of Medicine, 361,* 1963–1971. http://dx.doi.org/10.1056/NEJMsa0906126

Vevea, J. L., & Hedges, L. V. (1995). A general linear model for estimating effect size in the presence of publication bias. *Psychometrika, 60,* 419–435. http://dx.doi.org/10.1007/BF02294384

Vevea, J. L., & Woods, C. M. (2005). Publication bias in research synthesis: Sensitivity analysis using a priori weight functions. *Psychological Methods, 10,* 428–443. http://dx.doi.org/10.1037/1082-989X.10.4.428

Wagenmakers, E.-J., Wetzels, R., Borsboom, D., van der Maas, H. L. J., & Kievit, R. A. (2012). An agenda for purely confirmatory research. *Perspectives on Psychological Science, 7,* 632–638. http://dx.doi.org/10.1177/1745691612463078

Weber, W. E. J., Merino, J. G., & Loder, E. (2015). Trial registration 10 years on. *British Medical Journal, 351,* h3572. http://dx.doi.org/10.1136/bmj.h3572

Williamson, P. R., & Gamble, C. (2005). Identification and impact of outcome selection bias in meta-analysis. *Statistics in Medicine, 24,* 1547–1561. http://dx.doi.org/10.1002/sim.2025

5

CITING, BEING CITED, NOT CITING, AND NOT BEING CITED: CITATIONS AS INTELLECTUAL FOOTPRINTS

ALYSON L. LAVIGNE AND THOMAS L. GOOD

KEY POINTS

- Most published articles are never cited and hence make no contribution to the field.
- Most cited publications reach their prime within 5 years and then fade from memory.
- A rare number of articles go unread for a long period of time, only to be discovered and frequently cited.
- The highly skewed distribution of citations illustrates that only a handful of scholars influence any given field.
- Self-citations (when appropriate) often have good effects for the journal and the author in terms of garnering additional citations.
- Authors and editors illustrate a preference for newness as opposed to integrating new and old evidence.
- Authors, reviewers, and editors should become more conscious of who they cite and why.

We thank Karine Ivy and Natasha Sterzinger for their valuable assistance in chapter preparation. We also thank Julia Cohen, Erica Defrain, and Kathryn Wentzel for their helpful feedback.

http://dx.doi.org/10.1037/0000033-006
Toward a More Perfect Psychology: Improving Trust, Accuracy, and Transparency in Research, M. C. Makel and J. A. Plucker (Editors)

- Graduate students ideally will receive preparation in the ethics of the research process and guidelines for thinking about whom to read, how much to read, whom to cite, and the implications of citing and not citing.
- Researchers should consider the impact of a "more is better" orientation on the development of knowledge and determine whether or not more is indeed better.
- Given the number of articles that go unread or rarely read, it seems important to understand the economic cost of these professional activities and what might be done to improve the present publication process.

We write this chapter in the context of the growing criticism of science, and of psychology in particular (see Barrett, 2015; Bartlett, 2015; Meyer & Chabris, 2014; Voosen, 2015), and the continuing explosion of information. More scientific papers are being written than previously because of the expansion of the number of journals that are now available in print, online, and by means of the many Internet search engines that can locate more information more quickly. We address the information explosion later in this chapter, but for now it is important to note that many scholars have concluded that the role of publications has evolved in problematic ways. Indeed, current practices have led some scholars to question what is perceived to be the publication of many articles that hold little, if any, value for the field, providing special urgency for considering what we know about core aspects of publishing. Whom do we read and cite? Who cites us, and why? What are the implications of citing others, not citing others, and being cited? What are professional best practices in selecting and using others' work as we place our work into the larger literature that we address?

In the sections that follow we assess citation behaviors in academia, including the citation of others and self. We examine the nonscholarly motivations (intentional or not) of citation behavior, including trust, gender, and other knowledge about an author or his or her work. We use this analysis to propose and discuss a set of recommendations.

USING CITATIONS AND REFERENCE LISTS AS ARTIFACTS OF RESEARCH PRACTICE AND QUALITY

Examining an article's reference list and in-text citations provides considerable information: What is the author's theoretical or conceptual framework? Does the author read primarily contemporary work, historical work, or does he or she seek a balance? How much evidence does the author use to support the research presented, and what is its quality? The reference list should include the most important publications that inform the author's research, help readers understand the contribution an author's study makes to a field, and alert readers to the extent to which the study replicates or contradicts prior research (Brysbaert & Smyth, 2011).

THE LIFE CYCLE OF JOURNAL ARTICLES

Before delving into citing behavior, we consider the artifacts that scholars produce: journal articles. The average article's life cycle follows a fairly standard path. During the first years after publication, citations (per year) to any given article increase; a maximum is reached, followed by a decline (Glänzel & Schoepflin, 1995). Although a rare number of articles are cited even 100 years later after publication, most are gradually forgotten (Barnett, Fink, & Debus, 1989; Lange, 2005). However, an article's aging appears to be field specific, with citations per year peaking earlier in natural and life sciences (Year 2 or 3) and later in mathematics and social sciences. The relative frequency of citations for psychology articles, for example, peaks between Years 4 and 5 following an article's publication date (Glänzel & Schoepflin, 1995). Thus, the rates of knowledge use differ across fields, as do referencing practices (Cole, 2000).

There are a few outliers to the maturing and declining pattern of articles, including "Sleeping Beauties" and highly cited articles. Sleeping Beauties are articles that initially are either poorly cited or not cited at all and then suddenly receive recognition (Van Raan, 2005). These articles represent only 0.01% of all published articles (Glänzel & Garfield, 2004). Braun, Glänzel, and Schubert (2010) closely examined Sleeping Beauties in scientific fields and found that Sleeping Beauties were typically "awoken by a prince" 10 years after publication and, in 20% of the cases, the Sleeping Beauty received decent future citation success. Braun and colleagues' research reveals that articles with poor recognition in the first 5 years following publication are not doomed, but authors of such articles might be wise to seek out a prince because a large percentage of articles are cited only once or twice or never at all and remain asleep forever (Aksnes & Sivertsen, 2004).

Sleeping Beauties' more productive counterparts—highly cited articles— peak later in their citation life cycle and have more coauthors. These articles are more likely to involve international collaborations, be published in a high-impact journal, and be cited widely—in different journals and in close and remote fields (Aksnes, 2003). Highly cited articles also explain a large percentage of all citations because citation distributions are highly skewed. Across a

5-year window following publication, 40% of publications are cited only once or twice (Aksnes & Sivertsen, 2004; cf. de Solla Price, 1965). Furthermore, the most cited 50% of articles account for 90% of all citations to a journal, and the most cited half of articles are cited 10 times more than the least cited half of articles (Seglen, 1992).[1] Most articles are rarely cited, and thus only a small number of scholars influence the field (Endler, Rushton, & Roediger, 1978).[2]

CITATION BEHAVIOR: A BRIEF OVERVIEW

Citations can also be examined by what scholars read, whom they read, how much they read, and how they make sense of new knowledge. Pertinent to today's scholars is the "knowledge explosion" (Adair & Vohra, 2003)—the increasing amount of knowledge that is readily accessible to researchers. Reis and Stiller (1992) found a threefold increase in the number of references in articles published in the *Journal of Personality and Social Psychology*. Also, across the three decades (1968, 1978, 1988),[3] articles were longer, more procedural information and tables were included, research was based on more studies, more subjects were used per study, and more complex statistical methods were used. Renear and Palmer (2009) reported that the number of articles in which faculty report reading per year has steadily increased. They also reported that the amount of time they spent reading an article was 45 to 50 minutes between 1977 and the mid-1990s. However, they noted that, more recently, that amount of time has fallen to just over 30 minutes. Articles are now more numerous, and they tend to be longer. Hence, if we assume the amount of time scholars have to read has remained steady, in order for scholars to read the same percentage of the existing literature[4] authors must spend less time per article. This begs the question: Are scholars coping with the knowledge explosion by skimming and scanning rather than reading? If so, the effects on the acquisition and accumulation of knowledge could be highly detrimental.

---

[1]Citation distribution patterns were examined using a random sample of articles in 3,500 journals listed in the Science Citation Index from 1985 to 1989.

[2]There is some controversy concerning the number of articles that are read. For example, King, Tenopir, and Clarke (2006) noted that some of the claims suggesting that journal articles are rarely read are based on citation counts, and clearly articles could be read but not cited. They further noted that many articles are downloaded or examined online. We are comfortable with the conclusion that many articles are not given careful attention. If articles are read (or perused) but not cited, we conclude that these articles have little impact on the field. Actual citation seems to be a proxy that an article is being given serious thought; however, we wanted readers to be aware of counteropinions.

[3]The specific numbers were as follows: 1968 (n = 186), 1978 (n = 131), and 1988 (n = 188).

[4]It is unclear whether the growth in the number of articles scholars report reading matches the rate at which available literature has grown (number of articles published).

In-text citations also have increased. Adair and Vohra (2003) found that from 1972 to 1998, in-text citations increased to an average of 23 citations per article to 111 citations per article in the *Journal of Experimental Psychology: General* for articles published from 1996 to 1998. In one article, 18 citations were used in a single sentence! These findings illuminate the pressures under which authors are functioning—both in getting published (and the normative expectations and standards) and in reading and integrating existing knowledge. As more knowledge becomes available within an area of expertise, it will be important to determine whether researchers (or their graduate students) are becoming more narrow in their reading focus and/or better skimmers and to understand the impact of such practices on knowledge acquisition and use (because it appears that researchers are spending less time reading a given article). These findings also raise a question: Are we overciting? Oftentimes when authors claim a finding is well established, many citations follow, but if a finding is so well established it is practically common knowledge, will citing just one seminal or review article suffice? Citing all evidence available suggests to the reader that all studies are equal, when in reality some studies provide better, stronger, or more nuanced evidence than others. To avoid overcitation, we encourage authors to be mindful that their citing aligns with the specific claim being made and to cite only the appropriate evidence, not necessarily all the evidence.

Citing Others and Being Cited

In addition to quality, there are many reasons why we cite others and others cite us, including: "utility . . . availability . . . collaboration or camaraderie (in-house citations), chauvinism, mentoring, personal sympathies or antipathies, competition, neglect, obliteration by incorporation, argumentation, flattery, convention, reference copying, reviewing, and secondary referencing (MacRoberts & MacRoberts, 1989; Seglen, 1989)" (cited in Seglen, 1992, p. 636). Others may be motivated by mutual grooming with the hopes that if you cite someone, they will cite you (Hartley, 2012). Authors might even cite an editor with the hopes of gaining a favorable outcome (Romano, 2009) or be the victim of coercive self-citation by editors or peer reviewers (Martin, 2013; Straub & Anderson, 2009; Wilhite & Fong, 2012). Likewise, authors may be selective in what they cite and seek out citations that support their own personal views while ignoring existing counternarratives or opposing evidence. In addition to being unethical, according to Babor and McGovern (2008), this "publishing sin" hinders readers' ability to fully understand the implications of the present study in the context of the larger body of literature and may set scholars up to entertain analyses that are more likely to confirm their own hypotheses (Ferguson, 2015).

Another underlying mechanism that guides a researcher's reading and citing motivation is trust. Tenopir (2014)[5] explored how academics assign authority and trustworthiness to sources they read, cite, and publish. She found that as academics read, they read the abstract, assess the methodology, assess the credibility of the data and logic, and examine the source's references (i.e., are credible sources cited?). Academics read recommended works from colleagues as well as works from familiar scholars. Beyond this, they consider peer review, familiarity with the journal, and journal impact factors when deciding what to read. However, when they ultimately decide to cite a source, researchers use the following questions to guide their decision: Is the research group or institution, author, journal, or conference known and trusted? Is the work seminal in the field? Does the methodology support the research findings? Clearly, scholars use many measures in determining the credibility of a source.

Tenopir's (2014) research also underscores that science is a social enterprise. One might wonder, then—are we more likely to cite close acquaintances? It is clear that we might cite our peers more frequently because we know the extent to which we can trust their work, know their research, and/or have established open communication whereby we can inquire about their recent work when writing a new article or chapter. However, to what extent do we cite invisible (i.e., unknown) colleagues? (see de Solla Price, 1986; Lievrouw, 1990). Milard (2014)[6] interviewed authors about their relationship with the authors of each citation noted in the references of a given article. In 25% of the cited references, the author did not know the cited author(s). Authors were more likely to cite individuals who are known to some degree: In 75% of references (including self-citation), the author knew at least one of the cited authors in the reference, and in 3.2% of the cases the author was known because of self-citation. Milard found there were social structures at play that influence how *known* authors are cited and why: scholarly admiration or respect, notoriety, or author awareness through review processes. References are not always included or cited because they are essential to understand an argument or provide vital information to the reader; likewise, we are not always exclusively cited because of the quality of our work. Instead, citations may result from scholarly networks, and other factors, such as gender and status in the field, may guide both our citation practices and likelihood of being cited.

Gender

A gender citation bias has been documented in the fields of labor economics, mathematics, feminist economics, financial economics, and

---

[5]Fourteen focus groups were conducted in the United States and the United Kingdom (66 participants and 87 interviews), and a survey was administered to more than 3,600 respondents.
[6]The study included 32 tenured authors of chemistry publications comprising 1,410 references.

developmental psychology (Ferber, 1986, 1988). Nearly 30 years ago, Ferber (1988) found that, overall, both male and female scholars are more likely to cite the work of men. However, when comparing male- and female-authored work, women cite women (more often than men do), and men cite men (more often than women do). Women cite jointly authored articles more frequently than men—19.2% of the time—and these patterns are consistent. Mitchell, Lange, and Brus (2013)[7] found that women were more likely to cite female-authored work than works by men and mixed-gender teams (33%, 11%, and 11%, respectively). Simply put, men are cited more often than women. Why is this? One possibility is that women lose out on citations because they engage in self-citation less often. Although this pattern is true, when Mitchell et al. controlled for self-citation, the gender citation gap remained. Regardless of why these patterns emerge, what is clear is that references to women's publications (and to jointly authored publications) constitute a larger percentage of all citations among female authors than male authors, resulting in a substantial gender gap in citations. (In part, this gap materializes because men publish more than women.) Put another way, women can expect to receive approximately 80% of the citations that a similar male-authored article would (Maliniak, Powers, & Walter, 2013).[8]

Age

Do we change our citation practices as we age, or are we better able to use new knowledge given the expertise that often comes with experience and age? Milojević (2012)[9] examined the relationship between academic age (measured by span of years for a given author, between the first and most recent article) and referencing behavior in five disciplines. Senior authors were found to use the same number of references as more junior authors in mathematics and economics. In contrast, a downward trend was seen in astronomy, ecology, and robotics, and the decline was modest (a decrease of approximately 10% after 15–20 years). Senior authors were on par with more junior researchers in citing recent literature, yet senior authors were found to use more, on average, older references. The youngest references were used not by those who just entered the field but by scholars who had a decade under their belts; newcomers tended to use somewhat older references. Perhaps newcomers are still under the influence of more senior scholars who know and use historical references. A curious fact is that, within a decade, these

---

[7]The study included 57 articles published in two international studies journals in 2005 and the articles' references (n = 3,414).
[8]The sample included 3,000 peer-reviewed articles in international relations.
[9]The study sample consisted of 21,562 authors from 10 core journals in robotics, ecology, astronomy, mathematics, and economics across a 5-year period from 2006 to 2010.

newcomers lose sight of history and emphasize recent research. Without following these scholars over time it is unclear why this change occurs and what their motivations are for citing more recent work.

Milojević's (2012) findings suggest that at some point researchers display ingroup favoritism toward contemporary work. Likewise, studies spanning 50 years have documented a strong immediacy effect (Barnett et al., 1989; de Solla Price, 1965). Do scholars believe that more recent work is truly new, as opposed to projects that are merely confirming prior findings (see Good & Lavigne, 2015a)? Also, because of the knowledge explosion, might today's researchers be more likely to cite recent rather than historical research? Xhignesse and Osgood (1967) examined 21 psychology journals from 1950 to 1960 and found that 60% of all citations had publication dates within the past 10 years, and 1% had publication dates of 1900 or earlier. Citations of research published between 1901 and 1940 dropped significantly over the 10 years between 1950 and 1960, suggesting reduced attention to history. Yet, when Adair and Vohra (2003) examined older references (20–30+ years) in a subsample of articles published from 1972 to 1998 in two psychology journals, there was a noticeable, systematic increase in referencing studies that were 30 years or older. On closer examination, though, fewer than 1% of these citations were used to establish a historical understanding of the content of the research. Historical research has rarely been used to inform methodology (12.6% in the *Journal of Personality and Social Psychology* and 7.3% in the *Journal of Experimental Psychology*). When historical references have been used, it was to accompany more recent citations to illustrate patterns across time. In short, historical references may be making a comeback (at least in psychology), but in a fairly limited way. Still, it appears that attention to important work done in the past is a problem given that some editors continue to complain about authors' lack of historical knowledge (Knight et al., 2015).

Citing Self

Do we favor our own work over that of others? A study of four psychology journals revealed that a typical psychology article contains three to nine self-citations, whereas works by others received only one to three citations (Brysbaert & Smyth, 2011). In essence, authors are more likely to cite themselves rather than others when directing readers to relevant literature—a pattern otherwise known as the *self-citation bias*.

Scholars cite their own work for many reasons. First, we are more familiar with our own work than with that of others. Another reason to self-cite might be to tell readers where they can locate the material being discussed. Self-citation might help provide evidence for the researcher's claims, illustrate the researcher's scholarship and experience, or draw the reader's attention to unknown work. Similarly, the author could be building a body of work over time, and citing one's own previous work helps provide the reader with a clearer foundation for the current research being reported. Other reasons might include aligning the researcher with a particular school of thought or demonstrating the development of research (Hartley, 2012, p. 314). There are self-promotion reasons as well: inflating one's citation rates, self-enhancement, and ego fulfillment.

How common is the practice of self-citation in psychology? Nearly 40 years ago, Gottfredson (1978) found that 10% of citations in psychology journals were self-citations. More recent research suggests that 21% (Aksnes, 2003)[10] and 10% (Brysbaert & Smyth, 2011) of citations in psychology journals are self-citations. Over time, self-citation, although less common in psychology than in other fields, is maintaining or increasing in frequency.

Self-citation has the potential to inflate h-indexes (see http://research guides.uic.edu/c.php?g=252299&p=1683205), in particular for mid- and early career scholars. Likewise, the effect of self-citations typically decreases over time, as scholars gain recognition (Schreiber, 2007). But does it pay off? Medoff (2006) found, in a study of 400 economics articles, that self-cited articles are no more or less cited that articles not self-cited. However, in a study of 64,000 Norwegian publications, Fowler and Aksnes (2007) found that those who rarely cited themselves received fewer citations than authors who make self-citation a more regular practice. In essence, one self-citation yields an additional 3.6 citations across a 10-year span. Researchers who want to garner more attention to their work and themselves as a scholar should consider citing their own work when it is relevant. If you do not value your own work, you cannot expect others to either.

Not Citing

Unlike the previous topics we have addressed so far, there is not much literature to document the degree to which authors fail to cite previous research that is highly relevant to what they write about. This topic, although interesting in its own regard, takes on renewed importance in view of the recent media attention to the perceived lack of reproducibility of scientific research (Klein et al., 2014; Open Science Collaboration, 2015) and that number—as few as 0.13% of education articles in the top 100 education journals—are replication studies (Makel & Plucker, 2014). Failing to cite earlier work that is relevant to a present contribution helps create the impression that older

---

[10]The share of self-citations tends to be higher in bibliometric databases like those used by Aksnes (2003).

research is irrelevant and that the current contribution is more new than is actually the case. Failing to cite earlier work that is supportive of one's current work also contributes to the erroneous view that research does not accumulate over time.

Why Is Pertinent Research at Times Not Cited?

Perhaps the best explanation for why seemingly highly relevant research is not cited is a lack of awareness or knowledge of previous research. Although in this era of rapid online search engines it seems that, whether one's work on the topic of teacher effects on student achievement is in economics, sociology, or education, general searches would allow one to successfully remove disciplinary blinders and cross disciplinary boundaries. Yet the tons of available research studies, plus the putative ahistorical and narrow disciplinary nature of graduate programs, make this a real possibility.

Well-intentioned individuals can disagree on whether previous research is highly relevant or not. One strategy is to ask others about citation practices. The second author of this chapter contacted Richard Murnane, a noted researcher in economics education and a long-time contributor to research on effective teaching (T. Good, personal communication, April 11, 2014). In an email message, Murnane was asked why researchers with an economics background consistently moved from production function research (in which many economists have participated) to value-added research without any references to process–product research (in which economics researchers do not participate). He responded, "You ask a good question. I think at least part of the answer is that most of the value-added work is done by economists and they do not read outside of their own discipline" (R. J. Murnane, personal communication, April 12, 2014).

A more specific request was subsequently made to two other economists (T. Good, personal communication, June 28, 2015)—Rachel Garrett and Matthew Steinberg—because their careful study linking observed teaching to student achievement (Garrett & Steinberg, 2015) was very well done but included no reference to process–product research even though this topic was directly relevant to their reported research. Again, these authors were asked why they had not included earlier research that had also linked teaching to student achievement. They responded that they had limited knowledge of any work on teacher effects outside the field of economics (M. Steinberg, personal communication, June 29, 2015). After examples of this work were shared with them, both expressed appreciation for receiving useful information about previous research on the topic. Steinberg put it this way, "I think that this speaks to the need to coordinate the education research enterprise across disciplines" (personal communication, July 3, 2015). Thus, one plausible explanation as to why authors do not cite relevant work may be due to what is called the *academic silo effect* (whereby authors immerse themselves in their work and interact only minimally with colleagues) and a lack of awareness of relevant research conducted in other disciplines. However, even given the ahistorical stance of many authors it is considerably harder to understand why directly relevant research is not reported by scholars working in the same discipline.[11] Also, as we have found and have argued elsewhere, education research is often ahistorical (Good & Lavigne, 2015a, 2015b; Lavigne & Good, 2015).

WHAT HAVE WE LEARNED

So, what have we learned about citing, being cited, not citing, and not being cited? We have learned that not being cited is fairly common. Most published articles are never cited, and a rare number of those will be cited in the future. Being cited may be a function of the publication date of the work, as there appears to be a preference for more recent research. Also, one particular citation practice, self-citation, seems to yield adequate benefits for both authors and journals.

Recommendations for Scholars, Journal Editors, and Peer Reviewers

Where do we go from here? Various suggestions have been made for improving the credibility and integrity of the research process. Marcia McNutt (2014), the editor-in-chief of *Science*, proposed that authors be asked about their general considerations, such as what their thoughts were before data collection about issues like how to handle outliers, whether they conducted a power analysis to be sure their sample size was sufficient, and whether the sample was treated randomly. Similarly, we encourage authors (and editors) to become more reflective when selecting articles to cite, editors in making decisions on articles to publish, and reviewers in increasing the quality of feedback offered to authors. We also have a few recommendations of our own for improving the transparency and value of research.

Earlier in this chapter we briefly mentioned concerns about coerced citations. However, in the case of journal self-citation, Clarke (2009) argued that it is reasonably ethical for a journal to recommend that authors review prior journal issues for relevant literature and for a reviewer to ask the author to consider a specific reference in the revision process, as long as these two

---

[11]Another case can be found in *Experimental Economics*, where two authors wrote an erratum that acknowledged that they failed to note recent relevant research in their original article (Erat & Gneezy, 2015b) and included a description of the studies that they failed to cite (Erat & Gneezy, 2015a).

recommendations are within reason and are sufficiently relevant to the author's work. Likewise, we would imagine, and appropriately so, that authors intentionally seek out journal references that support a strong fit between their work and the journal (which they should), and that these references may come from the journal in which they submit.

Earlier we cautioned about the potential harm of the academic silo effect. The efforts made within the field of psychology to increase the interaction between applied behavior analysis and experimental analysis of behavior serves as an informative example. Since the 1990s, the *Journal of Applied Behavioral Analysis* (JABA) published articles on the applied significance of basic research, published the *Journal of Experimental Analysis of Behavior* (JEAB) abstracts in JABA, and appointed the editors of JEAB to the editorial board of JABA. From 1983 to 1992, the cross-citations between these two journals was fairly low: A little more than 2% (2.4%) of JABA citations were JEAB articles, and 0.6% of JEAB citations were JABA articles (Poling, Alling, & Fuqua, 1994). However, an analysis of data from 1993 to 2003 (after significant steps were made by JABA) indicated that 7.8% of JABA citations were JEAB articles, and 0.6% of JEAB citations were JABA articles (Elliott, Morgan, Fuqua, Ehrhardt, & Poling, 2005). These findings clearly are merely correlational, but they point to the possibility that journals can play an important role in broadening the knowledge and expertise of readers and, thus, respond to the challenge of narrowness.

Likewise, collaboration and cross-collaboration may help break down the borders between disciplines. Collaboration, as we discussed earlier in the chapter, seems to have significant benefits, particularly in reducing needless re-citation. We assume that coauthors gain access to new and different knowledge (of course it would be helpful to determine if this is better knowledge). Another way of broadening the scope of research is collaboration through interdisciplinary research, thereby including perspectives from various disciplines. There are some signs that interdisciplinary research is increasing. Van Noorden (2015) noted that interdisciplinary research is on the rise but that some fields are more interdisciplinary than others, as are some countries. He further noted that interdisciplinary research initially tends to pick up fewer citations than the average article but that over time it has more impact.

Editorial board members and peer reviewers are, in essence, gatekeepers who monitor and define citation practices and thus can help reduce problematic citation practices. This includes encouraging that relevant recent and historical work is cited. When asked to update their citations, authors should be asked to determine whether recent research adds more, new, or different knowledge to what is known about a given topic or area of research. Likewise, "drive-by citations" (whereby the author reports simply that there are many related articles, and provides a long list of citations but provides no explanation of any of them, even as a group) tell us little about how the author understands the cited work. These types of citations run the risk of diminishing the value of cited work. Ensuring that authors clearly illustrate how cited work informs their own research is crucial to helping ensure that citations of a work are more evident of a researcher's impact and that a researcher is basing citation decisions on scholarly motivations.

Editors, in addition to providing guidelines for reviewers, need to occasionally provide corrective feedback when warranted. If reviewers suggest that authors under review cite their own work too often, or in ways that seem unwarranted, there is nothing wrong with an editor asking an author if a particular citation is needed or requesting that the author demonstrate an illustrative connection. Good reviewers are not an unlimited resource; editors understandably need reviewers, and thus they may be unwilling to engage in such monitoring during an ongoing review; however, such feedback could also come after the review is completed. Another source of professional socialization is among reviewers themselves. In many journals, reviews are shared with everyone, and there is no reason to prevent reviewers from exchanging perspectives with one another in constructive ways. In our experience, when reviewers review a manuscript for the second time they rarely comment on remarks made by reviewers in the initial review. Most reviewers want to be fair and competent, and peer feedback about problematic or ambiguous issues might allow for conversations that improve transparency and good judgments.

Of course, the subjectivity of review work is reflected in the low to moderate correlations among reviewers in recommending manuscripts for publication. Some reviewers may see one particular review of literature as ahistorical, whereas another may describe it as excellent because it contains only the most recent references. Thus, journal editors and professional societies also have a responsibility to clarify expected professional behavior as it pertains to citing and including self-citation. Algorithms for making decisions are not possible given that the context (e.g., the purpose of the study) can vary sharply even within a discipline. Despite this complexity, editors can create guidelines for authors and reviewers.

Conscious Decisions

Although no prescription for citing is possible, because the range of reasons for choosing to cite or not cite and the purposes and context of articles vary markedly, it is possible to make decisions about citing others' work a conscious choice. Reviewers also have an obligation to examine the reasonableness of the cited literature. Editors have decisions to make about the extent to which they want to make the literature review an important part of the publication decision. Just as reviewers are encouraged to look for precise definitions of independent and dependent variables, clarity of research design, and the congruence between findings and recommended considerations, they also should examine the adequacy of the review as one determinant of a publication decision.

Although review adequacy is often on a prepublication checklist, we believe that the pertinent criteria are often passively applied. Likewise, just as prior literature should inform the rationale for and design of the study at hand, the value of the study inherently rests on the quality of review of literature. We suspect that many editorial boards are not strongly socialized (by their graduate training, the broader field, or by the journal editor) to closely attend to the literature review. Various questions could be raised to make the review of the literature section an active analysis. Questions that might help to make citations a more conscientious process include the following:

- Do the selected articles provide an overview of how theories and findings have evolved over time?
- Are the articles cited the best examples available?
- Could other articles have been cited? Why? Why not?
- Does the author provide a clear decision rule for how articles are cited?

Professional Socialization of Graduate Students

The guidelines just listed will also help support graduate students as they begin to navigate their practice as scholars. Many universities and organizations have provided handbooks or guidelines on research integrity and responsible research (see Committee on Professional Ethics, American Statistical Association, 1999, and Society for Neuroscience, 2015). Many of these are focused on responsible research and fail to tackle the complexity of scholarship that we described above. The recent edition of the *Publication Manual of the American Psychological Association* (American Psychological Association, 2010) provides some guidance as it pertains to citation practices and the literature review: "Discuss the relevant related literature, but do not feel compelled to include an exhaustive historical account . . . citation of and specific credit to the relevant earlier works are signs of scientific and scholarly responsibility" (p. 28). Here the emphasis is not on providing great detail of historical works but on establishing major historical findings or methodological issues. Scholars are encouraged to establish connections between previous and present work. Although no guidance is offered regarding the extent to which self-citation should be used, it is suggested that "a scholarly description of earlier work in the introduction provides a summary of the most recent directly related work and recognizes the priority of the work of others" (American Psychological Association, 2010, p. 28). In other words, the work of others should be given preference over an author's own work.

Graduate seminars can help with the socialization of new doctoral students and provide guidance beyond handbooks and guidelines. Such a seminar might include many of the issues presented throughout this book, help develop appropriate expectations for reviewing and preparing manuscripts, and provide normative expectations for sensible decisions with regard to citing oneself and others. Instructors might include an analysis of cited articles as part of evaluating a given article's value. Involving students in discussions about authors' decisions in choosing authors, and exploring whether other articles could have been cited, and why, would be valuable preparation for students who will be responsible for the future of the discipline. Writing and assessing a self-authored literature review would help students put these skills into practice.

CONCLUSION

We assume that the knowledge explosion will continue to contextualize the practices of today's researchers. Therefore, we believe that scholars should be cognizant of how they are reading and coping with "more." Likewise, researchers should be considerate of how they make choices about whom and what to read, and when to cite and why, because these decisions and actions help form their own intellectual footprints and that of others.

Given the knowledge explosion and the fact that many articles appear to have little to no impact, it is time to reconsider the current emphasis on the quantity of publications as the primary criterion for professional promotion and obtaining grants. Has the role of research in the academy shifted from the acquisition of important knowledge to an artificial sense of accountability? In the early stages of the information explosion, Merton (1973) wondered whether faculty motivation for publishing had moved away from intrinsic reasons to extrinsic ones. Binswanger (2015) not only reminded us of Merton's concern but also argued that the unreasonable pressure to publish has resulted in the publication of much nonsense. Is the present form of accountability in academia the best way to focus research time, money, and effort?

RECOMMENDED READING

Boote, D. N., & Beile, P. (2005). Scholars before researchers: On the centrality of the dissertation literature review in research preparation. *Educational Researcher, 34,* 3–15. http://dx.doi.org/10.3102/0013189X034006003

Brysbaert, M., & Smyth, S. (2011). Self-enhancement in scientific research: The self-citation bias. *Psychologica Belgica, 51,* 129–137. http://dx.doi.org/10.5334/pb-51-2-129

Campanario, J. M. (1998). Peer review for journals as it stands today—Part 2. *Science Communication, 19,* 277–306.

de Solla Price, D. J. (1965). Networks of scientific papers. *Science, 149,* 510–515.

de Solla Price, D. J. (1986). *Little science, big science.* New York, NY: Columbia University Press.

Ioannidis, J. P. A. (2015). A generalized view of self-citation: Direct, co-author, collaborative, and coercive induced self-citation. *Journal of Psychosomatic Research, 78,* 7–11. http://dx.doi.org/10.1016/j.jpsychores.2014.11.008

Knight, S. (2009). Journal self-citation XVI: Academic citations—A question of ethics? *Communications of the Association for Information Systems, 25,* 130–139.

Xhignesse, L. V., & Osgood, C. E. (1967). Bibliographical citation characteristics of the psychological journal network in 1950 and 1960. *American Psychologist, 22,* 778–791. http://dx.doi.org/10.1037/h0024961

REFERENCES

Adair, J. G., & Vohra, N. (2003). The explosion of knowledge, references, and citations: Psychology's unique response to a crisis. *American Psychologist, 58,* 15–23. http://dx.doi.org/10.1037/0003-066X.58.1.15

Aksnes, D. W. (2003). A macro study of self-citation. *Scientometrics, 56,* 235–246. http://dx.doi.org/10.1023/A:1021919228368

Aksnes, D. W., & Sivertsen, G. (2004). The effect of highly cited papers on national citation indicators. *Scientometrics, 59,* 213–224. http://dx.doi.org/10.1023/B:SCIE.0000018529.58334.eb

American Psychological Association. (2010). *Publication manual of the American Psychological Association* (6th ed.). Washington, DC: Author.

Babor, T. F., & McGovern, T. (2008). Dante's inferno: Seven deadly sins in scientific publishing and how to avoid them. In T. F. Babor, K. Stenius, S. Savva, & J. O'Reilly (Eds.), *Publishing addiction science: a guide for the perplexed* (2nd ed., pp. 153–171). Essex, England: Multi-Science.

Barnett, G. A., Fink, E. L., & Debus, M. (1989). A mathematical model of academic citation age. *Communication Research, 16,* 510–531. http://dx.doi.org/10.1177/009365089016004003

Barrett, L. F. (2015, September 1). Psychology is not in crisis. *The New York Times.* Retrieved from http://nyti.ms/1htGBo2

Bartlett, T. (2015, August 28). The results of the Reproducibility Project are in. They're not good. *The Chronicle of Higher Education.* Retrieved from http://chronicle.com/article/The-Results-of-the/232695/

Binswanger, M. (2015). How nonsense became excellence: Forcing professors to publish. In I. M. Welpe, J. Wollersheim, S. Ringelhan, & M. Osterloh (Eds.),

Incentives and performance: Governance of research organizations (pp. 19–32). New York, NY: Springer. http://dx.doi.org/10.1007/978-3-319-09785-5_2

Braun, T., Glänzel, W., & Schubert, A. (2010). On Sleeping Beauties, princes and other tales of citation distributions . . . *Research Evaluation, 19*, 195–202. http://dx.doi.org/10.3152/095820210X514210

Brysbaert, M., & Smyth, S. (2011). Self-enhancement in scientific research: The self-citation bias. *Psychologica Belgica, 51*, 129–137. http://dx.doi.org/10.5334/pb-51-2-129

Clarke, R. (2009). Self-plagiarism and self-citations—A practical guide based on underlying principles. *Communications of the Association for Information Sciences, 25*, 155–164.

Cole, J. R. (2000). A short history of the use of citations as a measure of impact of scientific and scholarly work. In B. Cronin & H. B. Atkins (Eds.), *The web of knowledge: A festschrift in honor of Eugene Garfield* (pp. 281–300). Medford, NJ: Information Today.

Committee on Professional Ethics, American Statistical Association. (1999). *Ethical guidelines for statistical practice.* Retrieved from http://www.amstat.org/about/ethicalguidelines.cfm

de Solla Price, D. J. (1965). Networks of scientific papers. *Science, 149*, 510–515.

de Solla Price, D. J. (1986). *Little science, big science.* New York, NY: Columbia University Press.

Elliott, A. J., Morgan, K., Fuqua, R. W., Ehrhardt, K., & Poling, A. (2005). Self- and cross-citations in the *Journal of Applied Behavior Analysis* and the *Journal of the Experimental Analysis of Behavior*: 1993–2003. *Journal of Applied Behavior Analysis, 38*, 559–563. http://dx.doi.org/10.1901/jaba.2005.133-04

Endler, N. S., Rushton, J. P., & Roediger, H. L., III. (1978). Productivity and scholarly impact (citations) of British, Canadian, and U.S. departments of psychology (1975). *American Psychologist, 33*, 1064–1082. http://dx.doi.org/10.1037/0003-066X.33.12.1064

Erat, S., & Gneezy, U. (2015a). Erratum to: Incentives for creativity. *Experimental Economics, 18*, 760. http://dx.doi.org/10.1007/s10683-015-9446-z

Erat, S., & Gneezy, U. (2015b). Incentives for creativity. *Experimental Economics, 19*, 269. http://dx.doi.org/10.1007/s10683-015-9440-5

Ferber, M. A. (1986). Citations: Are they an objective measure of scholarly merit? *Signs, 11*, 381–389. http://dx.doi.org/10.1086/494230

Ferber, M. A. (1988). Citations and networking. *Gender & Society, 2*, 82–89. http://dx.doi.org/10.1177/089124388002001006

Ferguson, C. J. (2015). Do Angry Birds make for angry children? A meta-analysis of video game influences on children's and adolescents' aggression, mental health, prosocial behavior, and academic performance. *Perspectives on Psychological Science, 10*, 646–666. http://dx.doi.org/10.1177/1745691615592234

Fowler, J. H., & Aksnes, D. W. (2007). Does self-citation pay? *Scientometrics, 72*, 427–437. http://dx.doi.org/10.1007/s11192-007-1777-2

Garrett, R., & Steinberg, M. P. (2015). Examining teacher effectiveness using classroom observation scores: Evidence form the randomization of teachers to students. *Educational Evaluation and Policy Analysis, 37*, 224–242. http://dx.doi.org/10.3102/0162373714537551

Glänzel, W., & Garfield, E. (2004). The myth of delayed recognition. *Scientist, 18*(11), 8–9.

Glänzel, W., & Schoepflin, U. (1995). A bibliometric study on ageing and reception processes of scientific literature. *Journal of Information Science, 21*, 37–53. http://dx.doi.org/10.1177/016555159502100104

Good, T. L., & Lavigne, A. L. (2015a). Issues of teacher performance stability are not new: Limitations and possibilities [Peer commentary on the paper "The Stability of Teacher Performance and Effectiveness: Implications of Policies Concerning Teacher Evaluation" by G. B. Morgan, K. J. Hodge, T. M. Trepinksi, & L. W. Anderson]. *Education Policy Analysis Archives, 23*(2). http://dx.doi.org/10.14507/epaa.v23.1916

Good, T. L., & Lavigne, A. L. (2015b). Rating teachers cheaper, faster, and better: No so fast [Peer commentary on the paper "Can We Identify a Successful Teacher Better, Faster, and Cheaper? Evidence of Innovating Teacher Observation Systems" by J. Gargani & M. Strong]. *Journal of Teacher Education, 66*, 288–293. http://dx.doi.org/10.1177/0022487115574292

Gottfredson, S. D. (1978). Evaluating psychological research reports: Dimensions, reliability, and correlates of quality judgments. *American Psychologist, 33*, 920–934. http://dx.doi.org/10.1037/0003-066X.33.10.920

Hartley, J. (2012). To cite or note to cite: Author self-citations and the impact factor. *Scientometrics, 92*, 313–317. http://dx.doi.org/10.1007/s11192-011-0568-6

King, D., Tenopir, C., & Clarke, M. (2006, October 12). Measuring total reading of journal articles. *D-Lib Magazine, 12*(10), 1–9.

Klein, R. A., Ratliff, K. A., Vianello, M., Adams, R. B., Bahník, S., Berstein, M. J., . . . Nosek, B. A. (2014). Investigating variability in replicability. A "many labs" replication project. *Social Psychology, 45*, 142–152. http://dx.doi.org/10.1027/1864-9335/a000178

Knight, S. L., Lloyd, G. M., Arbaugh, F., Gamson, D. A., McDonald, S. P., Nolan, J., Jr., & Whitney, A. E. (2015). Five-year retrospective. *Journal of Teacher Education, 66*, 410–414. http://dx.doi.org/10.1177/0022487115604839

Lange, L. L. (2005). Sleeping Beauties in psychology: Comparisons of "hits" and "missed signals" in psychological journals. *History of Psychology, 8*, 194–217. http://dx.doi.org/10.1037/1093-4510.8.2.194

Lavigne, A. L., & Good, T. L. (2015). *Improving teaching through observation and feedback: Going beyond state and federal mandates.* New York, NY: Routledge.

Lievrouw, L. A. (1990). Reconciling structure and process in the study of scholarly communication. In C. L. Borgman (Ed.), *Scholarly communication and bibliometrics* (pp. 59–69). Newbury Park, CA: Sage.

MacRoberts, M. H., & MacRoberts, B. R. (1989). Problems of citation analyses: A critical review. *Journal of the American Society for Information Science, 40*, 342–349. http://dx.doi.org/10.1002/(SICI)1097-4571(198909)40:5<342::AID-ASI7>3.0.CO;2-U

Makel, M. C., & Plucker, J. A. (2014). Facts are more important than novelty replication in the education sciences. *Educational Researcher, 43*, 304–316. http://dx.doi.org/10.3102/0013189X14545513

Maliniak, D., Powers, R., & Walter, B. F. (2013). The gender citation gap in international relations. *International Organization, 67*, 889–922.

Martin, B. R. (2013). Whither research integrity? Plagiarism, self-plagiarism and coercive citation in an age of research assessment. *Research Policy, 42*, 1005–1014. http://dx.doi.org/10.1016/j.respol.2013.03.011

McNutt, M. (2014). Reproducibility. *Science, 343*, 229. http://dx.doi.org/10.1126/science.1250475

Medoff, M. H. (2006). The efficiency of self-citations in economics. *Scientometrics, 69*, 69–84. http://dx.doi.org/10.1007/s11192-006-0139-4

Merton, R. K. (1973). The normative structure of science. In R. K. Merton (Ed.), *The sociology of science: theoretical and empirical investigations* (pp. 267–280). Chicago, IL: University of Chicago Press.

Meyer, M. N., & Chabris, C. (2014). Why psychologists' food fight matters [Blog post]. Retrieved from http://www.slate.com/articles/health_and_science/science/2014/07/replication_controversy_in_psychology_bullying_file_drawer_effect_blog_posts.html

Milard, B. (2014). The social circles behind scientific references: Relationships between citing and cited authors in chemistry publications. *Journal of the Association for Information Science and Technology, 65*, 2459–2468. http://dx.doi.org/10.1002/asi.23149

Milojević, S. (2012). How are academic age, productivity and collaboration related to citing behavior of researchers? *PLOS ONE, 7*(11), e49176. http://dx.doi.org/10.1371/journal.pone.0049176

Mitchell, S. M., Lange, S., & Brus, H. (2013). Gendered citation patterns in international relations journals. *International Studies Perspectives, 14*, 485–492. http://dx.doi.org/10.1111/insp.12026

Open Science Collaboration. (2015, August 28). Estimating the reproducibility of psychological science. *Science, 349*, aac4716. http://dx.doi.org/10.1126/science.aac4716

Poling, A., Alling, K., & Fuqua, R. W. (1994). Self- and cross-citations in the *Journal of Applied Behavior Analysis* and the *Journal of the Experimental Analysis of Behavior*:

1983–1992. *Journal of Applied Behavior Analysis, 27*, 729–731. http://dx.doi.org/10.1901/jaba.1994.27-729

Reis, H. T., & Stiller, J. (1992). Publication trends in *JPSP*: A three-decade review. *Personality and Social Psychology Bulletin, 18*, 465–472. http://dx.doi.org/10.1177/0146167292184011

Renear, A. H., & Palmer, C. L. (2009, August 14). Strategic reading, ontologies, and the future of scientific publishing. *Science, 325*, 828–832. http://dx.doi.org/10.1126/science.1157784

Romano, N. C. (2009). Journal Self-Citation V: Coercive journal self-citation—Manipulations to increase impact factors may do more harm than good in the long run. *Communications of the Association for Information Systems, 25*, 41–56.

Schreiber, M. (2007). Self-citation corrections for the Hirsch Index. *Europhysics Letters, 78*, 2007, 30002. http://dx.doi.org/10.1209/0295-5075/78/30002

Seglen, P. O. (1989). Evaluering av forskningskvalitet ved hjelp av siteringsanalyse og andre bibliometriske metoder [Evaluation of scientific quality using citation analysis and other bibliometric methods]. *Nordisk Medicin, 104*, 331–335, 341.

Seglen, P. O. (1992). The skewness of science. *Journal of the American Society for Information Science, 43*, 628–638. http://dx.doi.org/10.1002/(SICI)1097-4571(199210)43:9<628::AID-ASI5>3.0.CO;2-0

Society for Neuroscience. (2015). *Guidelines for responsible conduct regarding scientific communication.* Retrieved from http://www.sfn.org/member-center/professional-conduct/guidelines-for-responsible-conduct-regarding-scientific-communication

Straub, D. W., & Anderson, C. (2009). Journal Self-Citation VI: Forced journal self-citation—Common, appropriate, ethical? *Communications of the Association for Information Systems, 25*, 57–66.

Tenopir, C. (2014). Trust in reading, citing and publishing. *Information Services & Use, 34*, 39–48.

Van Noorden, R. (2015, September 17). Interdisciplinary research by the numbers. *Nature, 525*, 306–307. http://dx.doi.org/10.1038/525306a

Van Raan, A. F. J. (2005). Sleeping beauties in science. *Scientometrics, 59*, 467–472. http://dx.doi.org/10.1023/B:SCIE.0000018543.82441.f1

Voosen, P. (2015). Universities are falling behind on reproducibility reform, scientists say. *The Chronicle of Higher Education.* Retrieved from http://chronicle.com/blogs/ticker/universities-are-falling-behind-on-reproducibility-reform-scientists-say/104031

Wilhite, A. W., & Fong, E. A. (2012). Coercive citation in academic publishing. *Science, 335*, 542–543. http://dx.doi.org/10.1126/science.1212540

Xhignesse, L. V., & Osgood, C. E. (1967). Bibliographical citation characteristics of the psychological journal network in 1950 and 1960. *American Psychologist, 22*, 778–791.

II

PERSPECTIVES

6

THE PEER REVIEW PROCESS: USING THE TRADITIONAL SYSTEM TO ITS FULL POTENTIAL

JENNIFER J. RICHLER AND ISABEL GAUTHIER

KEY POINTS

- Authors and the field as a whole benefit from strong editorial oversight in peer review.
- Changes should be made with an eye toward improving the peer review process rather than overthrowing it altogether.
- The value of the traditional peer review system is realized only if it is used to its full potential.
- Flexible interactions among authors, reviewers, and editors lead to the best outcomes for authors and the strongest papers for the field.

Academic publishing has changed. The web makes the entire process, from submission to publication, faster, and it allows greater accessibility and dissemination of published work. This has inspired interesting new models of

http://dx.doi.org/10.1037/0000033-007
Toward a More Perfect Psychology: Improving Trust, Accuracy, and Transparency in Research, M. C. Makel and J. A. Plucker (Editors)

peer review that capitalize on what the web has to offer. For instance, *Frontiers* (http://home.frontiersin.org) and *PLOS ONE* (http://journals.plos.org/plosone/) have introduced publication models based on fast publication and public evaluation. At these journal sites, the purpose of peer review is to evaluate the technical soundness of methods and analyses, and a work's significance and impact are determined by crowd-sourced postpublication peer review based on comments posted to the article and impact metrics such as article views, downloads, social media buzz, posted comments, and citation counts. *Frontiers* also includes an interactive review phase in which authors and reviewers communicate in an online forum and all reviewers are identified on the final published paper. However, although these new models embrace the changes to academic publishing afforded by the rise of the Internet, some positive elements of the traditional peer review process are lost. What is critical, however, is that the value of what is lost depends on editors, reviewers, and authors using the more traditional system to its full potential.

It is certainly important for journals to make changes that reflect the current state of technology—it would, for instance, be ludicrous if authors were still required to submit a hard copy of their manuscript. Journals should adapt to the state of the field as well. For instance, the current wave of concerns about replicability and the open science movement has led top journals to add replication sections (e.g., *Journal of Experimental Psychology: General*) or create policies that aim to incentivize engagement in open science practices (e.g., *Psychological Science*). Changes should be made with an eye toward improving the process rather than overthrowing it altogether. For instance, following The Peer Reviewers' Openness Initiative proposal to provide open access to all data, materials, and programs (Morey et al., 2015) or adopting preregistration (Wagenmakers, Wetzels, Borsboom, van der Maas, & Kievit, 2012) would alleviate concerns about what Kerr (1998) called *HARKing* (hypothesizing after the results are found), and fraud, and allow reviewers to focus instead on substantive issues. Rapid communication by email allows editors to ask authors for minor revisions before a manuscript is sent out for review or to ask reviewers to clarify a comment before sending it to authors, which can improve the quality of the exchange on which a decision is ultimately made without significantly delaying the review process. Indeed, as we suggest in this chapter, making the most of the interactions among all the players (authors, reviewers, and editors) and appreciating the flexibility of these interactions can lead to the best outcomes for authors and, ultimately, the best papers for the field.

Evaluations and critiques of peer review are not new (e.g., Fletcher & Fletcher, 1997; Giner-Sorolla, 2012; Peters & Ceci, 1982), and many recent papers have outlined proposals for new journal policies (e.g., Koole & Lakens, 2012; Nosek, Spies, & Motyl, 2012; Wagenmakers et al., 2012). Instead of reviewing these arguments and suggestions, we aim to provide some balance by presenting a message we feel is lacking in this discussion, what we view to be the value of a traditional peer review process with strong editorial oversight. However, because this value is realized only if the process is used well, we then outline recommendations for authors, editors, and reviewers regarding how best to take advantage of what this system offers.

VALUE OF THE TRADITIONAL PEER REVIEW SYSTEM

The peer review system, although not perfect, does have specific advantages, both to authors and the field as a whole. Such a system also influences decisions related to hiring and promotions. In the following sections we elaborate on these in more detail.

Value to Authors

One value of the traditional peer review process is for a manuscript to receive attention from an experienced editor and reviewers before it is published. When a journal aims to publish work that is of broad appeal, this may be the only chance the paper has to be edited by people outside its immediate field of research, who are in a position to encourage the author to explore bridges to other literatures or clarify its message to make it more accessible. By taking risks on innovative work and publishing it in a top-tier journal, editors can exert an influence on the field that cannot be replaced by an open vote from those stakeholders who generally come to an article because it is relevant to their own work. Such a vote will tend by nature to support existing trends and theories. Indeed, one criticism of peer review is that reviewers are biased to favor work that is consistent with their own views (e.g., Mahoney, 1977). This criticism equally applies to forms of postpublication peer review. In fact, such biases may be even more likely in postpublication commentary because the people most likely to comment on a paper are those with a clear stake in the game.

Peer review also helps authors overcome their own biases. We all have pet theories or assumptions that we bring to an experiment or data set. Being forced to confront reviewers who disagree with us, though unpleasant, is an opportunity to refine and clarify arguments so that the strongest case is made in the final paper. This opportunity is completely lost in a model where reviewers comment only on technical aspects of the work, or provide ratings after the paper is published. Responding to criticisms in blog posts, online comments, or other forms of postpublication peer review may never be as effective as addressing those criticisms in the original paper, leaving a complicated trail that may confuse readers. In addition, we all know of heated exchanges on social media platforms that resulted in personal attacks that are difficult to forget. Although strong feelings can arise during the review process, an editor can take potential biases into account when evaluating and weighing reviews and ultimately help reviewers turn harsh criticism into constructive feedback and authors make the most of this feedback. In the end, consumers of the work may be better served by waiting for the outcome of this guided exchange.

Another component of the traditional peer review model is that, in particular at top journals, many papers are triaged, that is, rejected without being sent out for external review. At first blush this does not sound like a mechanism that provides value to authors, and many authors likely associate triage with some of the more discouraging action letters they have received. However, the value in triage for authors can be realized only in a model where editors are actively engaged. The motivation for triage should be to save authors precious time if there is a good reason that the paper is unlikely to ultimately be accepted and, because in a strong oversight editorial model the editor is responsible for the ultimate decision, she or he is often well positioned to make this decision with confidence. For instance, a paper may be triaged because of critical methodological flaws that would have come up during peer review. Triage on this basis provides authors with more rapid feedback on an issue that needs to be addressed: In the 2 to 3 months it would have taken to get reviews, authors can conduct a new experiment. In other cases, papers are triaged on the basis of fit with the journal. A triage decision can be frustrating, but not as frustrating as waiting several months for reviews only to hear back that the work is strong but not suited to that particular outlet. In that case, an author may receive little useful feedback from the reviewers and simply have to start from scratch at another journal. When triage rates are high, authors spend more time receiving constructive feedback, and reviewers and editors can devote more time and resources to promising papers that are in a position to benefit from a critical eye.

However, what is the risk that a high triage rate leads to the rejection of papers that could have survived the review process? This is a difficult question to answer because of course we do not send triaged papers out for review to compare with those we never considered triaging. However, we conducted an experiment to test how easy triage decisions are to make. The second author is the manuscript coordinator and an associate editor at the *Journal of Experimental Psychology: General*, which, as stated on the journal website, publishes "empirical work that bridges the traditional interests of two or more communities of Psychology." As she logged new submissions, she made final decision predictions (triage, reject after review, or accept) for 190 manuscripts on the basis of the title and abstract only. She correctly predicted triage for

71% of the articles that were ultimately triaged by action editors ($d' = 0.72$). These predictions were almost exclusively based on the sense that the article was not going to meet the criteria of relevance to multiple areas of psychology, which is the major reason for triage decisions at the journal (approximately 50% of all submissions are triaged).

To be clear, the actual triage decisions at the journal are based on a long reading of the paper, and we are certainly not advocating triaging on the basis of abstracts because authors benefit from triage only when they also receive feedback. Indeed, unless the reasons for triage are thoughtful and clearly articulated, authors may not understand the decision and may be unable to appeal it. In our view, the possibility of appeals by authors to learn editors' reasons for a decision is an integral part of a quality editorial process. Authors should not be made to feel like they are a nuisance when appealing a decision and, in our experience, when the decision is clear, appeals are rare and often well founded.

The fact that we are making a case for the value of peer review to authors does not mean that we are immune to some of the negative feelings that can arise as one takes part in the peer review process, especially as authors. We have certainly vented (sometimes using very colorful language) about reviews we found annoying or action letters we thought unfair. However, if we believe the editor or reviewers missed something critical, we are grateful for the opportunity to craft arguments to defend our work or question a decision. Regardless of whether this ultimately gets a paper published, provided the editor is engaged, this approach leads to better clarity on how we can improve the work, forces us to think about how we could sharpen our arguments in the paper, and generally hones our thinking. Because in our role as authors we see the value of such exchanges, it is important that we honor this option in our role as editors.

Finally, it is important to keep in mind that authors are also reviewers, and they benefit from this role as well. The current focus in the field on statistical issues, replication, and data transparency ignores the fact that results also have to be interpreted and situated within a literature. Disagreements between authors and reviewers on these latter aspects of a paper may seem to constitute the kind of bias that new models seek to remove as criteria for publication. However, this assumes that authors are infallible in these areas, or that there cannot be objective errors in a literature review, particularly when it comes to describing another author's work. As anyone who has been cited incorrectly knows, this is not the case. Peer review is one opportunity for authors, in their role as reviewer, to protect how their work is portrayed. Given how easy it is for published mischaracterizations to be repeated, it is more effective to point out these errors during peer review so that they are not published as opposed to trying to correct them in a postpublication outlet.

Value to the Field as a Whole

Whereas a journal's editorial decisions first affect authors, action editors can have an influential effect on the field as they work with authors during this crucial bottleneck of science dissemination. Authors are never as attentive to suggestions as when an editor has the fate of their paper in her or his hands. This vulnerability certainly should not be abused, and editors should be mindful of making suggestions and recommendations that are in the best interest of the field rather than imposing their own preferences. Our working principle at the *Journal of Experimental Psychology: General* has been to try to ensure that each published paper can be a clear example of best practices and what we would want to see in the future in the journal. For instance, sending a paper back to authors before review and asking them to clarify their sample size ensures that this information is added to the paper, regardless of whether it is ultimately published at our journal or elsewhere. If nothing else, it makes it clear to our reviewers that this information is expected. This small editorial exchange can help make reporting such information commonplace.

Value for Decisions Such as Hiring or Promotion

One of the values of the current system is that the journal in which a paper is published provides markers of its quality and impact to individuals who may not be specialists in the field or who may not have time to read all the relevant work, but participate in making important decisions, for instance, for hiring or promotion. One could argue that other markers of quality could replace this information. However, consider the fact that many important decisions affecting a young scientist's career are made before many of her or his papers have had time to gather significant post-external reviews or citations.

RECOMMENDATIONS FOR AUTHORS: BEFORE REVIEW

In this section we provide some recommendations regarding where and how to submit their work. Deciding where to submit a paper requires thoughtful consideration of several factors, and the cover letter provides an opportunity to exert some control over the peer review process.

Deciding Where to Submit

Where an article is published is a simple marker of its quality, and this naturally leads to a desire to aim for top journals. However, this should not be the only factor motivating journal choice. For example, it is also important that the manuscript meet other specific journal criteria. These are often clearly stated in the instructions for authors, but as any editor knows, authors often do not read these instructions very carefully. In fact, as editors lengthen their instructions, trying to ensure authors are better prepared to send papers that are a good fit, they might be discouraging more authors from reading them.

Judging the fit of an article with a journal's mission can be difficult if one does not have extensive experience with a particular journal in an editorial capacity. For example, another postdoctoral student with comparable research experience but without editorial experience at the *Journal of Experimental Psychology: General* was less accurate at predicting triage decisions based on title and abstract (a subset of 107 papers, triage accuracy = 57%, $d' = 0.56$; the second author's triage accuracy for that subset = 75%, $d' = 0.75$), suggesting less of a feel for journal fit. One tactic authors can use is to see which journals have published articles that are similar to theirs in terms of general approach, breadth, or impact.

Cover Letter

The cover letter is an author's first opportunity to exert control over the review process, and authors should not forgo this opportunity. Junior scientists often do not receive sufficient mentoring in the ways to get the most out of the review process and may suffer a disadvantage as a result.

The cover letter should be short and not redundant with the abstract. This is an opportunity for authors to explain why they are submitting to this journal and do so in a manner that is less formal than in the article: an elevator pitch for the paper, so to speak. The letter should address journal fit, the article's novelty, and its impact. To be effective, this should not be a reiteration of the journal description but instead should be specific. For example, do not say *that* your paper does X; explain *how* it does X. Indeed, formulating the arguments for a good cover letter is a good way to ensure a paper really should be submitted to that journal.

Even if there is no standard option to do so in a journal submission page, we recommend that authors suggest reviewers or, even better, kinds of reviewers, with examples. For instance, if the work bridges between work in memory and social psychology, suggesting appropriate reviewers in both of those fields helps make this case. Some scholars have suggested that requiring a list of potential reviewers reflects laziness on the part of the editor, but this is an argument we have trouble understanding, in particular when many editors act on papers outside of their immediate area of expertise. We believe seeking this information is part of recognizing that authors know their work best, especially at the outset of submission. Of course, editors are not obligated to take these suggestions. It is important not to suggest reviewers who may have a conflict of interest (e.g., individuals with whom you have published, former graduate students, postdoctoral students, or mentors), and avoid only listing very busy senior scientists, who are likely to decline. It should be acceptable to list nonpreferred reviewers, as this can avoid repeating the same disputes with each new submission. Authors should be aware that sometimes editors will nonetheless want to seek feedback from nonpreferred reviewers, but it is useful to prepare editors for possible bias or to ensure that they have the necessary information to gather opinions from a diverse set of experts.

RECOMMENDATIONS FOR EDITORS

In the traditional model we are supporting here, editors have the ultimate responsibility for the review process and the final decision. A good attitude to engage in this role is to consider oneself an advocate for the work and its potential readers. Editors do not need to find themselves needing to pick a side in debates between theoretical factions, or having to favor an author or a reviewer's point of view; instead, the editor needs to assess the potential value of the work to the readership and work with authors and reviewers to ensure this potential is delivered.

Editors should strive for clarity in their editorial policies (see Thompson, 2001) and action letters. Most action letters include a list of the reviewers' concerns, but because those are readily available, this list need not be exhaustive. In fact, the primary goal of the action letter is for authors to understand what aspect(s) of the reviews drove the editorial decision. Only then can they assess whether a revision (or even an appeal) could be successful. A secondary goal is for editors to highlight concerns of their own and to clarify any point on which they may disagree with reviewers. It is not uncommon for different reviewers to provide authors with feedback that may appear conflicting (e.g., add new experiments/make the paper shorter; cut this analysis/extend the results section), and editors need to integrate and settle any inconsistencies.

RECOMMENDATIONS FOR REVIEWERS

In the traditional peer review model reviewers play a critical role, without which an editor may not be able to make an informed decision. Although many reviewers like to address authors directly in their review, it may help for reviewers to address the editor instead, as a reminder to themselves that their comments are but one of several pieces of information that the editor will use to render a decision and provide guidance on a revision if it applies. Others have written good pieces of advice for reviewers; one of our favorites is Roediger's (2007) "Twelve Tips for Reviewers." Junior scientists will find in these simple tips a good basis to develop a fair and effective reviewing style, learning to become the reviewers they wish for their own work.

Even senior scientists who know a great deal about the research they are reviewing can sometimes produce surprisingly unhelpful reviews from an editorial point of view. To avoid getting lost in the details, it is very important to the effectiveness of the review process that reviewers separate major comments—those that are strongly linked to your recommendation—from minor comments that are really needed only if you encourage a revision.

Reviewers who are lucky to review for a journal in whose articles the power and strength of the methods are more important than p values should try to keep in mind the value of emphasizing transparency over perfect results. First, reviewers may want to encourage authors to explain their methodological choices (e.g., why was this measure used; why was this sample sized used; if the sample size varied between experiments, what rule was applied to stop data collection?). Second, if the methodological choices and power seem adequate, reviewers should avoid blaming researchers for less-than-perfect results. If results are inconsistent across studies, it surely may be appropriate to encourage a replication, but it is equally important to recognize that the same effect that is significant in one experiment and not in the next may in fact represent highly similar effect sizes that just happen to fall on either side of an arbitrary threshold.

Finally, reviewers may want to prepare for the not-so-uncommon situation in which they are asked to review a paper that they have already reviewed for another outlet. This situation should not surprise anyone and likely reflects a reviewer's clear relevant expertise. Although some people may feel that authors are entitled to fresh reviewers when they go to a new journal, we prefer not to think of the review process as a lottery in which authors get to draw a new number each time they submit; instead, we see the process as continuous across all journals that are part of the same field, with editors, reviewers, and authors working together with the ultimate goal of facilitating the publication of valuable scientific contributions. When a reviewer receives a repeat paper, it is a good idea to let the editor know. It may be sufficient to provide the original comments with a few notes on whether those comments were addressed and to keep in mind that other reviewers will be able to provide a complementary evaluation as they look at the paper for the first time.

HARSH REVIEWS

Just as we all have strong feelings about our own work, we often have strong feelings about papers we dislike. However, harshly written reviews come across as emotional rather than convincing, regardless of the solidity of the underlying arguments. Writing harsh reviews damages credibility and reduces the odds that the opinion will sway a decision. Consider that if a paper makes you mad, providing constructive advice is the best way to make sure it is not published elsewhere as is.

RECOMMENDATION FOR AUTHORS: AFTER REVIEW

Receiving an action letter is an emotional moment in the research process, and reviews often are difficult to read. However, it is important for authors to understand why the editor came to a particular decision; for example, what are the major comments driving the decision versus the minor ones? Authors should not hesitate to contact the editor if clarification is needed or if some of the major concerns are misguided or easily fixed. Such appeals need not be defensive: Like authors, editors are not infallible, and misunderstanding a critical aspect of a paper should not be interpreted as a malicious attack on the work. Appeals should also be brief but specific enough to demonstrate that a seemingly major concern does indeed have a straightforward solution.

Of course, appeals are not always appropriate, or successful, and in most cases manuscripts are submitted to another journal following a rejection. However, not having the opportunity to revise for one journal should not necessarily mean starting from scratch and therefore ignoring the current set of reviews. For instance, it may be useful to try to keep the same reviewers if their comments are constructive and can be addressed. Some publishers have a system in place to transfer reviews and reviewer identities between journals (this is something we would like to see more of). Even if there is no formal system, authors can ask the new editor if she or he would consider using the current reviewers and the previous editor if they would send the new editor the reviewers' identities. Previous reviews can also be sent in a new cover letter regardless, keeping in mind that it is entirely up to the editor what to do with them. Valid concerns should not be ignored. Failing to revise a manuscript after reviews just because the paper is being resubmitted elsewhere is a missed opportunity to submit a stronger manuscript, and it is a poor use of everyone's time to receive multiple sets of reviews that raise the same issues.

CONCLUSION

The appeal of new publication systems may be mainly due to a poor use of the current system instead of the constraints of the system per se. In this chapter we have provided some guidelines for making the most out of a traditional peer review system that cannot function without strong editorial oversight. The system works better when all stakeholders realize they play (even if only potentially) the role of author, editor, and reviewer at different times and apply the proverbial golden rule.

RECOMMENDED READING

Halsey, L. G., Curran-Everett, D., Vowler, S. L., & Drummond, G. B. (2015). The fickle *P* value generates irreproducible results. *Nature Methods, 12,* 179–185. http://dx.doi.org/10.1038/nmeth.3288

Roediger, H. L. (2007, April). Twelve tips for reviewers. *APS Observer, 20.* Retrieved from http://www.psychologicalscience.org/index.php/publications/observer/2007/april-07/twelve-tips-for-reviewers.html

Rotten reviews. (2015, October). *APS Observer.* Retrieved from http://www.psychologicalscience.org/index.php/publications/observer/2015/october-15/rotten-reviews.html

Stanley, D. J., & Spence, J. R. (2014). Expectations for replications: Are yours realistic? *Perspectives on Psychological Science, 9,* 305–318. http://dx.doi.org/10.1177/1745691614528518

REFERENCES

Fletcher, R. H., & Fletcher, S. W. (1997). Evidence for the effectiveness of peer review. *Science and Engineering Ethics, 3,* 35–50. http://dx.doi.org/10.1007/s11948-997-0015-5

Giner-Sorolla, R. (2012). Science or art? How aesthetic standards grease the way through the publication bottleneck but undermine science. *Perspectives on Psychological Science, 7,* 562–571. http://dx.doi.org/10.1177/1745691612457576

Kerr, N. L. (1998). HARKing: Hypothesizing after the results are known. *Personality and Social Psychology Review, 2,* 196–217. http://dx.doi.org/10.1207/s15327957pspr0203_4

Koole, S. L., & Lakens, D. (2012). Rewarding replications: A sure and simple way to improve psychological science. *Perspectives on Psychological Science, 7,* 608–614. http://dx.doi.org/10.1177/1745691612462586

Mahoney, M. J. (1977). Publication prejudices: An experimental study of confirmatory bias in the peer review system. *Cognitive Therapy and Research, 1,* 161–175. http://dx.doi.org/10.1007/BF01173636

Morey, R. D., Chambers, C. D., Etchells, P. J., Harris, C. R., Hoekstra, R., Lakens, D., . . . Zwaan, R. A. (2015). The Peer Reviewers' Openness Initiative: Incentivising open research practices through peer review. *Royal Society Open Science, 3,* 150547. http://dx.doi.org/10.1098/rsos.150547

Nosek, B. A., Spies, J. R., & Motyl, M. (2012). Scientific utopia: II. Restructuring incentives and practices to promote truth over publishability. *Perspectives on Psychological Science, 7*, 615–631. http://dx.doi.org/10.1177/1745691612459058

Peters, D. P., & Ceci, S. J. (1982). Peer-review practices of psychological journals: The fate of published articles, submitted again. *Behavioral and Brain Sciences, 5*, 187–195. http://dx.doi.org/10.1017/S0140525X00011183

Roediger, H. L. (2007, April). Twelve tips for reviewers. *APS Observer, 20*. Retrieved from http://www.psychologicalscience.org/index.php/publications/observer/2007/april-07/twelve-tips-for-reviewers.html

Thompson, B. (2001). Significance, effect sizes, stepwise methods, and other issues: Strong arguments move the field. *Journal of Experimental Education, 70*, 80–93. http://dx.doi.org/10.1080/00220970109599499

Wagenmakers, E.-J., Wetzels, R., Borsboom, D., van der Maas, H. L. J., & Kievit, R. A. (2012). An agenda for purely confirmatory research. *Perspectives on Psychological Science, 7*, 632–638. http://dx.doi.org/10.1177/1745691612463078

7

COMMUNICATING TO THE PUBLIC

HOWARD GARDNER

KEY POINTS

If you are considering writing regularly for a nonprofessional audience, ask yourself the following questions:

- Do you want to be known by individuals other than your friends and professional colleagues? Even recognized at parties or at the airport?
- Do you like to write?
- Can you write quickly and easily?
- Are you prepared to be edited by a nonpsychologist?
- Are you prepared to be misunderstood by well-intentioned (or perhaps not–well-intentioned) laymen?
- Do you want to spend significant time on social media?
- Would you like your ideas to reach a wide audience?

If you answer most of these questions in the affirmative, go for it!

http://dx.doi.org/10.1037/0000033-008
Toward a More Perfect Psychology: Improving Trust, Accuracy, and Transparency in Research, M. C. Makel and J. A. Plucker (Editors)

In the late 1970s, I was asked by *Psychology Today* to become a columnist. At the time, *Psych Today* was a much better publication than it is today. I consulted with two individuals about whether I should accept the invitation. One was Stephen Jay Gould, the great paleontologist, a peer in age who was already very well known for his monthly column in *Natural History*. His advice: "If you can do it in an evening, it is worth doing." The other counselor was psychologist Roger Brown, a treasured mentor. He thought for a few moments and said, "Well, all of your colleagues will advise you not to do it, but if asked, they would all jump at the chance."

I remember this experience quite vividly. This was the first time that I had to make a decision about whether to write popularly about my work, and—donning the title of columnist—about the work of other psychologists and social scientists. Since that time, decades ago, I have done a considerable amount of writing for the general public: two dozen books, hundreds of articles, op-eds, and, most recently, blogs. I have also had appearances on television and probably over 100 radio interviews, most typically on National Public Radio, the closest outlet in the United States to the British Broadcasting Corporation (BBC), where I have frequently appeared as well.

I welcome the opportunity to share my experiences, particularly with those readers who are young researchers. Perhaps the notes I present in this chapter will prove useful to you, allowing you to gain some of the pleasures of popular writing, while avoiding mistakes that I, and no doubt others, have made. Attempting to anticipate the issues that may arise in your mind, I've organized this chapter around a set of questions you should consider asking yourself. And because the work for which I am best known is about intelligence, I have drawn on that concept to illustrate some of my points.

1. DO YOU HAVE ANYTHING TO SAY THAT WOULD BE OF INTEREST TO THE BROADER PUBLIC, AND NOT JUST TO YOUR FELLOW RESEARCHERS?

In any field, much, if not most, of the work can be seen as "inside baseball"; that is, the work and the results may be of considerable, perhaps even great, interest and importance to practitioners within the field, even resolving some issues that have long been debated, but the work is either too esoteric to convey to the public or, if conveyed, would produce a humdrum reaction. One might, for example, find a quicker or more effective way to score an intelligence test, but this result would not arouse much interest. Or one might come up with a more effective measure of heritability of human traits, but the concept of heritability is difficult to convey succinctly and vividly.

In my own case, by the early 1980s I had published dozens of articles in peer reviewed journals. Few, if any of them, would have been of much interest to the general public. However, when in 1983 I published the book *Frames of Mind: The Theory of Multiple Intelligences*, I accomplished—unwittingly—two ends. First, I challenged a received wisdom: that intelligence is unitary; such a defiant, iconoclastic claim caught the attention of critics, commentators, and the general educated public. Second, one could convey the major point of a 400-page book in a not overly long sentence: "Most people think intelligence is a single capacity but now we know (!) that human beings have several semi-independent cognitive capacities, called the 'multiple intelligences.'"

2. DO YOU HAVE A STRONG DESIRE TO SHARE YOUR THOUGHTS WITH THE PUBLIC?

A good way to test yourself on this issue is to consider what happens when—say on a train or at a party—someone asks you about the nature of your work. It's easy to duck the question or to give a curt answer that tends to cordon off discussion: "Oh, I'm a psychologist"; or "Oh, I do research in psychology"; or (as I have sometimes said) "I'm not that kind of psychologist." But you can also invite conversation:

> I'm glad you asked. I'm actually excited about my recent work. A colleague and I just demonstrated that you can manipulate performance on the SAT (or some other instrument) simply by varying who else is sitting in the testing room. In other words, the company in which you are placed can make you smarter or dumber!

Of course, the public extends well beyond a relative, friend, or someone who happens to be sitting next to you on the subway. Which leads to the next question.

3. DO YOU ENJOY WRITING FOR A POPULAR AUDIENCE, AND CAN YOU DO IT EFFICIENTLY?

Ever since I was old enough to hold a writing implement or sit in front of a (at the time) manual typewriter, I have loved to write. I issued a newspaper when I was in second grade, edited my high school newspaper, wrote a lengthy novel after college, and have a vita that is too long ("no unpublished thought," as has sometimes been quipped). You should probably not become a researcher if you don't like to write, and you should certainly not consider writing for a popular audience unless you enjoy the experience.

Of course, not every researcher—no matter how gifted in creating questions or designing experiments—is going to be a natural or "easy" writer. That should not deter an otherwise-gifted scientist from a research career. But it places a premium on such a researcher to work on her writing skills, to find (and keep nearby) collaborators who enjoy writing, and to participate actively in a writing group; such steps may ultimately make one a decent if not fluent writer.

Those of us who are writers, by inclination, training, or necessity, feel the need to write to clarify our thoughts, even to know what those thoughts are. We write in different ways, but we all feel compelled to write. If you don't have that hanker, then probably you should leave popularization to others.

Which is perfectly OK. If you have something to say to the public, but don't like to write, then find (perhaps marry!) a gifted journalist. It can be a win–win situation.

It's possible to enjoy writing but to find that it is a time-consuming process. This is especially true for scientists, who are trained to write in a certain vein and must "unlearn" the stipulated style in order to reach an untrained readership. Since life is short, one has to decide how much time to devote to popular writing. Steve Gould's advice seems apt.

One more point about writing: There are some researcher–writers who are such excellent stylists that one reads them just to enjoy their choice of words and metaphors. In biology, Lewis Thomas was one such person; in astronomy, Carl Sagan. I'd love to have been such an individual, but I'm not. No one reads Howard Gardner principally for his style. I strive for clarity above all else and leave the poetic flourishes . . . to poets.

4. CAN YOU CONTINUE TO DO YOUR SCHOLARLY RESEARCH, OR ARE YOU DRAWN TO POPULARIZATION, TO THE DETRIMENT OF YOUR SCHOLARSHIP?

Having an audience, particularly one that awaits your every publication—indeed, nowadays, every blog and every tweet—can be a heady experience. But it can also come to dominate your life. There's nothing wrong with being a popularizer—many of us marvel at and even envy Malcolm Gladwell. But Gladwell is not a researcher-turned-popularizer, he is a popularizer through-and-through. In that way, he is quite different from Daniel Kahneman or Steve Pinker, two respected psychologists who also are effective public communicators.

I'd suggest keeping two things in mind. First, there's a difference between casual comments made in a posting to a friend or a tweet at a conference and writing about science for a general audience: When you popularize science, you need to be as careful as when you are writing for your peers. If you forget the nature of the media or of the audience, you may quickly get into trouble.

Second, you need to decide how to allot your time. A few scientists—like Gould and Sagan—are sufficiently fluent writers that they can maintain both a professional and a popular audience. Others—and I suspect that Kahneman is one of them—can write clearly and popularly, but it takes them far longer. And that is why one does not read many popular books by Kahneman.

5. HOW DO YOU DEAL WITH MISUNDERSTANDINGS OF YOUR IDEAS?

On the basis of my experiences with Multiple Intelligences Theory, I have lots to say. Albert Einstein famously said, "Explanations should be as simple as possible but no simpler." I feel the same way about popularization of scientific writing. One should write in such a way that the reader gets the points you are trying to make and does not take away points that are extraneous, irrelevant, or even fallacious.

But even if one's writing is beyond fault (clear as a bell, as the cliché has it), one cannot completely control how other people make use of it. When I first began to write popularly about intelligence I had the standard academic view: "It's my job to do the research and to describe the results clearly, but I am not responsible for how my ideas are interpreted by others."

For a while, that credo sufficed. But then I had an experience that was, within the academy, life transforming. I learned that in Australia, a curriculum had been developed based on "MI theory." Alas, as part of the curriculum, the authors had listed all of the major racial and ethnic groups in a particular state, along with the intelligences in which they were strong, and the intelligences in which they showed little strength.

This claim went beyond stupidity; it was actually damaging. Taken literally, it could lead teachers to make assumptions about their students that were groundless; it could actually have a negative impact on their learning and their sense of identity. And so I made the decision to appear on television in Australia and to denounce the curriculum as unfounded and "pseudoscience." Others joined the critique and, fortunately, the curricular initiative was suspended.

The Australian experience convinced me that, as a sometime popularizer of my research, I had responsibilities: to speak up, to correct the record, to prevent future misrepresentations. Shortly thereafter, I wrote an article that has become my most often cited: "Reflections on Multiple Intelligences: Myths and Realities." And, more recently, I created a website, http://multiple intelligencesoasis.org. This website explains the basic ideas of the theory, delineates some uses of the theory that I endorse, and, most important, throws the spotlight on what I call MISapplications of MI theory. I cannot prevent individuals from misinterpretation or misrepresentation (though I once undertook legal action against a company that produced "multiple intelligences toys for children" and indicated that I had approved this usage). But I can speak loudly and clearly about interpretations that are flawed and/or destructive.

I'd also like to turn to two other issues, which I've thought about a great deal in recent times. First, the issue of whether, and to what degree, publicity about research has changed over a 40-year period. The short answer is: a great deal, some ways good, some not.

While aware of the risks of seeing the past through gold-tinted lenses, I have considerable nostalgia with respect to the coverage of psychology in earlier decades. In the 1970s and 1980s, when I was much less well known, I appeared regularly on radio and television; I was frequently asked to write articles or review books for mainstream newspapers and magazines. When I wrote a book, the publisher arranged book tours, which even included airfare and accommodations in multistar hotels.

I was even asked to create a multiprogram television series on multiple intelligences for the BBC. The project fell apart when I refused to accommodate the theory to the ideas and methods that a new producer attempted to foist upon me. This is an example of drawing a line that needed to be drawn—even though it cost me a chance for possible fame and fortune. The producer was truly shocked that I withdrew from the project; as Roger Brown had opined, the mass media are sufficiently seductive that few can withstand their sirenic melody.

Currently, these opportunities do not exist, at least for me. No doubt, the number of flagship outlets (news magazines, review pages in newspapers) has been radically reduced, and the publishing and broadcast industries have been subject to massive disruption. A particular casualty is the so-called midlist book—a nonmonographic book for the general educated reader which, while never making the bestseller list, can remain in print for decades and continue to produce revenues for the publisher and author.

Indeed, publishers used to provide publicists, whose job it was to bring attention to the book. Nowadays, even scholars far better known than I am hire their own publicists—and pray that Oprah Winfrey or Stephen Colbert or Mark Zuckerberg will recommend their writings.

It is also possible, of course, that my own work is less original, even less interesting, even less well written, and so the judgment is chiefly about me, rather than about the sphere of popularization, writ large. I'll leave that verdict to others.

On the positive side, of course, there are many more outlets available, and anyone who wants to start a publication or a blog can do so. Though a good word from Oprah never hurts, we are not dependent on a few important curators or tastemakers. At least on rare occasions, a self-published book becomes a bestseller. But most scholars do not have the time or talent to maintain a full-time public relations campaign; we lose out to those individuals who have the time and/or resources to convert a random blog into a much-visited site. If you doubt this, go to a bookstore and look for a section called psychology. If it exists at all, it is stacked largely by self-help books, typically by individuals who are much better at selling a story than at designing an experiment, let alone developing a powerful new line of research or a comprehensive theory.

Finally, I turn to the question of whether, in a digital age, one should treat reports about research in a different way. Nowadays, many individuals, including scholars, write regularly about their emerging and often-changing ideas: they tweet, they blog, they communicate on platforms like Facebook, or Twitter, or Instagram. Part of the culture of these apps and platforms is that you communicate what you are thinking, often several times a day.

I know colleagues who believe that they can—indeed, they should—include in these informal reports the research on which they are working. They cheerfully and readily report preliminary findings, their reflections on these findings, changes of mind, heart, emphasis, interpretation. In a sense, they allow you to enter their mind on a daily basis or to eavesdrop on the conversations that take place in their laboratories.

Not to mince words: I deplore this practice. I consider scholarly research to be an endeavor in which one thinks carefully about the work that one does, carries it out as scrupulously as one can, reflects on what the findings mean, and reports them carefully and accurately. In the medical area, it seems self-evident that one does not want to prematurely claim a cure or, alternatively, dismiss a potential cure that has not been tested adequately. While most of us who conduct research in psychology do not deal with life-and-death issues, I recommend the same scrupulousness. One should not "go public" unless one is quite clear about the definitiveness of one's knowledge—though of course, we should always leave open the possibility of being wrong.

I don't expect to prevail in this debate. But when every thought—indeed, every whim—of a researcher becomes fuel for public circulation and speculation, something important and precious will be lost.

If you know this history of social psychology, you will remember a finding of Bela Zeigarnik, an early student of the great psychologist Kurt Lewin. According to the *Zeigarnik effect*, individuals remember better tasks that have not been completed than tasks that have been.

In the spirit of Zeigarnik, I bet that some of you are curious about what happened with the invitation to contribute a column to *Psych Today*—I wrote the column for 2 years and enjoyed doing so. But after a few years I ran out of things to say (as do most columnists). Rather than repeating myself, or turning to covering what others had done (thus becoming a reporter, rather than a publicist of my own work), I stopped writing the column. The time was hardly wasted. I enjoyed writing the columns, which I could do quickly, if not quite at Stephen Jay Gould speed. I then collected most of the columns in a book, *Art, Mind, and Brain: A Cognitive Approach to Creativity* (1982), which is still available. And thereafter, I returned full time to the conduct of research and the combination of scholarly and popular writings.

But with a nod to findings that are worthy of popularization, even a brief chapter deserves an ending. And so I close with the thought that most of us elect to become scholars, and (in the case of this readership) scientists, because we are fascinated by the world, want to understand it better, and to share our understandings with others. As scientists, we are obligated to make our findings public, but we are not obligated to popularize them. Yet, if you have the urge to do so, I encourage you to try. Writing popular science can be enjoyable, and you reach audiences of a size and variety that you could never have anticipated. Sometimes, you learn things that are helpful in your own work. Sometimes, you are surprised by what does or does not surprise your audience. And, as an unanticipated but important dividend, you contribute to a wider understanding of the work that you and others of your fellow professionals have undertaken. And since we are all dependent on the public support of science, and we all prefer science to folklore or mysticism, we are helping to preserve the calling in which we believe and to which we have devoted our working lives.

RECOMMENDED READING

Pinker, S. (2016). *The sense of style.* New York, NY: Penguin Books.

REFERENCES

Gardner, H. (1982). *Art, mind, and brain: A cognitive approach to creativity.* New York, NY: Basic Books.

Gardner, H. (1983). *Frames of mind: The theory of multiple intelligences.* New York, NY: Basic Books.

Gardner, H. (1995). Reflections on multiple intelligences: Myths and realities. *Phi Delta Kappan, 77,* 200–203, 206–209.

8

SHARING YOUR WORK: AN ESSAY ON DISSEMINATION FOR IMPACT

JONATHAN A. PLUCKER AND PAUL J. SILVIA

KEY POINTS

- Develop a coherent body of work that reflects a focused expertise; do not dabble in one-off projects early in your career.
- You'll write faster and better if you invest time in training, such as by reading practical books on grammar, style, and rhetoric.
- Write every week at consistent times, and defend those times.
- Focus on the traditional genres your department values (e.g., peer reviewed research articles and books). Other genres (e.g., social media) are frosting on the cake, not the core of your body of work.

Scholars conduct research not for its own sake, per se, but to shape the conversation in our field—to change beliefs, goals, and practices. The purpose of research is to have an influence. Of course, one must do good work to

http://dx.doi.org/10.1037/0000033-009
Toward a More Perfect Psychology: Improving Trust, Accuracy, and Transparency in Research, M. C. Makel and J. A. Plucker (Editors)

have an impact, and the strategies provided elsewhere in this book can help you create a robust, rigorous research program. But research eventually has to leave your laboratory and enter the scholarly community. What sort of reception will it get? Will people notice your research? Will some of them read and cite it? Or will your paper wander into the woods, never to be seen again?[1]

Much of your research's eventual influence will depend on how you share your ideas with the scholarly community and, from time to time, with broader audiences. Dissemination isn't everything, of course: You still need good ideas that are researched well. But many good ideas don't catch on, because they were shared poorly. In this chapter we discuss our thoughts on how to share research. We've had a certain amount of impact in our respective fields. That didn't happen by accident or because of well-timed envelopes of cash mailed to journal editors; instead, we have tried to learn from our many mistakes over the years, and we think and talk a lot about how to spread information about our work and use it to influence our fields and the public at large. This chapter grew out of our conversations, with each other, with colleagues, and with students, about how to help one's work become influential.

Our focus in this chapter is on influencing your community of academic scholars. We could write a similar chapter on interacting with the media, which carries its own significant benefits and drawbacks, but that widens our focus a bit too much. However, much of the advice we share about social media also applies to interacting with mass media (i.e., be careful and thoughtful about your approach).

WHAT ARE YOU GOING TO DISSEMINATE?

Before you share your research, you need research to share. Research matters more when it is systematic instead of scattered, deep instead of disparate, coherent instead of cobbled together with tape and roofing nails. A body of related publications, not lone articles published somewhere, are what attract attention and make an impact. As a researcher, you should avoid becoming a jack of all trades and aspire to be a master of no more than a handful. If you become well known in your field, you will be known as someone who studies some focused area or general problem, as revealed by a string of linked publications that all develop a theme.

Many students have the wrong goal when developing research ideas. They are looking for "an idea" that they can "get published somewhere"

---

[1]Most scholarly work gathers little attention, garners few if any citations, and has little impact. Bummer.

instead of identifying a theme that they can develop across a series of papers. Bodies of work attract more attention, for many reasons. So much gets published that the odds of a lone article hitting big are small—it takes a cluster of papers for people to notice. And one-off articles tacitly convey that the author isn't interested in the topic. If the person who developed the idea isn't committed to it and can't think of any important next step, why should a reader pick up the idea and run with it?

From this perspective, it helps to see dissemination as part of the research process, not the final step. If you're conducting one-shot studies that are not contributing to a focused line of research, then dissemination is probably your finish line. But for a well-considered body of research, dissemination should be intertwined with scholarship: You conduct good work, share it effectively, and then incorporate the feedback from your work into subsequent studies. As a result, the impact of dissemination efforts—and therefore of your work—builds over time.

For example, after one of us published an edited book, we did several presentations to both academic and nonacademic audiences, and we subsequently received feedback about what people enjoyed in the book and what they thought was missing. When we embarked on the second edition of the book, we incorporated this feedback with a critique from a book review (Worrell & White, 2009) to rethink our approach and improve the coverage of topics, which arguably resulted in a book that was better suited for both academics and practitioners (see Plucker & Callahan, 2008, 2014). Without the dissemination efforts, the information we could have used to improve the product would have been significantly limited.

It takes some effort and intention to think in terms of clusters of studies, and elsewhere in this book you will find advice for how to identify fertile ideas and develop a program of research. Most students find it difficult enough to come up with a single idea for a thesis or dissertation, so they don't want to puncture their relief by thinking about what, if anything, might come next. In most cases, merely posing the question "What would come next?" is enough to spark some ideas or, in some cases, to reveal that the idea is a one-off.

WRITE, WRITE, WRITE, READ, WRITE

One of us once had a professor in graduate school who illustrated the value of writing by passing out an article at the beginning of class. He asked us if we knew who the author was, and there was some light, under-the-breath recognition. The professor told us that we were holding the only major journal publication by that particular scholar, who was once very well-known because of his conference presentations and professional development work with teachers. The professor noted that this scholar's work had been largely forgotten—yet he had retired only a handful of years earlier.

The point was well taken: Your work has a lasting impact only if it is in writing. We can share our work in many ways, but some ways are ephemeral. For example, conference presentations are valuable—we discuss that in more detail later—but most of them vanish into history. The written word is what endures, so you will need to write a lot of words.

Arnold Schwarzenegger gave a commencement address a few years back, and one of his pieces of advice was not to sleep too much. As the crowd snickered, he observed that sleeping 9 to 10 hours per day was wasted time, but if you need that much sleep, he recommended learning to "sleep faster." Everyone laughed, but he was serious.[2]

Our advice for writing more efficiently is similar: Learn to write faster. Writing is not a gift handed down from a higher power to a select, lucky few; it is a craft that everyone can learn to do more efficiently and effectively. If you are a slow writer, it is because you have little experience and training in writing. You're not a failure, just a beginner. It would take you a long time to make lactofermented beets or rebuild a four-stroke lawnmower engine, too, if you hadn't done it before.[3]

Your writing will be faster, and better, if you do some training, so grab your headband and water bottle. Your writing workout has two main exercises. The first is reading about writing. Most people are slower writers than they should be because they lack confidence about grammar, usage, and style. We both reread our favorite writing and grammar books every year to keep from getting stale.[4] Reading a few books will improve the sound of your written voice and give you confidence (Baker, 1969; Hale, 2013; Plotnik, 2007; Zinsser, 2006); other books offer useful strategies for crafting tight and polished research articles (Goodson, 2012; Nygaard, 2015; Silvia, 2015; Sternberg, 2000; Sternberg & Sternberg, 2010). Beginners will save time and consternation if they learn how experienced researchers write articles, and we encourage you to learn from other people's mistakes.

The second exercise, of course, is writing. Unfortunately, reading other people's writing about how to write gets you only so far. In essence, all books about the practices of productive writers, be they poets or professors, show that they write often, usually every day (Boice, 1990; Perry, 1999; Silvia, 2007). We should take this lack of variance to heart and do what the experts

---

[2]It's funnier in an Austrian accent. Google it.
[3]Editor's note: This paragraph is more impactful if you know that the authors wrote this chapter in 9 days at the end of a semester.
[4]The books you choose don't matter that much. Anything that gets you reflecting on sentence construction and the craft of writing is helpful.

do. To write regularly, set up a schedule for writing, perhaps 2 to 8 hours a week, depending on how much you have to write. Slate it into your calendar like a class you're taking or teaching, and treat it with the same level of seriousness: Close your email, turn the phone off, squash potential distractions. This simple strategy ensures that your frenetic week will actually have time available for writing. A schedule is the only way to write productively during the normal work week. It sounds bland and mechanical, but we're not writing Broadway musicals here. The only alternative is to cannibalize your evenings and weekends or to hope that the future is miraculously less busy than the present.[5]

PUBLISH EFFICIENTLY

Academic writing has many genres. The most traditional genre is the empirical article published in a peer-reviewed journal, but researchers publish their scholarly ideas in many different forms. For example, you can write books, review papers, theory articles, chapters in edited books, book reviews, newsletter essays, blog posts, research or policy briefs, or white papers deposited into an online archive. What should you write?

For better or worse, your bosses and peers view some genres as more worthy than others. From the perspective of impact, this isn't mere prejudice: Some kinds of writing are more likely to have the influence you hope to have. Early in your career, journal articles—both empirical and conceptual—are what will get you hired and promoted. Peer-reviewed articles are the coin of the academic realm, and they are what you'll write if you want to influence fellow academics and begin to build your reputation. Some genres get more attention from other audiences. Books, for example, reach broader audiences, in particular if they are aimed at students or at a popular audience.

A few genres, however, don't attract much attention. At one time, book reviews and encyclopedia entries got solid readerships. Few journals still publish book reviews, and we doubt anyone consults hard-copy academic encyclopedias. Likewise, as odd as this is to say in a book chapter, chapters in edited books don't get the attention they once did, back when fewer were published and readers were willing to walk to the library to get a physical book.

A few genres are worth doing only if your main writing is getting done. Blogs, newsletter essays, and newspaper op-eds, for example, can reach surprisingly large audiences—audiences your journal articles won't. These pieces

---

[5]It won't be.

can often allow you to develop some ideas that don't easily fit into other formats. But beware of procrastination-by-writing, that peculiar form of time-wasting in which we put off writing our book by writing something shorter and breezier. There's a line between "writing for impact" and "wasting time on the Internet," and we trust that you know where it is; otherwise, you will quickly find it!

We should point out that we have conventional academic scholars in mind, so our advice about genres assumes your audience is composed of your scholarly peers. Academic researchers emphasize publications that are peer reviewed, documented, indexed, and archived, so they value articles and books vastly more than blogs and tweets. However, many academics write for several audiences. For example, it is common to see researchers who publish peer-reviewed articles aimed at their peers as well as books aimed at a different audience, such as textbooks for students, academic books intended for an interdisciplinary audience, and popular-press books written for the world's many curious readers. A few academics evolve into public intellectuals, spending their days writing popular-press books, traveling to give talks, and writing for mass-market outlets. These are all valuable profiles of scholarship. For some scholars, time spent blogging and tweeting is well spent, such as when a series of blog posts gauges readers' interest in a potential book topic, or when a new book is marketed via social media. Our broader point, however, remains true: Regardless of who your audience is, some forms of writing are a better use of your time than others in terms of influence, so reflect on what kinds of writing are most likely to get you where you want to go.

When writing for academic audiences, there are no hard-and-fast rules for which genres are most important. In some fields, such as the humanities, books are prestigious; in others, such as engineering and computer science, new ideas should appear first in a conference proceeding, and in others working papers are common and valued. It may be difficult to predict what genre will be most helpful to your work. As a case in point, the eminent psychologist Julian Stanley (1992) once wrote a column of advice for researchers in which he strongly cautioned against writing too many chapters for edited books, much as we did earlier. But then he noted that one of his most influential pieces was a chapter in a book on research methodology, which, as of the time of this writing, has been cited more than 18,000 times and is widely considered to be a seminal piece of scholarship in the social sciences. An invitation to contribute to a book edited by an eminent scholar and well-respected publisher on your main topic of interest is probably worth serious consideration; an invite to a book by editors you don't know, with a publisher you've never heard of, on a topic not central to your work should probably be politely declined. In a similar vein, being asked to write a post for a well-respected blog that garners lots of attention in your field may be a great opportunity, but a post on a blog with low readership and little connection to your fields of interest will probably do you and your work little good.

Keep in mind that you are constantly balancing opportunities with opportunity costs: What are you not able to do because you wrote that series of blog posts or decided to work on your book? A recent example was published in *Science* (Pennisi, 2015). Biologist Douglas Emlen was working on an invited review article on a topic that cut across much of his work. After finishing, he had far too much material and cut more than 10,000 words. He eventually turned that material into a book, noting that "it's the most important thing that I've ever done, and the most fun thing" (Pennisi, 2015, p. 1578). But when a journalist asked whether he planned to write another book, he was noncommittal, probably because of the many sacrifices he had to make in his professional and personal lives to get the book finished. As a researcher, time is your scarcest and thus most valuable resource. Spending 1,000 hours on Project Z means 1,000 fewer hours for Projects A, B, and C. As we have noted elsewhere in this chapter, learning to work more efficiently can help lessen opportunity costs—as can having a well-developed network of collaborators—but you can't add hours to a day or weeks to a year, nor can you magically prevent family members from getting sick, your furnace from breaking in the middle of the night, or someone rear-ending you on your way home from work.[6] Successful academics spend much of their time balancing opportunities with opportunity costs.

We offer one final caution about nonjournal publishing: Your name is still attached to your publications, and it represents a public display of your work. We have occasionally seen colleagues say things in blog posts that they would never write in a paper or chapter, which implies that the post is somehow less permanent or less serious. But the post should be seen as no less important in less formal of a setting. A recent example can be found in a well-known scholar who recently took to Twitter to protest proposed changes in his state's and university's policies.[7] The tweets got out of hand, and he said some edgy and questionable things. The situation quickly spiraled out of control when the mainstream media reprinted the tweets, and the professor found himself in the newspaper headlines (and not in a flattering way). The professor apologized but then (a) asserted that everyone knows social media is supposed to be unfiltered[8] and (b) immediately started tweeting the same sort of comments, in addition to taking shots at his critics. It is reasonable to respond to this anecdote with cries of "Free speech!" and "Academic freedom!" but one could also respond with "It's free speech, not guaranteed

---

[6]All of which feels most likely to happen about a week before a big deadline.

[7]Some details have been changed to keep things anonymous.

[8]In no way is this true.

acceptance of your message!" and "Your permanently damaged reputation doesn't care if your social media posts aren't supposed to be taken seriously!" Use discretion, and keep in mind that, regardless of your dissemination platform, you are representing yourself and your employer.

TALK ABOUT YOUR RESEARCH

In academia, writing and public speaking are two sides of the same low-denomination coin. Talking about your research feeds into publishing in some subtle ways. First, when you present at conferences, you will reach a large audience, and many people who hear about your research will look it up later. Second, you'll meet many other researchers in your scholarly niche, and those researchers are the people who are most likely to review, read, cite, and assign your articles. Many of the people you'll meet at conferences will invite you to contribute to special issues or edited books, and they may become future collaborators.[9] Finally, talking about your research gives you feedback and ideas for future studies.

Beyond presenting at conferences, you should get involved in scholarly societies devoted to your area of research. Although this might seem counterintuitive, we encourage you to devote more time to the smaller, niche societies than the huge groups. It is hard to stand out, be visible, and get involved in a huge national or international scholarly society. But in a small group—such as a regional society or a division or small society devoted to the narrow area of scholarship you study—you can stand out, meet people with similar interests, forge productive collaborations, and help craft the institutions that sustain and promote the field or subfield. Virtually all scholarly groups welcome graduate student members and early career scholars, and many have executive committee positions set aside for people at those stages of their careers. If so, get involved.

THINGS CHANGE

With the benefit of hindsight, the journal process at the start of our careers was surreal. Everything was in hard copy. To submit a manuscript to a journal, you would make the required number of copies on the photocopier (usually four or five), fret over whether the copies should be stapled or not, pillage the front office's cabinets for an envelope huge enough to fit 130 sheets of paper, and then mail the package to the editor, who then mailed

---

[9]We are a case in point.

a hard copy to each reviewer. If a reviewer didn't want to review it, he or she would mail it back. Many months and many dollars in postage later, you received a decision letter—an actual letter in your mailbox—from the editor, along with reviews and the occasional marked-up manuscript. Graduate students on the job market would haunt the mailroom, hoping for good news from the front lines. And if you revised and resubmitted the paper, the process started all over again. It was time consuming, resource intensive, and the way things worked.

The submission process feels radically different today, but many of the changes to the system were incremental and did not feel especially radical at the time. With the entire system now conducted online, from submission to reviews to communications to copyediting and proofing, the system is considerably faster and more efficient, and we certainly are not criticizing the improvements to the system; instead, we want to point out that the process will continue to change, and your probable knee-jerk reaction to some of the changes will be a healthy dose of skepticism. That's human nature, but you should also be open to new dissemination options.

What changes are coming next? Some fields, such as physics, have already moved in directions that would have seemed radical only a decade or two ago, with much less emphasis on double-blind, peer-reviewed journal articles. We're starting to see similar developments in the social sciences, with the Social Science Research Network and National Bureau of Economics Research white paper series as two higher profile examples. Our broader point here is that winter is indeed coming, but if you are prepared for it and stay open-minded, you may be able to capitalize on new dissemination strategies to enhance the impact of your work.

BRINGING IT ALL TOGETHER

It's hard to predict the future, of course, but researchers are probably best served by sticking to the following basic principles that are unlikely to change in the future:

- Develop a coherent program of research, not a scattered collection of one-off articles.
- Dissemination isn't the end of research. Ideally, you'll get feedback that will enrich and shape your research program.
- Write consistently, and schedule time to write during the work week. Protect that time like you protect your time for classes and other essential activities.
- No professor ever got fired for writing and publishing too many peer-reviewed articles.

- Don't dabble with lower prestige genres (e.g., social media) unless your most important writing is done. Treat them as "impact add-ons," not as the focus of your writing.
- Experiment with alternatives to traditional dissemination, including sharing your work in different genres, but keep their strengths and weaknesses in mind as you craft a comprehensive dissemination strategy.

RECOMMENDED READING

Boice, R. (1990). *Professors as writers*. Stillwater, OK: New Forums.

Garner, B. A. (2009). *Garner's modern American usage* (3rd ed.). New York, NY: Oxford University Press.

Silvia, P. J. (2007). *How to write a lot: A practical guide to productive academic writing*. Washington, DC: American Psychological Association.

Silvia, P. J. (2015). *Write it up: Practical strategies for writing and publishing journal articles*. Washington, DC: American Psychological Association.

Worrell, F. C., & White, L. H. (2009). Bringing evidence to bear on gifted education [Review of the book *Critical Issues and Practices in Gifted Education: What the Research Says*]. *Psychology of Aesthetics, Creativity, and the Arts, 3*, 259–261.

Zinsser, W. (2006). *On writing well* (30th anniversary ed.). New York, NY: HarperCollins.

REFERENCES

Baker, S. (1969). *The practical stylist* (2nd ed.). New York, NY: Thomas Y. Crowell.

Boice, R. (1990). *Professors as writers*. Stillwater, OK: New Forums.

Goodson, P. (2012). *Becoming an academic writer: 50 exercises for paced, productive, and powerful writing*. Los Angeles, CA: Sage.

Hale, C. (2013). *Sin and syntax: How to craft wickedly effective prose* (revised and updated ed.). New York, NY: Three Rivers Press.

Nygaard, L. (2015). *Writing for scholars: A practical guide to making sense and being heard* (2nd ed.). Los Angeles, CA: Sage.

Pennisi, E. (2015). Beetle horns and book writing. *Science, 350,* 1578. http://dx.doi.org/10.1126/science.350.6267.1578

Perry, S. K. (1999). *Writing in flow: Keys to enhanced creativity*. Cincinnati, OH: Writer's Digest Books.

Plotnik, A. (2007). *Spunk and bite: A writer's guide to bold, contemporary style*. New York, NY: Random House Reference.

−kin

Plucker, J. A., & Callahan, C. M. (Eds.). (2008). *Critical issues and practices in gifted education: What the research says*. Waco, TX: Prufrock Press.

Plucker, J. A., & Callahan, C. M. (Eds.). (2014). *Critical issues and practices in gifted education: What the research says* (2nd ed.). Waco, TX: Prufrock Press.

Silvia, P. J. (2007). *How to write a lot: A practical guide to productive academic writing*. Washington, DC: American Psychological Association.

Silvia, P. J. (2015). *Write it up: Practical strategies for writing and publishing journal articles*. Washington, DC: American Psychological Association.

Stanley, J. C. (1992). A slice of advice. *Educational Researcher, 21*(8), 25–26.

Sternberg, R. J. (Ed.). (2000). *Guide to publishing in psychology journals*. Cambridge, England: Cambridge University Press. http://dx.doi.org/10.1017/CBO9780511807862

Sternberg, R. J., & Sternberg, K. (2010). *The psychologist's companion: A guide to scientific writing for students and researchers* (5th ed.). Cambridge, England: Cambridge University Press. http://dx.doi.org/10.1017/CBO9780511762024

Worrell, F. C., & White, L. H. (2009). Review of Critical issues and practices in gifted education: What the research says. [Review of the book Critical issues and practices in gifted education: What the research says. Edited by J. A. Plucker & C. M. Callahan]. *Psychology of Aesthetics, Creativity, and the Arts, 3,* 259–261. http://dx.doi.org/10.1037/a0015410

Zinsser, W. (2006). *On writing well* (30th anniversary ed.). New York, NY: HarperCollins.

III

VIEWS FROM THE FIELD

9

THE PROMISES AND PITFALLS OF RESEARCH–PRACTICE PARTNERSHIPS

MARK BERENDS AND MEGAN J. AUSTIN

KEY POINTS

- The gap between research and practice has been a persistent challenge in education, but with the passage of the No Child Left Behind Act of 2001, there was a renewed federal focus on schools implementing scientifically based programs.
- Although making research evidence widely available through the What Works Clearinghouse was a significant step, the challenge of transferring research to practice remains.
- A further development in bridging the research–practice divide emerged when the Institute of Education Sciences promoted research–practice partnerships.

This chapter was supported by the University of Notre Dame's Center for Research on Educational Opportunity, Institute of Educational Initiatives. All opinions expressed in this chapter represent those of the authors and not necessarily the institutions with which they are affiliated. All errors in this chapter are solely the responsibility of the authors.

http://dx.doi.org/10.1037/0000033-010
Toward a More Perfect Psychology: Improving Trust, Accuracy, and Transparency in Research, M. C. Makel and J. A. Plucker (Editors)

- The Consortium on Chicago School Research is a model for research–practice partnerships, which are now spreading throughout the United States, with funding from the federal government and foundations.
- The promise of research–practice partnerships is that they have the potential to more closely connect research to practice, and the existing partnerships have many lessons to offer for those interested in this line of research.

When Congress passed the No Child Left Behind Act of 2001 (NCLB), researchers were enthusiastic that it required that federal funds be used for programs "based on scientifically based research"—a phrase mentioned more than 110 times in the legislation. This emphasis on research quality was a game changer in the educational research community. NCLB authorized the Institute of Educational Sciences (IES) within the U.S. Department of Education and thus increased the rigor of research through funding of research projects, development of interventions, testing them at scale, development of innovative measurement tools, and investment in predoctoral and postdoctoral training programs. The students who emerged from these programs took positions in universities, research firms, and government agencies, increasing the capacity to plan, conduct, and consume rigorous research studies.

As part of this development, IES funded and supported the What Works Clearinghouse (WWC), whose goal is to be a critical resource to inform decision making. "To reach this goal, the WWC identifies studies that provide credible and reliable evidence of the effectiveness of a given practice, program, or policy (referred to as 'interventions'), and disseminates summary information and free reports on the WWC website" (see http://ies.ed.gov/ncee/wwc/aboutus.aspx). Although WWC got off to an inconsistent start, it now has more than 700 publications available to the public and more than 10,500 studies that have been reviewed to help researchers and practitioners identify effective practices for improving student outcomes. WWC staff have worked diligently over nearly a decade to help the organization become the central resource for identifying the highest quality research on various policies, programs, and practices. They have strived to build trust by providing accurate information and transparent reviews of the available scientific evidence.

Yet despite the strengths of the development of IES and WWC and the improved quality of research and methodology, the problem of having an impact on changing practices in schools remains. Roderick, Easton, and Sebring (2009) described this development:

The strategy for influencing practice through model development is well established: (1) use existing research findings and theory to develop an effective intervention, (2) implement the model and test its effectiveness, (3) replicate the model in different settings and test scalability, and (4) move to rigorous evaluation of impact. The theory of action of such approaches is that practitioners need good models and evidence of effectiveness. By developing what works, we can then build knowledge of effective practice. . . . The role of the researchers, as described by IES, is to develop models, test their effectiveness, and then test the efficacy of bringing these ideas to scale using rigorous methods. (pp. 15–16)

The challenge with this approach is that such a model is premised on disseminating developed interventions and relies on improving the dissemination of research findings and interventions to states, districts, and schools to inform practice. In part, this approach stems back to the formation of IES and to its first director, Grover Whitehurst, who envisioned Thomas Edison's "invention pipeline," which moved "from inspiration through lab research to trials of effectiveness to promotion and finally to distribution and product support," as particularly applicable to education (Whitehurst, 2003, cited in Penuel, Allen, Coburn, & Farrell, 2015, p. 183).

However, this approach does not go far enough in establishing and nurturing relationships between researchers and practitioners (in states, districts, or schools) so that they can learn from each other when implementing interventions and modify and improve them on the basis of researchers' expert knowledge and practitioners' local expertise and experiences. Such relationships are key if the aim is to build the capacity to focus on what is happening to the core practices and processes in schools when various reforms are implemented (Roderick et al., 2009). Working collaboratively with school leaders and policy decision makers, the Consortium on Chicago School Research (CCSR) has addressed questions related to the daily workings of schools, such as research on new teacher evaluation systems, changes in high school requirements, the push for increasing algebra for all students, closing low-performing schools, and turning around schools (Sebring & Allensworth, 2012).

When John Easton succeeded Whitehurst at IES, he modified the IES approach to incorporate a broader vision whereby researchers and practitioners mutually inform one another within the context of research–practice partnerships. The idea is that by working together, the education agencies' use of research findings will increase, which in turn will have direct implications for improving educational practice, programs, and policy in ways that improve students' opportunities for learning and promote positive educational outcomes. In what follows, we describe CCSR as the model for research–practice partnerships, review how IES and other funders have financially supported such efforts, describe some other research–practice partnership models, and discuss opportunities and challenges for research–practice partnerships.

CONSORTIUM ON CHICAGO SCHOOL RESEARCH

The model for research–practice partnerships is CCSR at the University of Chicago Urban Education Institute, which recently celebrated its 25th anniversary. CCSR seeks "to expand communication among researchers, policymakers, and practitioners as we support the search for solutions to the problems of school reform [and] encourages the use of research in policy action and improvement of practice" (see https://consortium.uchicago.edu/about). CCSR points to a consistent focus on the following themes as key to its success: conducting research that is closely connected to the core problems and challenges confronting practitioners and decision makers; paying careful attention to the process by which people learn, internalize new information and ideas, and link it to their problems of the practice in order to make an impact; and requiring a change in the researcher's role from outside expert to interactive participant to build knowledge that matters for students' success in order to build capacity (Roderick et al., 2009, p. 3).

CCSR has put a great deal of time and effort into (a) developing a data system that allows researchers to monitor key education reforms, (b) engaging key stakeholders in ongoing relationships, (c) conducting rigorous studies to inform both research and practice, (d) accumulating knowledge over time by conducting coherent and connected studies, and (e) disseminating research findings and implications to the public (Roderick et al., 2009). In building the longitudinal data system over time, researchers have worked to ensure that test score gains and academic productivity could be measured in a valid and reliable manner, included high school transcripts, and linked students to the National Student Clearinghouse (NSC; http://www.studentclearinghouse.org/) on enrollment and educational attainment in higher education. In addition, because extant student and school records provide useful yet limited information for school improvement, CCSR researchers have supplemented the data system with surveys to measure key aspects of schools. For example, Bryk and Schneider (2002) developed measures of relational trust between teachers, between teachers and students, and between teachers and administrators in ways that reveal how higher levels of positive social relationships and social capital are important predictors of higher academic achievement.

Building on these surveys, Bryk and colleagues have developed the "essential supports for school improvement" to measure principal leadership; collaborative work among teachers; involved families; and supportive environments to support ambitious instruction, school improvement, and student achievement. These essential support measures were positively correlated with test score gains in Chicago (Bryk, Sebring, Allensworth, Luppescu, & Easton, 2010) and Illinois (Klugman, Gordon, Sebring, & Sporte, 2015). In addition, educators and school leaders have used these essential support measures to help guide school improvement and monitor progress over time (Roderick et al., 2009).

Engaging stakeholders and developing ongoing relationships are also critical for CCSR's success. These are challenging tasks, in particular when researchers provide findings that run counter to school district leaders' hopes and expectations. However, CCSR's experience reveals that policymakers and educators can handle bad news as long as all participants trust that they seek a common purpose: improving reform efforts that lead to school improvement and student success. For example, in the 1990s, CCSR reported on the problem of high school students dropping out of Chicago schools. In addition, CCSR researchers found a positive relationship between students performing well in their ninth-grade courses and high school graduation (Roderick & Camburn, 1999). Chicago Public Schools incorporated CCSR findings to assess high schools according to a broader set of criteria beyond test scores, including dropout rates and the percentage of ninth graders who were on track to graduate (Roderick et al., 2009).

Although school principals appreciated the expansion of accountability indicators beyond high school test scores, they were critical of these indicators because they lacked adequate information in their schools to understand and address the dropout problem. In response, CCSR researchers returned to the initial studies that revealed the importance of the on-track indicator systems and clearly communicated, through presentations and research briefs to Chicago high schools, the practical details of their findings. Roderick et al. (2009) noted that the continuous collaborative research informing a challenging problem of high school dropouts—consistently bad news to the district and school leaders—resulted in an on-track indicator system becoming "an important lever for coherence among high school reform efforts in Chicago" (p. 23). Engaging policymakers and educators takes time, involving consistent and regular communication; reporting of findings to the district before they are made public; and requesting input and feedback from stakeholders throughout the study on research questions, design, data collection, findings, reporting, and dissemination (Roderick et al., 2009).

Conducting rigorous studies that inform research and practice is a challenge that CCSR has addressed by attending to the technical issues of research (e.g., measurement of test score growth and indicators of school improvement) and translating the technical details in ways that are accessible to the wider education community. CCSR not only provides the details for researchers to assess the quality of the research but also distills the key findings and implications in short research briefs for policymakers and educators to allow them to reflect on the findings in ways that may change their practice. CCSR both engages in technical analyses of student administrative records and other quantitative data and supplements this research with qualitative case studies and interviews to provide a richer context for reform implementation and effects; this "not only enhances the rigor and validity of reports but also makes researchers credible in the eyes of practitioners" (Roderick et al., 2009, p. 10).

CCSR conducts research not merely to accumulate fragmented findings but also to accumulate and further systematic knowledge building and revision of policies so that there is growth in our understanding of the policies and research (see Cohen, 2003). As Roderick et al. (2009) described,

> The release of a report should not be the last word on a research topic; it must be thought of as the first word or next word. . . . We focus on developing a series of reports that releases critical findings over time and focuses attention on the key determinants of the problem. (p. 10)

CCSR also aims to make the research accessible to a wide-ranging set of audiences. Because researchers often do not attend to the manner in which research findings make their way into policymakers' and practitioners' views, CCSR seeks to change the way that researchers, policymakers, and practitioners interact in regard to research. By using a variety of communication strategies (e.g., face-to-face meetings, presentations, policy briefs, reports), CCSR wants to help decision makers and educators understand the findings, connect them to the problems they face on a day-to-day basis, and incorporate that knowledge in what they do in schools on a daily basis (Roderick et al., 2009).

When he was director of IES, Easton expanded the CCSR model by directing research funding to research–practice partnerships:

> The Researcher–Practitioner Partnerships in Education Research (Research Partnerships) . . . supports partnerships composed of research institutions and state or local education agencies that have identified an education issue or problem of high priority for the education agency that has important implications for improving student education outcomes. These partnerships are to carry out initial research on that education issue and develop a plan for future research on it. Through this joint research, the education agency's capacity for taking part in research and using research results is expected to increase. The ultimate goal of the partnerships . . . is to conduct and promote research during and after the grant that has direct implications for improving programs, processes, practices, or policies that will result in improved student education outcomes. (https://ies.ed.gov/funding/ncer_rfas/partnerships.asp)

Since 2014, IES has funded 28 different projects at approximately $400,000 each (over $11 million total) to help establish and sustain research–practice partnerships across the United States. With this IES funding, as well as additional funding from foundations, several efforts have been made across the United States to extend the success of CCSR to other cities and states. In what follows, we highlight just some of these partnerships. Each differs in their focus, location, and strategies; some of them modeling what CCSR has done, but others pursuing different strategies. We describe them here to suggest the possibilities for research–practice partnerships in using research to inform decision making.

THE HOUSTON EDUCATION RESEARCH CONSORTIUM

The Houston Education Research Consortium (HERC) is led by Ruth López Turley at Rice University and Carla Stevens of the Houston Independent School District (see López Turley & Stevens, 2015). López Turley started the initiative at HERC in 2011 after researching other research–practice partnerships, developing relationships with district leaders in Houston, Texas, and writing a grant proposal to provide funding for the partnership. University and district leaders met together to help define and build the partnership and set priorities.

In the beginning, HERC spent time building organizational infrastructure, which involved hiring staff, setting up a data-sharing agreement with the school district, and selecting an advisory board (university, district, funder, and nonprofit and for-profit representation) to guide the research agenda. HERC's research focus was on closing socioeconomic achievement gaps. According to López Turley and Stevens (2015), "The goal of closing these gaps served as a guiding principle for selecting research projects, the first of which was to monitor and analyze these gaps longitudinally" (p. 9S).

Although it is a relatively new partnership, HERC has been able to inform district programs such as Project Grad, which aims to increase high school graduation and college attendance, and Reasoning Mind, a technology-based program to teach elementary and middle school students mathematics and logical reasoning skills. After reviewing the existing empirical literature on these programs, HERC researchers found that few studies met rigorous standards of evaluation that could inform the programs, so they established an external third-party review process to provide independent assessments of district programs: "research that evaluates [district] programs, curricula, interventions, or policies that affect a large portion of the student body and that addresses a forthcoming school board meeting agenda item" (López Turley & Stevens, 2015, p. 9S). HERC provided the district with a database of external reviewers and guidelines for the review so that it could inform district decision making.

In addition, HERC built a longitudinal data system that enables researchers to conduct analyses on the effects of district policies, programs, and practices. HERC developed the data system in such a way that they could make it available for outside researchers to analyze a variety of district reforms. This helped increase the timeliness of research, allowed the district access to a deeper pool of research expertise, and provided the district with further opportunities to rely on independently produced research.

BALTIMORE EDUCATION RESEARCH CONSORTIUM

The Baltimore Education Research Consortium (BERC) was formally launched in 2006 as a partnership between researchers at Johns Hopkins University and Morgan State University in Baltimore, Maryland, and Baltimore City Public Schools. BERC's establishment formalized an informal partnership in which the district shared data and partnered with researchers to examine "accountability-focused reform efforts" and "equity of learning opportunities across Baltimore's public schools" (Durham et al., 2015, p. 121). BERC is supported by Baltimore foundations and a coalition of agencies, including Head Start, the Baltimore City Health Department, and others; it also includes researchers from other Baltimore colleges.

BERC's partnership relies on ongoing stakeholder meetings, with representatives from universities, the district, and community partners, to develop a shared research plan that prioritizes research on issues with the greatest potential to influence school reform and improvement in Baltimore City Public Schools. Research topics that directly address district needs are prioritized over topics of interest to researchers but without clear applications to policy issues and concerns. In 2008, a long-term research agenda was developed with a focus on "keeping on-level students on track to educational success (particularly on-time high school graduation) and decreasing the dropout rate" (Durham et al., 2015, p. 122). In early 2009, the district granted researchers access to their NSC data so they could pursue questions that extended this research agenda into postsecondary educational outcomes.

THE MINORITY STUDENT ACHIEVEMENT NETWORK

A different model of a research–practice partnership is provided by the Minority Student Achievement Network (MSAN), a self-organized "network of 29 suburban and small urban districts committed to eliminating the achievement gaps between their white and Asian students and their African American and Latino students" (Booth et al., 2015, p. 79). MSAN recognized that district staff did not have the capacity to build and maintain a sustainable research–practice partnership, so in 2006 they partnered with the Strategic Education Research Partnership (SERP), whose mission is to facilitate partnerships between districts and researchers.

SERP is a stand-alone nonprofit organization, started in 2003, that establishes long-term partnerships with school districts to address critical problems of practice. Unlike many research–practice partnerships, research projects are initiated by school districts, which identify a problem and reach out to SERP for help connecting with researchers. SERP then recruits researchers to investigate the problem in partnership with the district, with the dual goals of (a) producing a practical solution to the district's problem and (b) contributing more broadly to the field of education research through scalable solutions designed with a firm grounding in existing theory and research and tested using rigorous methods. SERP brings researchers and practitioners into partnership for specific projects instead of a long-term, open-ended partnership. A significant outcome of a 7-year research–practice partnership between five districts in MSAN and SERP was the development of AlgebraByExample, a set of 42 math assignments that can be incorporated into existing algebra curricula (Booth et al., 2015).

NOTRE DAME'S CENTER FOR RESEARCH ON EDUCATIONAL OPPORTUNITY AND INDIANA DEPARTMENT OF EDUCATION

In 2011, the Center for Research on Educational Opportunity (CREO), as part of the University of Notre Dame's Institute for Educational Initiatives, established a partnership with the Indiana Department of Education. The mission guiding the partnership was to conduct independent, rigorous research to inform educational policy and decision making in Indiana. Conversations at the time established research priorities. When the partnership began, the state had a Republican governor; a significant majority of Republicans in both houses of the state legislature; and a Republican State Superintendent of Public Instruction (Tony Bennett), an elected position. Within this context the Indiana Department of Education's focus was on market-based reforms and accountability, which included grading schools on an A–F scale, closing failing schools, considering teacher merit pay, evaluating teacher accountability on the basis of value-added test scores, and expanding school choice (charter schools and voucher program).

However, running against this conservative agenda, with a significant amount of support from the teachers union, Democrat Glenda Ritz won the election for the state superintendent in 2012, thus expanding the research priorities of the partnership from issues of school choice and teacher effectiveness to students' transitions into higher education, student mobility, and the teacher labor market and shortages.

LESSONS LEARNED

The various experiences of existing research–practice partnerships have yielded important lessons for others, including the importance of cultivating trust, finding a common language, building longitudinal data systems, communicating effectively with various stakeholders, meeting timelines, and rethinking university reward structures.

Cultivating Trust

Researchers frequently conduct research that leads to distrust rather than trust. Too often, researchers make commitments to schools and districts to provide feedback in return for access so they can collect various kinds of data but fail to deliver on this feedback. This kind of "drive-by" research may be beneficial to researchers and their careers, but it leaves schools and teachers frustrated, without potential direction, and skeptical toward the research and its usefulness. In addition, educators may look at the research being done as evaluative, "which can lead to defensiveness and apprehension about collaborating with researchers and letting them into their schools" (Coburn, Penuel, & Geil, 2013, p. 14).

Thus, cultivating trust poses a significant challenge to effective research–practice partnerships (Coburn et al., 2013; Coburn & Penuel, 2016; López Turley & Stevens, 2015; Roderick et al., 2009). López Turley and Stevens (2015) emphasized the importance of developing trust:

> Perhaps the most significant lesson we have learned through this partnership is the importance of developing relationships of trust, in which leaders from both institutions mutually agree with and are invested in the larger mission of the partnership, can communicate effectively across institutions, and are open and willing to learn from each other. (p. 10S)

To get to this point of trust and mutual collaboration takes time: time to establish priorities, to come to a consensus about feasible research projects that are informative within a reasonable time frame, and to build relationships grounded on a common mission. For example, some organizations are able to dedicate key personnel to coordinating and managing the partnerships, whereas university-based partnerships, for example, require dedicated faculty to coordinate and manage the work in addition to their other responsibilities (Coburn et al., 2013). The first model is more attractive but requires resources, something that some university-based partnerships lack.

An example of the challenge of sustaining trust comes from the Notre Dame partnership with the Indiana Department of Education. The transition from Republican State Superintendent of Public Instruction Bennett's administration to Democrat Ritz's was fraught with conflict and contentiousness, which had significant implications for the partnership with Notre Dame. With a focus on school choice issues, especially the impact of the voucher program on student outcomes, it was no surprise that the new Indiana Department of Education's staff were skeptical about the research–practice partnership with Notre Dame. However, over time, a commitment to conducting independent research that was not made publicly available until it had passed a peer review, and an expansion of research priorities helped the Indiana Department of Education's administrative staff and Notre Dame researchers to build a foundation of trust to sustain the research–practice partnership. CREO researchers have expanded the research agenda to include examination of the influence of peers on student achievement, expectations, engagement, and motivation; the extent and sources of the perceived teacher shortage in Indiana; and student mobility across schools in the state.

Another way research–practice partnerships can build trust is to commit to a "no surprises" policy (Coburn et al., 2013; Roderick et al., 2009). For example, researchers agree not to release findings or a report to the general public until key stakeholders in the partnership have had the opportunity to read the report, provide feedback, and digest the findings and implications. It is particularly important for stakeholders to have some time to review the report if the findings reflect negatively on a district policy, program, or practice. This does not mean that the findings are buried or rewritten by stakeholders; instead, having the opportunity to see the report before the general public allows stakeholders to develop a response when the findings are made public.

For example, BERC researchers' initial report on the NSC data was a descriptive analysis of the percentage of Baltimore students who enrolled in college, the type of college in which they enrolled, and whether they completed college. As is the case for national data on low-income and racial/ethnic minority students' college participation trends, the results indicated that fewer than half of students enrolled in college, and far fewer completed a degree. The report was not well received by the district, for a number of reasons. The results were descriptive, were not actionable, did not point to policies or practices the district could influence to change the results, and did not account for the recent successes the district had in raising graduation rates or the fact that this focus took attention and resources away from initiatives around postsecondary outcomes (Durham et al., 2015). To overcome these challenges, BERC members built trust by holding frequent conversations with district staff and establishing an agreement that researchers will keep district staff informed throughout the process, from research design through implementation and reporting. BERC's agreement provides Baltimore City Public Schools a 30-day review period for drafts that are ready for public release.

It is important for researchers and research organizations to maintain their independence and objectivity, especially when partnering with organizations that may be advocacy groups. In the American Psychological Association's (2017) *Ethical Principles of Psychologists and Code of Conduct* (http://www.apa.org/ethics/code/principles.pdf), fidelity, responsibility, and integrity are mentioned in the General Principles. When working with others, researchers are to establish trusting relationships. Moreover, in their work researchers are to be accurate, honest, and truthful. In addition, if conflicts of interest emerge from working with other organizations, reasonable steps should be taken to resolve the conflict. Toward these ethical aims, after discussing findings with the research partner it is helpful for researchers to submit their research to rigorous peer review, such as that established by many journals and book publishers. Such peer review helps buttress the legitimacy of the social science of the study and trust in the findings and interpretation.

Finding a Common Language

Coburn et al. (2013) raised one of the challenges in establishing an effective research–practice partnership as "bridging the different cultural worlds of researchers and practitioners" (p. 14). In other words, researchers and practitioners typically come from different work settings, everyday tasks, incentive systems, and ways of describing what they do. Coburn et al. pointed to the contrasting examples of how district leaders often feel a sense of urgency, in that they need answers to questions immediately, and often research-based answers are not readily available, contrasted with researchers' reluctance to provide quick answers to complex research questions that may take a multi-year, longitudinal study to produce some answers.

For example, BERC's research on postsecondary outcomes benefited from the active participation of all stakeholders in the consortium. Researchers at Morgan State University and district staff worked with the university's office of institutional research to start participating in the NSC, and an external partner program, College Bound (http://collegebound.org/), provided a forum in which BERC researchers can present their findings to school principals and counselors. These logistical projects also contributed to building a sense of trust among partners as well as further communicating the relevance and applicability of the findings.

Researchers and practitioners eventually came to a common language and revised their approach to the postsecondary reports—connecting results back to students' high school experiences and pointing to potential initiatives that Baltimore City Public Schools could develop to make an impact on their postsecondary outcomes. The district recently implemented an Office of Secondary Education Services, which is partnering with BERC researchers to look at college matching and undermatching and consulting about the most useful ways researchers can look at students' data. Furthermore, Baltimore City Public Schools are developing a new strategic plan that focuses on four pillars that have the potential to improve students' postsecondary outcomes (Durham et al., 2015). In return, BERC researchers are preparing a continuous improvement research project that will track how school leaders use data to influence students' college attendance and completion. Researchers and practitioners in BERC have highlighted that the consortium provides the long-term stability to facilitate this kind of planning and implementation, along with cumulative learning, that is often not possible with turnover and shorter timelines at the district level (Durham et al., 2015).

It takes time to find a common language and set of expectations for researchers and practitioners to carry on their work together. Sifting through the academic and bureaucratic acronyms to distill the key policy and practice issues to research requires multiple conversations, arguments, and solutions. At a more aggregate level, it parallels teacher learning communities, characterized by Fred Newmann (2002) as having a mutual commitment to the schools' mission and goals related to improving student outcomes; the resulting crucial arguments and self-reflection to accomplish those goals among trusted colleagues; and cooperation, coordination, and learning from each other for the benefit of school improvement and positive student outcomes.

Building Longitudinal Data Systems

One key to good research is good data. With cuts in the federal budget for national data collection efforts and the growth of longitudinal student data systems in states and school districts, data systems are critical resources going forward for educational researchers. Over the past decade, there has been significant growth in data systems that track entire populations of students from elementary through secondary school, through college, and potentially into the labor force. Some student data systems are also linked to data from teachers, including some sites that link the students and the teachers who teach them (e.g., McCaffrey, Lockwood, Koretz, Louis, & Hamilton, 2004).

Although they are becoming widespread, many of these data systems are going unanalyzed. López Turley and Stevens (2015) made the following point:

> There is no shortage of data, but often there is not enough time and resources for in-depth analyses on issues such as student development and persistence, changes in achievement gaps over time and across grade levels, and the short- and long-term effects of curricula, programs, and interventions. (p. 7S)

Researchers and practitioners have a great deal to gain by entering into research–practice partnerships to build the capacity to analyze the rich data sources that have thus far been compiled as well as to build better data systems that can address key policy and practice issues that districts confront. Although building longitudinal data systems may not be an option for researchers outside of research–practice partnerships, some partnerships, such as CCSR and HERC, have included other researchers to help build the capacity for the expertise and analysis needed to conduct studies that inform the partnerships.

Even with longitudinal records on students and schools, additional data may be necessary to address some key policy issues. For example, conducting additional surveys of principals, teachers, and students within districts can provide information on how schools differ in their improvement efforts (Bryk et al., 2010). Conducting such surveys over time can provide information on how schools are changing in ways that are positively associated with student achievement and other outcomes, or perhaps changing in negative ways.

One of the key issues in building longitudinal data systems is data confidentiality. Fortunately, there are ways for districts to deidentify the data so that researchers do not know students' names or other identifying information, thereby maintaining confidentiality. Although researchers have developed sophisticated ways of preserving confidentiality, this issue is likely to pose a continuing challenge as the public and policymakers become increasingly concerned about data privacy issues.

Communicating Effectively With Various Stakeholders

When conducting research within a research–practice partnership, there are a variety of stakeholders with whom establishing effective communication is critical if the partnership is to be built and trust established among members. For example, stakeholders may include state and district leaders, state and district data and information technology staff, research staff, external researchers, school board members, organizations devoted to developing and implementing educational products (including vendors), principals and teachers, students, and parents. Each group may have different priorities and ways to articulate those priorities. The various communication strategies to keep all stakeholders informed may include different types of meetings, presentations, discussion groups, retreats, research briefs, website dashboards, and social media. For example, in addition to a longer report or research article, researchers can provide shorter executive summaries or two-page research briefs to highlight the research problem, design, findings, and implications. The goal is to disseminate key information to ensure that the leaders on the practitioner side of the partnership are not surprised by any findings or reports and are fully in the loop throughout the research development and design phases as well as the dissemination and reporting phases.

Meeting Timelines and Rethinking University Reward Structures

One of the many challenges facing researchers is that state and district leaders need to make decisions in a much shorter time frame than academics are used to. Rigorous longitudinal research studies can take several years to yield results, especially results that give districts and states information on which to act. Successful partnerships are the ones that are able to provide timely research without sacrificing rigorous analyses of policies, programs, and practices (Coburn et al., 2013; Coburn & Penuel, 2016; Conaway, Keesler, & Schwartz, 2015; López Turley & Stevens, 2015; Roderick et al., 2009).

Balancing the long- and short-term priorities within research–practice partnerships presents a continuous challenge, and negotiating the research products that provide the timely results that decision makers need with the longer term results of larger scale studies may involve different strategies and options. For example, BERC conducts not only long-term research projects but also "rapid response" studies—providing data analyses to the Baltimore City Public Schools—with projects that take a month or less to complete, such as examining the relationships between rates of student and teacher absenteeism (see Coburn et al., 2013; Connolly, Plank, & Rone, 2012). Some partnerships may not choose this type of strategy unless they have the capacity to do so, as they may not want to be involved in work that has little payoff within the academy.

However, universities may need to change the ways they evaluate and incentivize faculty who become involved in research–practice partnerships to make rapid response studies more feasible. Universities currently do not value many of the activities that are necessary for effective research–practice partnerships (Coburn et al., 2013; Coburn & Penuel, 2016). Research briefs and short-term rapid response studies in response to district and state priorities do not have the same impact as articles and books published in top journals and presses, yet these activities may be critical for building relationships among researchers and practitioners. In the future, if research–practice partnerships are to increase and thrive, university leaders may need to rethink how the necessary activities benefit the university as its faculty engages in the local community. Such a rethinking of research–practice partnerships and the activities involved will need to consider how to value the time involved, the products produced, the policies and programs developed and changed, and the several team members involved on various projects.

CONCLUSION

The increasing number of research–practice partnerships has great promise for improving education systems across the United States. Although the payoffs of the significant federal and foundation investments may be a few years off, we are beginning to learn from the various research–practice partnerships that have been established in different districts and states. We certainly have more to learn about how to improve their effectiveness.

Establishing research–practice partnerships is not for the faint of heart. It takes a great deal of patience and perseverance to do the diligent work of establishing partnerships, building the capacity within them, developing data sharing agreements, coming to a consensus about research priorities, and agreeing on timelines for the research. It takes a significant amount of time and energy from both university researchers and district or state practitioners to make research–practice partnerships happen and to make them work well. Despite the many challenges and potential pitfalls confronting research–practice partnerships, the promise is that, over time, they will conduct rigorous research to directly inform policymakers and educators in ways that bridge the historically persistent divide between research and practice. If successful, research–practice partnerships have the potential to build the capacity of education systems to improve educational policy, programs, and practice and thereby improve student outcomes, in particular for students who have been historically disadvantaged.

REFERENCES

American Psychological Association. (2017). *Ethical principles of psychologists and code of conduct* (2002, Amended June 1, 2010 and January 1, 2017). Retrieved from http://www.apa.org/ethics/code/index.aspx

Booth, J. L., Cooper, L. A., Donovan, M. S., Huyghe, A., Koedinger, K. R., & Paré-Blagoev, E. J. (2015). Design-based research within the constraints of practice:

Algebra By Example. *Journal of Education for Students Placed at Risk, 20,* 79–100. http://dx.doi.org/10.1080/10824669.2014.986674

Bryk, A. S., & Schneider, B. (2002). *Trust in schools: A core resource for improvement.* New York, NY: Russell Sage Foundation.

Bryk, A. S., Sebring, P. B., Allensworth, E., Luppescu, S., & Easton, J. Q. (2010). *Organizing school for improvement: Lessons from Chicago.* Chicago, IL: University of Chicago Press.

Coburn, C. E., & Penuel, W. R. (2016). Research–practice partnerships in education: Outcomes, dynamics, and open questions. *Educational Researcher, 45,* 48–54. http://dx.doi.org/10.3102/0013189X16631750

Coburn, C. E., Penuel, W. R., & Geil, K. E. (2013). *Research–practice partnerships: A strategy for leveraging research for educational improvement in school districts.* New York, NY: William T. Grant Foundation.

Cohen, D. (2003). *Workshop on understanding and promoting knowledge accumulation in education: Tools and strategies for education research.* Washington, DC: National Academy of Sciences.

Conaway, C., Keesler, V., & Schwartz, N. (2015). What research do state education agencies really need? The promise and limitations of state longitudinal data systems. *Educational Evaluation and Policy Analysis, 37*(Suppl. 1), 16S–28S. http://dx.doi.org/10.3102/0162373715576073

Connolly, F., Plank, S., & Rone, T. (2012). *Baltimore Education Research Consortium: A consideration of past, present, and future.* Baltimore, MD: Baltimore Education Research Consortium. Retrieved from http://baltimore-berc.org/past-present-and-future/

Durham, R. E., Bell-Ellwanger, J., Connolly, F., Robinson, H. R., Olson, L. S., & Rone, R. (2015). University–district partnership research to understand college readiness among Baltimore city students. *Journal of Education for Students Placed at Risk, 20,* 120–140. http://dx.doi.org/10.1080/10824669.2014.987278

Klugman, J., Gordon, M. F., Sebring, P. B., & Sporte, S. E. (2015). *A first look at the 5 Essentials in Illinois Schools.* Chicago, IL: The Consortium on Chicago School Research at the University of Chicago Urban Education Institute. Retrieved from https://consortium.uchicago.edu/sites/default/files/publications/Statewide%205E%20Report.pdf

López Turley, R. N., & Stevens, C. (2015). Lessons from a school district–university research partnership: The Houston Educational Research Consortium. *Educational Evaluation and Policy Analysis, 37*(18), 6S–15S.

McCaffrey, D. F., Lockwood, J. R., Koretz, D., Louis, T. A., & Hamilton, L. (2004). Models for value-added modeling of teacher effects. *Journal of Educational and Behavioral Statistics, 29,* 67–101. http://dx.doi.org/10.3102/10769986029001067

Newmann, F. M. (2002). Achieving high-level outcomes for all students: The meaning of staff-shared understanding and commitment. In W. D. Hawley (Ed.), *The keys to effective schools: Educational reform as continuous improvement* (pp. 28–42). Thousand Oaks, CA: Corwin Press.

No Child Left Behind Act of 2001, Pub. L. 107–110, 20 U.S.C. §§ 6301-8962.

Penuel, W. R., Allen, A. R., Coburn, C. E., & Farrell, C. (2015). Conceptualizing research–practice partnerships as joint work at boundaries. *Journal of Education for Students Placed at Risk, 20,* 182–197. http://dx.doi.org/10.1080/10824669.2014.988334

Roderick, M., & Camburn, E. (1999). Risk and recovery from course failure in the early years of high school. *American Educational Research Journal, 36,* 303–343. http://dx.doi.org/10.3102/00028312036002303

Roderick, M., Easton, J. Q., & Sebring, P. B. (2009). *The Consortium on Chicago School Research: A new model for the role of research in supporting urban school reform.* Chicago, IL: The Consortium on Chicago School Research at the University of Chicago Urban Education Institute.

Sebring, P. B., & Allensworth, E. (2012, April). *The development, challenges and lessons of the Consortium on Chicago School Research.* Paper presented at the annual meeting of the American Educational Research Association, Vancouver, British Columbia, Canada.

10

CONDUCTING COGNITIVE NEUROSCIENCE RESEARCH

AMY LYNNE SHELTON

KEY POINTS

- The first step in understanding how brain imaging techniques can effectively answer questions is to recognize the limitations of what the different techniques (e.g., electroencephalography, positron emission tomography, magnetic resonance imaging) can and cannot measure.
- Effective brain imaging studies require the same rigor associated with experimental design for strong behavioral experiments but within the limitations of the methods.
- Brain imaging techniques introduce a set of unique challenges due to the massive spatial and temporal territory covered in data acquisition.
- The high cost of many brain imaging techniques poses additional challenges in balancing good research practice with affordability.
- The field of functional brain imaging requires diligence to enable research designs and analyses.

http://dx.doi.org/10.1037/0000033-011
Toward a More Perfect Psychology: Improving Trust, Accuracy, and Transparency in Research, M. C. Makel and J. A. Plucker (Editors)

Cognitive neuroscience sits at a critical intersection of the psychological and biological aspects of human behavior. As a field, cognitive neuroscience was born out of methodological advances that allowed researchers new ways to think about cognitive functions in light of brain mechanisms, distinguishing it from many closely related areas, such as cognitive psychology, cognitive science, and systems neuroscience. Today, cognitive neuroscience may be viewed as an orientation toward questions rather than being tied strictly to methods. However, the primary advantages and limitations of the field still rest heavily on the methods that defined this field in the space of where structure meets function: brain imaging techniques.

The exploration of cognitive functions in the awake behaving human brain dates back to the mid-20th century, when some of the earliest studies using electroencephalography (EEG) began (e.g., Davis, 1939; Sutton, Braren, Zubin, & John, 1965; Walter, Cooper, Aldridge, McCallum, & Winter, 1964). The interest in functional imaging has exploded since the 1980s, when additional noninvasive techniques were adapted to measure changes in brain activation over time. Positron emission tomography (PET) and single-photon emission computed tomography (SPECT) began to offer better spatial resolution at the cost of temporal resolution compared with EEG (e.g., Wernick & Aarsvold, 2004). In the 1990s, the development of functional magnetic resonance imaging (fMRI) to measure blood-oxygen-level-dependent (BOLD) changes over time offered both spatial resolution superior to EEG and temporal resolution superior to tomography (Aine, 1995).

The availability of functional imaging facilities and automation in the processing and analysis programs has opened the door for researchers from nearly any area of human cognitive and behavior research to launch investigations. This proliferation in the use of functional imaging puts a premium on understanding the strengths and limitations of these techniques (e.g., Aguirre, 2014; Logothetis, 2008). The following discussion offers a summary of these limitations and the demands that come from the psychological aspects of cognitive neuroscience.

FUNCTIONAL IMAGING AS THE NEW PHRENOLOGY

In the late 18th century, Franz Joseph Gall promoted the idea that different parts of the brain were responsible for different functions, and individual differences in abilities attributable to different brain regions could be understood by feeling bumps on the skull (Simpson, 2005). Although phrenology has since been debunked, the basic concept of mapping brain function has enjoyed a rich history that continues to be of interest today (Toga, 2015).

In the early days of the functional imaging boom, the dominant work was on mapping well-known functions to macro regions of the human brain—most notably, regions of the cerebral cortex. For example, some of the earliest PET and fMRI studies were used to identify the regions of the brain responsible for basic sensory functions (e.g., Belliveau et al., 1991; Rao et al., 1996; Wessinger et al., 2001), supporting the previous results from studies of patients with brain damage due to development, injury, or pathology. Subsequent work revealed specific areas of the brain that were associated with more specific kinds of cognitive processes, such as processing face stimuli relative to other objects (fusiform face area; Kanwisher, McDermott, & Chun, 1997), viewing images of scenes relative to objects (parahippocampal place area; Epstein, Harris, Stanley, & Kanwisher, 1999), learning large-scale environment (navigational network or spatial learning network; Shelton & Gabrieli, 2002; Maguire et al., 1998), and directing attention to one hemifield of space versus another (attentional control network; Kelley, Serences, Giesbrecht, & Yantis, 2008).

One cynical view of the brain mapping approach is that it largely validated the existence of distinct functions, but it would be remiss not to acknowledge that these findings elaborated the organizational structure of the behaving brain and identified potential constraints that the organization would place on the kinds of functional models that were possible. For example, the observation that viewing faces activated a different but nearby part of the brain than viewing other objects suggested new ways of thinking about the psychological similarities and differences involved in processing these two kinds of stimuli (Haxby et al., 2001; Kanwisher et al., 1997). These efforts also served as the critical foundation for using these same imaging techniques to test ideas about not only where cognitive functions happen in the brain but also how they might operate. For example, the vast literature on the regions of the brain associated with learning a novel large-scale environment (e.g., Maguire et al., 1998; Shelton & Gabrieli, 2002) opened the door to asking about how individuals might differentially engage this learning network to support successful navigation (e.g., Furman, Clements-Stephens, Marchette, & Shelton, 2014; Hartley, Maguire, Spiers, & Burgess, 2003; Marchette, Bakker, & Shelton, 2011). Such advances have the potential to shape our thinking about what it means to have an individual learning profile, extending this work to a wide range of issues in neuroscience, psychology, and even educational practice (for a brief discussion, see Furman et al., 2014).

In more recent years, the field of functional neuroimaging has become fertile ground for a much wider range of research questions in terms of both psychological scope and the detailed level of function. A salient example of this breadth has been the many advances in our understanding of social cognition that have been studied directly with, or influenced by results from, functional imaging. In the complex case of two social interactions, brain imaging has revealed the conditions under which brain activation can become synchronized across individuals (Abrams et al., 2013; Dumas, Nadel, Soussignan, Martinerie, & Garnero, 2010; Nummenmaa et al., 2012, 2014). This interbrain synchronization has taken the imaging world beyond the individual and into the world of humans as social beings, offering important complements to the cognitive social psychology.

In addition, the repertoire of brain imaging techniques has continued to grow. Given these advances, this is a good time to examine the standards and controversies in research practice. For example, an entire subfield of cognitive neuroscience has focused on how functional activity during a state of rest can inform us about the connections among brain areas (Cole, Smith, & Beckmann, 2010). The use of multiple imaging techniques has allowed us to dramatically improve our understanding of the relationships among structural and functional connections. Perhaps more interesting, it has also offered new ideas about how to diagnose a variety of neurological disorders and predict the cognitive decline in degenerative brain diseases (e.g., Lee, Smyser, & Shimony, 2013).

The following discussion focuses on fMRI as a central technique, but the same issues are relevant to multiple methods. Critical points for specific methodologies are highlighted as needed.

BEHAVIORAL DESIGNS FOR BRAIN IMAGING

As with any effort to understand human behavior through experimentation, the foundation of a functional imaging study starts with strong experimental design. A good study will adhere to the features associated with good behavioral experiments (see the chapters in Part II of this volume) but will also address a number of additional issues brought on by the features and limitations of the functional imaging techniques.

One of the first challenges in designing a functional imaging study is adapting paradigms that are effective in purely behavioral experiments to fit the demands of the imaging technique. The environments that are required for many functional imaging techniques pose limitations that can conflict with what might be best approaches for capturing the desired behavior. For example, if one is interested in spatial learning from exploratory wayfinding, it might be ideal to place a participant in a standing position (as in walking) or a seated position (as in driving) and allow him or her to have freedom of head and arm movement. However, the specific network of regions that have been implicated in navigation will best be examined in an fMRI study, which requires a highly restricted supine position with the head and upper body fully restrained.

Moreover, the appropriate design to capture a behavioral difference may not be the same as the appropriate design to capture a difference in the relevant brain activation. Consider the example of trying to understand whether people learn an environment differently when they view it from a ground-level perspective (akin to learning by walking around) than when they view it from an aerial overview (akin to scanning a map). One strong behavioral approach might be to have an individual learn and test a single environment from one perspective and then, after a delay, learn and test on the second environment from the other perspective. We would want to counter-balance factors such as the assignment of the environment to perspective and the order of the environments learned. By encapsulating the learning and testing of each environment, and the order of perspectives across participants, we control for interference effects. We could also use the two perspectives as between-subjects manipulation and randomly assign participants to the conditions. In the end, we would compare the measures obtained during testing to evaluate whether the two perspectives showed differences, either in a within-subject or between-subjects comparison (for the within-subject example of this behavioral paradigm, see Shelton & McNamara, 2004).

Now, imagine we wish to understand the brain mechanisms that are associated with learning the two different perspectives to understand what might give rise to the observed behavioral differences. First, to really under-stand how the learning is occurring, the scanning needs to be done during initial encoding of the environment, when there is arguably no behavior to readily measure. Next, we would need to consider how the learning progresses. In the typical setup, the participant learns only one environment at a time, but most of our measures of brain activation depend on showing relative acti-vation: the change in the brain activation for one stimulus/condition/process compared with the brain activation of another stimulus/condition/process. For example, using fMRI for this purpose, we would clearly need to have both kinds of perspectives and the relevant control condition. These would need to alternate within a time period that allows interspersing these conditions throughout a set of scans, resulting in a paradigm that has potential con-sequences for the desired behavior (for an example of an fMRI-adapted para-digm, see Shelton & Gabrieli, 2002).

A major strength of the cognitive neuroscience community has been the emphasis placed on understanding how these adaptations influ-ence the cognitive functions of interest in order to make informed decisions about how to work within these constraints. This is often accomplished through extensive behavioral piloting with the goal of optimizing the brain imaging results without compromising the integrity of the original research question.

ISOLATING FUNCTION AND MEASURING ACTIVATION

In addition to the practical aspects of having multiple conditions, studies of brain function require that the function or functions of interest be defined clearly. As with any laboratory research, tight experimental designs are critical to be able to isolate the functions of interest. For example, consider this seemingly simple question: Does the brain have distinct areas associated with processing faces? We start with this case because the fusiform face area is a well-established functional region of the human brain (Haxby et al., 2001; Kanwisher et al., 1997), but it illustrates the need for tight experimental control. To isolate the region or regions associated with processing faces using fMRI, one needs to ask what the relevant comparison should be. If we think about processing faces compared with processing nothing, then we might think we should compare activation during the presentation of a face to activation during presentation of a blank screen. However, such a comparison would reveal a vast range of processing that occurs any time visual information is presented. As such, the question itself must be refined to include what we mean by *distinct*. In the case of face processing, the real question was about face processing relative to processing other kinds of objects. As such, the design needed to allow a contrast between faces and other objects. Moreover, the faces and objects needed to be matched on all of the visual properties that might incidentally produce processing differences—such as how much of the visual field was occupied, the complexity of the color profile, and so on.

As another concrete example, consider that when studying the networks associated with learning a large-scale space, we use virtual reality to have a participant move through a space during learning (e.g., Marchette et al., 2011). The processes we hope to isolate are those associated with the acquisition of the spatial information distinct from the visual stimulation coming from the shapes and colors, the optic flow coming from the movement through space, and even the semantic knowledge and automatic naming that occurs when one sees an identifiable object.

This issue of baseline, in particular in fMRI, has been so critical to the field that there has been a line of research devoted specifically to understanding how to find an appropriate control task for a brain imaging study (e.g., Gusnard, Raichle, & Raichle, 2001; Stark & Squire, 2001). This work highlights the fact that the brain is always in action, and one can really think about brain activation only in terms of relative states that are changing moment to moment. Whether designing a study or evaluating the importance of a set of results, concerns about baseline in the context of any given technique raise the issue of whether isolation of activation is or is not synonymous with isolation of function. The upshot is that knowing whether activation is absolute or relative (and relative to what) is an important consideration.

Finally, all of these design issues must also be coupled with the critical issue of what is actually being measured. It is easy to fall into the trap of assuming that "activation" in some region of the brain can be easily interpreted as a region that is directly supporting some function. However, the assumptions about what is happening in the brain depend on whether the technique measures electrical signals, metabolic processes, or vascular changes. In each case, the "activation" can be associated with different aspects of processing (for a review, see Aguirre, 2014). For example, BOLD fMRI identifies regions where the oxygen in the blood has been depleted and flooded with freshly oxygenated blood. Through physics and physiology, we know that this oxygenation occurs in response to neurons firing; however, neurons can utilize oxygenated blood for multiple reasons (Logothetis, 2008). As such, the full understanding of how a particular region might participate in a function often rests on having converging evidence from multiple techniques, including those that go beyond brain imaging (e.g., animal models, clinical patients).

SAMPLE SIZE, POWER, AND BREAKING THE BANK

A priori power analysis has long been the standard for determining the necessary sample size for any study. In the best case, this is a quantitative approach in which there are some previous data available on which the researcher can base estimates of expected effect sizes (Cohen, 1992). However, power analysis in the field of functional imaging has been difficult and contentious for several reasons (for a review, see Mumford, 2012). First, traditional methods for calculating power generally deal with one effect size, but in functional imaging the results are taking place over multiple electrodes (e.g., EEG) or thousands of voxels (e.g., fMRI). As a result, the functional imaging field has had to evolve the techniques. Early attempts to provide sample size calculations met with a great deal of skepticism (e.g., Desmond & Glover, 2002; Hayasaka, Peiffer, Hugenschmidt, & Laurienti, 2007; Mumford & Nichols, 2008), but the development of more transparent approaches and convenient calculators has improved the prospect for adhering to more rigorous standards (Durnez et al., 2016; Mumford, 2012).

Despite the growing availability of power analysis tools, sample size in functional imaging has always been influenced by basic research economics. Depending on the technique, studies that use brain imaging methods can be costly. For example, a typical fMRI research scan session can cost from

$400 to $700 per hour depending on the infrastructure of the research center. In addition, participants in the study are compensated for their time at an average rate of about $40 per hour. This means that just collecting pilot data on six to eight participants can cost thousands of dollars. Therefore, one of the never-ending debates in the cognitive neuroscience literature is the need to balance cost against power and sample size. This issue goes beyond just sensible cost–benefit analysis, given the heavy dependence on grant funding. In the case of federal funding, researchers owe it to taxpayers to use funds wisely so they can provide quality research. It also means that all of the research issues are essentially high stakes.

In making decisions about how to balance cost against power there are no easy answers, but knowingly setting out with an underpowered study is generally ill-advised in any domain. The fact that each participant can be very costly should actually serve as an argument for, rather than against, making sure power is sufficient. Despite the growing awareness of this need to address sample sizes through statistically valid approaches, small, seemingly arbitrary sample sizes continue to be among the questionable research practices lingering in the field (e.g., Button et al., 2013; David et al., 2013; for similar concerns raised in the EEG/event-related potential community, see Larson & Carbine, 2016).

Therefore, the key to producing higher quality, replicable studies is to marshal the resources needed to make a statistically sound decision. In addition to the obvious need to incorporate power analyses in some form, the field has also put a premium on understanding how other factors, such as the way the brain images are collected (size and scope of the units) and the number of trials conducted, affect the ability to detect changes in activation. Having this big-picture approach at the earliest stages of design can optimize the study in terms of statistical standards. A tightly designed study on an important topic for human cognition with appropriate power will have the highest likelihood of success and will thereby justify the cost.

BIG DATA AND MULTIPLE COMPARISONS

Among the decisions that affect power is the question of what will be tested: How many different conditions, how many tests, and where in the brain? The brain is made up of billions of neurons, with recent estimates hovering around 86 billion (e.g., see Herculano-Houzel, 2009). Brain imaging techniques generally measure activity at the scale of millimeters. For example, a typical fMRI study breaks the brain up into volumes, called *voxels*, that are approximately 27 mm^3 (cubes at 3 mm per dimension) in size. Each voxel contains hundreds of thousands of neurons, and a single image of the brain at one time point will contain thousands of voxels. If we then conduct a whole brain image analysis, we will be doing statistical tests at the level of each of these voxels. With a standard hypothesis testing framework, this means that, just by chance, with a standard alpha of .05 as the allowable false-alarm rate, we may expect to find significant activation in about 5% of the voxels, whether looking for active regions or regions that correlate with some external measure. This has been exemplified in "phantom" scans, the most notorious of which is the "Dead Salmon" study, which showed significant activation in an fMRI image of a dead Atlantic salmon (Bennett, Baird, Miller, & Wolford, 2010).

The solution to this problem of multiple comparisons in a typical cognitive experimental paradigm might be to predetermine the number of comparisons and adjust the alpha level for each comparison so that the overall false-alarm rate is controlled at the desired level. This use of the Bonferroni correction method works well for designs with a small number of desired comparisons, but the consequences for functional imaging studies of the brain are dire given the number of comparisons. This correction is based on dividing the intended familywise error rate (P_{FWE}) among the number of tests conducted. For any family of n values, the probability that all n tests will be less than α is $(1 - \alpha)^n$, which essentially allows us to adjust the FWE by simply testing each voxel at $\alpha_n = P_{FWE}/n$. The problem with such a correction harkens back to the wealth of data in standard fMRI. Imagine we had 1,000 voxels at which we were testing for an effect of our experimental manipulation. Any one voxel would have to reach a probability of less than 0.00005 before we would be willing to say it was in the acceptable limit. For a whole brain, with a conservative estimate of 66,000 voxels, the appropriate correction for a desired alpha of .05 would make require voxels to be significant at height thresholds of 7.6×10^{-7}.

Several approaches have been put forward to address this issue, many of which take into account the spatial correlation in the brain; the number of independent values is actually smaller than the number of voxels because of correlations nearby voxels (due to physiology, preprocessing, etc.). For example, one approach has been to address data locally to control for the FWE. These are akin to some of the less conservative versions of the Bonferroni method (e.g., Hochberg, 1988; Holm, 1979). *Random field theory* (RFT) offers a theoretical distribution to find an appropriate correction (Worsley & Friston, 1995). Put in simplified form, RFT correction involves first establishing the number of resolution elements (*resels*) on the basis of the total number of voxels and the degree to which the data have been smoothed as part of the image preprocessing ($n_{resels} \ll n_{voxels}$). On the basis of these resel counts it is possible to estimate how many blobs of activation would be expected at different thresholds. In practice, RFT correction also adjusts the probabilities on the basis of the size and shape of the activated blobs.

Another alternative is to control the expected proportion of false positives using the *false discovery rate* (FDR; Chumbley & Friston, 2009; Genovese, Lazar, & Nichols, 2002). The FDR is determined from the distribution of probability values in the data. At a given threshold, some number of voxels will emerge as significant (N_S). FDR techniques then estimate how many of these are expected to be false positives. In general, this method is adaptive for neuroimaging because it depends on the amount of signal present and thus it may allow for weaker designs, assuming the data behave according to the assumptions.

For all of these approaches, we can also correct thresholds by considering how meaningful it is to see activation in a single voxel. The first general approach that can address this issue is to constrain the search for activation to hypothesized regions and networks. However, even small brain regions (e.g., the amygdala) are made up of multiple voxels. Therefore, one or two disparate voxels are probably not indicative of an active brain region, and the real interest is in groups of active voxels. Therefore, we can also set the probability of having significant voxels (at a given height threshold) in close spatial proximity. Different combinations of height and extent can be used to establish the same corrected value, allowing some flexibility as a function of the regions one is most interested in observing and how they interact with the critical questions.

CONCLUSION

Although the field of cognitive neuroscience has made efforts to standardize approaches (e.g., Ashby, 2011; Shelton & Greenberg, 2009; Worsley, 1997), the ever-changing scope of the questions being addressed by brain imaging means that the application of statistics must also evolve. Moreover, we need to continue to consider how both the power and limitations of these methods might require more integration into other research domains that address the same research questions (e.g., Pasco Fearon, 2016; Schwartz, Lilienfeld, Meca, & Sauvigné, 2016). In such a dynamic environment, problems will emerge, but an important feature of a rapidly growing research domain is its ability to respond (see Chapter 1, this volume). One of the more encouraging aspects of the field has been its ability to respond to changes and problems as a community. For example, when controversies arose over studies of individual differences in social cognitive neuroscience (e.g., Kriegeskorte, Simmons, Bellgowan, & Baker, 2009; Vul, Harris, Winkielman, & Pashler, 2009), the response was extensive and has led to additional efforts to more carefully address statistical and methodological issues.

Recognizing the many limitations and the approaches to addressing them is a critical part of any research field, and one of the key take-home messages from the preceding discussion is that good research practices in brain imaging are largely good research practices nuanced by the nature of the data that can be acquired. The need to adhere to both the psychological concerns of behavioral experimentation and the physiological and environmental limitations of specific imaging techniques requires that we make decisions about how to balance competing interests. However, the success of cognitive neuroscience in advancing our understanding of how the human mind–brain works suggests that it is well worth the effort.

RECOMMENDED READING

Cabeza, R., & Kingstone, K. (Eds.). (2006). *Handbook of functional neuroimaging of cognition*. Cambridge, MA: MIT Press.

Cacioppo, J. T., Tassinary, L. G., & Berntson, G. G. (2007). *Handbook of psychophysiology*. New York, NY: Cambridge University Press.

Hillary, F. G., & DeLuca, J. (2007). *Functional neuroimaging in clinical populations*. New York, NY: Guilford Press.

Johnston, J. & Parens, E. (Eds.). (2014) *Interpreting neuroimages: An introduction to the technology and its limits*. Garrison, NY: Hastings Center. Retrieved from http://www.thehastingscenter.org/publications-resources/special-reports-2/interpreting-neuroimages-an-introduction-to-the-technology-and-its-limits/

Kanwisher, N., & Duncan, J. (Eds.). (2004). *Functional neuroimaging of visual cognition*. New York, NY: Oxford University Press.

Schwartz, S. J., Lilienfeld, S. O., Meca, A., & Sauvigné, K. C. (2016). The role of neuroscience within psychology: A call for inclusiveness over exclusiveness. *American Psychologist, 71*, 52–70. http://dx.doi.org/10.1037/a0039678

Silbersweig, D., & Stern, E. (2001). *Functional neuroimaging and neuropsychology fundamentals and practice: Convergence, advances and new directions*. Lisse, the Netherlands: Swets & Zeitlinger.

Thatcher, R. W., Hallett, M., Zeffiro, T., John, E. R., & Huerta, M. (Eds.). (1994). *Functional neuroimaging: Technical foundations*. New York, NY: Academic Press.

REFERENCES

Abrams, D. A., Ryali, S., Chen, T., Chordia, P., Khouzam, A., Levitin, D. J., & Menon, V. (2013). Inter-subject synchronization of brain responses during natural music listening. *European Journal of Neuroscience, 37*, 1458–1469. http://dx.doi.org/10.1111/ejn.12173

Aguirre, G. K. (2014). Functional neuroimaging: Technical, logical, and social perspectives. *The Hastings Center Report, 44*, S8–S18. http://dx.doi.org/10.1002/hast.294

Aine, C. J. (1995). A conceptual overview and critique of functional neuroimaging techniques in humans: I. MRI/fMRI and PET. *Critical Reviews in Neurobiology*, *9*, 229–309.

Ashby, F. G. (2011). *Statistical analysis of fMRI data*. Cambridge, MA: MIT Press.

Belliveau, J. W., Kennedy, D. N., Jr., McKinstry, R. C., Buchbinder, B. R., Weisskoff, R. M., Cohen, M. S., . . . Rosen, B. R. (1991, November 1). Functional mapping of the human visual cortex by magnetic resonance imaging. *Science*, *254*, 716–719. http://dx.doi.org/10.1126/science.1948051

Bennett, C. M., Baird, A. A., Miller, M. B., & Wolford, G. L. (2010). Neural correlates of inter-species perspective taking in the post-mortem Atlantic salmon: An argument for proper multiple comparisons correction. *Journal of Serendipitous and Unexpected Results*, *1*(1), 1–5. Retrieved from http://jpeelle.net/reprints/Bennett-2011-Neural_correlates_of_interspecies_perspective_taking.pdf

Button, K. S., Ioannidis, J. P. A., Mokrysz, C., Nosek, B. A., Flint, J., Robinson, E. S. J., & Munafò, M. R. (2013). Power failure: Why small sample size undermines the reliability of neuroscience. *Nature Reviews Neuroscience*, *14*, 365–376. http://dx.doi.org/10.1038/nrn3475

Chumbley, J. R., & Friston, K. J. (2009). False discovery rate revisited: FDR and topological inference using Gaussian random fields. *NeuroImage*, *44*, 62–70. http://dx.doi.org/10.1016/j.neuroimage.2008.05.021

Cohen, J. (1992). A power primer. *Psychological Bulletin*, *112*, 155–159. http://dx.doi.org/10.1037/0033-2909.112.1.155

Cole, D. M., Smith, S. M., & Beckmann, C. F. (2010). Advances and pitfalls in the analysis and interpretation of resting-state fMRI data. *Frontiers in Systems Neuroscience*, *4*, 8. http://dx.doi.org/10.3389/fnsys.2010.00008

David, S. P., Ware, J. J., Chu, I. M., Loftus, P. D., Fusar-Poli, P., Radua, J., . . . Ioannidis, J. P. (2013). Potential reporting bias in fMRI studies of the brain. *PLOS ONE*, *8*(7), e70104. http://dx.doi.org/10.1371/journal.pone.0070104

Davis, P. A. (1939). Effects of acoustic stimuli on the waking human brain. *Journal of Neurophysiology*, *2*, 494–499.

Desmond, J. E., & Glover, G. H. (2002). Estimating sample size in functional MRI (fMRI) neuroimaging studies: Statistical power analyses. *Journal of Neuroscience Methods*, *118*, 115–128. http://dx.doi.org/10.1016/S0165-0270(02)00121-8

Dumas, G., Nadel, J., Soussignan, R., Martinerie, J., & Garnero, L. (2010). Inter-brain synchronization during social interaction. *PLOS ONE*, *5*(8), e12166. http://dx.doi.org/10.1371/journal.pone.0012166

Durnez, J., Degryse, J., Moerkerke, B., Seurinck, R., Sochat, V., Poldrack, R., & Nichols, T. (2016). Power and sample size calculations for fMRI studies based on the prevalence of active peaks. *BioRxiv*. Advance online publication. http://dx.doi.org/10.1101/049429

Epstein, R., Harris, A., Stanley, D., & Kanwisher, N. (1999). The parahippocampal place area: Recognition, navigation, or encoding? *Neuron*, *23*, 115–125. http://dx.doi.org/10.1016/S0896-6273(00)80758-8

Furman, A. J., Clements-Stephens, A. M., Marchette, S. A., & Shelton, A. L. (2014). Persistent and stable biases in spatial learning mechanisms predict navigational style. *Cognitive, Affective, & Behavioral Neuroscience, 14*, 1375–1391.

Genovese, C. R., Lazar, N. A., & Nichols, T. (2002). Thresholding of statistical maps in functional neuroimaging using the false discovery rate. *NeuroImage, 15*, 870–878. http://dx.doi.org/10.1006/nimg.2001.1037

Gusnard, D. A., Raichle, M. E., & Raichle, M. E. (2001). Searching for a baseline: Functional imaging and the resting human brain. *Nature Reviews Neuroscience, 2*, 685–694. http://dx.doi.org/10.1038/35094500

Hartley, T., Maguire, E. A., Spiers, H. J., & Burgess, N. (2003). The well-worn route and the path less traveled: Distinct neural bases of route following and wayfinding in humans. *Neuron, 37*, 877–888. http://dx.doi.org/10.1016/S0896-6273(03)00095-3

Haxby, J. V., Gobbini, M. I., Furey, M. L., Ishai, A., Schouten, J. L., & Pietrini, P. (2001, September 28). Distributed and overlapping representations of faces and objects in ventral temporal cortex. *Science, 293*, 2425–2430. http://dx.doi.org/10.1126/science.1063736

Hayasaka, S., Peiffer, A. M., Hugenschmidt, C. E., & Laurienti, P. J. (2007). Power and sample size calculation for neuroimaging studies by non-central random field theory. *NeuroImage, 37*, 721–730. http://dx.doi.org/10.1016/j.neuroimage.2007.06.009

Herculano-Houzel, S. (2009). The human brain in numbers: A linearly scaled-up primate brain. *Frontiers in Human Neuroscience, 3*, 31. http://dx.doi.org/10.3389/neuro.09.031.2009

Hochberg, Y. (1988). A sharper Bonferroni procedure for multiple tests of significance. *Biometrika, 75*, 800–802. http://dx.doi.org/10.1093/biomet/75.4.800

Holm, S. (1979). A simple sequentially rejective multiple test procedure. *Scandinavian Journal of Statistics, 6*, 65–70.

Kanwisher, N., McDermott, J., & Chun, M. M. (1997). The fusiform face area: A module in human extrastriate cortex specialized for face perception. *The Journal of Neuroscience, 17*, 4302–4311.

Kelley, T. A., Serences, J. T., Giesbrecht, B., & Yantis, S. (2008). Cortical mechanisms for shifting and holding visuospatial attention. *Cerebral Cortex, 18*, 114–125. http://dx.doi.org/10.1093/cercor/bhm036

Kriegeskorte, N., Simmons, W. K., Bellgowan, P. S. F., & Baker, C. I. (2009). Circular analysis in systems neuroscience: The dangers of double dipping. *Nature Neuroscience, 12*, 535–540. http://dx.doi.org/10.1038/nn.2303

Larson, M. J., & Carbine, K. A. (2016). Sample size calculations in human electrophysiology (EEG and ERP) studies: A systematic review and recommendations for increased rigor. *International Journal of Psychophysiology*. Advance online publication. http://dx.doi.org/10.1016/j.ijpsycho.2016.06.015

Lee, M. H., Smyser, C. D., & Shimony, J. S. (2013). Resting-state fMRI: A review of methods and clinical applications. *American Journal of Neuroradiology, 34*, 1866–1872. http://dx.doi.org/10.3174/ajnr.A3263

Logothetis, N. K. (2008, June 12). What we can do and what we cannot do with fMRI. *Nature, 453,* 869–878. http://dx.doi.org/10.1038/nature06976

Maguire, E. A., Burgess, N., Donnett, J. G., Frackowiak, R. S. J., Frith, C. D., & O'Keefe, J. (1998, May 8). Knowing where and getting there: A human navigation network. *Science, 280,* 921–924. http://dx.doi.org/10.1126/science.280.5365.921

Marchette, S. A., Bakker, A., & Shelton, A. L. (2011). Cognitive mappers to creatures of habit: Differential engagement of place and response learning mechanisms predicts human navigational behavior. *The Journal of Neuroscience, 31,* 15264–15268.

Mumford, J. A. (2012). A power calculation guide for fMRI studies. *Social Cognitive and Affective Neuroscience, 7,* 738–742. http://dx.doi.org/10.1093/scan/nss059

Mumford, J. A., & Nichols, T. E. (2008). Power calculation for group fMRI studies accounting for arbitrary design and temporal autocorrelation. *NeuroImage, 39,* 261–268. http://dx.doi.org/10.1016/j.neuroimage.2007.07.061

Nummenmaa, L., Glerean, E., Viinikainen, M., Jääskeläinen, I. P., Hari, R., & Sams, M. (2012). Emotions promote social interaction by synchronizing brain activity across individuals. *Proceedings of the National Academy of Sciences of the United States of America, 109,* 9599–9604. http://dx.doi.org/10.1073/pnas.1206095109

Nummenmaa, L., Smirnov, D., Lahnakoski, J. M., Glerean, E., Jääskeläinen, I. P., Sams, M., & Hari, R. (2014). Mental action simulation synchronizes action–observation circuits across individuals. *The Journal of Neuroscience, 34,* 748–757. http://dx.doi.org/10.1523/JNEUROSCI.0352-13.2014

Pasco Fearon, R. M. (2016). Looking beyond the horizon—innovation in child psychology and psychiatry [Editorial]. *Journal of Child Psychology and Psychiatry, 57,* 213–215. http://dx.doi.org/10.1111/jcpp.12545

Rao, S. M., Bandettini, P. A., Binder, J. R., Bobholz, J. A., Hammeke, T. A., Stein, E. A., & Hyde, J. S. (1996). Relationship between finger movement rate and functional magnetic resonance signal change in human primary motor cortex. *Journal of Cerebral Blood Flow & Metabolism, 16,* 1250–1254. http://dx.doi.org/10.1097/00004647-199611000-00020

Schwartz, S. J., Lilienfeld, S. O., Meca, A., & Sauvigné, K. C. (2016). The role of neuroscience within psychology: A call for inclusiveness over exclusiveness. *American Psychologist, 71,* 52–70. http://dx.doi.org/10.1037/a0039678

Shelton, A. L., & Gabrieli, J. D. E. (2002). Neural correlates of encoding space from route and survey perspectives. *Journal of Neuroscience, 22,* 2711–2717.

Shelton, A. L., & Greenberg, A. S. (2009). Statistical tests and inferences. In L. R. Squire (Ed.), *Encyclopedia of neuroscience* (Vol. 9, pp. 393–400). Oxford, England: Academic Press.

Shelton, A. L., & McNamara, T. P. (2004). Orientation and perspective dependence in route and survey learning. *Journal of Experimental Psychology: Learning, Memory, and Cognition, 30,* 158–170.

Simpson, D. (2005). Phrenology and the neurosciences: Contributions of F. J. Gall and J. G. Spurzheim. *ANZ Journal of Surgery, 75*, 475–482. http://dx.doi.org/10.1111/j.1445-2197.2005.03426.x

Stark, C. E. L., & Squire, L. R. (2001). When zero is not zero: The problem of ambiguous baseline conditions in fMRI. *Proceedings of the National Academy of Sciences of the USA, 98*, 12760–12766. http://dx.doi.org/10.1073/pnas.221462998

Sutton, S., Braren, M., Zubin, J., & John, E. R. (1965, November 26). Evoked-potential correlates of stimulus uncertainty. *Science, 150*, 1187–1188. http://dx.doi.org/10.1126/science.150.3700.1187

Toga, A. W. (Ed.). (2015). *Brain mapping.* London, England: Academic Press.

Vul, E., Harris, C., Winkielman, P., & Pashler, H. (2009). Puzzlingly high correlations in fMRI studies of emotion, personality, and social cognition. *Perspectives on Psychological Science, 4*, 274–290. http://dx.doi.org/10.1111/j.1745-6924.2009.01125.x

Walter, W. G., Cooper, R., Aldridge, V. J., McCallum, W. C., & Winter, A. L. (1964, July 25). Contingent negative variation: An electric sign of sensorimotor association and expectancy in the human brain. *Nature, 203*, 380–384. http://dx.doi.org/10.1038/203380a0

Wernick, M. N., & Aarsvold, J. N. (2004). *Emission tomography: The fundamentals of PET and SPECT.* Amsterdam, the Netherlands: Elsevier.

Wessinger, C. M., VanMeter, J., Tian, B., Van Lare, J., Pekar, J., & Rauschecker, J. P. (2001). Hierarchical organization of the human auditory cortex revealed by functional magnetic resonance imaging. *Journal of Cognitive Neuroscience, 13*, 1–7. http://dx.doi.org/10.1162/089892901564108

Worsley, K. J. (1997). An overview and some new developments in the statistical analysis of PET and fMRI data. *Human Brain Mapping, 5*, 254–258. http://dx.doi.org/10.1002/(SICI)1097-0193(1997)5:4<254::AID-HBM9>3.0.CO;2-2

Worsley, K. J., & Friston, K. J. (1995). Analysis of fMRI time-series revisited—Again. *NeuroImage, 2*, 173–181. http://dx.doi.org/10.1006/nimg.1995.1023

11

SCIENCE IN CLINICAL PSYCHOLOGY

BRIAN M. D'ONOFRIO, RICHARD J. VIKEN,
AND WILLIAM P. HETRICK

KEY POINTS

- The field of clinical psychology must be grounded in scientific epistemology. Both researchers and clinicians must embrace not knowing the answers to key questions and rigorously test competing hypotheses in an iterative manner instead of solely searching for evidence to support one's own hypothesis.
- Research in clinical psychology must leverage major advances and understanding from related disciplines, especially to facilitate the construct, statistical, internal, and external validity of studies.
- Major advances in clinical psychology will require researchers to explore multiple levels of analysis and break down barriers in translational research whereby basic research informs and is informed by applied research.
- Training in clinical psychology must integrate research and clinical activities, with a scientific approach serving as the foundation for both.

http://dx.doi.org/10.1037/0000033-012
Toward a More Perfect Psychology: Improving Trust, Accuracy, and Transparency in Research, M. C. Makel and J. A. Plucker (Editors)

Although there is debate about the role of science in the field of psychology as a whole (e.g., Lilienfeld, 2012), there is great disagreement about the importance (or lack thereof) of science in clinical psychology (Baker, McFall, & Shoham, 2008; McFall, 1991, 2006). In this chapter we emphasize the importance of training and research in clinical psychology that (a) is fundamentally grounded in scientific epistemology, (b) leverages advances in understanding and methods from related disciplines, (c) explores multiple levels of analysis and advances our understanding of questions spanning the continuum from basic to applied research to policy, and (d) integrates experiences from both applied clinical work and research activities. Failing to emphasize these four core principles limits the field's ability to advance knowledge as well as clinical practice. In contrast, training in these principles is now enabling a growing group of clinical scientists to shed great light on the nosology, assessment, etiology, treatment, and prevention of psychological and substance use disorders in their work, both research and clinical. Thus, in this chapter we underscore the importance of training and research to each of these four principles. This is not merely an intellectual exercise; advancing the understanding, treatment, and prevention of psychological and substance use disorders is critically important because of the enormous pain, suffering, and disability such disorders cause (e.g., Murray et al., 2012).

GROUNDING IN SCIENTIFIC EPISTEMOLOGY

In our view, the distinction between clinical scientists and other scientists is primarily one of problem focus. Clinical scientists are focused on describing, measuring, predicting, explaining, preventing, and ameliorating psychopathology problems. Apart from this distinctive problem focus, however, clinical scientists should not differ significantly from other scientists, especially in their epistemology. Not all clinical psychologists or clinical programs share this view, unfortunately. We frequently hear three claims: (a) the foundational research knowledge in clinical psychology is insufficient to guide decision making; (b) clinical issues are too complex to study from a research perspective; and (c) mental health professionals are just trying to help others, so it does not matter what the research states. We would like to briefly address each of these because they greatly influence the amount and quality of clinical research.

First, in our view, complaints about the limited knowledge in clinical psychology are based on a very limited understanding of the very essence of science, which is not a list of facts. We view science instead as an epistemological framework for guiding how we gain knowledge. Instead of basing our beliefs on our assumptions and initial thoughts, scientists seek to test competing hypotheses (e.g., Platt, 1964). By systematically searching for disconfirming evidence—rather than information that merely supports our hypotheses—rigorous research is a safeguard that helps guard against fundamental human biases, such as confirmation bias (Dawes, 1986; O'Donohue, Lilienfeld, & Fowler, 2007) and the availability and representativeness heuristics (Tversky & Kahneman, 1974). Researcher bias certainly can greatly undermine scientific progress, which further highlights the importance of explicitly testing competing hypotheses. Unfortunately, few clinical psychology programs provide training in the philosophy of science (for an accessible introduction, see Chalmers, 2013), even though there have been major calls for such training (O'Donohue, 1989, 2013). A limited understanding of the process of science has therefore also resulted in many clinical psychologists conducting research that solely involves collecting evidence to support their theories. We believe research in the field would be greatly aided by some introductory training in epistemology, emphasizing that science is not memorizing facts; instead, those who excel in research embrace not knowing (a.k.a. "the importance of stupidity"; Schwartz, 2008) and creatively using advances within and outside of psychology to test competing hypotheses.

Second, many clinical psychologists are explicitly trained to believe that clinical issues are too complex to study scientifically. This has been an ongoing debate in clinical psychology (Meehl, 1973a). We acknowledge that we will never truly understand human behavior in all of its complexity, yet researchers must balance this view with the understanding that models of human behavior, which by definition are simplifications of a complex reality, may provide great insight into mental illness. There are countless topics in other disciplines that are complex, but researchers in those fields do not throw up their hands, saying "It's too complex." Would it make sense for researchers to say the world economy or global warming (to give just two examples) are too complex, so we are not going to study them?

Third, many of the debates about the role of science in clinical psychology center on what types of therapy are supported (or not) by scientific evidence, which we discuss below. However, many clinical psychologists dismiss the importance of using empirically supported treatments or revising their treatments on the basis of recent scientific evidence because of the altruistic motives of mental health professionals. However, we want to stress that only a scientific approach can provide critical information about the benefits and risks of interventions. It was only when scientists dared to test the possibility that some treatments may actually cause harm that professionals in the field actually found that many interventions cause more harm than good (Lilienfeld, 2007).

In sum, we believe that research in clinical psychology would be greatly aided if researchers received training in scientific epistemology, embracing not knowing the answers to key questions, and then rigorously testing competing hypotheses, instead of solely trying to gain support for their own hypotheses. This will help guide research that will help us better understand the complexity of mental illness while being cognizant of the fact that throughout history many "interventions" for mental illness actually caused more harm than good.

Making research advances in clinical psychology now frequently requires that individuals and research teams take advances from neighboring disciplines and apply them to clinical questions. Thus, we believe clinical research that relies solely on traditional psychological methods will have a limited ability to answer important clinical questions. Using the four criteria (construct, statistical conclusion, internal, and external validity) set out by Shadish, Cook, and Campbell (2002) to test causal inferences, we now highlight several examples of how clinical psychologists can take advances from neighboring areas to inform clinical research.

There is a rich history in psychology of understanding the importance of construct validity (i.e., the degree to which a measure truly reflects the higher order construct one is studying) when conducting research (Cronbach & Meehl, 1955). Although construct validity is important for many areas, it is particularly important to the field of clinical psychology because of the fuzzy definition of a "mental illness" (Kendler, Zachar, & Craver, 2011; Lilienfeld & Marino, 1995). In fact, a lack of standardized assessments and unlimited flexibility in the creation of variables can lead to unacceptable rates of false positive findings (Simmons, Nelson, & Simonsohn, 2011). Conducting rigorous clinical research therefore requires detailed measurement and the use of sophisticated statistical tools. Unfortunately, the authors of many clinical psychology studies make inferences without considering the limitations in the construct validity and/or do not use modeling techniques that could further enhance the construct validity of a study. To advance the field, clinical psychology researchers should use advanced analytical methods that are focused on measurement, such as latent variable modeling, item response theory, and signal detection theory techniques (e.g., Treat & Viken, 2012).

The field of psychology has not always uniformly embraced advances in statistics. This has greatly limited statistical conclusion validity, the use of the appropriate statistical techniques to examine research questions. For example, the field has been overly reliant on statistical significance levels ($p < .05$) and has failed to appreciate the importance of considering statistical power when designing research studies (Cohen, 1990). Recent major initiatives, however, have called for changes in the manner in which researchers conduct and report their statistical analyses (e.g., focusing on effect sizes and the precision of the estimates; Cumming, 2014). Furthermore, there is a growing awareness that standard analytic practices, such as statistically controlling for measured covariates to account for confounding factors, have many limitations that researchers must consider (Westfall & Yarkoni, 2016). Although controlling for measured covariates may be helpful, this approach can provide quite biased estimates (e.g., regression parameters going in the opposite direction) when assumptions that are unknown to many psychologists are violated (Greenland, Pearl, & Robins, 1999). Although recent initiatives focused on statistics in the field of psychology represent important advances, many researches in clinical psychology have not embraced them fully; many, in fact, have not been trained to do so.

Although many clinical psychology studies are randomized controlled trials, which enable researchers to draw strong causal conclusions, most research in the field must rely on other types of methods. Unfortunately, most studies in the field have limited internal validity (the extent to which one can draw causal conclusions about the relation between two variables). Although most psychologists have been trained to believe that "correlation does not mean causation," many make inappropriate leaps when interpreting their findings. First, they use inappropriate language (e.g., concluding that an exposure "affects" an outcome, although they were not able to test a causal influence) when discussing their results (Kraemer et al., 1997). Second, most studies rely solely on measured covariates to rule out confounding factors, an approach that has significant limitations (Shadish et al., 2002). As a result, researchers in numerous fields have called for studies to use designs that can rule out alternative hypotheses for why an exposure could be associated with an outcome, including the use of family-based designs (see the review in D'Onofrio, Lahey, Turkheimer, & Lichtenstein, 2013). We thus encourage clinical researchers to incorporate design features that rule out alternative explanations for statistical associations.

Finally, there is a growing awareness of the potential limited generalizability of findings from setting to setting, that is, the external validity. Given this, clinical psychologists need to collaborate with researchers in the field of epidemiology to take advantage of sampling strategies and larger sample sizes in observational studies that will enable analyses to explore whether research findings apply across, for example, different racial and/or ethnic groups. Given concerns about discrepancy between findings from highly controlled efficacy and "real-world" effectiveness studies, clinical psychologists also need to collaborate with researchers in basic sciences, such as social psychology, as well as community partners, as exemplified by the growing field of dissemination and implementation science (e.g., Brownson, Colditz, & Proctor, 2012).

Major advances in clinical psychology research now require interdisciplinary training and collaboration. Although many researchers acknowledge the necessity of such efforts, we want to emphasize the importance of interdisciplinary collaboration at all phases of a research project, including the conceptualization, design, implementation, analysis, and interpretation of the results.

EXPLORING MULTIPLE LEVELS OF ANALYSIS
AND TRANSLATIONAL RESEARCH

We believe a very useful heuristic for guiding clinical psychology research is the intersection of two key considerations: (a) exploring multiple levels of analysis and (b) the importance of translational science. We believe that this framework can help guide student training and best help researchers conduct studies that will solve clinical problems.

There is a growing realization that risk factors and protective factors at multiple levels of analysis (i.e., from genes to neighborhoods) are critically important to understanding mental health problems (e.g., Kendler, 2012), but there are two critical questions facing the field when exploring factors at multiple levels. First, there is increasing acknowledgment that the factors underlying mental illness do not operate on the level of psychiatric diagnoses (Persons, 1986). Thus, there are major initiatives from the National Institute for Mental Health, including the Research Domain Criteria (Cuthbert & Insel, 2013), that are focusing on how factors at multiple levels influence underlying processes across multiple disorders. Second, exploring multiple levels brings up the challenging concerns about how reductionist models can explain complex behavior (e.g., Kendler, 2012; Miller & Keller, 2000). Therefore, researchers will need to explore how the factors at lower levels of analysis may profoundly change when exploring higher level phenomena (Anderson, 1972). Thus, we believe that advances in clinical psychology research will rest, in part, on how studies can help us understand processes at multiple levels of analysis, including the difficult job of integrating information across levels.

Translational science can be conceptualized as an emerging discipline dedicated to the transfer of basic scientific methods and findings to human clinical research and then disseminating and implementing human clinical research findings into best practices and public policy (Westfall, Mold, & Fagnan, 2007). This process is depicted as unfolding across a continuum from basic science to human applications and practice-based research, with translational blocks between stages. Appropriately trained clinical scientists are uniquely positioned both to contribute to each stage of research and to develop innovative applications that break through the translational blocks.

Clinical psychologists should be challenged to conceptualize psychopathology by identifying dimensional domains of functioning and using multiple units of analysis to uncover mechanisms that predispose, precipitate, perpetuate, and protect individuals from psychological disorders. Simultaneously, researchers must learn to situate their research questions along the translational continuum to anticipate blocks and expedite innovation. Thus, advances in clinical psychology will come from those with expertise at the intersection of these two frameworks.

INTEGRATING APPLIED CLINICAL WORK
AND RESEARCH ACTIVITIES

One fundamental problem with clinical psychology research is the lack of integration of applied clinical work and research training (Chorpita & Daleiden, 2014). It is no wonder that so many clinical psychologists have difficulty combining research and applied work when training in the two areas is conducted separately. Yet we believe that a scientific approach is absolutely essential in clinical training. For example, there are major reviews of the importance of understanding one's own biases and the major implications this has for conducting clinical work (Meehl, 1973b). In fact, we believe it is unethical to not take a scientific approach to clinical work (Gambrill & Dawes, 2003). Below we provide several examples.

First, there is a rich history of research highlighting the importance of empirically supported assessments (Chapman & Chapman, 1967), which requires training in such assessments and an understanding of how to improve them (Hunsley & Mash, 2007). Second, extensive research has illustrated the importance of using actuarial methods guiding decision making instead of relying on subjective impressions (Grove & Meehl, 1996), in particular because of our innate biases (Dawes, 1986). Third, the importance of using empirically supported interventions has received great attention in the past several decades (e.g., Chambless & Ollendick, 2001), which has been controversial. Yet there is a growing awareness that only by taking a scientific approach to identifying and implementing interventions/preventions can improvements occur in the lives of those who are suffering with mental illness and substance use problems (Institute of Medicine, 2015). Finally, taking a scientifically informed approach to clinical work does not rest solely on using interventions that have been shown to be efficacious or effective in research studies; instead, a scientific approach requires therapists to continually monitor their clients' progress to refine case conceptualization, which can then inform subsequent therapeutic activities (Scott & Lewis, 2015).

Applied clinical work can inform more basic science questions. The translational research framework we discussed above frequently is used to illustrate how basic science can inform more applied work, but we want to stress the importance of the reverse. In fact, this is one of the major advantages of receiving training in clinical psychology: Research should inform, and be informed by, applied clinical work.

There should be no distinction between research and clinical work and practice with regard to scientific process and principles—both should follow the same process. It is critically important to gather information, identify multiple hypotheses, develop creative ways of testing those hypotheses, refine the hypotheses, and continue the process of hypothesis testing in an iterative fashion, regardless of whether one is engaged in research or clinical work.

CONCLUSION

Major advances in clinical psychology research will be made only when the field and researchers (a) embrace the scientific process, (b) collaborate with neighboring disciplines, (c) conduct research that explore multiple levels of analysis and helps break down blocks in translational research, and (d) integrate research and clinical activities. Given this view, there is a growing movement in the field of clinical psychology to specifically train students in these principles, which together are known as the clinical science model of training (McFall, Treat, & Simons, 2015). Again, failing to advance our basic understanding of the field and clinical practice has life-and-death consequences because of the enormous burden of mental and substance use disorders (e.g., Murray et al., 2012).

RECOMMENDED READING

Baker, T. B., McFall, R. M., & Shoham, V. (2009). Current status and future prospects of clinical psychology. *Psychological Science in the Public Interest, 9*, 67–103.

Cummings, G. (2014). The new statistics: Why and how. *Psychological Science, 25*, 7–29.

Kendler, K. S. (2012). The dappled nature of causes of psychiatric illness: Replacing the organic–functional/hardware–software dichotomy with empirically based pluralism. *Molecular Psychiatry, 17*, 377–388.

Lilienfeld, S. O. (2007). Psychological treatments that cause harm. *Perspectives on Psychological Science, 2*, 53–70.

Meehl, P. E. (1973b). Why I do not attend case conferences. In P. E. Meehl (Ed.), *Psychodiagnosis: Selected papers* (pp. 225–302). Minneapolis: University of Minnesota Press.

REFERENCES

Anderson, P. W. (1972, August 4). More is different: Broken symmetry and the nature of the hierarchical structure of science. *Science, 177*, 393–396. http://dx.doi.org/10.1126/science.177.4047.393

Baker, T. B., McFall, R. M., & Shoham, V. (2008). Current status and future prospects of clinical psychology: Toward a scientifically principled approach to mental and behavioral health care. *Psychological Science in the Public Interest, 9*, 67–103. http://dx.doi.org/10.1111/j.1539-6053.2009.01036.x

Brownson, R. C., Colditz, G. A., & Proctor, E. K. (2012). *Dissemination and implementation research in health: Translating science to practice.* New York, NY: Oxford University Press. http://dx.doi.org/10.1093/acprof:oso/9780199751877.001.0001

Chalmers, A. (2013). *What is this thing called science?* Indianapolis, IN: Hacket.

Chambless, D. L., & Ollendick, T. H. (2001). Empirically supported psychological interventions: Controversies and evidence. *Annual Review of Psychology, 52*, 685–716. http://dx.doi.org/10.1146/annurev.psych.52.1.685

Chapman, L. J., & Chapman, J. P. (1967). Genesis of popular but erroneous psychodiagnostic observations. *Journal of Abnormal Psychology, 72*, 193–204. http://dx.doi.org/10.1037/h0024670

Chorpita, B. F., & Daleiden, E. L. (2014). Structuring the collaboration of science and service in pursuit of a shared vision. *Journal of Clinical Child & Adolescent Psychology, 43*, 323–338. http://dx.doi.org/10.1080/15374416.2013.828297

Cohen, J. (1990). Things I have learned (so far). *American Psychologist, 45*, 1304–1312. http://dx.doi.org/10.1037/0003-066X.45.12.1304

Cronbach, L. J., & Meehl, P. E. (1955). Construct validity in psychological tests. *Psychological Bulletin, 52*, 281–302. http://dx.doi.org/10.1037/h0040957

Cumming, G. (2014). The new statistics: Why and how. *Psychological Science, 25*, 7–29. http://dx.doi.org/10.1177/0956797613504966

Cuthbert, B. N., & Insel, T. R. (2013). Toward the future of psychiatric diagnosis: The seven pillars of RDoC. *BMC Medicine, 11*, 126. http://dx.doi.org/10.1186/1741-7015-11-126

Dawes, R. M. (1986). Representative thinking in clinical judgment. *Clinical Psychology Review, 6*, 425–441. http://dx.doi.org/10.1016/0272-7358(86)90030-9

D'Onofrio, B. M., Lahey, B. B., Turkheimer, E., & Lichtenstein, P. (2013). Critical need for family-based, quasi-experimental designs in integrating genetic and social science research. *American Journal of Public Health, 103*(Suppl. 1), S46–S55. http://dx.doi.org/10.2105/AJPH.2013.301252

Gambrill, E., & Dawes, R. M. (2003). Ethics, science, and the helping professions: A conversation with Robyn Dawes. *Journal of Social Work Education, 39*, 27–40.

Greenland, S., Pearl, J., & Robins, J. M. (1999). Causal diagrams for epidemiologic research. *Epidemiology, 10,* 37–48. http://dx.doi.org/10.1097/00001648-199901000-00008

Grove, W. M., & Meehl, P. E. (1996). Comparative efficiency of informal (subjective, impressionistic) and formal (mechanical, algorithmic) prediction procedures: The clinical–statistical controversy. *Psychology, Public Policy, and Law, 2,* 293–323. http://dx.doi.org/10.1037/1076-8971.2.2.293

Hunsley, J., & Mash, E. J. (2007). Evidence-based assessment. *Annual Review of Clinical Psychology, 3,* 29–51. http://dx.doi.org/10.1146/annurev.clinpsy.3.022806.091419

Institute of Medicine. (2015). *Psychosocial interventions for mental and substance use disorders: A framework for establishing evidence-based standards.* Washington, DC: National Academies Press.

Kendler, K. S. (2012). The dappled nature of causes of psychiatric illness: Replacing the organic–functional/hardware–software dichotomy with empirically based pluralism. *Molecular Psychiatry, 17,* 377–388. http://dx.doi.org/10.1038/mp.2011.182

Kendler, K. S., Zachar, P., & Craver, C. (2011). What kinds of things are psychiatric disorders? *Psychological Medicine, 41,* 1143–1150. http://dx.doi.org/10.1017/S0033291710001844

Kraemer, H. C., Kazdin, A. E., Offord, D. R., Kessler, R. C., Jensen, P. S., & Kupfer, D. J. (1997). Coming to terms with the terms of risk. *Archives of General Psychiatry, 54,* 337–343. http://dx.doi.org/10.1001/archpsyc.1997.01830160065009

Lilienfeld, S. O. (2007). Psychological treatments that cause harm. *Perspectives on Psychological Science, 2,* 53–70. http://dx.doi.org/10.1111/j.1745-6916.2007.00029.x

Lilienfeld, S. O. (2012). Public skepticism of psychology: Why many people perceive the study of human behavior as unscientific. *American Psychologist, 67,* 111–129. http://dx.doi.org/10.1037/a0023963

Lilienfeld, S. O., & Marino, L. (1995). Mental disorder as a Roschian concept: A critique of Wakefield's "harmful dysfunction" analysis. *Journal of Abnormal Psychology, 104,* 411–420. http://dx.doi.org/10.1037/0021-843X.104.3.411

McFall, R. M. (1991). Manifesto for a science of clinical psychology. *Clinical Psychologist, 44,* 75–91.

McFall, R. M. (2006). Doctoral training in clinical psychology. *Annual Review of Clinical Psychology, 2,* 21–49. http://dx.doi.org/10.1146/annurev.clinpsy.2.022305.095245

McFall, R. M., Treat, T. A., & Simons, R. F. (2015). Clinical science mode. In R. Cautin & S. Lilienfeld (Eds.), *Encyclopedia of clinical psychology* (pp. 1–9). Cambridge, MA: Wiley-Blackwell. http://dx.doi.org/10.1002/9781118625392.wbecp458

Meehl, P. E. (Ed.). (1973a). *Psychodiagnosis: Selected papers.* Minneapolis, MN: University of Minnesota.

Meehl, P. E. (1973b). Why I do not attend case conferences. In P. E. Meehl (Ed.), *Psychodiagnosis: Selected papers* (pp. 225–302). Minneapolis, MN: University of Minnesota.

Miller, G. A., & Keller, J. (2000). Psychology and neuroscience: Making peace. *Current Directions in Psychological Science, 9*, 212–215. http://dx.doi.org/10.1111/1467-8721.00097

Murray, C. J. L., Vos, T., Lozano, R., Naghavi, M., Flaxman, A. D., Michaud, C., . . . Lopez, A. D. (2012). Disability-adjusted life years (DALYs) for 291 diseases and injuries in 21 regions, 1990–2010: A systematic analysis for the Global Burden of Disease Study 2010. *The Lancet, 380*, 2197–2223. http://dx.doi.org/10.1016/S0140-6736(12)61689-4

O'Donohue, W. (1989). The (even) bolder model. The clinical psychologist as metaphysician–scientist–practitioner. *American Psychologist, 44*, 1460–1468. http://dx.doi.org/10.1037/0003-066X.44.12.1460

O'Donohue, W. (2013). *Clinical psychology and the philosophy of science*. New York, NY: Springer. http://dx.doi.org/10.1007/978-3-319-00185-2

O'Donohue, W. T., Lilienfeld, S. O., & Fowler, K. A. (2007). Science is an essential safeguard against human error. In S. O. Lilienfeld & W. T. O'Donohue (Eds.), *The great ideas of clinical science: 17 principles that every mental health professional should understand* (pp. 3–17). New York, NY: Routledge.

Persons, J. B. (1986). The advantages of studying psychological phenomena rather than psychiatric diagnoses. *American Psychologist, 41*, 1252–1260. http://dx.doi.org/10.1037/0003-066X.41.11.1252

Platt, J. R. (1964). Strong inference: Certain systematic methods of scientific thinking may produce much more rapid progress than others. *Science, 146*, 347–353. http://dx.doi.org/10.1126/science.146.3642.347

Schwartz, M. A. (2008). The importance of stupidity in scientific research. *Journal of Cell Science, 121*, 1771. http://dx.doi.org/10.1242/jcs.033340

Scott, K., & Lewis, C. C. (2015). Using measurement-based care to enhance any treatment. *Cognitive and Behavioral Practice, 22*, 49–59. http://dx.doi.org/10.1016/j.cbpra.2014.01.010

Shadish, W. R., Cook, T. D., & Campbell, D. T. (2002). *Experimental and quasi-experimental designs for generalized causal inference*. New York, NY: Houghton Mifflin.

Simmons, J. P., Nelson, L. D., & Simonsohn, U. (2011). False-positive psychology: Undisclosed flexibility in data collection and analysis allows presenting anything as significant. *Psychological Science, 22*, 1359–1366. http://dx.doi.org/10.1177/0956797611417632

Treat, T. A., & Viken, R. J. (2012). Measuring test performance with signal detection theory techniques. In H. Cooper (Ed.), *APA handbook of research methods in psychology* (pp. 723–744). Washington, DC: American Psychological Association. http://dx.doi.org/10.1037/13619-038

Tversky, A., & Kahneman, D. (1974, September 27). Judgment under uncertainty: Heuristics and biases. *Science, 185,* 1124–1131. http://dx.doi.org/10.1126/science.185.4157.1124

Westfall, J. M., Mold, J., & Fagnan, L. (2007). Practice-based research—"Blue Highways" on the NIH roadmap. *JAMA, 297,* 403–406. http://dx.doi.org/10.1001/jama.297.4.403

Westfall, J., & Yarkoni, T. (2016). Statistically controlling for confounding constructs is harder than you think. *PLOS ONE, 11*(3), e0152719. http://dx.doi.org/10.1371/journal.pone.0152719

12

THE MESSY ART OF DOING SCIENCE: AVOIDING ETHICAL PITFALLS AND PROBLEMATIC RESEARCH PRACTICES

JONATHAN A. PLUCKER AND MATTHEW C. MAKEL

KEY POINTS

- Reading about ethical quandaries is not the same as engaging with them.
- Problematic research practices and false findings can cause public mistrust and be difficult to remove from the public sphere, so avoiding them in the first place is essential.
- Every researcher encounters and must address ethical issues related to their work.

How do we conduct ourselves in ethical ways as scholars? Introductory methods courses and textbooks provide a good outline and framework for appropriate research practices and general ethical guidelines (see the Additional Resources section at the end of this chapter). However, in our

http://dx.doi.org/10.1037/0000033-013
Toward a More Perfect Psychology: Improving Trust, Accuracy, and Transparency in Research, M. C. Makel and J. A. Plucker (Editors)

experience, ethics in the abstract is a different animal from ethical practices in context. Indeed, as one of our colleagues noted in response to a question about how often he faced ethical dilemmas, "If you're actively engaged in research, you're dealing with ethical issues nearly every day." We have certainly found that to be true in our careers.

Our approach in this chapter, therefore, is not to provide a lecture on how one should behave as a researcher; instead, we provide a series of scenarios involving key issues for readers to consider regarding acceptable research practices. The scenarios are based on real situations, although details have occasionally been changed for clarification or simplification purposes. Some scenarios are based on multiple, similar real-life situations, some of which are part of the public record, others of which we have personally observed or with which we ourselves have wrestled. All center on the themes of potential conflicts of interest, uncovering previous errors, issues of authorship, and replicating research. Readers should note, however, that research misconduct and problematic practices are certainly not limited to these themes. Many of these examples are set within the context of psychology, and others come from the medical and other social science fields, but the general principles of research methods and statistical analysis easily extend across many social sciences.[1]

After each scenario, we provide questions to consider, although the questions are not meant to be (and are not) exhaustive. Almost every scenario, like ethical issues in real life, touches on multiple ethical and moral issues that can be weighed and deliberated. As you read through the scenarios, consider not only how you would react within each context but also how you would advise a friend or close colleague who was wrestling with a similar situation. Consider whether your personal decisions and collegial advice would always be the same, or under which conditions they would differ.

WHY IS MISCONDUCT SUCH A BIG DEAL?

People-pleasing tendencies combined with opportunities for self-benefit can contribute to some motivated decision making, especially when the "losers" in the decision can often be a distant, invisible, or unknown "other." Fraud and false findings are particularly troublesome in science because they can

---

[1]We also refer readers and instructors to other sources of vignettes and case studies, including those from the National Science Foundation (http://www.nsf.gov/bfa/dias/policy/hsfaqs.jsp) and the American Psychological Association (http://www.apa.org/monitor/2014/01/research-misconduct.aspx).

often be sticky (Heath & Heath, 2007; Lewandowsky, Ecker, Seifert, Schwarz, & Cook, 2012). By *sticky*, we mean that they are still believed to be true even after they have been debunked. In the case of a researcher who falsely linked autism with vaccinations, the article was brought under scrutiny relatively quickly but was not retracted until nearly a decade later (Editors of *The Lancet*, 2010). In the intervening time, it was cited by thousands of researchers and, perhaps more dangerously, became the foundation of many activist groups advocating against vaccinations. Even though the research—and the researcher's motivations—have been widely discredited, the original study and resulting conspiracy theories remain a major public health issue 20 years later. In a more recent case, in which a junior scholar was found to have misrepresented survey incentives and sponsorship as well as likely fabricated analyses, which happened after the reproducibility movement had begun to grow, retraction came much more quickly (within 5 months; McNutt, 2015). This shrinking of time to retraction is heartening but may not be representative of the lag time for all retractions.

Retractions on the whole have been rapidly increasing for the past decade, increasing from 30 to more than 400 each year (Van Noorden, 2011). When we lose confidence in the veracity of research, the entire foundation of science within a field can be destroyed. Also, given the public and private investment in research, misconduct and questionable practices extend credibility crises and eat up precious resources that could be put to better use by other researchers. In other words, psychology needs to get its ethical house in order, which was one of the driving factors for us to put together this book.

CONFLICTS OF INTEREST

Scenario A

A colleague approaches you and asks for your help with a delicate situation. She has been conducting several externally funded research projects, some through her university center and some through a private company that she set up. She is wondering if you would be willing to serve as a "principal investigator in name only" on a pending project. You learn that the funder strongly prefers that the study be run through the university, and your colleague wants you to serve as principal investigator, then subcontract much of the work to her private company. You agree, but you learn soon thereafter that your colleague had not declared any potential conflicts of interest to the university for the projects run through her private company and not the university.

- Is it the responsibility of individuals to report on their colleagues' potential conflicts of interest?
- If the work is being done successfully and "no one is being hurt," do you have the same obligations to act as when things are not going well?
- To whom should you turn to take appropriate action?
- If all explicit regulations have been followed, but you are still not comfortable with being involved, what is the best course of action?

Scenario B

A researcher has a financial interest in a new vaccine to prevent a common and serious childhood illness. However, there is a well-established, widely used alternative vaccine, and there is little market pressure for a new option. The researcher publishes an article containing a series of case studies of children with developmental disabilities, positing that all of them developed symptoms for the first time after receiving the long-standing vaccine. The article concludes with a strong cautionary note about the possibility that the vaccine causes developmental disabilities. However, the conflict of interest is not discovered for several years, at which point the article has helped fuel conspiracy theories that the vaccine is dangerous for children. Subsequent replication efforts find no evidence of a vaccine–disability link, and the journal is forced to retract the article after the conflict of interest and possible data fabrication are discovered. However, the researcher continues to give public talks and appear in the media to make claims based on the original, now-debunked study.[2]

- What are a researcher's ethical obligations if his or her work is retracted?
- Is the lack of contrition relevant here, or is that just human nature?
- Does the journal in which the original research was published share some of the blame for publishing a controversial article that was easily debunked on closer examination?
- What do such examples do to your confidence in other research? Is this an isolated incident, or an indication of a flawed system?

---

[2]Data from Editors of *The Lancet* (2010).

Scenario C

As part of a large research team, you are asked to step in to help run a project when the project director has to take some time away from work to deal with some personal issues. The research goes well, and the project is renewed for the next grant cycle. A similar issue occurs as the extension nears its end, and you and your colleagues again assume responsibility for the grant activities and construction of the final report. The funder, unaware of the behind-the-scenes complications but quite happy with the results, offers to support a third year of the research project. But the project director announces she is moving to a new institution and has convinced the funder to move the project to the new organization, putting at risk the jobs of the colleagues who helped rescue the project.

- Does this scenario represent any ethical issues, or is it "just one of those things that happens?"
- Where do an individual researcher's ethical responsibilities lie in a choice between protecting the research team/center/ institution versus protecting the integrity of the research?
- Are there steps that could have been taken earlier to communicate effort of various contributors so the funder would be aware of what was happening? Would such steps be necessary or helpful?

Scenario D

Your employer has a strict antinepotism policy that does not allow spouses to hire or supervise each other. One of your colleagues asks you to serve as the supervisor of record for one of his graduate students, whom he recently married, with the understanding that you wouldn't have any real responsibility, given that student will actually be working directly for her husband. You are also led to believe that your bosses are willing to turn a blind eye to the arrangement. Things proceed without incident for a couple years, until a routine audit leads to questions about the supervisory relationship, and you are asked to speak to the auditors.

- Who should have been responsible for reporting (or preventing) the conflict of interest? Or for reporting the violation of university policy?
- Who is the best person to turn to in your department, school, or university when approached with such a proposition?
- To what extent should your actions be to extricate yourself from this situation, and to what extent is it your responsibility to make sure that you aren't simply passing the buck to someone else in your center, program, or department?

UNCOVERING PREVIOUS ERRORS
AND POSSIBLE MISCONDUCT

Scenario E

A research team from a prestigious institution publishes findings that strongly advocate for a particular policy (and a controversial one, at that). These suggestions are taken up by numerous policymakers and implemented in many locations. A few years later, a graduate student contacts the research team, asking for their data and analysis plan. The authors oblige, but the graduate student then uncovers that the original research team had mistakenly left some relevant data out of their analyses. With the full data included, the results show the *opposite* of the original results, suggesting a policy that completely contradicts the original authors' suggestion. They acknowledge their mistake but stand firmly behind their original conclusions.[3]

- What is the correct action in this case for a journal editor? Retraction? Correction?
- Is it the responsibility of the original source of publication to deal with the error?
- What is the role of the reviewers in this case? Should they have been expected to re-create and recalculate all analyses to check all calculations?
- Should the article be sent back through the review process to assess whether the authors should be allowed to maintain their original position within the peer review environment?
- Given the attention the original article received, not to mention the error, any subsequent peer review would not be blind. How should this influence the editor's decision?

Scenario F

Within a few years of the death of an eminent psychologist, who often espoused controversial, provocative views, evidence is found of his possible data fabrication. Many of the statistical results in the famous researcher's studies are determined to be highly unlikely and probably the result of fabricated data. Furthermore, there are accusations that two of his coauthors did not exist and were in fact created by the researcher to help distract reviewers from his fabrications. The psychologist's supporters push back aggressively on

---

[3]Data from http://www.bbc.com/news/magazine-22223190

the accusations, hypothesizing that some of the data may have been lost during a fire that destroyed many of the team's records, that unlikely results do not necessarily always reflect fraud, and that the psychologist may have used pseudonyms for his coauthors. One of the psychologist's strongest defenders eventually writes a biography of the researcher, in which he concludes that some form of misconduct probably occurred.[4]

- How should the field respond to the ethical cloud now hanging over this body of research?
- What if subsequent work by other scholars, not tainted by concerns about misconduct, found results similar to the possibly fraudulent research?
- To what degree should a researcher receive the benefit of the doubt when such concerns are raised? Does the eminence of the researcher matter?
- To what degree is due process important in such instances?

Scenario G

A junior researcher, in reading a senior colleague's application for research funding, suspects that the section on "prior research" being used to justify the proposed research and provide evidence of successful pilot work is fabricated. The junior researcher looks through prior proposals submitted by her colleague, some of which have been funded, and finds several similarly questionable sections. In the course of a subsequent investigation, the senior researcher admits to fabricating prior research sections in many proposals over the course of his career.[5]

- Given that the fabricated sections were used to obtain public research funding, what are reasonable penalties for these actions?
- To whom should the junior researcher report this type of concern (e.g., the department chair, the university research office, the funding agencies)? What are pros and cons of each strategy?
- What checks and balances could be implemented to avoid such problems in the future?

Scenario H

One of the country's top psychologists fabricates data used in several dozen papers. The researcher eventually admits his misconduct, which

---

[4]Data from http://www.intelltheory.com/burtaffair.shtml
[5]Data from http://ori.hhs.gov/press-release-poehlman

includes providing fake data for a number of his students' doctoral dissertations. Several investigations conclude that he was able to perpetrate his fraud for many years because he was viewed as a superstar, and anomalous results were therefore not questioned. In addition, his work was "replicated," which helped mask his deceit, but the replications appeared only in multistudy papers on which he was an author. Despite the damage done to his university, his former students' and collaborators' careers, and the funding agencies who supported his research, he is punished with community service and a loss of retirement benefits that many feel are rather minor. Reviewers note that the psychologist's seemingly contrite memoir, published a couple years after the misconduct was admitted, contains several lines from other authors that are not identified as quotes and only attributed in the book's appendix.[6]

- Should the scale of the fraud influence the punishments for the misconduct?
- Should the number and type of victims influence the punishments for the misconduct?
- How could the students have better protected themselves during the dissertation process?
- Do your feelings change if the findings had been applied to a particularly vulnerable group (e.g., the homeless) versus being entirely laboratory based and never implemented in policy?

Scenario I

An article is published indicating that x is highly correlated with y, and the research receives significant coverage in the media and significant attention among policymakers. Several years later, better, more psychometrically sound measures of both x and y are developed. Research relying on these new measures finds that x is only moderately correlated with y, suggesting implications different from those of the original study.

- How should the new results be reported to researchers, the public, and policymakers?
- Should the older article be retracted?
- What if the new research finds that x is now negatively related with y?

---

[6]Data from http://retractionwatch.com/category/by-author/diederik-stapel/

Scenario J

You are reviewing a manuscript, and you feel confident that the authors made an error in the statistical analysis that they chose to use to answer their research questions.

- Are the data now worthless, or can the authors ethically run a different set of analyses?
- Do the authors have to disclose that they originally ran a different set of analyses on their data?
- What if the authors disagree with your conclusion that different analyses are needed? Can they make the claim that reanalyzing their data a different way could consist of "double dipping?"
- What if the authors agree to post their data for any reader to reanalyze?

Scenario K

An article on the efficacy of a particular clinical trial is published in a journal that requires that all data be shared publicly, and the article receives substantial media attention. The data are initially shared online but then are taken down, with the authors claiming that they do not have permission to share their data. A well-established researcher, not affiliated with the article, questions the findings publicly on social media and provides detailed questions about how he believes the study to be faulty in its methods, analyses, and conclusions. The researcher also points out that although the consent form did not specifically ask for permission to share data, it uses language similar to those in consent forms for studies in which data have been shared.[7]

- If the data are not posted, should the journal retract the article?
- If journals require data to be shared, should they require that the data be sent to the journal rather than have the authors post it on a departmental or third-party site?
- If the authors had published in a journal that did not require data sharing, would the skeptic have less firm grounds to lodge his complaints?
- Given that the external researcher cannot substantiate many of his questions without access to the data, should he have aired his accusations publicly before confirming his suspicions?

---

[7]Data from http://retractionwatch.com/2015/12/16/plos-one-issues-editors-note-over-disputed-chronic-fatigue-research/

AUTHORSHIP ISSUES

Scenario L

A student completes a master's thesis in which his major advisor carries much of the load: suggesting the study idea, arranging for access to the participants, funding the costs of the study, connecting the student with a statistician to help crunch the numbers, and so on. The student shows no interest in publishing the study but decides to convert the thesis into an article after encouragement from his advisor. During the manuscript preparation, much of the Introduction and Discussion sections are written by the advisor. When order of authorship is discussed, the advisor recommends that the order be: the advisor, the student, then the statistician. The student agrees, but as they prepare the final manuscript the statistician objects, noting that students are almost always first author on the paper emanating from their thesis or dissertation, regardless of the actual division of labor during the research and manuscript preparation.

- To what degree should actual effort be reflected in order of authorship?
- Should effort be a factor in authorship if the individual is paid for the work?
- Should authorship be determined by the "inspiration" for developing the study?
- Does it matter whether the paper in question is based on a thesis/dissertation or a regular research project?
- Would things differ if those involved were a postdoctoral trainee/supervisor or assistant professor/department chair?
- How could this dilemma have been avoided?

Scenario M

A famous scientist files a formal misconduct complaint against a junior colleague working in his laboratory; specifically, the scientist claims that the junior colleague copied sections from one of their published articles and used that section in one of the junior colleague's subsequent articles. When the investigating committee noted that the famous scholar was an author on both articles and therefore carried some level of responsibility for any plagiarism, the senior researcher becomes indignant, noting that he was an author but hadn't written any of either article; therefore, he was not responsible for any issues with the articles.

- What are the ethical responsibilities of an author or a principal investigator on a grant?
- Do the content and length of the potentially plagiarized material matter in the determination of misconduct?
- Does it matter which sections were copied? What if the sections were from the Method section or from the literature review summarizing previous work?
- Does the Association for Psychological Science practice (and others like it) of listing how each author contributed to the article help alleviate this problem?

Scenario N

Reviews for one of your manuscripts are positive, and the editor indicates a willingness to accept the paper after minor revisions. But the editor suggests that a revised paper will stand a better chance of success if you (a) drop Study 2 because it makes the paper too complicated and (b) cite more of the editor's own research.

- What are the pros and cons of agreeing to the editor's "suggestions"?
- How should you respond to the editor?
- Would it make a difference if the suggestion came from a reviewer?
- Would it be appropriate to make the editor's request public by posting it in a blog (or an edited book), or should you get the editor's consent prior to posting?
- Is there a cost to adding more citations to your manuscript? If so, what is it?

Scenario O

A senior researcher is invited to contribute to an edited volume. She asks her graduate student to take the lead on the chapter. The two of them draft a chapter and receive positive initial feedback from the book editors, who submit a lightly revised version of the chapter along with the rest of the chapters to the publisher for external review. However, the editors then send a copyright permission form to the chapter authors, and the graduate student feels strongly that she should maintain copyright of her own work. After several rounds of discussion and negotiation with the publisher (who feels they need to maintain copyright so that, among other reasons, foreign translation rights for the entire book can be sold), the graduate student withdraws the chapter from the book.

- When should authors maintain copyright of their own work?
- Would the situation be different if it were an invitation to write a commentary in a journal?
- If the publisher routinely grants republication and reuse rights to authors, is it acceptable to jeopardize the publication of the book—or at least seriously delay it—over a matter of principle?
- Should the editors have sent the copyright permission form to authors before the writing of the chapter, or perhaps immediately after the chapter authors agreed to write a chapter?
- Does the senior researcher have a role to play in this scenario?

REPLICATING RESEARCH

Scenario P

When attempting to replicate their previously published study, a research team simply copies and pastes the Method section from the previous article, rather than rewrite it for the replication manuscript. One member of the team worries that this is a form of self-plagiarism, whereas other team members scoff at the suggestion that reusing their own material in this way could be viewed as improper.

- Is this plagiarism? Can you plagiarize yourself in this way, or is it reasonable to copy highly technical methods descriptions (e.g., if you use the same instrument in most of your work, should you be expected to rewrite the instrument description in every article)?
- What if the researchers begin the Method section with, "Replicating the method from . . ." and cite their previous article? Is that sufficient attribution to communicate to readers?

Scenario Q

A researcher unsuccessfully attempts to replicate a study and contacts the original authors to determine whether she made a mistake when replicating the methods. The researchers of the original study reveal that they attempted the study six times and were successful only on the final attempt but that they published only the results of that sixth attempt and neglected to note the five failed trials.[8]

- What obligation do researchers have to describe their efforts fully and transparently?
- What pressures would lead authors to omit information about failed experiments?
- How would you respond to this new information about the original study? Does it alter your confidence in the published findings?

CONCLUSION

We have our own answers for how we would react (and how we would hope our colleagues would react) to these scenarios, but we are purposefully not sharing them. We won't be there when readers face these or other ethical situations, and there likely will not be someone with you who can tell you what to do, although getting input from an external source (or sources) whom you trust may be helpful.

If your answers to any of these scenarios came to you quickly and easily, this may mean you have a clear understanding of your ethical grounding. However, readers may want to consider how others might come to an alternative conclusion. At what points do the contrasting decisions differ, and is there any room for "reasonable" minds to differ at any of these junctures? We purposefully chose scenarios in which at least one professional has held in the past contrasting views from his or her colleagues. If the answers were all easy, then this chapter (and this book) wouldn't be necessary, and many of the problems that are discussed in this chapter would never have happened. But they did happen, sometimes very publicly, sometimes to us as we did our own work. As we noted at the beginning of this chapter, you will run into ethical dilemmas if you are actively doing research. The key is to be self-vigilant and self-reflective as you build your career.

ADDITIONAL RESOURCES

American Psychological Association. (n.d.). *Research misconduct.* Retrieved from http://www.apa.org/research/responsible/misconduct/
This is a great source for information about misconduct and best practices in teaching and research.

---

[8]Data from http://www.reuters.com/article/us-science-cancer-idUSBRE82R12P20120328

U.S. Department of Health and Human Services, Office of Research Integrity: http://ori.hhs.gov

The Office of Research Integrity is considered one of the best resources for information on research ethics and misconduct.

Resnik, D. B. (2015). *What is ethics in research & why is it important?* Retrieved from http://www.niehs.nih.gov/research/resources/bioethics/whatis/

This is a solid, if life sciences focused, overview of key issues of research ethics and norms of practice.

Committee on Publication Ethics: http://publicationethics.org/

This organization provides advice to editors and publishers on publication ethics.

REFERENCES

Editors of *The Lancet.* (2010). Retraction—Ileal-lymphoid-nodular hyperplasia, non-specific colitis, and pervasive developmental disorder in children. *The Lancet, 375,* 445. http://dx.doi.org/10.1016/S0140-6736(10)60175-4

Heath, C., & Heath, D. (2007). *Made to stick: Why some ideas survive and others die.* New York, NY: Random House.

Lewandowsky, S., Ecker, U. K. H., Seifert, C. M., Schwarz, N., & Cook, J. (2012). Misinformation and its correction: Continued influence and successful debiasing. *Psychological Science in the Public Interest, 13,* 106–131. http://dx.doi.org/10.1177/1529100612451018

McNutt, M. (2015, February 20). Editorial retraction. *Science, 347,* 834. http://dx.doi.org/10.1126/science.347.6224.834-a

Van Noorden, R. (2011, October 5). Science publishing: The trouble with retractions. *Nature, 478,* 26–28. http://dx.doi.org/10.1038/478026a

IV

REPRODUCIBILITY

13

DATA REANALYSIS AND OPEN DATA

JELTE M. WICHERTS

KEY POINTS

- Research data need to be kept after publication for at least 5 years and should be shared with scientific peers for verification purposes.
- Data can also be shared openly (by means of data repositories or data papers) or with other researchers for secondary use.
- Despite a common reluctance to share data, sharing is associated with many benefits for science and the sharing researcher.
- Benefits of data sharing include abiding by the scientific norms of openness and communality and increased credits and citations.
- Keeping and sharing data require solid data management, including safe storage of raw and processed data, meta-data, and syntaxes used in analyses.

http://dx.doi.org/10.1037/0000033-014
Toward a More Perfect Psychology: Improving Trust, Accuracy, and Transparency in Research, M. C. Makel and J. A. Plucker (Editors)

Although data sharing, open data, reanalyses, and secondary analyses are of general scientific interest, in this chapter I introduce them by sharing the personal experiences that shaped my thinking about these issues. My PhD dissertation concerned generational increases in average IQs that have been documented in much of the western world (Flynn, 1987). I found this so-called Flynn effect puzzling; how could validated IQ tests, with their high heritabilities and solid interindividual stabilities (e.g., Mackintosh, 2011), also show such strong mean increases in as little as a decade? I set out to study this question by testing for measurement invariance of IQ tests across cohorts of test-takers. Applying a psychometric technique called *multigroup confirmatory factor analysis* to data from different cohorts could help answer whether people have truly become smarter or instead simply somewhat better at completing IQ subtests. I needed IQ data. Yet most of the researchers or test publishers I contacted simply had not kept those data.

This struck me as weird given that the very phenomenon I was studying meant that IQ norms become obsolete quite quickly and that collecting data with individually administered IQ tests for norming purposes is expensive. Most of the researchers I contacted admitted to having lost data files from older articles, or lacking the time to retrieve them in useful format. In the end, I found old (and new) IQ data reported in a test manual, in an article's data table, in a (dusty, I suppose) file drawer of a Belgian intelligence researcher in his late 80s, in a data repository that had recently gone online, on a floppy disk (remember those?) from a test publisher, and in the archives of a group of behavior geneticists who have long acknowledged the value of solid data management. The secondary analyses of the old data showed a consistent pattern of failures of measurement invariance over time, indicating that the Flynn effect is at least in part an artifactual. The reanalysis article (Wicherts et al., 2004), which included as coauthors several researchers who shared their data, has now been cited more than 180 times.

My quest for older IQ data highlighted the fact that potentially valuable data are often hard to locate and/or reuse and might get lost fairly rapidly. The problem of data loss over time is increasingly being noted in many scientific fields (Alsheikh-Ali, Qureshi, Al-Mallah, & Ioannidis, 2011; Freese, 2007; Vines et al., 2014) and is rightly denoted in the medical sciences as "research waste" (Chan et al., 2014). Waste of data is problematic because it prevents data reuse in secondary analyses that address novel questions and impedes (independent) verification of results through reanalysis. At the same time, the sharing of research data is associated with many benefits for both science and the sharing scientist (Wicherts, 2013), including increased citation scores (Piwowar, Day, & Fridsma, 2007).

REQUESTING DATA FOR VERIFICATION PURPOSES

There is wide agreement that researchers should keep their data after publication for a number of years to allow for verification of the results. Most ethical guidelines of professional organizations, academic institutions, and academic publishers indicate that data should not only be kept safely for at least 5 (sometimes even 10) years but also should be made available in a useful format to academic peers who wish to verify the results in the published article through reanalysis. For instance, the American Psychological Association's (APA's; 2017) *Ethical Principles of Psychologists and Code of Conduct* (http://www.apa.org/ethics/code/) contains the following statement:

> After research results are published, psychologists do not withhold the data on which their conclusions are based from other competent professionals who seek to verify the substantive claims through reanalysis and who intend to use such data only for that purpose, provided that the confidentiality of the participants can be protected and unless legal rights concerning proprietary data preclude their release.

The sharing of data for this purpose aligns well with the core scientific norms of openness and communality (Merton, 1973; Hartgerink & Wicherts, 2016). Data should also be made available to editors during the review process, with a failure to comply potentially leading to rejection of the manuscript (APA, 2010).

Among its other publication rights forms, APA lets its authors sign a formal statement that includes the guideline given above. Despite these steps, many authors fail to share their data upon request after publication. After several instances of a failure to share data, my colleagues and I decided to check the availability of data from 141 articles published in four of APA's top journals (Wicherts, Borsboom, Kats, & Molenaar, 2006). Our request was specifically designed to follow APA's standard and referred to our wish to check the robustness of the published results against the potential influence of outliers through reanalysis (the text of the email is available in Wicherts, Bakker, & Molenaar, 2011). Notwithstanding the signed statements and the fact that the articles from which we requested data were fairly recent (all were about 18 months old at the time), many corresponding authors proved unwilling or unable to share.

"I will send you the data within a few days" is what one corresponding author wrote us. It has been more than 10 years now, and so this promise has not been kept (although in all honesty we did not pursue the question further after having sent two reminders). This author's unfulfilled promise to share was quite common; it happened for about 20% of the articles. So many corresponding authors were at least willing to share but simply lacked the time to either locate the data files and/or to organize and document them in such a way that we, as peers, would be able to use them. Some of the data sets that were shared were poorly documented, with authors apologizing that they (and this was a year and a half after publication) no longer remembered what the variables named VAR00001, VAR00002, and so on (i.e., the default SPSS variable names) actually represented or how certain variables were coded (e.g., whether the "1" represented male or female for the variable gender). Thus, the failure to share was often due to both substandard archiving and poor documentation of the data files, although a more critical interpretation would be that at least some researchers might have had something to hide. The modal response, occurring with 35% of the articles, was a refusal or expressed inability to share the data, for reasons such as a loss of files on old computers, or because the student or research assistant keeping the data had left, and so on. In a handful of cases the refusal was caused by ethical guidelines stipulated by institutional review boards or ownership issues; one author stated that (s)he was "afraid" that our request was "not possible." In several cases, we were asked to seek institutional review board approval for our reuse, or to send formal letters, sometimes even including our full resumés. In the end, after sending two reminders as well as these letters and our resumes, 27% of the 141 authors we had contacted shared some data (Wicherts et al., 2006). Some of the shared data were very well documented, whereas others were rather difficult to reuse. Note that the APA guideline does refer to legal propriety rights that might impede sharing. The refusals because of ownership were seldom legally supported (e.g., by ownership documents or contracts), although in some cases we were referred to others, or our request was forwarded without us getting a response. A few corresponding authors indicated that the data could not be shared because they were also meant to be used in further studies. I discuss these reasons for not sharing below.

Our study showed that almost three quarters of psychology researchers could not or did not share their data for verification purposes. Earlier similar studies in the 1960s (Wolins, 1962) and 1970s (Craig & Reese, 1973) had yielded positive response rates of 24% and 38%, respectively. A recent conceptual replication of Wicherts et al.'s (2006) study (Vanpaemel, Vermorgen, Deriemaecker, & Storms, 2015) involving 394 articles published in four APA journals in 2012 showed a positive response rate of 38% and hence little sign of improvement. This low sharing rate occurred despite the recent wide debate on reproducibility in psychology and in spite of the fact of the many benefits associated with sharing (Destro Bisol et al., 2014; Nosek & Bar-Anan, 2012; Nosek, Spies, & Motyl, 2012; Wicherts & Bakker, 2012).

BENEFITS OF DATA SHARING

The first benefit of data sharing is somewhat negative. Albeit a rare occurrence, some researchers feel inclined to present data that are falsified or fabricated altogether (see Hartgerink & Wicherts, 2016). Exposure of research misconduct is greatly facilitated by having the raw data (Simonsohn, 2013). Diederik Stapel is a case in point, because his fraudulent data included weird patterns that led the junior researchers who worked with him to eventually blow the whistle in 2011. The patterns that they discovered included large effect sizes despite scales showing very low reliabilities (rendering such large effects psychometrically curious) and apparently copy-and-pasted sections of data that appeared in files from different studies that Stapel had presented as being completely different in terms of design and sample. The later investigation into Stapel's work exposed further blatant problems in the data files, which helped determine which articles needed to be retracted for reporting on fabricated data (Levelt, Drenth, & Noort, 2012).

One of Stapel's now-retracted papers was among the 141 articles from which we requested the data in 2005, so hindsight bias forces me to claim that Stapel's exposure could have been greatly expedited had we gotten a hold of those data at that time (although we had no reason to doubt his integrity then). Another recent case of potential research misconduct leading to a retraction of a widely publicized *Science* paper also came to light after scrutiny of the raw data file, which also showed anomalies and signs of copying and pasting (Broockman, Kalla, & Aronow, 2015; McNutt, 2016). In that study, which was in the field of political science, the data were available because it is more common in political science to share data as a so-called replication file, which in this case led a shift retraction of the contested article. Thus, having the data available for verification is seen as an effective method to deter and detect scientific misconduct (Simonsohn, 2013; Wicherts, 2011), and it greatly helps subsequent investigations of the works by the supposed perpetrator.

The second benefit of sharing data after publication is that results are typically reported only very succinctly in research articles, thereby leaving out a great deal of information that can be crucial for certain readers and interesting for future use. Such information is often more relevant for readers than authors themselves might realize, and in some cases a lack of information may even amount to questionable research practices (see also Hartgerink & Wicherts, 2016). One often-heard reason for incompleteness in presenting results is readability. Another reason for the brevity of reporting results is, or actually was, a "limitation of journal space," which has become an anachronism with the vast majority of journals nowadays offering the option to include links to data repositories or the option to upload supplementary online materials (including full materials and data). Future readers might want to obtain information about the results that are not reported in the article but can be readily retrieved from the data file. For instance, someone reading the article might want to conduct a replication that requires item-level statistics on a certain test, or correlations between variables not given in the article. Obtaining this information will assist in setting up the new study in which the authors will certainly acknowledge the original authors by citing them. In fact, research has found that sharing data is associated with an increase in citations (Piwowar et al., 2007). In addition, sharing data might open the door for future collaborations and will almost certainly be seen as positive by one's scientific peers (Wicherts, 2013; Wicherts & Bakker, 2012).

A common reason for requesting data (or additional summary results that require an analysis of the data) is the desire to include the study in a meta-analysis or systematic review. Many meta-analyses require such additional information (e.g., means and standard deviations for subgroups not analyzed in the original article), and a recent development in meta-analysis involves the use of raw data that can help answer many more questions related to person-level moderators (Cooper & Patall, 2009). Similarly, computing standard errors for within-subject designs often requires correlations typically missing from articles. Also, it may well be that a meta-analysis concerns certain results that were not of interest to the original research and hence not reported, such as a meta-analysis considering gender or age differences in variables that were merely used as covariates in the original paper. In such instances, too, one's original study could be included in the meta-analysis only if the data are still available and the required results are shared. Such sharing also potentially increases the impact of the original paper and so is not only beneficial for science but also for the sharing researcher.

A third advantage of sharing data concerns the value of verification and emerges because statistical analyses of data are complex and therefore prone to error. Sharing can help correct these errors and might even help avoid having them appear in print altogether. Older studies (Rossi, 1987; Wolins, 1962) and more recent ones indicate a worryingly high rate of statistical errors in articles published in psychology (Bakker & Wicherts, 2011, 2014; Petrocelli, Clarkson, Whitmire, & Moon, 2013; Wicherts et al., 2011), and there is little reason to believe that related fields are not similarly affected. Large-scale studies that have addressed errors in the reporting of p values from F, t, z, and chi-square tests show errors in about half of psychology articles, with about 12% of articles showing at least one statistical conclusion that appears to be erroneous (Nuijten, Hartgerink, van Assen, Epskamp, & Wicherts, 2016). Because their methods entail the recomputation of p values on the basis of test results (e.g., F values and associated dfs), the check for errors in these studies is conservative and hence the actual error rate is likely to be higher. Reanalysis of the data is the preferred way to detect reporting errors or other mistakes in the analysis, and it is quite likely that researchers who know that their data could be scrutinized might double-check their results more diligently before publication, thereby lowering the error rate in the literature (as has happened with image checks in some biomedical journals, as discussed by Hartgerink & Wicherts, 2016).

In a follow-up study of our 2005 data request (Wicherts et al., 2011), we found that articles from which the data were not shared showed appreciably more reporting errors than articles from which data were shared for verification purposes. Even though the misreporting of nonsignificant p values as being significant is seen as a (deliberate) questionable research practice (John, Loewenstein, & Prelec, 2012), the appearance of such erroneous results might be due to honest error. It is possible that the association between errors and failure to share data is caused by poor data documentation, which heightens both the likelihood of error and the possibility that the data cannot be shared later (Wicherts et al., 2011). Regardless of the reasons why researchers failed to share data of articles with more errors, our result indicated that it will be hard to get to the bottom of the errors reported in the articles from which data were lost or unavailable. Hence, the failure to share data greatly impedes the self-correcting mechanisms of science.

Errors are easily made when analyzing data and presenting the results, and so it is desirable to have the data available to correct those errors later, or even to avoid errors in the first place. Moreover, it is good practice to always share data with one's coauthors and to have them double-check the results before an article is submitted. A recent survey among more than 700 psychologists suggested that this best practice is common but certainly not always used, with 20% of the articles having only one researcher holding the data (Veldkamp, Nuijten, Dominguez-Alvarez, van Assen, & Wicherts, 2014). Sharing data with coauthors has the additional advantages that multiple researchers have access to the data (avoiding loss) and that the coauthors could check whether the data are sufficiently well documented to allow a competent peer to independently use them.

A fourth benefit of sharing data is related to these errors but concerns researchers' susceptibility to biases when analyzing the results of their own studies and presenting the results (Barber, 1976; Firebaugh, 2007; Mahoney, 1976; Simmons, Nelson, & Simonsohn, 2011; Wicherts et al., 2011). Whereas expectancy effects (Rosenthal, 1966) are typically controlled by blinding procedures during the data collection (Shadish, Cook, & Campbell, 2002), the data from behavioral and social science studies are typically analyzed by a researcher who has clear expectations about the outcomes and a vested interest in finding and presenting a particular result. Given that such data can often be analyzed in different ways, the original researcher has certain degree of maneuverability in how to analyze the data (Simmons et al., 2011), which may lead to bias (Bakker, van Dijk, & Wicherts, 2012; Wicherts et al., 2011). The relevance of the choices made by the original researcher for the substantive conclusions is subject to peer review and editorial oversight. However, the summary of results presented in the final article often is insufficient for a critical reader to fully grasp the relevance of analytic choices. For instance, suppose a researcher presents the F test from an analysis of covariance bearing on the main hypothesis, but the result without the covariate is not given. The analysis has certain assumptions (e.g., normality, variance homogeneity, independence of data points) that may not hold and that might affect the final conclusion. A critical reader is entitled to request the data to verify the robustness of results against such potential violations or with respect to choices made by the original researcher. In other words, any reader is allowed to disagree with the original researcher's analysis, and the preferred way to solve the disagreement is to have the critical reader look at the data him- or herself, reanalyze the data, and independently conclude what those data actually show. Whether the reanalysis results are relevant enough for publication can subsequently be judged by the editor and peer reviewers as in any critique of a published article.

It may not appear in the original authors' best interest to share the data with a critical reader after publication, but this is how science works. Presenting one's results to the academic community entails an invitation to that community to either disagree or agree with one's conclusions. Withholding the data of published studies for independent reanalysis is not merely impeding the debate; it actually represents a violation of scientific integrity according to most ethical standards. Note that there might be propriety rights that render data sharing problematic, but even in these cases the data owners need to allow independent verification of the results (e.g., by having the verifying researcher conduct the reanalysis in a supervised setting). If this were not so, companies could sponsor studies highlighting the effectiveness of their products (drugs or treatments), publish the results in an academic journal, and subsequently disable any possibility of verification by other researchers. Thus, publishing results requires one to allow verification, and vice versa: If one dislikes verification, then one should not publish. It is interesting that some researchers in our request for data from 141 articles were unwilling to share their data because these were part of an ongoing project. This, however, cannot be a reason to not share the data if the request concerns the verification of the specific results that were already presented in an academic journal.

The fifth benefit of sharing data is that it may help answer novel questions in the context of an analysis or study that goes beyond the one(s) presented in the original article. My request for older IQ data in which I applied relatively novel psychometric models to data that predated these models is an excellent example of such a secondary analysis; it dealt with a new research question and so was not aimed at verifying earlier conclusions based on those data. Keeping the data for a number of years after publication will enable new research questions to be answered because novel insights might force researchers to revisit their data, newly developed analyses might allow us to learn more from the data, or a creative fellow researcher might come up with a brilliant idea that could be studied with data that have already been published. Use of shared data for secondary analysis may be done with or without the original researcher's involvement, but it will often lead to collaboration with the original researchers who collected the data and hence are intimately familiar with them.

A sixth benefit of sharing data is that it is an effective way for publishing researchers to show that they strongly believe in their results and they are willing to let others scrutinize their data. As Hartgerink and Wicherts (2016) discussed, sharing data fits the core norms of science. A researcher who has analyzed the data in many different ways and subsequently presents the only analysis out of many that yielded a significant outcome likely would not be very willing to share the data. However, those who have carefully analyzed the data and are quite certain that alternative analyses corroborate the results probably would be happy to share their data and let anyone verify the robustness of results. The sharing of data for independent reanalysis could be seen as a fairly direct way to replicate the results (Freese, 2007), and allowing replication is more convincing than disallowing it.

In addition to opening the door to collaboration, sharing data for secondary analysis leads to more citations and a recognition among peers of the willingness to share data with others in the interest of scientific progress. For this reason, some colleagues and I started the *Journal of Open Psychology Data* (*JOPD*), which publishes peer-reviewed data papers describing openly available psychological data sets that can be reused by others in education and research (Wicherts, 2013). The Nature Publishing Group recently launched the multidisciplinary journal *Scientific Data*, which similarly publishes data papers, and APA launched the Archives of Scientific Psychology, which publishes regular research articles and uses a data-sharing format called *collaborative data sharing*. The goals of these journals (all open access) is to promote reuse of the data to answer novel questions, with the only real difference among them is the procedure to obtain the data, which for *Archives of Scientific Psychology* involves a requirement to always invite the original authors to collaborate, which is not required for *Scientific Data* or *JOPD*.

THE DIFFERENCE BETWEEN VERIFICATION
AND SECONDARY ANALYSES

The APA Ethics Code indicates that "psychologists who request data from other psychologists to verify the substantive claims through reanalysis may use shared data only for the declared purpose. Requesting psychologists obtain prior written agreement for all other uses of the data" (APA, 2017). This highlights the importance of distinguishing a request for data for verification purposes from a request for data in the context of a secondary analysis. The former request bears on the conclusions drawn in the paper and is one that the original researcher cannot refuse. The latter request concerns another (new) research question that normally would be part of another publication or research project. Although not the most collegial choice, an original researcher can refuse to share data if the goal of the reanalysis is to address novel research questions, which are often already part of different publications even if these were based on the same data. For instance, in complex longitudinal studies the original authors might already have plans to study supplementary relations not studied in the earlier paper (such questions need to be different for the new paper to be publishable), and a requesting author cannot then request the data to scoop the original authors. For secondary analyses it is often reasonable that the original researcher, as the person who invested time and resources in collecting the data, has a say in what can be done with the reused data and perhaps should be a collaborator on (and coauthor on publications arising from) such a new project. My request for IQ data was one such secondary analysis, which was also my reason to invite the original researchers to join as coauthors.

Unfortunately, the latest version of the APA (2010) *Publication Manual* does not clearly distinguish requests for verification from requests for secondary analysis (Wicherts & Bakker, 2009); specifically, it refers to the necessity of always having an explicit agreement between the original researcher and the requesting researchers on (a) how the data would be analyzed; (b) whether the results of the analysis will be disseminated and, if so, how; and (c) coauthorship expectations. Such agreements make perfect sense if the goal goes beyond verification and is a true secondary analysis of the data. However, it makes little sense when the request is for verification purposes. If I were to read a certain weird result in a paper, I can request the data and verify the results in any way I like and subsequently submit the results of my critical reanalysis for publication to see whether the editor and reviewers consider my critique publishable. If the reanalysis is done for verification purposes, the original researcher is not in a position to demand (and is unlikely to want) to be a coauthor on the paper criticizing his or her own work, cannot force the requesting researcher to not write about the reanalysis results, and can certainly not stipulate the use of an analytic approach that lies at the heart of the contention about the results. Nonetheless, it is important to be always clear about the reasons for the data request: If it is for verification, this needs to be stated in the requesting correspondence; the following is an example:

> I would like to verify your conclusions through an independent reanalysis of your data. I will not share the data with others and will follow relevant codes of conduct with respect to confidentiality of the research participants and care for the data file.

Moreover, a researcher cannot refuse to share data for which he or she has further research plans if the request concerns verification of the *published* results (such a practice would obstruct verification because it would allow all researchers to refuse to share data by invoking unspecified further research plans with the same data).

DATA MANAGEMENT

The low rate of data sharing in psychology may be attributed to widespread poor data management. Introductory textbooks in research methods and/or statistics in the social sciences normally have a chapter on research ethics that discusses issues such as confidentiality, informed consent, institutional review boards, potential risks to participants, the problem of deceit, debriefings, and the general care of researchers for the well-being of the people (or animals) taking part in their research. APA's Ethics Code also states the following:

> Psychologists create, and to the extent the records are under their control, maintain, disseminate, store, retain, and dispose of records and data relating to their professional and scientific work in order to . . . allow for replication of research design and analyses. (Section 6.01)

Yet introductory textbooks in methods and statistics seldom discuss data management. Recently, Michèle Nuijten and I looked at all 30 introductory methods textbooks and 21 introductory statistics textbooks that were sent to our Department of Methodology and Statistics by publishers in the hope that we would use them in our freshman psychology and social sciences courses. Only three of these textbooks discussed the importance of data storage, and 27 of them (90%) contained a chapter on research ethics. Of the 21 statistics textbooks, none discussed data storage in such a way that the relevant terms appeared in the index. So, although students are clearly taught how to collect and analyze data, they are barely taught to keep them for future use and verification.

In 2009, the organization that hosts a large data repository in the Netherlands (Data Archiving and Network Services) decided to study why it had obtained so few data sets from the relatively large field of psychology. The subsequent survey of nearly 200 researchers from the different subdisciplines in psychology threw interesting light on this question (Voorbrood, 2010). Most of the respondents indicated that they kept the data of their studies after results were published. Yet when asked *how* they kept their data, the modal answer (given by 32% of respondents) was that they saved the data on their own computer. Many researchers appeared to confuse pressing "save file" on one's computer with robust and properly documented archiving. Other common methods to archive the data were on CDs/DVDs (18%), in the filing cabinet (20%), or on a central server at the department (21%). Apart from the last option, all methods of keeping data are problematic. Saving a file on a single computer could easily lead to a loss of the data; the computer might get stolen or replaced by a new one. Also, the computer software needed to open and use the data may not be available after a while. For instance, older versions of the popular statistical program SPSS provided files that could not be opened with more recent versions of the same program.

What does solid data management entail? Since the Stapel affair (Stapel was the dean at my current faculty), our faculty has installed a guideline concerning data management. The guideline "data package" provides a good example of a data management plan. It involves a specification of the general ethical standards, similar to those from APA and other professional societies, concerning how data should be handled during the study and after publication. The first author of a publication is obliged to keep a digital data folder (the data package) that follows the eight criteria:

1. It has to include metadata specifying when, where, and by whom the data were collected, who analyzed the data, and where non-digital source material is kept.
2. The data package should contain the raw data in unaltered (read-only) form (the raw data file is defined as the first digital file that was available to the researcher).
3. The data package should be stored safely, with automated backups.
4. The data package should include materials (questionnaires, stimuli, instructions) used to run (and hence replicate) the study.
5. The data package should include a syntax or codebook specifying how data were processed and analyzed.

6. The data package should include a processed data file that is sufficiently well documented (e.g., it includes informative variable names, value labels, etc.) so that any competent peer would be able to use it.
7. The data package should be accessible by at least two persons.
8. The data package should be safely stored for at least 10 years after publication.

Our faculty conducts random audits of published articles to check whether researchers follow these guidelines. A recent article on researcher practices (Hartgerink & Wicherts, 2016) provides more practical advice on proper data management.

OPEN DATA

Some social and behavioral science data sets cannot be openly shared because of propriety rights (e.g., when companies own the data), ethical considerations related to privacy issues (Finkel, Eastwick, & Reis, 2015), or insurmountable logistical issues (e.g., very large physiological data sets or big streaming data from social media). However, the preponderance of data sets in the social and behavioral sciences are not owned by companies or organizations that would oppose sharing openly. If research is financed by public money, one could argue (Ceci & Walker, 1983) that the wider scientific community and even the general public should be able to use the data after the original researchers have had a chance to publish their research (e.g., after a certain period of time, or after conclusion of the funded research project). An increasing number of funding organizations either strongly support or even demand eventual publication of the data (Destro Bisol et al., 2014).

Sharing data is not free of costs, but an increasing number of data repositories, such as Dataverse, Figshare, or the Open Science Framework, offer free capabilities to host data from most types of social and behavioral research (the *Journal of Open Psychology* website offers a list of established repositories: http://openpsychologydata.metajnl.com/about/#repo). These repositories offer good places to host data and have excellent features, such as version control, persistent identifiers that allow data to be found and cited (e.g., digital object identifiers), metadata, and safe storage. If one is willing and able to openly share data, such repositories are greatly preferred over the use of personal or faculty websites (which often lead to dead/expired links after a while; Klein et al., 2014) or promises to share data on request (which are often not fulfilled; Krawczyk & Reuben, 2012).

When openly sharing data, it is important to consider issues of confidentiality. Personal information should not enable any potential user to identify participants, and so data should be either rigorously made anonymous or shared only in a way that ensures compliance with legal and ethical guidelines. It is also important to consider including plans to share data in the informed-consent forms participants sign. This allows participants to express their wish to have their data shared or not.

Preparing data files for sharing or publication also requires some additional work by the authors (although they are actually already obliged ethically to rigorous record keeping), so there is a need to incentivize sharing. For this reason it is important to have potential outlets for data papers such as *JOPD* and *Scientific Data*, but other publishers can help promote this kind of transparency (Nosek et al., 2015). An increasing number of journals are adhering to guidelines that require sharing of data for all articles (as long as this is ethically and legally feasible). For instance, the journal *PLOS ONE* has installed a requirement to have explicit data-sharing statements for all articles in 2014, leading to a massive and almost overnight increase in the number of articles accompanied by open data. Other journals, such as *Psychological Science*, have started active promotion of open data (and open materials) by offering so-called open data badges (and open material badges) to appear on the front page of articles accompanied by open data (and/or open materials; Eich, 2014). At *Psychological Science* this has led to an apparent increase in the number of articles sharing data (Kidwell et al., 2016).

With funders, journal editors, academic societies, the general public, and researchers increasingly becoming aware of the many benefits (and relatively minor disadvantages) to sharing data, I expect more and more articles to be accompanied by open data in the near future. My colleague Denny Borsboom (Borsboom, 2013) compared not sharing data in the future with how we now consider people who smoke on an airplane. Thirty years ago, smoking on an airplane was considered normal. It is my hope and expectation that 15 years from now not sharing data would be just as weird as lighting a Marlboro while one is getting settled in seat 21C, and that we will look back on today's lack of data sharing with the same astonishment as when we imagine the smoke-filled planes of the previous century.

RECOMMENDED READING

Ceci, S. J., & Walker, E. (1983). Private archives and public needs. *American Psychologist, 38*, 414–423. http://dx.doi.org/10.1037/0003-066X.38.4.414

Freese, J. (2007). Replication standards quantitative social science—Why not sociology? *Sociological Methods & Research, 36*, 153–172. http://dx.doi.org/10.1177/0049124107306659

Nosek, B. A., & Bar-Anan, Y. (2012). Scientific utopia: I. Opening scientific communication. *Psychological Inquiry, 23,* 217–243. Science revolves around the data. Journal of Open Psychology Data, 1, e1.

Wicherts, J. M., & Bakker, M. (2012). Publish (your data) or (let the data) perish! Why not publish your data too? *Intelligence, 40,* 73–76. http://dx.doi.org/10.1016/j.intell.2012.01.004

REFERENCES

Alsheikh-Ali, A. A., Qureshi, W., Al-Mallah, M. H., & Ioannidis, J. P. A. (2011). Public availability of published research data in high-impact journals. *PLOS ONE, 6,* e24357. http://dx.doi.org/10.1371/journal.pone.0024357

American Psychological Association. (2010). *Publication manual of the American Psychological Association* (6th ed.). Washington, DC: Author.

American Psychological Association. (2017). *Ethical principles of psychologists and code of conduct* (2002, Amended June 1, 2010 and January 1, 2017). Retrieved from http://www.apa.org/ethics/code/index.aspx

Bakker, M., van Dijk, A., & Wicherts, J. M. (2012). The rules of the game called psychological science. *Perspectives on Psychological Science, 7,* 543–554. http://dx.doi.org/10.1177/1745691612459060

Bakker, M., & Wicherts, J. M. (2011). The (mis)reporting of statistical results in psychology journals. *Behavior Research Methods, 43,* 666–678. http://dx.doi.org/10.3758/s13428-011-0089-5

Bakker, M., & Wicherts, J. M. (2014). Outlier removal, sum scores, and the inflation of the Type I error rate in independent samples *t* tests: The power of alternatives and recommendations. *Psychological Methods, 19,* 409–427. http://dx.doi.org/10.1037/met0000014

Barber, T. X. (1976). *Pitfalls in human research: Ten pivotal points.* New York, NY: Pergamon Press.

Borsboom, D. (2013). *Smoking on an airplane.* Retrieved from http://centerforopenscience.github.io/osc/2013/10/02/smoking-on-an-airplane/

Broockman, D., Kalla, J., & Aronow, P. (2015, May 19). *Irregularities in LaCour (2014).* Unpublished manuscript, Stanford University, Stanford, CA. Retrieved from https://web.stanford.edu/~dbroock/broockman_kalla_aronow_lg_irregularities.pdf

Ceci, S. J., & Walker, E. (1983). Private archives and public needs. *American Psychologist, 38,* 414–423. http://dx.doi.org/10.1037/0003-066X.38.4.414

Chan, A.-W., Song, F., Vickers, A., Jefferson, T., Dickersin, K., Gøtzsche, P. C., . . . van der Worp, H. B. (2014). Increasing value and reducing waste: Addressing inaccessible research. *The Lancet, 383,* 257–266. http://dx.doi.org/10.1016/S0140-6736(13)62296-5

Cooper, H., & Patall, E. A. (2009). The relative benefits of meta-analysis conducted with individual participant data versus aggregated data. *Psychological Methods, 14*, 165–176. http://dx.doi.org/10.1037/a0015565

Craig, J. R., & Reese, S. C. (1973). Retention of raw data: A problem revisited. *American Psychologist, 28*, 723. http://dx.doi.org/10.1037/h0035667

Destro Bisol, G. D., Anagnostou, P., Capocasa, M., Bencivelli, S., Cerroni, A., Contreras, J., . . . Boulton, G. (2014). Perspectives on Open Science and scientific data sharing: An interdisciplinary workshop. *Journal of Anthropological Sciences, 92*, 179–2000. http://dx.doi.org/10.4436/JASS.92006

Eich, E. (2014). Business not as usual. *Psychological Science, 25*, 3–6. http://dx.doi.org/10.1177/0956797613512465

Finkel, E. J., Eastwick, P. W., & Reis, H. T. (2015). Best research practices in psychology: Illustrating epistemological and pragmatic considerations with the case of relationship science. *Journal of Personality and Social Psychology, 108*, 275–297. http://dx.doi.org/10.1037/pspi0000007

Firebaugh, G. (2007). Replication data sets and favored-hypothesis bias. *Sociological Methods & Research, 36*, 200–209. http://dx.doi.org/10.1177/0049124107306663

Flynn, J. R. (1987). Massive IQ gains in 14 nations: What IQ tests really measure. *Psychological Bulletin, 101*, 171–191. http://dx.doi.org/10.1037/0033-2909.101.2.171

Freese, J. (2007). Replication standards quantitative social science—Why not sociology? *Sociological Methods & Research, 36*, 153–172. http://dx.doi.org/10.1177/0049124107306659

Hartgerink, C. H. J., & Wicherts, J. M. (2016). Research practices and assessment of research misconduct. *ScienceOpen Research.* http://dx.doi.org/10.14293/S2199-1006.1.SOR-SOCSCI.ARYSBI.v1

John, L. K., Loewenstein, G., & Prelec, D. (2012). Measuring the prevalence of questionable research practices with incentives for truth telling. *Psychological Science, 23*, 524–532. http://dx.doi.org/10.1177/0956797611430953

Kidwell, M. C., Lazarević, L. B., Baranski, E., Hardwicke, T. E., Piechowski, S., Falkenberg, L. S., . . . Nosek, B. A. (2016). Badges to acknowledge open practices: A simple, low-cost, effective method for increasing transparency. *PLOS Biology, 14*, e1002456. http://dx.doi.org/10.1371/journal.pbio.1002456

Klein, M., Van de Sompel, H., Sanderson, R., Shankar, H., Balakireva, L., Zhou, K., & Tobin, R. (2014). Scholarly context not found: One in five articles suffers from reference rot. *PLOS ONE, 9*, e115253. http://dx.doi.org/10.1371/journal.pone.0115253

Krawczyk, M., & Reuben, E. (2012). (Un)available upon request: Field experiment on researchers' willingness to share supplementary materials. *Accountability in Research, 19*, 175–186.

Levelt, W. J. M., Drenth, P., & Noort, E. (Eds.). (2012). *Flawed science: The fraudulent research practices of social psychologist Diederik Stapel.* Max Planck Institute for Psycholinguistics. Retrieved from http://www.mpi.nl/publications/escidoc-1569964

Mackintosh, N. J. (2011). *IQ and human intelligence*. Oxford, England: Oxford University Press.

Mahoney, M. J. (1976). *Scientist as subject: The psychological imperative*. Cambridge, MA: Ballinger.

McNutt, M. (2016, February 5). Editorial retraction [Letter to the editor]. *Science, 351*, 569. http://dx.doi.org/10.1126/science.351.6273.569-a

Merton, R. K. (1973). *The sociology of science: Theoretical and empirical investigations*. Chicago, IL: University of Chicago Press.

Nosek, B. A., Alter, G., Banks, G., Borsboom, D., Bowman, S., Breckler, S., . . . Yarkoni, T. (2015, June 26). Promoting an Open Research culture: Author guidelines for journals could help to promote transparency, openness, and reproducibility. *Science, 348*, 1422–1425. http://dx.doi.org/10.1126/science.aab2374

Nosek, B. A., & Bar-Anan, Y. (2012). Scientific utopia: I. Opening scientific communication. *Psychological Inquiry, 23*, 217–243. http://dx.doi.org/10.1080/1047840X.2012.692215

Nosek, B. A., Spies, J. R., & Motyl, M. (2012). Scientific utopia: II. Restructuring incentives and practices to promote truth over publishability. *Perspectives on Psychological Science, 7*, 615–631. http://dx.doi.org/10.1177/1745691612459058

Nuijten, M. B., Hartgerink, C. H. J., van Assen, M. A. L. M., Epskamp, S., & Wicherts, J. M. (2016). The prevalence of statistical reporting errors in psychology (1985–2013). *Behavior Research Methods, 48*, 1205–1226. http://dx.doi.org/10.3758/s13428-015-0664-2

Petrocelli, J., Clarkson, J., Whitmire, M., & Moon, P. (2013). When ab≠c − c′: Published errors in the reports of single-mediator models. *Behavior Research Methods, 45*, 595–601. http://dx.doi.org/10.3758/s13428-012-0262-5

Piwowar, H. A., Day, R. S., & Fridsma, D. B. (2007). Sharing detailed research data is associated with increased citation rate. *PLOS ONE, 2*, e308. http://dx.doi.org/10.1371/journal.pone.0000308

Rosenthal, R. (1966). *Experimenter effects in behavioral research*. New York, NY: Appleton-Century-Crofts.

Rossi, J. S. (1987). How often are our statistics wrong—A statistics class exercise. *Teaching of Psychology, 14*, 98–101. http://dx.doi.org/10.1207/s15328023top1402_8

Shadish, W. R., Cook, T. D., & Campbell, D. T. (2002). *Experimental and quasi-experimental designs for generalized causal inference*. New York, NY: Houghton Mifflin.

Simmons, J. P., Nelson, L. D., & Simonsohn, U. (2011). False-positive psychology: Undisclosed flexibility in data collection and analysis allows presenting anything as significant. *Psychological Science, 22*, 1359–1366. http://dx.doi.org/10.1177/0956797611417632

Simonsohn, U. (2013). Just post it: The lesson from two cases of fabricated data detected by statistics alone. *Psychological Science, 24*, 1875–1888. http://dx.doi.org/10.1177/0956797613480366

Vanpaemel, W., Vermorgen, M., Deriemaecker, L., & Storms, G. (2015). Are we wasting a good crisis? The availability of psychological research data after the storm. *Collabra, 1*(1), 3. Advance online publication. http://dx.doi.org/10.1525/collabra.13

Veldkamp, C. L. S., Nuijten, M. B., Dominguez-Alvarez, L., van Assen, M. A. L. M., & Wicherts, J. M. (2014). Statistical reporting errors and collaboration on statistical analyses in psychological science. *PLOS ONE, 9*, e114876. http://dx.doi.org/10.1371/journal.pone.0114876

Vines, T. H., Albert, A. Y. K., Andrew, R. L., Débarre, F., Bock, D. G., Franklin, M. T., . . . Rennison, D. J. (2014). The availability of research data declines rapidly with article age. *Current Biology, 24*, 94–97. http://dx.doi.org/10.1016/j.cub.2013.11.014

Voorbrood, C. (2010). *Archivering, beschikbaarstelling en hergebruik van onderzoeksdata in de psychologie* [Archiving, sharing, and reusing of psychological research data]. The Hague, the Netherlands: Data Archiving and Networked Services.

Wicherts, J. M. (2011, November 5). Psychology must learn a lesson from fraud case. *Nature, 480*, 7. http://dx.doi.org/10.1038/480007a

Wicherts, J. M. (2013). Science revolves around the data. *Journal of Open Psychology Data, 1*, e1. http://dx.doi.org/10.5334/jopd.e1

Wicherts, J., & Bakker, M. (2009, October 22). Sharing: Guidelines go one step forwards, two steps back. *Nature, 461*, 1053. http://dx.doi.org/10.1038/4611053c

Wicherts, J. M., & Bakker, M. (2012). Publish (your data) or (let the data) perish! Why not publish your data too? *Intelligence, 40*, 73–76. http://dx.doi.org/10.1016/j.intell.2012.01.004

Wicherts, J. M., Bakker, M., & Molenaar, D. (2011). Willingness to share research data is related to the strength of the evidence and the quality of reporting of statistical results. *PLOS ONE, 6*, e26828. http://dx.doi.org/10.1371/journal.pone.0026828

Wicherts, J. M., Borsboom, D., Kats, J., & Molenaar, D. (2006). The poor availability of psychological research data for reanalysis. *American Psychologist, 61*, 726–728. http://dx.doi.org/10.1037/0003-066X.61.7.726

Wicherts, J. M., Dolan, C. V., Hessen, D. J., Oosterveld, P., van Baal, G. C. M., Boomsma, D. I., & Span, M. M. (2004). Are intelligence tests measurement invariant over time? Investigating the nature of the Flynn effect. *Intelligence, 32*, 509–537. http://dx.doi.org/10.1016/j.intell.2004.07.002

Wolins, L. (1962). Responsibility for raw data. *American Psychologist, 17*, 657–658. http://dx.doi.org/10.1037/h0038819

14

REPLICATION

STEFAN SCHMIDT

KEY POINTS

- Within the social sciences, replications have a history of not being acknowledged and very few researchers conduct them.
- From a theoretical point of view, replications are at the heart of science, because they transfer single observations into scientific knowledge.
- A recent assessment in the field of psychology showed that only about one third of published findings are replicable.
- There are several forms of replications; in this chapter a functional approach that helps design and to assess replication studies is presented.
- Recent changes in daily scientific practice are targeting a more positive attitude toward replications; several instruments and incentives in support of this goal have been developed.

http://dx.doi.org/10.1037/0000033-015
Toward a More Perfect Psychology: Improving Trust, Accuracy, and Transparency in Research, M. C. Makel and J. A. Plucker (Editors)

In August 2015, the results of a large collaboration that determined the rate of replication in the field of psychology was published (Open Science Collaboration, 2015). The authors had replicated 100 studies published in psychology journals in 2008. Why would such a research project, demanding immense resources, be of importance? The reason is that there is long-standing and ongoing debate on the question of the robustness of the findings reported in the social sciences. The authors assumed that the social practice of modern empirical sciences in the social sciences would yield a large amount of false-positive results (Horton, 2015; Ioannidis, 2005). The pressure to be innovative and to publish positive results in a highly competitive system in which financial resources are distributed in relation to success, and in which success most often is quantified by bibliometric and economic figures, are reasons why false-positive results may be prevalent. However, the aforementioned replication project itself is also subject to a lively debate (Gilbert, King, Pettigrew, & Wilson, 2016; but cf. Anderson et al., 2016).

The actual practices leading to the publication of false-positive research are manifold. Most severe, but maybe also the rarest cases, are those of fraud. More common are so called *questionable research practices* (QRPs; John, Loewenstein, & Prelec, 2012), such as fishing for significance, reporting only positive variables, recruiting more participants based on current results, hypothesizing after the results are known (also called *HARKing*; Kerr, 1998), arbitrarily excluding outliers, selective publication, nonpublication of nonsignificant results, and so on, with many of them addressed in this book (see also Neuroskeptic, 2012, for a creative approach). Added to this pile are several fallacies (e.g., only seeking evidence that supports one's prior beliefs and ignoring all else) resulting from self-deception (see, e.g., Nuzzo, 2015). The crucial questions now are: How big is the damage? To what extent have these practices biased published results? Are most of the reported findings false, or does the system have self-correcting capacities and the problem applies to only a minority of publications?

Although there are many ways false-positive publications can occur, there is only one way to assess whether an article reports false-positive results: replication. This is the reason why Brian Nosek and the Open Research Collaboration started the Reproducibility Project (Open Science Collaboration, 2012). The idea is to empirically assess the reliability of published reports by the systematic replication of a large set of studies. The Reproducibility Project selected the studies published in 2008 from three major journals: (a) *Psychological Science*; (b) *Journal of Personality and Social Psychology*; and (c) *Journal of Experimental Psychology: Learning, Memory, and Cognition*. Researchers interested in participating in this project could select among the studies and then develop a protocol for a planned direct replication by prespecified methods that guaranteed (among other aspects) that replications were adequately powered. All procedures of this project are publicly available through the Open Science

Framework (http://osf.io/ezcuj). In the end, 100 studies were replicated. Of interest is that the final article did not specify a measure that indicated whether Experiment B (the replication study) was a successful replication of Experiment A (the original study). Thus, the project authors relied on several indicators in parallel to get an overall view of the reproducibility rate. The first indicator was a dichotomous one and counted the percentage of studies in which a significant p value in the original experiment could be reproduced (in the same direction) by the replication study. Only 35 of 97 original studies that reported a significant p value ($p \leq .05$) also yielded a significant p value in the replication; this is a reproducibility rate of 36%. The second indicator was a comparison of the mean effect size of the original studies with one of the replication studies. All effect sizes were converted into correlation coefficients as common metric. The 2008 studies had an average effect size of $r = .403$ ($SD = .188$), and the replication studies had an average effect size of $r = .197$ ($SD = .257$), which is less than the half that of the original studies and significantly different from that of the original studies. Next, the project authors assessed whether the original effect size was within a 95% confidence interval of the effect size of the replication study. This was the case for 47% of the 95 studies included in this analysis. Finally, they added a subjective criterion by asking the replication team whether they believed their finding replicated the original study. A subjective reproducibility rate of 39% was obtained. This project was the first empirical assessment to find out whether the assumption of a crisis of confidence in psychology (Pashler & Wagenmakers, 2012) is really justified. The answer is yes. According to the criteria, only 36% to 47% of the findings published in top psychology journals in 2008 passed the most important test for a scientific finding: They survived replication.

At least two important questions arise from this story. First, why is replication so important? Second, if this is the case, why hasn't anybody tried before to replicate important findings? In the following sections I examine the logic behind the concept of replication, what the term *replication* exactly means, and clarify distinctions among various types of replication. Next, I address the problem of what exactly constitutes one experiment as a replication of a prior one and explain how taking a functional approach toward designing replication studies in a more systematic fashion is a potential solution. I then discuss replication statistics, addressing the question of how one can quantify whether a replication is successful or not. In the final sections of this chapter I address the social practice of science with respect to replication. On the one hand, direct replications have thus far been generally disregarded and are thus very rare in the social sciences. On the other hand, there are some implicit procedures that at least partially support the idea behind replication. I close the chapter by discussing the issue of unconventional claims in science and showing how the role and handling of replication change decisively within such a context.

WHY REPLICATION?

The fact that replication is one of the most important tools in science results from the perspective that a single observation cannot be trusted. A single observation, as well as a single scientific finding, may not necessarily reflect a regularity that can be found again. It might just be a chance finding, an artifact or a misinterpretation of the experimental procedures. But the aim of science is to obtain stable and systematic descriptions about its subjects, which in turn should also allow for making predictions. A single observation that does not occur again is of only very limited use. Only if the same initial conditions and the same way of conducting the experiment lead to identical—or at least similar—findings can one assume that some regularity was found that is beyond the specific circumstances of the first observation. Therefore, replication has the function of establishing *stability* in our knowledge of nature (Radder, 1996). By replicating, we sort the findings that are stable from those that are chance findings or artifacts.

Starting from this point, *replication* can be defined as "the set of technologies which transforms what counts as belief into what counts as knowledge" (Shapin & Schaffer, 1985, p. 225). In other words, replication is a methodological tool based on a *repetition procedure* that is capable of transforming an observation into a *fact*, or *piece of knowledge* (Schmidt, 2009). The basic assumption entailed in this definition is that the respective part of the world that is investigated by this procedure behaves lawfully. Dilworth (1996) called this the *principle of uniformity of nature* (p. 53). Science sets this principle as an axiom, which is rarely questioned. Similarly, the procedure of replication itself can be considered a basic assumption of science. This means that scientists have agreed on the basis of logical reasoning as well as social interaction on the importance of this principle. That many findings in the social sciences are taken for granted without having their reproducibility demonstrated indicates that this cornerstone of science does not always get the attention it deserves.

TYPES OF REPLICATION

The above definition does not tell us exactly how a replication should be performed. Also, if one looks into the literature, one can see that there many types of replication mentioned. Authors have differentiated between *literal, operational,* and *constructive* replication (Lykken, 1968); *exact, partial,* and *conceptual* replication (Hendrick, 1991); and *exact* and *inexact* replication (Keppel, 1982). The most refined differentiation came from the Dutch philosopher Radder, who also discriminated the types of people conducting these replications and thus arrived at a 3 × 4 grid with 12 different types of replication (Radder, 1992).

Seen from a distance, all types of replication refer to the question of whether the replication is conducted with the same experimental and material realization or with a different experimental setup. Let me provide a simple example. The famous American psychologist Robert Rosenthal demonstrated empirically that the expectation of an experimenter regarding the outcome of an experiment can influence the results of this experiment. In his experiment he gave students some rats and asked them to train them in a simple T maze. One group of students was told that they received a strain of "maze-bright" rats, and the other group was told their rats were "maze dull." The maze-bright rats showed a significantly better performance than the maze-dull ones, although they were all from the same breed (Rosenthal & Fode, 1963). Now, imagine you wanted to replicate this experiment. There are two principal avenues by which to proceed. One would be to repeat the rat experiment; this could either be done in the same laboratory or in a different one, according to the details described in the publication's Method section. However, instead of repeating the rat experiment, one could also invent another experimental idea to test the general assumption that the student's expectation had an influence on the results. For example, one could assess the effect of caffeinated coffee on blood pressure and heart rate in students. The experimenters interacting with the students could either be told, correctly, that the coffee administered would be decaffeinated or they could be deceived by telling them that the coffee contains an extra dose of caffeine. Both experiments can be considered a replication in the sense that they are a repetition procedure that is capable of transforming an observation into a piece of knowledge by demonstrating the stability of the effect. At this fundamental level two basic notions of replication can be differentiated (Schmidt, 2009):

1. Narrow bounded notion of replication: This refers to the repetition of an experimental procedure and will be termed *direct replication*.
2. Wider notion of replication: This refers to the repetition of a test of a hypothesis or of a result of an earlier research work with different methods and will be referred to as a *conceptual replication*.

WHAT CONSTITUTES A REPLICATION?

The above-mentioned example has already made one thing clear: Many different studies and experiments can be considered as a replication of the original experiment. Now a difficult question arises: What conditions have to be fulfilled to ensure that an Experiment B is a replication of an Experiment A?

And once a replication is conducted, a second question comes up: What conditions have to be fulfilled to ensure that the results of Experiment B are a successful replication of the results of Experiment A? There are no clear-cut answers to these two questions. Despite the fact that most scientists would agree to the statement that reproducibility is one of the most important criteria in science, there seems to be no agreement regarding the questions of what qualifies as a replication and how it is evaluated for success.

What would qualify an Experiment B to be a replication of an Experiment A? The most logical answer seems to be that it assesses the same hypothesis (in the case of a conceptual replication) or that it applies the same experimental procedures (in the case of a direct replication). *Sameness* seems to be the key, and the closer the experiment is to the original one, the more one may be justified in calling it a replication. In this sense, the best direct replication would be to perform an experiment that is as close as possible to the original one. However, this is not always the case. One has to consider that a given Experiment B can never be the exact replication of Experiment A because there is no such thing as an exact repetition. The reproduced experimental procedure can be more or less similar to the original one, but it can never be the same in all possible aspects. If this were the case, then Experiment A and its replication, Experiment B, would be the same experiment. But this is, of course, not only impossible but also in contradiction of the very idea of replication, which is finding the results of A again in a different experiment, B. One can see that sameness is not the only aspect that defines a replication. Although a certain amount of sameness is necessary to guarantee that the second experiment addresses the same observations as the first one, it also is necessary to have differences between the two experiments in order to arrive at *confirmatory power* (Collins, 1985). Confirmatory power is the reason to conduct a replication in the first place. A replication needs a mixture of sameness and differences (for a more detailed account, see Schmidt, 2009). Thus, the interesting question is, what should be kept, and what should be changed?

THE FUNCTIONAL APPROACH

The answer to this question depends on the reason why one wants to conduct a replication. In addition to the more general function of demonstrating the stability of a finding, it is also necessary to define the aim of the replication experiment more specifically. Only when this more specific function is determined can the problem of what to keep constant and what to change can be solved. This is what I have previously called a *functional approach to replication* (Schmidt, 2009). This approach enables a more systematic method toward the design of a replication experiment, especially with respect to whether

Experiment B can be considered a replication of Experiment A. The specific functions of a replication are to

- control for sampling error (chance result);
- control for artifacts (lack of internal validity);
- control for the impact of QRPs, as well as fraud;
- to generalize results to a larger or a different population; and
- to verify the underlying hypothesis of the earlier experiment.

Depending on the specific function of the replication, several aspects of the new experiment need to be similar or different compared with the original one. Hendrick (1991) proposed eight classes of variables that define the total research reality. A simplified model of four classes consists of (a) primary information focus (i.e., how the independent variable is presented to participants), (b) context variables that are assumed to be irrelevant to the study outcomes (e.g., participant background), (c) procedures for selecting participants from a population, and (d) procedures for assessing the dependent variable (e.g., statistical analysis). The demands for each of the functions mentioned above can be specified into four functions of replications:[1]

> *Function 1: To control for sampling error (chance result).* Any reported effect may be due to a type 1 [*sic*] error. This is targeting class 3 (participant selection). But there is no possibility of ruling out a type 1 error completely by any changes in any of the classes. The only possibility is to reduce its likelihood. If for instance the chances of obtaining a false positive result are set to $p = .05$ (i.e., 1:20) then the probability of obtaining a second false positive finding is much lower: $p = .05 \times .05 = .0025$ (i.e., 1:400). Thus, if one wants to replicate a study to test for chance finding then the advice would be to repeat the experiment in all classes 1, 2, 4 as exactly as possible but on a different sample (class 3). But also the procedures in class 3 have to be kept constant as they describe the way in which a random sample is drawn from the population. If this procedure is repeated then drawing a second random sample from the same population will in almost all cases result in a sample that is different from the first one. Very often this is done when the original researcher simply uses more participants from the same population.
>
> *Function 2: To control for artefacts (lack of internal validity).* The artefact hypothesis assumes that class 1 (primary information focus) is not solely responsible for the changes in the dependent variables or in other words a lack of internal validity. The reasons may be that either one or several variables from class 2 or 4 (or both) interact with one or several variables

---

[1]Text excerpts reprinted from "Shall We Do It Again? The Powerful Concept of Replication is Neglected in the Social Sciences," by S. Schmidt, 2009, *Review of General Psychology, 13,* pp. 93–94. Copyright 2009 by the American Psychological Association.

from class 1 in an unexpected way. A replication testing for this assumption should aim to duplicate the primary information focus as closely as possible while, at the same time, as many variables as possible from class 2 and 4 should be changed. This is especially true for the sub-classes of class 2 (i.e., contextual background) general physical setting, specific task variables and control agent. Usually this is obtained when an experiment is reproduced in a different lab by a different investigator. Such a replication is usually done when the findings of the original study are in doubt without any specific hypothesis. Here differences in the results between original and replicated study might not necessarily identify the source of the artifact because changes in the contextual variables will be confounded. But of course if there are more specific hypotheses regarding the source of the assumed artefact only the aspects and details dealing with these specific circumstances have to be changed.

Function 3: To control for the impact of questionable research practices (QRPs) as well as fraud. This functions tests for the idea that certain practices in setting up, conducting and evaluation of the original experiment introduced a bias in the results with fraud being the worst case. This case demands for changes in two categories. One is the personnel involved in the original study referring to class 2. The second one deals with all aspects that constitute the dependent variable in a wider sense (class 4). This means not only how the specific dependent variable is generated (e.g., the EEG amplifier or the specific questionnaire) but also all procedures involved in data handling, data evaluation and analysis until the final results of the experiments are obtained. With respect to QRPs a prespecified research protocol giving a detailed description of sample size and planned analyses is necessary and ideally this study protocol should be published in a register beforehand like this is compulsory in the medical sciences (De Angelis et al., 2004) and now also taking occasionally place for psychological studies (Nosek & Lakens, 2014). (from Schmidt, 2009, p. 94)

Function 4: To generalize results to a larger or to a different population. In this case a researcher replicates an experiment to investigate whether the result obtained on a sample from a specific population can be generalized to a larger or a different population. In this case class 1 has to be kept constant and class 3 has to be changed. Class 2 and 4 should be kept constant, but can also be slightly changed, which is often determined by pragmatic considerations. If the same investigator/same lab is conducting the replication class 2 or 4 may be closest to the original study. If the experiment is rebuilt in a different lab one cannot avoid changes in these variables. All this is fine as long as none of them interacts with class 1.

Function 5: To verify the underlying hypothesis of the earlier experiment. Stepping beyond the objectives of confirming results and generalizing to other samples a simple repetition of the experimental procedure is no longer sufficient. To verify the underlying hypothesis one needs to construct a different experimental setup that conveys the same primary information focus (class 1) by a radically different material realization. This will result in large changes of class 2 and 4 as well as changes of the material and procedural aspects of class 1. Class 3 should be kept constant if it is possible to run the new study on the same population. But this might not be achievable if e.g., the new experimental idea targets a different population. (Schmidt, 2009, pp. 93–94)

Function 5 is called a *conceptual replication*, and I will illustrate it by again using the example of Rosenthal's experimenter effect. Rosenthal's research on experimenter effects (Rosenthal & Rubin, 1978) started with studies on animal learning. The experiment with allegedly maze-bright and maze-dull rats was published in 1963 (Rosenthal & Fode, 1963):

> Some years later the same hypothesis was tested with teachers and pupils. Here the teachers were told that based on a specific test result some of their pupils would show remarkable gains in intellectual competence within the next months. But this was also done only to elicit positive expectations in the teachers while the pupils were selected randomly from the class. It is obvious that these two studies differ in all four classes. But the immaterial information focus, (i.e., the information conveyed to the participants) is the same for both studies. Both students and teachers were manipulated in a way to raise positive expectations about some of the rats/pupils they had to teach. The material realization of this information differed according to the experimental idea (experimental instructions read to the students or test results about the pupils handed out to the teacher). (Schmidt, 2009, p. 94)

An overview of how the classes and functions fit together to create different types of replications can be found in Figure 1 of Schmidt (2009). However, replications may not always be driven by such a methodological rationale; pragmatism may be the driving force and thus limit replication efforts (e.g., not every variable can be kept exactly the same as in the original study). Nevertheless, it is important to remember that making multiple changes (even small ones) renders interpretation of replication results more difficult, in particular when results differ from the original experiment. That is why replications should alter only one variable at a time, keeping all others constant (or as constant as possible).

To see how this functional approach could work in daily life, let us analyze how the Reproducibility Project (Carpenter, 2012; Open Science Collaboration, 2012, 2015) has approached this issue. The rationale for why they conducted replications was the assumption that many of the original studies had reported false-positive results. The likely reasons for this, discussed beforehand, were sampling or Type I error (Function 1); artifacts that went so far undetected (Function 2); or QRPs (Function 3), such as HARKing, fishing for significance, optional stopping, recruiting more participants, inclusion/exclusion of outliers, or selective reporting (John et al., 2012; Simmons, Nelson, & Simonsohn, 2011). All three functions are associated with a direct replication. This means that the primary information focus of the original study has to be kept constant with regard to its material as well as its immaterial realization. Also, the participants should be recruited from the same population by the same sampling procedures. The assumption that QRPs and artifacts involved will necessitate that a different team in a different laboratory conduct the direct replication.

Furthermore, the constitution of the dependent variable needs to be changed to rule out the artifact hypothesis and some potential QRPs. The latter refers in particular to the way data are handled once they are obtained. This exactly what happened in the Reproducibility Project. The replication teams rebuilt the original experiments as close as possible in their own laboratories. They also applied the same procedures to recruit their sample, but they might have made changes to the way they handled their data given that one cannot be sure that the original report, for example, contained selected findings or results trimmed toward significance by either excluding or including outliers. It is also interesting to note that within the Reproducibility Project several functions were assessed simultaneously, and thus several aspects were changed. In such a case, and this is true for most direct replications, it is impossible to identify the reasons for a failed replication because the changed aspects are confounded and compounded.

Implementation is not necessarily simple or easy. To make it easier, answering the questions "Why do I want to replicate Experiment A?" and "What are my specific hypotheses regarding Experiment A? (e.g., specific hypotheses on interactions between Class 1 and Class 2 or 4)" (Schmidt, 2009, p. 94) before beginning the study will clarify replication efforts for both researchers and readers. All five functions maintain a constant primary information focus. Thus, an Experiment B can be considered a replication of Experiment A if Experiment B maintains the primary information focus of Experiment A.

Direct replications (Functions 1–4) make a smaller reach than conceptual replications (Function 5). With a direct replication, a researcher produces facts (i.e., are the data in Experiment A correct?), whereas a conceptual replication helps produce greater understanding of the concept. Greater understanding is crucial in science (Edge, 1985). Conceptual replications corroborate and develop the theory behind the general hypothesis being replicated by testing it by means of a unique experiment. Both are derived from the same underlying theory but seek to confirm it in different ways. However, conceptual replication is also more risky than direct replication because interpretation of results can be more difficult. A successful conceptual replication can be interpreted as a successful extension of the theory, but a failed conceptual replication can be viewed as worthless because the root of the failure is unknown. Whether it failed because of a flaw in the original findings, the underlying theory, or an error in the new implementation remains unknown without further investigation.

REPLICATION STATISTICS

Because the functional approach presented above offers a solution to the question of whether Experiment B is a replication of Experiment A, we can now turn to the question of how to determine whether the results of Experiment B are a successful replication of the results of Experiment A. Because replications are rarely done, it is not surprising that no standard approach exists for this question. Within the daily science practices this problem is often solved only after the results of the replication study are known (Braude, 1979). If the results of the replication study confirm the finding of original study, this is called a "successful replication." However, in the case of inconsistent results, the researchers of the replication study will often address the differences between the original study and the replication, and there are always differences. This will often lead to a judgment that the new study was not in fact a replication. Some approaches on how to deal statistically with this issue are presented below (see also Open Science Collaboration, 2015).

Comparison of p Values

In this approach, the obtained p values of the respective studies are dichotomized at a criterion for significance (.05 or .01) as either being significant or not. The two studies can then be compared with regard to whether they have the same status regarding significance. The advantage of this procedure is that it is easy to understand and gives a clear statement (yes or no). The disadvantage, however, is that p value criteria are arbitrary, and dichotomizing removes a lot of variance in the data. For example, a study pair of $p_A = .040$ and $p_B = .051$ would be categorized as a failed replication, whereas a pair of $p_A = .040$ and $p_B = .049$ would be deemed a replication success. Another point that needs to be taken into consideration is that the p value is related to the size of the sample.

Replication Plane

Another approach was proposed by Rosenthal (1991) and is called the *replication diagonal* or *replication plane*. It is also suitable for the comparison of two studies. For both studies an effect size has to be calculated (e.g., a correlation coefficient [r] or Cohen's d). Next, the relationship of the two effect sizes is displayed in a chart by indicating the spot representing when the effect size of the first study is displayed on the x-axis and the result of the replication study on the y-axis (see Rosenthal, 1991, p. 19, for an example).

In the case of a perfect replication the resulting spot will be exactly on the diagonal representing all combinations of same effect sizes in the two studies. The less similar the results of the two studies are, the larger the distance from the diagonal will be. In contrast to p values, the effect sizes themselves are not dependent on sample size. The advantage of this graphical display is that one can get a quick impression and easily compare the similarity of sets of two studies with each other. The disadvantage of this method is that it does not provide a clear-cut criterion for a success or failure of replication.

Statistical Comparison of Effect Sizes

Here the idea is to compare the effect sizes of the two studies regarding a significant difference. This approach also goes back to Rosenthal (1991). In the case of r-type effect sizes, the respective r values or correlation coefficients have to be converted into a Fisher's Z metric (Rosenthal, 1991, p. 19) by the following formula:

$$Z_r = \frac{1}{2} \log_e \left(\frac{1+r}{1-r} \right)$$ (Rosenthal & Rosnow, 1991, p. 448).

In the case of two experiments, A and B, one obtains Z_{rA} and Z_{rB} from the two effect sizes r_A and r_B. The difference between Z_{rA} and Z_{rB} is Cohen's q (Rosenthal, 1991, p. 19). Cohen's q gets larger with larger difference and can also be tested for significance because a z score can be obtained by this formula:

$$Z = \frac{q}{\sqrt{\frac{1}{N_1 - 3} + \frac{1}{N_2 - 3}}}$$ (Rosenthal, 1991, p. 20).

For d effect sizes, one can either convert the d effect size into an r effect size using the following formula:

$$r = \frac{d}{\sqrt{d^2 + 4}}$$ (Rosenthal & Rosnow, 1991, p. 442)

(which is applicable only if d is derived from a between-subjects design) and then applying the procedure described above or simplifying the formula for a test on homogeneity (Shadish & Haddock, 1994, p. 266) to two studies only. For two effect sizes d_A and d_B, this results in:

$$Q = \frac{\left(d_A - \bar{d}\right)^2}{v_A} + \frac{\left(d_B - \bar{d}\right)^2}{v_B},$$

where $\bar{d} = \dfrac{d_A + d_B}{2}$ and v_A and v_B are the conditional variances of d_A and d_B, respectively. The calculation of this variance is dependent on the structure and distribution of the data. In the case of a between-subjects design with experimental (ex) and control group (co), for example, this variance calculates as follows:

$$v_i = \frac{n_{ex} + n_{co}}{n_{ex} n_{co}} + \frac{d^2}{2\left(n_{ex} + n_{co}\right)} \text{ (Shadish \& Haddock, 1994, p. 268).}$$

Q is χ^2 distributed with $df = k - 1$, which is $df = 1$ in this case. The disadvantage of the latter procedure is that the Q statistic has weak power, especially for small and/or unequal data sets (Hardy & Thompson, 1998; Petitti, 2001), whereby a two-study set is the smallest data set possible. Thus, it is best to apply a more liberal criterion for a difference between the study pairs (e.g., $p < .10$), or to convert effect sizes into r-type effect sizes.

SOCIAL PRACTICE OF SCIENCE

The need to conduct replications of single findings is obvious and necessary in order to arrive at sound scientific knowledge. This is made clear from a theoretical and epistemological perspective. Obviously, however, hardly any replications are conducted in the social sciences. The consequence, as I have empirically demonstrated, is that the combination of QRP and a lack of direct replications was found for more than the half of the published results, which implies a lack of reliability. This circumstance clearly demonstrates that, consistent with what is written in textbooks, there is also a social practice of science that develops its own tacit and implicit standards and procedures. The latter ones are not found in textbooks but learned directly in the laboratory. Obviously these more implicit procedures vary across different fields. In the field of physics, direct replications are well respected and published; in psychology, the situation is the opposite. Direct replications are considered to be more or less useless because they "do not provide anything new" (see Schmidt, 2009) and reduce the likelihood of getting a paper published.

Makel, Plucker, and Hegarty (2012) empirically assessed the replication rate in psychology by analyzing the 100 most important journals back to the year 1900. They arrived at a replication rate of 1.07%. On closer inspection they demonstrated that this already very small rate is mostly due to the same authors conducting these replications and they are also mostly either published subsequent to the same article, as a follow-up study, or in the same journal. Thus, it is not surprising that only 9.6% of these replications failed. It is obvious that a replication by the same authors is not fulfilling the function to control for QRPs or fraud. Ioannidis (2012) addressed the social aspects of same-team replication and scientific inbreeding and wrote of obedient and obliged replication. For the educational sciences, the same approach yielded an even lower replication rate of 0.13% (Makel & Plucker, 2014).

The reason for this lack of direct replications in the social sciences is obviously the pressure on researchers to publish as many articles as possible with the goal of obtaining the highest possible impact factor and best bibliographic figures. Makel and Plucker (2014) listed eight different biases within the field of stakeholders in the scientific field (e.g., journal editors, funding agencies, scientific institutions) that lead to this situation. On the basis of these analyses, one can clearly see that there exists a culture within the social sciences that strongly discourages conducting and publishing replications. With the additional implicit agreement on QRPs within the same stakeholders, this combination obviously results in the present situation: that the majority of the published results cannot be trusted (Laws, 2013). The field remains, in almost all cases, on the level of single observations, and such observations are not the same as facts or knowledge. One can only hope that this crisis will stimulate a change within these practices, but, as with all cultural changes, this will take time.

IMPLICIT REPLICATION PROCEDURES

Although it is obvious that open direct replications are a rare occurrence in the social sciences, there are some implicit procedures that nevertheless function to establish knowledge and facts out of single observations. These are follow-up studies, disguised conceptual replications, and the principle of heterogeneity of irrelevances.

A *follow-up study* combines a direct replication with new elements, for example, in an additional condition as an additional study arm, or with a new experiment in the same publication (Schmidt, 2009, p. 96). This may be done either by the original research team or a different one. Because the follow-up study will also create findings not reported earlier, the bias against direct replications does not apply to these types of studies.

A *disguised conceptual replication* tests a hypothesis from an earlier study with a different experimental setup. These procedures are not done very often. The point here is that it is not called explicitly a *conceptual replication*. This is understandable given the disregard for the term *replication* in the social sciences. The second reason may simply be that the respective researchers do not realize that what they are doing is a conceptual replication. They may think that they are expanding on prior findings or transfer interesting results to a different experimental paradigm.

The *principle of heterogeneity of irrelevancies* addresses explicitly those replication studies in which more than one aspect has been changed. From a perspective of conducting a replication, this is not a clever idea. If the replication fails, the reasons remain unclear because of the confounding of several changes. However, if these studies still replicate the original findings, then the aspects that have undergone changes can be judged as irrelevant to the primary information focus of the concept under investigation (Schmidt, 2009, p. 96). Considered from this perspective, many aspects that are considered irrelevant should be varied to achieve what is called a heterogeneity of irrelevancies (Cook, 1990; Shadish, 1995).

EXEMPTIONS: UNCONVENTIONAL CLAIMS

An exception to the above-stated circumstances of disregarding direct replications is worth considering. This refers to unconventional claims often derived from theories that are considered interesting (Schmidt, 2009). Davis (1971) described interesting theories in science as those that "deny certain assumptions of their audience" (p. 309). Claims often made regarding evidence for telepathy (Bem & Honorton, 1994) or precognition (Bem, 2011) serve as an example. Such claims are clearly in contradiction of the current scientific worldview and are therefore in conflict with accepted understanding. Some theories even challenge the basic unproven presuppositions and axioms of science in general (Walach & Schmidt, 2005). Although scientific findings that fit the current paradigm and worldview are usually accepted blindly on the basis that they affirm the assumptions of the audience, one can find usually a different reaction to all claims challenging the generally agreed-on scientific worldview. On the basis of reasoning according to Bayesian statistics, one could state that the prior probabilities for unconventional effects are largely different from those of well-accepted paradigms. Thus, the scientific communities immediately give up their reservations about direct replications and call for them. Also, here the likelihood of getting a replication, especially a failed one, published in a respected journal is much higher than with a study that has made conventional claims (e.g., Colwell, Schröder, & Sladen, 2000; Milton & Wiseman, 1999; Ritchie, Wiseman, & French, 2012).

It is interesting that researchers in the field of parapsychology have established some procedures that help prevent some of the known QRPs in psychology. Replications of experiments, independent of their success, as well as experiments with nonsignificant results, are usually accepted for publication (Johnson, 1976). This leads to some rather homogeneous databases that are then subject to meta-analyses (e.g., Bösch, Steinkamp, & Boller, 2006; Storm, Tressoldi, & Di Risio, 2010). Also, a practice called *optional stopping* is explicitly identified as a QRP in various textbooks (e.g., Irwin & Watt, 2007). In optional stopping the researcher evaluates the overall results after every trial or session and stops including new participants once a significant result is reached. Researchers in the field of parapsychology are clearly encouraged to prespecify their sample size, to stick to this number, and to report this procedure in the respective publication.

In 2012, a study register for the preregistration of planned experiments was opened (Watt & Kennedy, 2015). This register is designed according to the principles of medical registers (De Angelis et al., 2004). Researchers are asked to distinguish between confirmatory and exploratory analyses and to define a precise analysis plan for confirmatory research. This research plan is then reviewed for completeness and deficiencies. According to the authors, nearly every plan is sent back at least once for the researchers to complete minor details to make the analysis unambiguous (Watt & Kennedy, 2015). Thus, this register is in some respect more straightforward than the current possibilities at the Open Science Framework (Nosek & Lakens, 2014).

RECOMMENDATIONS AND FURTHER DEVELOPMENTS

Since the discovery of the crisis of credibility in psychology, many recommendations have been made as to how scientific practices need to be changed so scholars in the field can devise procedures that can unfold the full potential of the scientific method within psychology (Asendorpf et al., 2013; Ioannidis, Munafò, Fusar-Poli, Nosek, & David, 2014; Nosek et al., 2015). In this chapter I have shown that conducting and publishing replication experiments is the number one procedure to consolidate knowledge and to sort out false-positive from true findings. Thus, the stakeholders of science now generally agree that incentives are needed for researchers to conduct and publish replications and that practices that discourage replications need to be changed.

The Association for Psychological Science started an initiative on Registered Replication Reports (http://www.psychologicalscience.org/index.

php/replication) in which they emphasize the crucial role of direct replications and offer a modified submission and review process for such studies. Researchers planning a direct replication of a study submit their research plan, which is then in turn reviewed by the authors of the original study. Once there is an agreement between the two parties, the method and analysis plan is made publicly available and more researchers are invited to conduct replications according to this plan. Finally, the results of all these replications are published as a Registered Replication Report in *Perspectives on Psychological Sciences*, irrespective of their outcome. A similar initiative was started by the journal *Cortex* with the publication category Registered Replication (Chambers, 2013). Here the study plan is also reviewed before the replication starts, and the plan will be granted *in-principle acceptance*. Once the study has been conducted, the authors will publicly share their data and logs and submit a final manuscript, which will be judged for quality and sensible interpretations but not regarding a specific outcome. A list of other journals that have adopted the registered report principle can be found at https://osf.io/8mpji/wiki/home/.

These new incentives are steps in the right direction, but they are also quite demanding. One can assume that more changes are needed to give replications the same high reputation in daily scientific practice as they have from an epistemological perspective. One must also keep in mind that the practices addressed in this chapter are social practices and thus part of a culture. Cultures do change, especially when there is such an intensive discussion as has occurred in the social sciences in the past 5 years, but nevertheless these changes will need some time to be implemented and will be subject to further debate. When Neuliep and Crandall (1990) conducted a survey of editors of journals from the natural sciences regarding their policy on publishing replications, one editor answered, "Replication is rarely an issue for us . . . since we publish them." The recent discussions and developments in the social sciences indicate that this field is now also moving in a direction in which replications are both published and appreciated.

RECOMMENDED READING

Ioannidis, J. P. A. (2005). Why most published research findings are false. *PLOS Medicine*, 2(8), e124. http://doi.org/10.1371/journal.pmed.0020124

John, L. K., Loewenstein, G., & Prelec, D. (2012). Measuring the prevalence of questionable research practices with incentives for truth telling. *Psychological Science*, 23, 524–532. http://dx.doi.org/10.1177/0956797611430953

Open Science Collaboration. (2015, August 28). Estimating the reproducibility of psychological science. *Science*, 349, aac4716. http://doi.org/10.1126/science.aac4716

Pashler, H., & Wagenmakers, E.-J. (2012). Editors' introduction to the Special Section on Replicability in Psychological Science: A Crisis of Confidence? *Perspectives on Psychological Science, 7*, 528–530. http://doi.org/10.1177/1745691612465253

Rosenthal, R. (1991). Replication in behavioral research. In J. W. Neuliep (Ed.), *Replication research in the social sciences* (pp. 1–39). Newbury Park, CA: Sage.

REFERENCES

Anderson, C. J., Bahník, Š., Barnett-Cowan, M., Bosco, F. A., Chandler, J., Chartier, C. R., . . . Zuni, K. (2016, March 4). Response to comment on "Estimating the Reproducibility of Psychological Science." *Science, 351*, 1037. http://dx.doi.org/10.1126/science.aad9163

Asendorpf, J. B., Conner, M., De Fruyt, F., De Houwer, J., Denissen, J. J. A., Fiedler, K., . . . Wicherts, J. M. (2013). Recommendations for increasing replicability in psychology. *European Journal of Personality, 27*, 108–119. http://dx.doi.org/10.1002/per.1919

Bem, D. J. (2011). Feeling the future: Experimental evidence for anomalous retroactive influences on cognition and affect. *Journal of Personality and Social Psychology, 100*, 407–425. http://dx.doi.org/10.1037/a0021524

Bem, D. J., & Honorton, C. (1994). Does psi exist? Replicable evidence for an anomalous process of information transfer. *Psychological Bulletin, 115*, 4–18.

Bösch, H., Steinkamp, F., & Boller, E. (2006). Examining psychokinesis: The interaction of human intention with random number generators—A meta-analysis. *Psychological Bulletin, 132*, 497–523. http://dx.doi.org/10.1037/0033-2909.132.4.497

Braude, S. E. (1979). *ESP and psychokinesis: A philosophical examination.* Philadelphia, PA: Temple University Press.

Carpenter, S. (2012, March 39). Psychology's bold initiative. *Science, 335*, 1558–1560. http://dx.doi.org/10.1126/science.335.6076.1558

Chambers, C. D. (2013). Registered reports: A new publishing initiative at *Cortex. Cortex, 49*, 609–610. http://dx.doi.org/10.1016/j.cortex.2012.12.016

Collins, H. M. (1985). *Changing order: Replication and induction in scientific practice.* London, England: Sage.

Colwell, J., Schröder, S., & Sladen, D. (2000). The ability to detect unseen staring: A literature review and empirical tests. *British Journal of Psychology, 91*, 71–85. http://dx.doi.org/10.1348/000712600161682

Cook, T. D. (1990). The generalization of causal connections: Multiple theories in search of clear practice. In L. Sechrest, E. Perrin, & J. Bunker (Eds.), *Research methodology: Strengthening causal interpretations of non-experimental data* (pp. 9–30). Washington, DC: U.S. Department of Health and Human Services.

Davis, B. M. (1971). That's interesting! Towards a phenomenology of sociology and a sociology of phenomenology. *Philosophy of the Social Sciences*, *1*, 309–344. http://dx.doi.org/10.1177/004839317100100211

De Angelis, C., Drazen, J. M., Frizelle, F. A., Haug, C., Hoey, J., Horton, R., . . . Van Der Weyden, M. B. (2004). Clinical trial registration: A statement from the International Committee of Medical Journal Editors. *The New England Journal of Medicine*, *351*, 1250–1251. http://dx.doi.org/10.1056/NEJMe048225

Dilworth, C. (1996). *The metaphysics of science: An account of modern science in terms of principles, laws and theories*. Dordrecht, the Netherlands: Kluwer.

Edge, H. (1985). The problem is not replication. In B. Shapin & L. Coly (Eds.), *The repeatability problem in parapsychology* (pp. 53–64). New York, NY: Parapsychology Foundation.

Gilbert, D. T., King, G., Pettigrew, S., & Wilson, T. D. (2016, March 4). Comment on "Estimating the Reproducibility of Psychological Science." *Science*, *351*, 1037–1037. http://dx.doi.org/10.1126/science.aad7243

Hardy, R. J., & Thompson, S. G. (1998). Detecting and describing heterogeneity in meta-analysis. *Statistics in Medicine*, *17*, 841–856. http://dx.doi.org/10.1002/(SICI)1097-0258(19980430)17:8<841::AID-SIM781>3.0.CO;2-D

Hendrick, C. (1991). Replication, strict replications, and conceptual replications: Are they important? In J. W. Neuliep (Ed.), *Replication research in the social sciences* (pp. 41–49). Newbury Park, CA: Sage.

Horton, R. (2015). Offline: What is medicine's 5 sigma? *The Lancet*, *385*, 1380. http://dx.doi.org/10.1016/S0140-6736(15)60696-1

Ioannidis, J. P. A. (2005). Why most published research findings are false. *PLOS Medicine*, *2*(8), e124. http://dx.doi.org/10.1371/journal.pmed.0020124

Ioannidis, J. P. A. (2012). Scientific inbreeding and same-team replication: Type D personality as an example. *Journal of Psychosomatic Research*, *73*, 408–410. http://dx.doi.org/10.1016/j.jpsychores.2012.09.014

Ioannidis, J. P. A., Munafò, M. R., Fusar-Poli, P., Nosek, B. A., & David, S. P. (2014). Publication and other reporting biases in cognitive sciences: Detection, prevalence, and prevention. *Trends in Cognitive Sciences*, *18*, 235–241. http://dx.doi.org/10.1016/j.tics.2014.02.010

Irwin, H. J., & Watt, C. (2007). *An introduction to parapsychology* (5th ed.). Jefferson, NC: McFarland.

John, L. K., Loewenstein, G., & Prelec, D. (2012). Measuring the prevalence of questionable research practices with incentives for truth telling. *Psychological Science*, *23*, 524–532. http://dx.doi.org/10.1177/0956797611430953

Johnson, M. (1976). On publication regarding non-significant results. *European Journal of Parapsychology*, *1*(2), 1–5.

Keppel, G. (1982). *Design and analysis: A researcher's handbook*. Englewood Cliffs, NJ: Prentice Hall.

Kerr, N. L. (1998). HARKing: Hypothesizing after the results are known. *Personality and Social Psychology Review, 2*, 196–217. http://dx.doi.org/10.1207/s15327957pspr0203_4

Laws, K. R. (2013). Negativland—A home for all findings in psychology. *BMC Psychology, 1*, 2. http://dx.doi.org/10.1186/2050-7283-1-2

Lykken, D. T. (1968). Statistical significance in psychological research. *Psychological Bulletin, 70*, 151–159. http://dx.doi.org/10.1037/h0026141

Makel, M. C., & Plucker, J. A. (2014). Facts are more important than novelty: Replication in the education sciences. *Educational Researcher, 43*, 304–316. http://dx.doi.org/10.3102/0013189X14545513

Makel, M. C., Plucker, J. A., & Hegarty, B. (2012). Replications in psychology research: How often do they really occur? *Perspectives on Psychological Science, 7*, 537–542. http://dx.doi.org/10.1177/1745691612460688

Milton, J., & Wiseman, R. (1999). Does psi exist? Lack of replication of an anomalous process of information transfer. *Psychological Bulletin, 125*, 387–391. http://dx.doi.org/10.1037/0033-2909.125.4.387

Neuliep, J. W., & Crandall, R. (1990). Editorial bias against replication research. *Journal of Social Behavior and Personality, 5*, 85–90.

Neuroskeptic. (2012). The nine circles of scientific hell. *Perspectives on Psychological Science, 7*, 643–644. http://doi.org/10.1177/1745691612459519

Nosek, B. A., Alter, G., Banks, G. C., Borsboom, D., Bowman, S. D., Breckler, S. J., . . . Yarkoni, T. (2015, June 26). Promoting an open research culture. *Science, 348*, 1422–1425. http://dx.doi.org/10.1126/science.aab2374

Nosek, B. A., & Lakens, D. (2014). Registered reports. *Social Psychology, 45*, 137–141. http://dx.doi.org/10.1027/1864-9335/a000192

Nuzzo, R. (2015, October 7). How scientists fool themselves—And how they can stop. *Nature, 526*, 182–185. http://dx.doi.org/10.1038/526182a

Open Science Collaboration. (2012). An open, large-scale, collaborative effort to estimate the reproducibility of psychological science. *Perspectives on Psychological Science, 7*, 657–660. http://dx.doi.org/10.1177/1745691612462588

Open Science Collaboration. (2015, August 28). Estimating the reproducibility of psychological science. *Science, 349*, aac4716. http://dx.doi.org/10.1126/science.aac4716

Pashler, H., & Wagenmakers, E.-J. (2012). Editors' introduction to the Special Section on Replicability in Psychological Science: A Crisis of Confidence? *Perspectives on Psychological Science, 7*, 528–530. http://dx.doi.org/10.1177/1745691612465253

Petitti, D. B. (2001). Approaches to heterogeneity in meta-analysis. *Statistics in Medicine, 20*, 3625–3633. http://dx.doi.org/10.1002/sim.1091

Radder, H. (1992). Experimental reproducibility and the experimenters' regress. In D. Hull, M. Forbes, & K. Okruhlik (Eds.), *Proceedings of the Biennial Meeting of the Philosophy of Science Association* (pp. 63–73). Chicago, IL: University of Chicago Press.

Radder, H. (1996). *In and about the world: Philosophical studies of science and technology.* Albany: State University of New York Press.

Ritchie, S. J., Wiseman, R., & French, C. C. (2012). Failing the future: Three unsuccessful attempts to replicate Bem's "retroactive facilitation of recall" effect. *PLOS ONE, 7*(3), e33423. http://dx.doi.org/10.1371/journal.pone.0033423

Rosenthal, R. (1991). Replication in behavioral research. In J. W. Neuliep (Ed.), *Replication research in the social sciences* (pp. 1–39). Newbury Park, CA: Sage.

Rosenthal, R., & Fode, K. L. (1963). The effect of experimenter bias on the performance of the albino rat. *Behavioral Science, 8,* 183–189. http://dx.doi.org/10.1002/bs.3830080302

Rosenthal, R., & Rosnow, R. L. (1991). *Essentials of behavioral research: Methods and data analysis.* Boston, MA: McGraw-Hill.

Rosenthal, R., & Rubin, D. B. (1978). Interpersonal expectancy effects: The first 345 studies. *Behavioral and Brain Sciences, 1,* 377–415. http://dx.doi.org/10.1017/S0140525X00075506

Schmidt, S. (2009). Shall we really do it again? The powerful concept of replication is neglected in the social sciences. *Review of General Psychology, 13,* 90–100. http://dx.doi.org/10.1037/a0015108

Shadish, W. R. (1995). The logic of generalization: Five principles common to experiments and ethnographies. *American Journal of Community Psychology, 23,* 419–428. http://dx.doi.org/10.1007/BF02506951

Shadish, W. R., & Haddock, C. K. (1994). Combining estimates of effect size. In H. Cooper & L. V. Hedges (Eds.), *The handbook of research synthesis* (pp. 261–281). New York, NY: Russell Sage Foundation.

Shapin, S., & Schaffer, S. (1985). *Leviathan and the air-pump: Hobbes, Boyle, and the experimental life.* Princeton, NJ: Princeton University Press.

Simmons, J. P., Nelson, L. D., & Simonsohn, U. (2011). False-positive psychology: Undisclosed flexibility in data collection and analysis allows presenting anything as significant. *Psychological Science, 22,* 1359–1366. http://dx.doi.org/10.1177/0956797611417632

Storm, L., Tressoldi, P. E., & Di Risio, L. (2010). Meta-analysis of free-response studies, 1992–2008: Assessing the noise reduction model in parapsychology. *Psychological Bulletin, 136,* 471–485. http://dx.doi.org/10.1037/a0019457

Walach, H., & Schmidt, S. (2005). Repairing Plato's life boat with Ockham's Razor: The important function of research in anomalies for mainstream science. *Journal of Consciousness Studies, 12,* 52–70.

Watt, C., & Kennedy, J. E. (2015). Lessons from the first two years of operating a study registry. *Frontiers in Psychology, 6,* 173. http://dx.doi.org/10.3389/fpsyg.2015.00173

15

META-ANALYSIS AND REPRODUCIBILITY

RYAN T. WILLIAMS, JOSHUA R. POLANIN, AND TERRI D. PIGOTT

KEY POINTS

- A series of research replications provides more reliable evidence than single studies do.
- Systematic reviews and meta-analysis are tools for combining replication research and exploring sources of heterogeneity in individual study findings.
- High-quality systematic reviews and meta-analysis can provide optimally reliable research findings by minimizing the effects of the flaws associated with individual studies.
- Recent advances in research synthesis methodology, namely, individual participant data meta-analysis, will expand opportunities for conducting unplanned replication research.
- Fostering a culture of scientific collaboration and open data remains the best safeguard against bias.

http://dx.doi.org/10.1037/0000033-016
Toward a More Perfect Psychology: Improving Trust, Accuracy, and Transparency in Research, M. C. Makel and J. A. Plucker (Editors)

Single studies are unreliable. Science is a cumulative process: Theories are devised, hypotheses are formed, studies are designed, and data are collected with relentless attempts to disprove those hypotheses. Social and behavioral researchers are excellent at devising theories, forming hypotheses, designing studies, and collecting data. Where we fail is in the relentless pursuit of disproving our hypotheses. Too often, research is conducted in isolation, as single "one-off" studies or experiments. Also too often, isolated study results are considered the "truth," thereby suppressing rich and systematic culminations of scientific knowledge across multiple endeavors.

Primary research studies can be thought of as indicators of the underlying theories they investigate. Like items on a standardized assessment, each study provides additional information about the viability of the theories it investigates. One study may produce evidence consistent with a theory by testing various research hypotheses, and that study may inform the field about new techniques, practices, policies, and programs. Another study may produce evidence that is contrary to the theory. In an ideal world, both findings are equally likely to emerge and made available for external scientific and public scrutiny.

As Ioannidis (2005) discussed, most published studies have a number of flaws that must be considered in the interpretation of individual study findings. Individual research studies can suffer from selection bias, measurement bias, or poor sampling procedures. Errors in design and analysis (e.g., missing data, attrition, dependent observations) may be overlooked or go uncorrected. Errors in reporting also may occur. This is, of course, not to say that individual research studies are futile efforts at uncovering truth, but a reliable understanding of research findings in a particular field is rarely clear from one or two studies.

A series of studies, on the other hand, can account for some of these issues. Multiple studies on the same topic can be more robust to differences in sampling procedures or unobservable biases due to the randomization of groups. More saliently, multiple studies simply include more participants, thus improving the accuracy of the statistical analyses. Put simply, the addition of studies on the same topic provides greater confidence in the overall results. A *research synthesis* is designed to locate, code, and analyze multiple studies, thus providing the strongest evidence possible for or against a research hypothesis.

Replication research, by default, is ideal for research synthesis. The goal of replication is to test research hypotheses across independent samples, time frames, and observations, thus providing a robust understanding of a specific research hypothesis and its underlying theory. The goal of research synthesis is to combine multiple independent studies to provide a generalized understanding of specific research hypotheses and the viability of the theories underlying those hypotheses.

RESEARCH SYNTHESIS

Research synthesis (also called *synthesis research*) is a set of methods for combining scientific evidence with the goal of better understanding questions related to intervention effectiveness or complex social and psychological relationships. For example, one might synthesize the extant research on the effectiveness of behavioral interventions for aggressive behavior among adolescents. Alternatively, one might synthesize the existing evidence of the relationship between high school grade-point average and college completion. Synthesis research is particularly valuable to practitioners and policymakers because it provides a consolidated summary of existing evidence.

Most synthesis research falls into one of three categories—(a) qualitative narrative review, (b) systematic review, or (c) meta-analysis—or into (d) some combination of these. Narrative reviews are common in psychology and the social sciences. These reviews encompass traditional literature reviews of existing research and do not impose a specific set of criteria for selecting which studies to include in the review. Narrative reviews are not without value, and they exist, at least in part, in most scientific works. For example, introductory or background sections of empirical research often include brief narrative reviews. They are useful for illustrating a theoretical rationale for an investigator's hypotheses. Narrative reviews involve, however, almost exclusively what we will refer to as *high-level inferences* (e.g., Valentine & Cooper, 2008), which are conscious or unconscious decisions about the relative merits of a scientific contribution that happen during the review process. High-level inferences are not explicit and are often unreproducible. For example, one might review an article on the effects of cognitive behavior therapy (CBT) on depression among adults over age 65 and find that the study included 28 individuals who were not randomly assigned to the CBT condition. A narrative reviewer may decide to exclude this study from his or her review because of inadequate methodological quality, a decision that may be defensible. In this context, however, the evaluative criteria the reviewer used are neither transparent nor reproducible. Furthermore, traditional narrative reviews are typically incomprehensive, including only the aspects of a scientific body of literature that are easily accessible. Without a clear understanding of the literature that was searched, how it was searched, how studies were included in the review, and what kinds of information they provided for the review, the validity of the review's findings remains tenuous. For these reasons, we argue that traditional narrative syntheses are ill-suited for synthesis research that intends to summarize a body of scientific evidence.

Systematic reviews, the second category of synthesis research methods, comprise a set of procedures designed explicitly to avoid the limitations of traditional narrative reviews. Systematic reviews are intended to be explicit, transparent, and reproducible, and they may or may not contain a quantitative synthesis. One way to think about systematic reviews is that they provide a paper trail of all decisions made during a review. Cooper and Patall (2009) provided a framework for systematic reviewing that includes the following six steps: (a) problem formulation, (b) systematic search of the literature base, (c) gathering information from studies, (d) evaluating the quality of studies, (e) analyzing and interpreting the evidence, and (f) presenting the results. Under this framework, one may decide to exclude studies that had inadequately defined samples or used methods that are poorly suited for answering the primary questions, but these decisions must be identifiable and consistent throughout the review. Defining these decisions early on makes the final product available to scientific scrutiny, debate, and even replication. Moreover, discussing findings and conclusions with blind generality is avoided within this framework; the units, treatments, outcomes, and settings (UTOS; Cronbach, 1982) to which the findings pertain are explicitly defined, thereby avoiding, or at least minimizing, high-level inferences.

Meta-analysis is the third category of synthesis research. Traditional narrative reviews and some systematic reviews may not include a quantitative summary of the scientific evidence. Without a quantitative summary, even a well-implemented systematic review can yield unclear results and conclusions. When the goal of synthesis research is to generate a consolidated finding, the reviewers should include a meta-analysis whenever possible.

Meta-analysis involves a suite of statistical methods that are used to combine effect size estimates. Effect size estimates have two important features: They encode (a) the direction and (b) the magnitude of a relationship. Meta-analysis is most commonly used in the social and behavioral sciences to estimate mean effects of interventions (e.g., Sokolowski, Li, & Willson, 2015; Steenen et al., 2016), as represented by standardized mean differences or odds ratio effect sizes. Meta-analysis is also commonly used to combine bivariate correlations (e.g., Vasquez, Patall, Fong, Corrigan, & Pine, 2015) or information about a population proportion (e.g., Williams & Murray, 2015).

Glass (1976) coined the term *meta-analysis*, and Hedges and Olkin (1985) developed a theoretical and statistical foundation for combining and analyzing effect size estimates. Since then, meta-analytic work, including substantive and methodological research, has increased substantially. Figure 15.1 displays the PsycINFO citation returns for a search for "meta-analysis" OR "systematic review" OR "research synthesis" between 1985 and 2015.

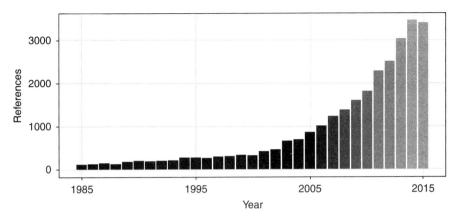

Figure 15.1. Historical synthesis research activity in psychology.

It is important to note that meta-analysis, on its own, is a purely a statistical procedure for combining quantitative data in an optimally efficient manner. For example, within a randomized-block design experiment, one might use a meta-analysis to combine the effects of the intervention effects in each of the blocks. In such scenarios, synthesizing an entire body of evidence is not the intention. Meta-analysts conducting synthesis research must take care to document the data-generating mechanisms. Without the careful design and implementation of a systematic review for information retrieval, a meta-analysis may contain many of the inferential flaws of traditional narrative reviews. For example, a poorly planned meta-analysis conducted on the basis of an unsystematic search may include studies only from the peer-reviewed, published literature. It is a well-known phenomenon that studies and effect sizes from the published literature tend to be larger than those from the unpublished literature (Polanin, Tanner-Smith, & Hennessy, 2015).[1] For these reasons, we recommend that reviewers use systematic reviewing and meta-analysis and, in the sections that follow we refer to meta-analysis as a scientific enterprise that includes a comprehensive and systematic review. Even though some readers may disagree with the decisions made during a systematic review and meta-analysis, the fact that they are presented and can be retraced is a defining feature of these methods.

---

[1] Some (e.g., Ferguson & Brannick, 2012) believe that unpublished literature induces bias into a systematic review. We do not take this position and instead recommend using publication status to facilitate empirical investigations of its effects. See Rothstein and Bushman (2012) for a more thorough discussion of the potential dangers of excluding unpublished literature.

WHEN IS A META-ANALYSIS NEEDED?

One of the most common questions from researchers interested in conducting a meta-analysis is, "How many studies do I need?" Technically, the answer to this question is: two (Valentine, Pigott, & Rothstein, 2010). Again, meta-analysis on its own is purely a set of statistical procedures, so simply asking how many studies are needed does not quite address the impetus for synthesis research. We argue that, regardless of the number of studies needed, synthesis research is healthy scientific practice.

The scope of a meta-analysis is tied to the research questions being addressed and the inferences the investigators intend to make. Many systematic reviews and meta-analyses may be small (e.g., fewer than 10 studies included); others may be larger. If, for example, someone wanted to understand the effects of cognitive therapy on the treatment of anxiety, without qualifying the characteristics of the samples, the outcomes, the treatments, or the settings, they would uncover a very large body of relevant research. Alternatively, they could specify that they are interested in conducting a systematic review and meta-analysis of cognitive therapy interventions for generalized anxiety disorder among African American men, between ages 18 and 25, in studies that randomly assigned treatment, used a manualized treatment implementation, and measured anxiety using the Beck Anxiety Inventory (Beck, Epstein, Brown, & Steer, 1988), which would yield a much smaller pool of studies eligible for synthesis. Meta-analysts must find a balance between pursuing unrealistically narrow research questions as well as questions so broad that they prevent one from making practical or actionable conclusions.

Sometimes, well-constructed research questions with appropriate inclusion criteria may return no studies that meet the inclusion criteria. A meta-analysis with no included studies is sometimes referred to as an "empty" review. Identifying a research literature that is undeveloped or underdeveloped is valuable information and perhaps just as important as knowing how effective a single treatment is across many studies. The fewer the number of studies, the less reliable the cumulative evidence is. For example, perhaps there exist only two, small, randomized experiments of cognitive therapy for treating generalized anxiety disorder among African American men between ages 18 and 25. And perhaps someone conducts a meta-analysis of these two treatment effect estimates. The mean estimate from that study is much more likely to change when a third, larger, study emerges in the literature as opposed to an estimate from a meta-analysis based on 30 small randomized experiments. Thus, one main benefit from synthesizing a larger rather than smaller body of evidence is stability in the estimated average effect.

Some meta-analyses, on the other hand, contain many studies. A great example from the Campbell Collaboration is Wilson, Lipsey, Tanner-Smith,

Huang, and Steinka-Fry's (2011) review of school dropout prevention programs. The authors conducted an exhaustive search of the literature and ultimately included 167 studies. It is clear that for this body of literature, at this particular time, a meta-analysis was needed. Moreover, the results revealed a significant treatment effect, but, as the authors pointed out, the programs varied considerably in their implementation, populations, and findings. Larger meta-analyses such as this one (a) will often have more heterogeneous effects and (b) will have greater statistical power to investigate potential sources of heterogeneity (Hedges & Pigott, 2004).

The decision to begin a systematic review or meta-analysis should be determined not solely on the basis of the number of studies one expects to include but instead by the need for understanding specific and well-constructed research questions. Understanding the state of the science in regard those questions is critical for advancing future research in a targeted manner. Of course, a larger number of studies provides greater stability and statistical power, and, regardless of the number of studies needed for a synthesis, meta-analyses, especially those with relatively low between-study heterogeneity, are often more powerful than their individual studies (Cohn & Becker, 2003).

META-ANALYSIS FOR UNDERSTANDING HETEROGENEITY

In addition to understanding the magnitude of the mean intervention effect or an average bivariate correlation, meta-analysis is an important tool for understanding the variation, or heterogeneity, across the synthesized study effects (Cook et al., 1992; Stuart, Cole, Bradshaw, & Leaf, 2011; Weiss, Bloom, & Brock, 2014). This information is as important as understanding the strength of the relationship because practitioners and policymakers care about consistency as much as they do about magnitude. A program with a highly variant yet large average treatment effect may not be as useful as a program that is relatively stable with a small average treatment effect.

Consider Figure 15.2, which depicts two hypothetical forest plots. Forest plots are useful for graphically illustrating both the mean effect and the variance among the individual effects that contributed to the mean. Each individual study effect is represented by a small dot (i.e., the effect size) and a horizontal line (i.e., the 95% confidence interval [CI]). The larger diamond at the bottom of the plot represents the overall mean effect estimate.

The first forest plot represents a relatively homogeneous group of studies, with an average treatment effect of 0.05 (95% CI [0.01, 0.10]). Each of the individual effects deviates from the overall mean by only a small amount, less than 0.10 standard deviations. With these effects it is possible to draw a vertical line through the plot that intersects with all of the individual effect CIs.

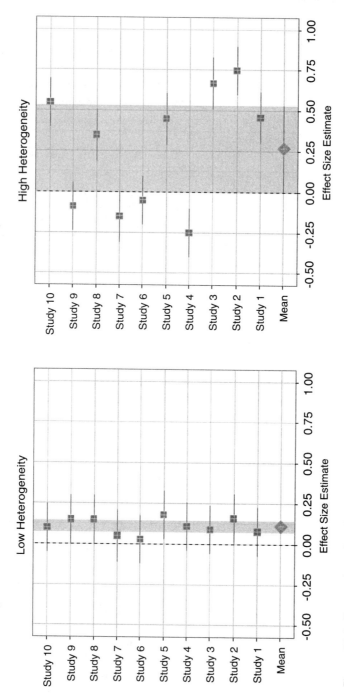

Figure 15.2. Forest plots showing low and high levels of heterogeneity.

The second forest plot represents a heterogeneous set of effects. The average treatment effect is much larger, 0.27 (95% CI [0.004, 0.53]), indicating a moderate treatment effect. However, Studies 4, 6, 7, and 9 are noticeably different from the others. Perhaps there was something specific about the composition of those samples that is moderating the magnitude of the observed effects (e.g., gender, grade level, age, ethnicity). In fact, the mean effect for those four samples may be negative. Without such information, a practitioner or policymaker may inaccurately assume that the mean effect generalizes to all subpopulations.

The second plot in Figure 15.2 is by far the most commonly encountered scenario in meta-analytic work, which may be a symptom of synthesizing uncoordinated replications in a body of research. An important aspect of any meta-analysis is the attempt to make sense of heterogeneity among effect sizes, most commonly using sources about sample composition, treatment components implemented, outcome measures, methods, and study settings. However, there often remain significant amounts of between-study heterogeneity that is not explained by study characteristics.

META-ANALYSIS AND REPLICATION

Meta-analysis is an opportunity to take stock of what is known and what is not known across different scientific endeavors. Allen and Preiss (1993) discussed the symbiotic relationship between meta-analysis and replication more than 20 years ago, noting that although meta-analysis inextricably relies on replication, future directions for research, practice, and policy are often tied to the results of meta-analytic work. Unfortunately, coordinated replication research remains rare in the social and behavioral sciences (Makel & Plucker, 2014; Makel, Plucker, & Hegarty, 2012). Systematic reviewers and meta-analysts are therefore tasked with sifting through vast literatures to identify studies that address specific research questions and making decisions about the comparability of those investigations.

Schmidt (2009) described a continuum for replication research. On one end of the continuum are tightly controlled laboratory replications in which the research questions, measures, methods, and populations are identical across each study or trial. This is what Schmidt referred to as *direct replication*. In a direct replication study, the investigators exactly replicate the population from which study units were drawn, the study design, and the measures. On the other end of the continuum are replications that use different methods (e.g., sampling and study designs, outcome measures) for addressing the same questions. Schmidt called this *conceptual replication*. In a conceptual replication study the investigators address the same general research questions, with the same general target population, use similar (though not identical) methods for answering those questions, and measure the same constructs, but perhaps with different instruments. Consider an investigation of the effectiveness of CBT for treating depression among young adults. An example of a direct replication would be a series of at least two experiments of manualized CBT for treating depression among college students, conducted by the same research team, in the same research laboratory, sampling students from the same university health care system, and using the Beck Depression Inventory (BDI; Beck, Ward, Mendelson, Mock, & Erbaugh, 1961) as an outcome measure. An example of a conceptual replication of the CBT experiment would be a series of at least two experiments of a nonmanualized CBT experiment; at different universities; using college-age students in one and adults between the ages of 18 and 30 in the other, one using the Patient Health Questionnaire–9 (Kroenke, Spitzer, & Williams, 2001) as the depression outcome measure and the other using the BDI. In the direct replication example there is little argument needed for the comparability of the units, treatments, outcomes, and settings that the studies comprised. In the conceptual replication a meta-analyst is charged with making the argument for the comparability of the different research constructs across the two investigations, which ultimately becomes an exercise in generalizability (Shadish, Cook, & Campbell, 2002). Because of the very low prevalence of direct replication research, nearly all meta-analytic research focuses on identifying and combining conceptual replicates.

Although we have thus far discussed meta-analysis as a tool for studying replication research, replications of meta-analyses are needed, too. Meta-analysts face the challenge of identifying research questions and locating the sources of information that will inform those questions. In that process, myriad decisions are made regarding the sources of information that are searched, the terms used in the search, the qualifying features of candidate study reports (e.g., populations, treatments, outcomes, settings, methods), and methods for computing and combining effect sizes. With so many potential sources of variance across these decisions, it is easy to imagine investigators coming to conclusions that differ, at least slightly. High-quality systematic reviews and meta-analyses will typically include a number of procedural replications within the review process. For example, many systematic reviews and meta-analyses include two or more independent searches of the literature, screening of titles and abstracts, and coding of studies. Discrepancies are discussed and a consensus is met, ensuring optimal fidelity to the a priori study operations. Because systematic reviews and meta-analyses are intended to summarize extant findings, many researchers try to keep them updated (e.g., Gouvas, Tan, Windsor, Xynos, & Tekkis, 2009; Griffeth, Hom, & Gaertner, 2000; Smith et al., 2007). Unfortunately, replications of meta-analytic research using the same operational definitions is extremely rare, perhaps nonexistent.

INDIVIDUAL PARTICIPANT DATA META-ANALYSIS

Meta-analysis, like other methods, evolves to meet the demands of the research community. Up to this point, we have discussed meta-analysis in its traditional form, whereby study reports are identified as being relevant to a specific research question and they report the necessary information from which to calculate an effect size estimate. Such a meta-analysis might be considered an "aggregate data" meta-analysis because it relies on the investigator-generated summary statistics for effect size computation. Another form of meta-analysis that is gaining traction in the biomedical research fields is *individual participant data (IPD) meta-analysis*, which is a synthesis that uses the raw data generated from primary research studies. One recent example of this kind of research is Lejoyeux and Lehert's (2011) study. The authors conducted an IPD meta-analysis using data from 10 randomized experiments on the effects of acamprostate for treating alcohol-use disorders. Another example is Suciu et al. (2014), who conducted an IPD meta-analysis of 15 data sets from randomized experiments of adjunctive interferon-a for treating high-risk melanoma.

Cooper and Patall (2009) identified three main advantages of conducting an IPD meta-analysis instead of a traditional aggregate-data meta-analysis. First, an IPD meta-analysis provides an opportunity to conduct analyses that were not presented in published research reports. Meta-analysts often need additional information from a study, such as a correlation matrix, an intraclass correlation, or even simple means or standard deviations. Having IPD allows meta-analysts to conduct these auxiliary analyses that are otherwise irrelevant to the published research that used the data. Second, subgroup analyses can be conducted. Although a research publication may present an overall mean difference between a treatment group and a control group, the authors may not have looked at an interaction with, for example, gender. A meta-analyst then has an opportunity to extract a larger quantity of information using IPD, which is often helpful for understanding heterogeneity in effect size estimates. Third, with IPD the meta-analyst has an opportunity to conduct analyses independently. Here the advantage is that the meta-analyst can make decisions about the analysis that may differ from those of the primary researchers. For example, the meta-analyst may choose to multiply impute their missing data rather than using listwise deletion.

There are three approaches to IPD meta-analysis. The first approach is what Cooper and Patall (2009) referred to as the *two-stage approach*, in which IPD data sets are analyzed separately, effect sizes are computed, and they are combined using traditional meta-analytic methods. The second approach is a *one-stage analysis*, whereby the IPD is combined into a single data file and analyzed simultaneously. The one-stage approach is often difficult to implement in practice because outcome and covariate measures vary, often dramatically, across investigations. The third approach is a combination of IPD meta-analysis and aggregate data meta-analysis. In the context of systematic reviewing, a meta-analyst may uncover a large number of relevant studies. It is very unlikely that all studies that are flagged as eligible will also have available IPD. Therefore, a meta-analyst may combine the aggregate data and IPD in a single multilevel model (e.g., Goldstein, Yang, Omar, Turner, & Thompson, 2000; Pigott, Williams, & Polanin, 2012). Although IPD meta-analysis is still in its infancy, especially in the social and behavioral sciences, it offers tremendous potential for advancing replication research. Researchers frequently collect a wide range of data in their investigations. For example, researchers conducting a randomized experiment on the effects of an antidepressant medication may collect data on multiple depressions measures, other measures of affect and psychopathology, satisfaction with life, functional independence, demographic data, religiosity, political affiliation, and general health. With troves of data collected as part of single investigations, IPD meta-analysts have opportunities to identify unplanned replications and study them in a systematic fashion.

Prospective meta-analysis is a special example of IPD meta-analysis. In its basic form, a prospective meta-analysis identifies all studies for inclusion before their individual study findings become available. These studies could be coordinated or not. The key purpose of prospective meta-analysis is to alleviate any investigator biases that may affect traditional retrospective meta-analyses, in which investigators may be aware of study findings (Higgins & Green, 2011).

Data availability remains the biggest hurdle for advancing IPD meta-analysis. Only recently have federal organizations begun implementing policies that promote data sharing and collaboration within their respective communities. The National Institutes of Health (2003) requires that funded projects greater than or equal to $500,000 provide the institutes with a final research data set. The National Science Foundation (2013) also requires investigators to share the primary data they collect as part of funded research activities. And during the 2012–2013 fiscal year, the Institute of Education Sciences (2013) published its first data-sharing policy, targeting projects funded through the National Center for Education Research and the National Center for Special Education Research. Federally funded research constitutes only a portion of active research endeavors in a given field. To change the way we do science requires a change in the culture of the scientific community. It requires a culture of systematic and collaborative investigation, and it requires research transparency. A good first step would be making data available to prospective collaborators.

Data sharing is often a complicated matter. Data security, confidentiality, coauthorship, and ownership are all important considerations. We believe it is likely that these issues, though nontrivial, can most often be addressed in a fashion that facilitates a successful and productive collaboration between primary study researchers and meta-analysts.

Although federal funding agencies are advancing data release policies, the scientific community can contribute to this endeavor as well. Scientific journals have an opportunity to help identify investigators who are interested in sharing their data. As part of standard documentation with manuscript submission and publication, journals can survey investigators and ask if they have the rights to the data that generated the reported findings and, if they do, whether they would be willing to share their data with potential collaborators. Although this seems like a small step, it may help change the standard operating assumption that researchers are unwilling to let others use any of their data whatsoever.

CONCLUSION

Meta-analysis is an invaluable suite of methods for summarizing bodies of scientific findings and for understanding variation in those findings and is why synthesis research activity in psychology has increased exponentially over the past 30 years. Unfortunately, coordinated research endeavors involving systematic replications are rare. Thus, meta-analysis is most often retrospective, with researchers identifying conceptual replications, often with a large amount of construct variability. Recent advances in meta-analytic methods, namely, IPD meta-analysis, may provide increased opportunities for both collaborative research and systematic replication research. Federal funding agencies are advancing policies to encourage data sharing among investigators, but researchers must also help advance a culture of collaboration.

RECOMMENDED READING

Cook, T. D., Cooper, H., Cordray, D. S., Hartmann, H., Hedges, L. V., & Light, R. J. (1992). *Meta-analysis for explanation: A casebook*. New York, NY: Russell Sage Foundation.

Cooper, H., Hedges, L. V., & Valentine, J. C. (2009). *The handbook of research synthesis and meta-analysis*. New York, NY: Russell Sage Foundation.

Valentine, J. C., & Cooper, H. (2008). A systematic and transparent approach for assessing the methodological quality of intervention effectiveness research: The Study Design and Implementation Assessment Device (Study DIAD). *Psychological Methods, 13*, 130–149. http://dx.doi.org/10.1037/1082-989X.13.2.130

Valentine, J. C., Pigott, T. D., & Rothstein, H. R. (2010). How many studies do you need? A primer on statistical power for meta-analysis. *Journal of Educational and Behavioral Statistics, 35*, 215–247. http://dx.doi.org/10.3102/1076998609346961

Weiss, M. J., Bloom, H. S., & Brock, T. (2014). A conceptual framework for studying the sources of variation in program effects. *Journal of Policy Analysis and Management, 33*, 778–808. http://dx.doi.org/10.1002/pam.21760

REFERENCES

Allen, M., & Preiss, R. (1993). Replication and meta-analysis: A necessary connection. *Journal of Social Behavior and Personality, 8*, 9–20.

Beck, A. T., Epstein, N., Brown, G., & Steer, R. A. (1988). An inventory for measuring clinical anxiety: Psychometric properties. *Journal of Consulting and Clinical Psychology, 56*, 893–897. http://dx.doi.org/10.1037/0022-006X.56.6.893

Beck, A. T., Ward, C. H., Mendelson, M., Mock, J., & Erbaugh, J. (1961). An inventory for measuring depression. *Archives of General Psychiatry, 4*, 561–571. http://dx.doi.org/10.1001/archpsyc.1961.01710120031004

Cohn, L. D., & Becker, B. J. (2003). How meta-analysis increases statistical power. *Psychological Methods, 8*, 243–253. http://dx.doi.org/10.1037/1082-989X.8.3.243

Cook, T. D., Cooper, H., Cordray, D. S., Hartmann, H., Hedges, L. V., & Light, R. J. (1992). *Meta-analysis for explanation: A casebook.* New York, NY: Russell Sage Foundation.

Cooper, H., & Patall, E. A. (2009). The relative benefits of meta-analysis conducted with individual participant data versus aggregated data. *Psychological Methods, 14*, 165–176. http://dx.doi.org/10.1037/a0015565

Cronbach, L. J. (1982). *Designing evaluations of educational and social programs.* San Francisco, CA: Jossey-Bass.

Ferguson, C. J., & Brannick, M. T. (2012). Publication bias in psychological science: Prevalence, methods for identifying and controlling, and implications for the use of meta-analyses. *Psychological Methods, 17*, 120–128. http://dx.doi.org/10.1037/a0024445

Glass, G. V. (1976). Primary, secondary, and meta-analysis of research. *Educational Researcher, 5*, 3–8. http://dx.doi.org/10.3102/0013189X005010003

Goldstein, H., Yang, M., Omar, R., Turner, R., & Thompson, S. (2000). Meta-analysis using multilevel models with an application to the study of class size effects. *Journal of the Royal Statistical Society: Series C. Applied Statistics, 49*, 399–412. http://dx.doi.org/10.1111/1467-9876.00200

Gouvas, N., Tan, E., Windsor, A., Xynos, E., & Tekkis, P. P. (2009). Fast-track vs standard care in colorectal surgery: A meta-analysis update. *International Journal of Colorectal Disease, 24*, 1119–1131. http://dx.doi.org/10.1007/s00384-009-0703-5

Griffeth, R. W., Hom, P. W., & Gaertner, S. (2000). A meta-analysis of antecedents and correlates of employee turnover: Update, moderator tests, and research implications for the next millennium. *Journal of Management, 26*, 463–488. http://dx.doi.org/10.1177/014920630002600305

Hedges, L. V., & Olkin, I. (1985). *Statistical methods for meta-analysis*. New York, NY: Academic Press.

Hedges, L. V., & Pigott, T. D. (2004). The power of statistical tests for moderators in meta-analysis. *Psychological Methods, 9*, 426–445. http://dx.doi.org/10.1037/1082-989X.9.4.426

Higgins, J. P., & Green, S. (Eds.). (2011). *Cochrane handbook for systematic reviews of interventions* (Version 5.1.0). Retrieved from http://handbook.cochrane.org/

Institute of Education Sciences. (2013, August). *Implementation guide for public access to research data*. Retrieved from http://ies.ed.gov/funding/datasharing_implementation.asp

Ioannidis, J. P. A. (2005). Why most published research findings are false. *PLOS Medicine, 2*(8), e124. http://dx.doi.org/10.1371/journal.pmed.0020124

Kroenke, K., Spitzer, R. L., & Williams, J. B. (2001). The PHQ-9: Validity of a brief depression severity measure. *Journal of General Internal Medicine, 16*, 606–613. http://dx.doi.org/10.1046/j.1525-1497.2001.016009606.x

Lejoyeux, M., & Lehert, P. (2011). Alcohol-use disorders and depression: Results from individual patient data meta-analysis of the acamprosate-controlled studies. *Alcohol and Alcoholism, 46*, 61–67. http://dx.doi.org/10.1093/alcalc/agq077

Makel, M. C., & Plucker, J. A. (2014). Facts are more important than novelty: Replication in the education sciences. *Educational Researcher, 43*, 304–316. http://dx.doi.org/10.3102/0013189X14545513

Makel, M. C., Plucker, J. A., & Hegarty, B. (2012). Replications in psychology research: How often do they really occur? *Perspectives on Psychological Science, 7*, 537–542. http://dx.doi.org/10.1177/1745691612460688

National Institutes of Health. (2003, March). *NIH data sharing policy and implementation guidance*. Retrieved from http://grants.nih.gov/grants/policy/data_sharing/data_sharing_guidance.htm#goals

National Science Foundation. (2013, January). *Chapter VI—Other post award requirements and considerations*. Retrieved from http://www.nsf.gov/pubs/policydocs/pappguide/nsf13001/aag_6.jsp#VID4

Pigott, T., Williams, R., & Polanin, J. (2012). Combining individual participant and aggregated data in a meta-analysis with correlational studies. *Research Synthesis Methods, 3*, 257–268. http://dx.doi.org/10.1002/jrsm.1051

Polanin, J. R., Tanner-Smith, E. E., & Hennessy, E. A. (2015). Estimating the difference between published and unpublished effect sizes: A meta-review. *Review of Educational Research, 86*, 207–236. http://dx.doi.org/10.3102/0034654315582067

Rothstein, H. R., & Bushman, B. J. (2012). Publication bias in psychological science: Comment on Ferguson and Brannick (2012). *Psychological Methods, 17*, 129–136. http://dx.doi.org/10.1037/a0027128

Schmidt, S. (2009). Shall we really do it again? The powerful concept of replication is neglected in the social sciences. *Review of General Psychology, 13*, 90–100.

Shadish, W. R., Cook, T. D., & Campbell, D. T. (2002). *Experimental and quasi-experimental designs for generalized causal inference*. Boston, MA: Houghton Mifflin.

Smith, J. S., Lindsay, L., Hoots, B., Keys, J., Franceschi, S., Winer, R., & Clifford, G. M. (2007). Human papillomavirus type distribution in invasive cervical cancer and high-grade cervical lesions: A meta-analysis update. *International Journal of Cancer, 121*, 621–632. http://dx.doi.org/10.1002/ijc.22527

Sokolowski, A., Li, Y., & Willson, V. (2015). The effects of using exploratory computerized environments in Grades 1 to 8 mathematics: A meta-analysis of research. *International Journal of STEM Education, 2*, 8–17. http://dx.doi.org/10.1186/s40594-015-0022-z

Steenen, S. A., van Wijk, A. J., van der Heijden, G. J., van Westrhenen, R., de Lange, J., & de Jongh, A. (2016). Propranolol for the treatment of anxiety disorders: Systematic review and meta-analysis. *Journal of Psychopharmacology, 30*, 128–139. http://dx.doi.org/10.1177/0269881115612236

Stuart, E. A., Cole, S. R., Bradshaw, C. P., & Leaf, P. J. (2011). The use of propensity scores to assess the generalizability of results from randomized trials. *Journal of the Royal Statistical Society: Series A. Statistics in Society, 174*, 369–386. http://dx.doi.org/10.1111/j.1467-985X.2010.00673.x

Suciu, S., Ives, N., Eggermont, A. M., Kirkwood, J. M., Lorigan, P., & Markovic, S., . . . Wheatley, K. (2014). Predictive importance of ulceration on the efficacy of adjuvant interferon-a (IFN): An individual patient data (IPD) meta-analysis of 15 randomized trials in more than 7,500 melanoma patients (pts). *ASCO Meeting Abstracts, 32*(Suppl. 15), 9067.

Valentine, J. C., & Cooper, H. (2008). A systematic and transparent approach for assessing the methodological quality of intervention effectiveness research: The Study Design and Implementation Assessment Device (Study DIAD). *Psychological Methods, 13*, 130–149. http://dx.doi.org/10.1037/1082-989X.13.2.130

Valentine, J. C., Pigott, T. D., & Rothstein, H. R. (2010). How many studies do you need? A primer on statistical power for meta-analysis. *Journal of Educational and Behavioral Statistics, 35*, 215–247. http://dx.doi.org/10.3102/1076998609346961

Vasquez, A. C., Patall, E. A., Fong, C. J., Corrigan, A. S., & Pine, L. (2015). Parent autonomy support, academic achievement, and psychosocial functioning: A meta-analysis of research. *Educational Psychology Review, 28*(3). Advance online publication. http://dx.doi.org/10.1007/s10648-015-9329-z

Weiss, M. J., Bloom, H. S., & Brock, T. (2014). A conceptual framework for studying the sources of variation in program effects. *Journal of Policy Analysis and Management, 33*, 778–808. http://dx.doi.org/10.1002/pam.21760

Williams, R., & Murray, A. (2015). Prevalence of depression after spinal cord injury: A meta-analysis. *Archives of Physical Medicine and Rehabilitation, 96*, 133–140. http://dx.doi.org/10.1016/j.apmr.2014.08.016

Wilson, S. J., Lipsey, M. W., Tanner-Smith, E., Huang, C. H., & Steinka-Fry, K. T. (2011). Dropout prevention and intervention programs: Effects on school completion and dropout among school-aged children and youth. *Campbell Systematic Reviews, 7*(8). Retrieved from http://www.campbellcollaboration.org/lib/project/158/

V

SYNTHESIS

16

THE REPRODUCIBILITY CRISIS IN PSYCHOLOGY: ATTACK OF THE CLONES OR PHANTOM MENACE?

JEFFREY K. SMITH, LISA F. SMITH, AND BENJAMIN K. SMITH

KEY POINTS

- Replication is an important component of scientific research, but it is not the essential component.
- HARKing (hypothesizing after the results are known) is a problem only if done deceitfully; otherwise, it is what science is all about.
- There is little evidence to support the argument that important findings in psychology research are not sufficiently replicated.
- What is needed in psychological research are better ideas to study and a infrastructure that encourages and promotes responsible behavior, collaboration, and creativity, not one that sets up impediments and assumes unethical behavior.

http://dx.doi.org/10.1037/0000033-017
Toward a More Perfect Psychology: Improving Trust, Accuracy, and Transparency in Research, M. C. Makel and J. A. Plucker (Editors)

Consider this thought experiment: If you could change one thing about psychology research in order to improve the field, what would that one thing be, and how would it change psychology? More replication (Chapter 14, this volume)? Less HARKing (hypothesizing after results are known; Chapter 4)? Obtaining larger sample sizes (Chapters 2 and 3)? Using more rigorous and appropriate data analysis (Chapter 2)? Less selective outcome reporting (Chapter 4)? Downgrading the influence of statistical significance testing in favor of reporting effect sizes (Chapter 4)? Registering hypotheses at a central registry before conducting a study analysis (Chapter 2)? Using more directed acyclic graphs (Chapter 3)? Keeping a closer eye on research misconduct (Chapter 17)?

An argument can be made for each of these options; indeed, arguments *have* been made for each of them in this volume. Most would make a contribution to the development of the field—but what would the effect size be? Against a standard of making only one change to improve the field, perhaps none of these would be a first choice. We argue that a better choice for a single change would be this: Generate ideas that better explain psychological phenomena. The short form of this is: Better ideas. That's it. That's our choice. It is fairly closely aligned with the arguments presented by Vartanian (Chapter 1). In this chapter, we take a look at some of the alternatives presented in this book and then make an argument for better ideas, and some corollaries that arise from it.

WHAT ARE WE TRYING TO DO?

Many of the chapters of this book have as their underlying premise that the field of psychology has a problem, perhaps even a crisis (Makel, Plucker, & Hegarty, 2012; Pashler & Harris, 2012; Chapter 14, this volume). But what exactly is that crisis? That the public does not have enough faith in the field? That research findings are not replicated with sufficient frequency? That the field is rife with questionable research practices, approaching outright fraud?

Although it is no doubt true that some of these things go on in the field of psychology, as they no doubt do in every field, where is the evidence that this is a common problem, much less a crisis? Following the logic of Ioannidis (2005), Pashler and Harris (2012) began their argument for the crisis with the supposition that one can reasonably set a prior probability that an effect actually exists at 10%. *What?* Who goes through the trouble of conducting a study when they believe that what they are looking for to confirm their theoretical argument has a 90% chance of being false? The authors then claimed that a power level of 80% "exceeds any realistic assumptions about psychology studies in general" (p. 532). *It does?* In the Open Science Framework Reproducibility Project (Open Science Collaboration, 2015), power levels above 80% were obtained in almost all 100 replications, apparently without too much stress on the replicators. Although Pashler and Harris allowed for consideration of a prior probability as high as 75%, in doing so they lowered the power of their study to 35% and concluded that false positives are therefore rampant. Even if one accepted this intriguing line of argumentation, where is the evidence that this is a problem in psychology?

In this chapter we look at some of the claims of problems that supposedly are plaguing the field, in particular, lack of replication, hypothesizing after results are known (HARKing), and selective outcome reporting. After that, we look at some of the broader issues that these concerns raise and then examine our argument that better ideas would be the change that would benefit the field the most.

REPLICATION

Although HARKing and selective outcome reporting are argued to be serious problems, lack of replication is the concept that most often has the descriptor *crisis* attached to it (Maxwell, Lau, & Howard, 2015). Being opposed to replication would be like being opposed to apple pie; it is an essential aspect of every academic discipline that relies on research studies. The question with respect to replication is not whether it is a good thing but whether there is currently a critical dearth of replication in psychology. Citing the Reproducibility Project study (Open Science Collaboration, 2012, 2015), Schmidt (Chapter 14, this volume) concluded that the answer is yes. We draw a different conclusion based on three arguments. First, the Reproducibility Project does not speak to the issue of whether enough replication occurs in psychology. The results from the Reproducibility Project would not change if there were a surfeit of replication studies in psychology— or none at all. Thus, the results of the Reproducibility Project, as popular as they are (and, as this chapter was being written, the project won an award from *Science* as one of the findings of the year in 2015 having the greatest impact on science), simply do not speak to the question.

Second, the important question is not the proportion of research findings that replicate; the question is whether key research findings, ones on which scholars base subsequent work, receive sufficient replication to establish the reliability of the findings. Here we think the answer is clearly yes. Why? One simply has to look at the proliferation of meta-analytic studies in the field of psychology to come to this simple and convincing conclusion: Important findings in psychology are replicated. Meta-analysis is not possible without replication. If one asked, "What are the 20 most important research findings in the field of psychology in the past 10 years?" different scholars might generate different lists, but some level of consensus could probably be reached. If one then asked, "Are the findings on that list reliable? Have they been replicated?" the answer almost assuredly would be yes. There is a Darwinian process that exists with such research. The good work, the work that is exciting, advances the field, and causes a buzz in the research community, gets replicated. Sometimes those replications reproduce the original findings; sometimes they do not. But they get done. And within 5 to 10 years, meta-analyses of those studies get done. It happens with such amazing regularity that it is hard to imagine why anyone would think there is a problem with replication. Work that is important to the field gets replicated. It is the stuff of meta-analyses that populate our journals.

To put some hard figures on this argument, consider the fact that just the first 10 original studies listed on the Reproducibility Project site (https://osf.io/ezcuj/; Open Science Collaboration, 2015) have received 939 citations as of the time of this writing (ranging from a low of 18 to a high of 218). Many of those citations are articles that replicate or extend the work of the original study. Most of those studies combined the information from a range of original studies, and the authors' original thinking, to generate new and refined hypotheses to investigate. Had the Reproducibility Project simply looked at the extant record of refereed publications using those articles as part of their research, they might have saved a lot of time with needless replications of works already thoroughly examined. And they would have found that some of the works replicated successfully in direct or conceptual replications, whereas others did not. At the end of the articles, they would have seen scientists working to reconcile and extend findings that were either congruent or not congruent with the original studies. That is how science actually proceeds. What one does not see in these later studies are scientists who bemoan having been led completely in the wrong direction by the results of a single study failing to replicate. The crisis is fugitive at best.

In contrast to the 20 most important research findings, it would be difficult to list the 20 least important research findings in the past 20 years. There would be many contenders. One thing they would almost all have in common is that they have not been replicated. Why not? Because *why bother*? They were not interesting studies to begin with. Thus, if we let the interchange of ideas play out here, the work that is likely to advance the field will be replicated, and it will not be relied upon until it *is* replicated. And those works that do not generate interest in the scientific community will languish and die.

Third, the Reproducibility Project has been accepted widely at face value. It is at least a meme, and growing toward being a law, that only 36% of findings in psychology are not false positives (see, e.g., Chapter 14, this volume). Such logic assumes that the 100 replication studies in the Reproducibility Project were of high quality, reasonably close to being direct replications instead of conceptual replications, did not have design flaws or stray so far away from the original study to be of questionable value, and had sufficient statistical power to anticipate a positive finding if the original finding were true. But a cursory look at the Reproducibility Project immediately calls into question a number of those assumptions. An admirable part of the Reproducibility Project is that the replication study reports are all available on the site. But in reading the reports one finds numerous examples of difficulties in executing the replications that would lead one to question whether some of the studies could fairly be called replications.

One study in the Reproducibility Project replicated an original study conducted with Princeton University undergraduates in a laboratory setting with some students from the University of South Alabama also participating, online. Another study used a false newspaper article about the underlying stability of the country as an intervention designed to set up a level of ambivalence in the male participants. The original study was conducted in Canada; the replication was done in Germany. How is this a direct replication? Surely one would have to take into consideration the relative historical stability of the two societies before thinking that the settings would be comparable. As a cross-cultural replication it is fine, and important, but it can hardly be considered a direct replication. On that front, a number of the studies were conducted in a language different from the original language in the replication, with no evidence that the outcome measures translated were measuring the same constructs. In particular for the *Journal of Personality and Social Psychology*, but also for the social-oriented articles from *Psychological Science*, one would anticipate that different cultural and social norms of different samples might influence outcomes. And in fact, the articles from those two sources showed significant replications in 25% of the studies, whereas the articles from the *Journal of Experimental Psychology: General*, and the cognitive articles from *Psychological Science* showed significant replications in 50% of the studies. A quick chi-square calculation of the difference between the two rates is significant at $p = .013$.

When one reads that only 36% of the studies in the Reproducibility Project successfully replicated, one naturally uses 100% as a comparison. But it is the cumulative power of the replications that would provide the expectation for how many positive replications would result, not the alpha levels of the original studies. The Reproducibility Project report stated that, given the mean power of the studies conducted, a replication rate of 89 positive results would have been expected. The report further stated that, of 97 successful attempts at replication, 35 obtained positive results, yielding a 36% success rate ($35/97 = 36\%$). But if only 89 positive results would have been expected, why is the success rate not presented as $35/89 = 39\%$?

One study attempted to replicate a part of an original study using a sample size of eight, which was one quarter as large as the original sample. In an email exchange with one of the authors of the original study (E. Nurmsoo, personal communication), she pointed out that although the Reproducibility Project had failed to replicate the first part of her study, Yow and Markman (2009) had published a replication of the second part. She also stated that there were aspects of the study that required good acting skills on the part of the investigator to convince the participating children that the investigator did not know where an object was hidden when, in fact, the investigator did know. Without that minor deception being successful, the study could not be considered a replication.

There are many instances of problems such as this, and several of the original authors have written to the Reproducibility Project to argue that their study was not faithfully replicated. Of interest is that the Reproducibility Project used the opinions of the replicating authors as one measure of whether the original finding was replicated, but it does not appear to have solicited the opinions of the original authors. One of the arguments made with regard to the general issue of false-positive findings is that the researchers in such studies have a vested interest in finding positive results (Fraenkel, Wallen, & Hyun, 1993). But what was the goal of the Reproducibility Project? What was the motivation of the teams that engaged in the studies, and what was their level of expertise in regard to the ability to faithfully execute the replications?

It would appear to be the case that the Reproducibility Project may have had some reproducibility problems of its own. Even without such problems, it does not make the case for additional replication studies to be conducted because it does not speak to that issue. So how would we know if there were a replication crisis? Would verifying this not have to do with finding example after example of results that were presented and relied on for some time to further progress in the field and then were found out not to be replicable? Where are those situations? What we see instead is many situations in which a very interesting finding is presented, and then a number of replications and extensions are conducted, and we learn more about the phenomenon under examination. If all or most attempts at replication fail, the argument tends to die out. On occasion, a finding will persist in popular opinion, but not because it has been supported through replication (e.g., the Mozart effect; see http://lrs.ed.uiuc.edu/students/lerch1/edpsy/mozart_effect.html).

HYPOTHESIZING AFTER RESULTS ARE KNOWN

HARKing, as mentioned earlier, is the practice of hypothesizing after results are known (Kerr, 1998; Chapter 3, this volume). There is a more common term for HARKing: *science*. HARKing is what we do as researchers. The problem with HARKing occurs only when researchers go back and change their initial hypotheses in the write-up of their research in order to make the results appear to be consistent with original hypotheses. This is dishonest practice. How prevalent it is in psychology is difficult to know. There have been calls to solve this problem by having a registry of research hypotheses to which researchers submit before conducting a study, so that all will know that they have not gone back and altered their original hypotheses to fit their data (Asendorpf et al., 2013).

The problem is that we have set up a set of circumstances that encourages a fundamentally dishonest practice. But, who, exactly, is at fault here? The researchers who dishonestly refabricate hypotheses are, to be sure, but might we not also cast an eye on our publication system? If authors were *encouraged* to engage in post hoc speculation and reformulation of hypotheses when original results are surprising, and if manuscripts with findings that are not consistent with original hypotheses were not denigrated for those results, we might make this problem go away without adding a wing to the Office of Research Prevention in Psychology. Consider the New Horizons probe that flew by Pluto in 2015 and sent back extensive data on the dwarf planet for the first time. Do we really want to wait until a second probe is sent to confirm findings before we revise our theoretical models about the solar system? No, we want to HARK! Now is exactly the time to be theorizing, not last year before the results were in and not in 10 years should another probe go by. We are adult enough to understand that hypotheses are just that, and await confirmation, but if the science of psychology is to advance, we must think about our results and generate better hypotheses based on those results.

SELECTIVE OUTCOME REPORTING

Selective outcome reporting is the practice of gathering a number of outcome measures together and then reporting only those that produce positive results (Dwan et al., 2008; Chapter 4, this volume). In our opinion, this is probably the most severe problem that exists with regard to false positives in psychology. It may exist because researchers do not feel it is a questionable research practice, or at least not a *highly* questionable research practice. If that speculation is true, then selective outcome reporting is not only a problem, it is a pernicious one. Researchers may feel that to get the results of a study published, they have to go with their best, strongest, largest effect size material. If they have given six outcome measures for a given study, and only two of them have turned out to be significant, they may feel that they have significant results and proceed to publish the article, ignoring the nonsignificant findings. Leaving those findings out not only presents a unified argument for the study but also eliminates the need to have a section on each of the nonsignificant measures that argues their worth and why they should be in the study. It simply makes life easier.

To paraphrase a famous politician, "You could do that, but it would be wrong." Instead of going the preregistration route, we suggest an alternative. Encourage authors to spend less space in an article explaining and defending all the measures used in a given study and to instead describe them briefly and provide references to studies in which their quality has been assessed. In the Results section, mention all nonsignificant findings at a given p value and include the following statement: "All outcome measures used in this research have been reported on here," or something to that effect. If other measures are going to be discussed in a separate article, that could be stated as well. This would be the same as requiring authors to say that they have received permission to conduct the study from their institutional review board or ethics committee. With a statement declaring complete reporting, noncompliant authors are not simply failing to mention something that did not turn out significant; they are being deceitful. They are no longer playing around the fringes of dishonesty. We suspect (with no evidence other than a faith in our fellow psychologists) that this would solve what we believe to be the biggest problem in nonreplicable findings, without invoking an agency whose existence is justified by mistrust.

THE "BETTER IDEAS" APPROACH
TO IMPROVING PSYCHOLOGY

We turn now to some alternative suggestions for improving the progress of the field of psychology. We begin with a claim we believe to be self-evident: Science is a creative endeavor. What we do as scientists is "invent understanding." We observe a phenomenon of interest and try to explain it with theoretical concepts that we believe will work under a variety of conditions. Then we conduct research to see whether our inventions of understanding hold up. Sometimes they do, and other times they do not. The "do not's" frequently never see the light of day in terms of communication. There is no *Journal of Bad Ideas*. Much of science is what Kuhn (2012) called *normal science*. It is the working out and testing of ideas. This work is the building block part of science. It is how we construct the edifices of our strongest understandings. But the design, the architecture of those understandings, comes from the interaction of creative thinking and what is currently known in the field. Sometimes the architecture is broadly defined, such as behaviorism or cognitivism; sometimes it is the creative application of a breakthrough to a new area, such as neuroaesthetics (Chatterjee & Vartanian, 2014); and sometimes it is a clever extension of an established method, such as graded response version of the Rasch model in psychometrics (Samejima, 1997).

INVENTING UNDERSTANDING

Ioannidis (2005) argued that in any field there are a certain number of true hypotheses and a certain number of false ones, and that an estimate of these figures can provide a prior probability that can be combined with the results of an investigation that will yield a posterior probability that will more accurately reflect the status of a hypothesis than would the research results alone. His work stemmed from biological/medical research, and he provided a setting involving genetics where such a set of assumptions might be worthwhile. What would those assumptions be in psychology? Would one set for the entire discipline work? Are hypotheses that are studied in psychology really a random sample from some definable population of hypotheses? Ioannidis's argument seems so far removed from the reality of psychology research as to not merit serious consideration. Psychology researchers do not go to a store of hypotheses and draw one at random to study. They work from a theory to come to a conclusion about a psychological phenomenon and then develop a study to shed light on the status of that conclusion. They typically begin the study with the expectation that the conclusion will turn out to be correct. They argue, "If what we believe to be true is, in fact, true, then if we set up this set of conditions, we should see X." Sometimes X can be established through a hypothesis test, and other times it can be established by estimating the magnitude of X to see if it is within an expected area.

Nosek, Spies, and Motyl (2012) discussed a study that was part of Motyl's PhD dissertation. They conducted a study with 1,979 participants and got a result that was significant ($p = .01$). But then, because of their firm belief in replication, they decided to run the study again. The replication had more than 1,000 participants, but this time the resulting p value was .59. They concluded that the result cast doubt on the original finding, and rightly so. But then they stated, "Our immediate reaction was 'Why the #&@! did we do a direct replication?'" (p. 616). Their question should have been, "Why did this show significance there and not here?"

What we do in psychology is not tick off true and false hypotheses and throw mounds of data into The Great Data Pile to be sifted through in the pursuit of truth. Think of who the great psychologists were and are, and why we revere them: James, Piaget, Wundt, Ainsworth, Hollingworth, Skinner, Bandura, Kahneman, Milner. They are revered not because they had great data but because they had great ideas. To be sure, they used data in the development of those ideas, but they made equal use of their intelligence and their creativity. They invented understanding in their various fields within the discipline.

What we do as research psychologists—indeed, as researchers in almost all fields—is invent understanding. We try to explain what we see in how individuals behave, learn, interact with others, think, see, smell, and so on. We develop theories about how what we observe works. And then we test those theories, usually by working within a theoretical framework, finding a problem or interesting issue within it, proposing a possible explanation of it, and creating a set of conditions that would shed light on the accuracy of that explanation. We do not study hypotheses drawn randomly from some large bank of hypotheses. We do not study whether ducks can fly upside down, or if screaming at newborns will make them more resilient in later life. We study possibilities drawn from theory and prior research that seem like good explanations of phenomena of interest. The quality of our work depends on a number of factors, the first of which has to do with the value of the question being asked. In working with PhD students, the first two authors of this chapter frequently tell them that the standard for having a good research question is the following: "Will people who are generally interested in your area of research want to know what you found no matter what you find?" If the answer is yes, you have a good question. If the answer is, "If your study comes out positive, let me know," then you should continue to work on your question.

Nosek et al. (2012) bemoaned the fact that journals prize novelty over truth. They made the rather astonishing distinction between new ideas (novelty) and truth as if they were a dichotomy. Truth certainly is a wonderful thing. But sometimes it is boring. Ducks do not fly upside down. No matter how many times that might be established, it will never be very interesting. It fails the interest test from A to Z: It will not advance our understanding of anything from aeronautics to zoology. On the other hand, a bold claim, even if later proven to be false, spurs debate, replication, and sometimes methodological and substantive gains. Cold fusion, facilitated communication, and phlogiston all had their day, only to fall by the wayside. New claims are made every day that will join them in that fate. There will always be something new to occupy a place in The Pantheon of Questionable Claims, but that does not mean that we should not encourage bold thinking. In fact, each of the three examples just given, even though they were all essentially debunked, led to robust examination and debate within their fields at the time.

RELIABILITY AND VALIDITY IN RESEARCH

In Chapter 15 of this volume, Williams, Polanin, and Pigott discuss research synthesis, using the example of studying the relationship between high school grade-point averages and college completion. The relationship between grades in high school and college graduation is low to moderate, as has been shown in many, many studies (Camara & Echternacht, 2000). It is lower than one might think it would be. Why is that? Instead of running another 10 replications to examine the relationship, would it not be more productive to stop and ask *why* the relationship is not as strong as we think it should be? An example of such thinking is the creative work of Young (1990), who has shown that much of the problem occurs simply because higher achieving students often pick the most challenging majors (and hence reduce their chances for success and high grades). Without the contributions of innovative ideas such as this, we are stuck in misperceptions of the situation because we believe the finding (low correlation between high school grades and college success) to be reliable. And it is reliable; it just is not valid.

So, what we need are good proposals for solutions to the problems of psychology. There is a surfeit of good problems to work on, and for most of those problems there is an abundance of data to ponder. Why does stereotype threat (Steele & Aronson, 1995) obtain in some settings and not in others? Is homework effective (Cooper, 1989)? Why does the Pygmalion effect seem to occur only for researchers who believe in it and not for those who do not (Rosenthal & Jacobson, 1968)? Simply adding weight to one side of the argument or the other with additional studies does not really advance the field in any of these areas. What is needed are insights into these issues that resolve the disputes, that explain why we see differing results from differing studies.

DO LESS, BETTER

One way to improve the situation is to think more before collecting data. Run one careful study instead of two slipshod ones. Think. Replications take time, effort, and often funding. Are they really the best way to spend one's time? If an effect has been replicated in three studies and not in a fourth and fifth, what is the best way to proceed? Run a sixth? Or perhaps, instead, take all five replications, and the original study, and think about why some replications were positive and others negative, and then run a sixth. Although more data in a given study is always better than less, sometimes two studies with smaller samples, one based on the findings from the first, are a better allocation of resources than one larger study—not always, but sometimes. In either case, a study that is based on a better, more completely thought out, more inventive idea, will be better than one run on an idea of lesser quality. The problem, of course, is that if 15 refereed journal articles is the mark for tenure, the real pressure is on the count, not necessarily the quality. Unfortunately, H-indices present the same problem. One hundred citations spread evenly over 10 articles is seen by many a tenure panel as roughly 10 times better than one highly influential article with 100 citations. And so we stack the incentive deck in favor of the good at the expense of the great.

WORKING TOGETHER

We also have a tendency to discourage collaborative efforts. This problem is perhaps waning as articles with multiple authors become much more the norm and highly multiple authored articles are gaining in popularity (Bandyopadhyay, 2001). But such authorships are usually research teams working together in an institution. Although this is desirable, what might we do to encourage collaboration across institutions? Our goals often tend to be personal ones rather than ones aimed at advancing the field. It is difficult to strike a proper balance between collaboration and competition among researchers. Perhaps this has always been the case in all fields, but might there be ways of encouraging more collaborative thinking about common problems? Perhaps a website where researchers could post short pieces, with or without data, for purposes of discussion, refinement, and collaborative thinking about a problem would be helpful. This would allow researchers to establish their ownership of a given idea and still be able to work with others on the refinement of the idea, generation of insightful hypotheses, and a powerful research plan.

JOURNAL EDITORS, HOW ABOUT A LITTLE SLACK?

Finally, we might make more progress as a field if we could encourage journal editors to show a bit of flexibility in what researchers write, in two fashions. First, a better way to solve the problem of selective reporting of results is to let researchers know that they are welcome to present nonsignificant findings along with significant ones. All findings should be welcome. Second, let authors speculate. Two of the present authors (with James C. Kaufman) were founding coeditors of the journal *Psychology of Aesthetics, Creativity, and the Arts*. We frequently encouraged authors to take the Discussion section of their manuscript and speculate a bit on what they had found. Nobody knows more about what is happening in a particular study than the people who have conducted the research. We invited those people to go beyond their data and let the field know their thoughts, ideas, and concerns. If authors were permitted to state that they are "now going beyond what we know from our data," and let us know what their hunches are (clearly presented as hunches), we might actually accelerate the progress of the field.

We also encouraged HARKing at that point, as long as the authors make clear that that is what they are doing. Researchers should start with what has been learned from their study; relate those findings to the established research; and then engage in a blend of results, logic, and creativity in an effort to move the research ball down the field.

CONCLUSION AND RECOMMENDATIONS

We fundamentally do not believe that the field of psychology is at some crisis point with regard to replication. We believe that there are false positives, but we think they are mostly the result of journals not being interested in negative findings, and researchers tending to focus only on their positive results, and nothing more nefarious than that. Furthermore, we think that this problem, and others in the field, can be ameliorated through positive steps rather than punitive ones. We would, instead, encourage an ethic of honest reporting by putting incentives in front of such behavior rather than inventing punishments for bad behavior—or, worse yet, creating obstacles to productivity. We need not impede the work of all researchers in order to deter a few, all to solve a problem that has yet to be clearly established.

Replication is a good thing; we think it currently exists to a sufficient degree for those findings that are of interest to the field. We think that HARKing is what science is all about, as long as researchers clearly state that this is what they are doing. We think that asking researchers to state that all of their dependent measures have been accounted for in the publication could solve selective reporting of results. More than anything else, we think that the field will be advanced through careful consideration of what we already know, bringing to those deliberations a strong dose of clear thinking, creativity, and inventiveness. What we need are strong minds, not strong minders.

REFERENCES

Asendorpf, J. B., Conner, M., De Fruyt, F., De Houwer, J., Denissen, J. J., Fiedler, K., . . . Wicherts, J. M. (2013). Recommendations for increasing replicability in psychology. *European Journal of Personality, 27,* 108–119. http://dx.doi.org/10.1002/per.1919

Bandyopadhyay, A. K. (2001). Authorship pattern in different disciplines. *Annals of Library and Information Studies, 48,* 139–147.

Camara, W. J., & Echternacht, G. (2000). *The SAT I and high school grades: Utility in predicting success in college* [Research Note]. The College Board. Retrieved from http://research.collegeboard.org/sites/default/files/publications/2012/7/researchnote-2000-10-sat-high-school-grades-predicting-success.pdf

Chatterjee, A., & Vartanian, O. (2014). Neuroaesthetics. *Trends in Cognitive Sciences, 18*, 370–375. http://dx.doi.org/10.1016/j.tics.2014.03.003

Cooper, H. (1989). *Homework*. London, UK: Longman. http://dx.doi.org/10.1037/11578-000

Dwan, K., Altman, D. G., Arnaiz, J. A., Bloom, J., Chan, A.-W., Cronin, E., . . . Williamson, P. R. (2008). Systematic review of the empirical evidence of study publication bias and outcome reporting bias. *PLOS ONE, 3*(8), e3081. http://dx.doi.org/10.1371/journal.pone.0003081

Fraenkel, J. R., Wallen, N. E., & Hyun, H. H. (1993). *How to design and evaluate research in education* (Vol. 7). New York, NY: McGraw-Hill.

Ioannidis, J. P. A. (2005). Why most published research findings are false. *PLOS Medicine, 2*(8), e124. http://dx.doi.org/10.1371/journal.pmed.0020124

Kerr, N. L. (1998). HARKing: Hypothesizing after the results are known. *Personality and Social Psychology Review, 2*, 196–217. http://dx.doi.org/10.1207/s15327957pspr0203_4

Kuhn, T. S. (2012). *The structure of scientific revolutions*. Chicago, IL: University of Chicago Press. http://dx.doi.org/10.7208/chicago/9780226458144.001.0001

Makel, M. C., Plucker, J. A., & Hegarty, B. (2012). Replications in psychology research: How often do they really occur? *Perspectives on Psychological Science, 7*, 537–542. http://dx.doi.org/10.1177/1745691612460688

Maxwell, S. E., Lau, M. Y., & Howard, G. S. (2015). Is psychology suffering from a replication crisis? What does "failure to replicate" really mean? *American Psychologist, 70*, 487–498. http://dx.doi.org/10.1037/a0039400

Nosek, B. A., Spies, J. R., & Motyl, M. (2012). Scientific utopia: II. Restructuring incentives and practices to promote truth over publishability. *Perspectives on Psychological Science, 7*, 615–631. http://dx.doi.org/10.1177/1745691612459058

Open Science Collaboration. (2012). An open, large-scale, collaborative effort to estimate the reproducibility of psychological science. *Perspectives on Psychological Science, 7*, 657–660. http://dx.doi.org/10.1177/1745691612462588

Open Science Collaboration. (2015, August 28). Estimating the reproducibility of psychological science. *Science, 349*, aac4716. http://dx.doi.org/10.1126/science.aac4716

Pashler, H., & Harris, C. R. (2012). Is the replicability crisis overblown? Three arguments examined. *Perspectives on Psychological Science, 7*, 531–536. http://dx.doi.org/10.1177/1745691612463401

Rosenthal, R., & Jacobson, L. (1968). Pygmalion in the classroom. *The Urban Review, 3*, 16–20. http://dx.doi.org/10.1007/BF02322211

Samejima, F. (1997). Graded response model. In W. J. van der Linden & R. K. Hambleton (Eds.), *Handbook of modern item response theory* (pp. 85–100). New York, NY: Springer. http://dx.doi.org/10.1007/978-1-4757-2691-6_5

Steele, C. M., & Aronson, J. (1995). Stereotype threat and the intellectual test performance of African Americans. *Journal of Personality and Social Psychology, 69,* 797–811. http://dx.doi.org/10.1037/0022-3514.69.5.797

Young, J. W. (1990). Adjusting the cumulative GPA using item response theory. *Journal of Educational Measurement, 27,* 175–186. http://dx.doi.org/10.1111/j.1745-3984.1990.tb00741.x

Yow, W. Q., & Markman, E. M. (2009). Understanding a speaker's communicative intent: Bilingual children's heightened sensitivity to referential gestures. In J. Chandlee, M. Franchini, S. Lord, & G. Rheiner (Eds.), *Proceedings of the 33rd Annual Boston University Conference on Language Development* (Vol. 2, pp. 646–657). Somerville, MA: Cascadilla Press.

17

REPRODUCIBLE SCIENCE: A NEW HOPE

MATTHEW C. MAKEL AND JONATHAN A. PLUCKER

Writing a summary of an edited book full of provocative ideas is never an easy task, and writing one for this book is no exception. But here are a couple of our initial impressions from working with the chapter authors over the past several months: (a) We know how to improve social science research, and (b) we have a lot of improving to do. This should provide social scientists with a healthy dose of optimism.

The authors of the chapters in this book, despite writing on often-disparate topics, hit on several cross-cutting themes, suggesting a degree of consensus on how to move from existing practice to preferred practice. So then why, if these strategies are well-known and agreed on, aren't the recommended practices being used? We suspect that the lack of action may be a by-product of the long time it takes to change the course of a ship as large and unwieldy as the modern academic research infrastructure—and the culture that surrounds it. The fact that such infrastructure lacks a clear hierarchy or

http://dx.doi.org/10.1037/0000033-018
Toward a More Perfect Psychology: Improving Trust, Accuracy, and Transparency in Research, M. C. Makel and J. A. Plucker (Editors)

central authority (which is probably a good thing) with numerous interwoven stakeholders only complicates such changes.

Smith, Smith, and Smith, in the preceding synthesis chapter, suggest that the path forward is to "have better ideas." The importance of great ideas is probably something we as a field overlook too often. But one weakness of this proposal is that we don't know how to make it actually happen. The Smiths' suggestions of "do less, better" and increased collaborative work would likely help, but we're not sure that those are the sole hurdles between current practice and creating the next 100 William Jameses.

This is not to say that we should give up on creating better ideas, but we view that road as much more difficult than improving many of the structural processes discussed throughout this book. Even if such improvements only nibble at the edges of improvement, the relative costs in fixing these problems seem remarkably low, especially for a field whose purpose is to help show society better ways of doing things. If it's broke, let's fix it. Continuing to do things ineffectively or inefficiently undermines the credibility of a field that already often struggles to get attention for its work. And recent changes appear to be following such a perspective.

As for whether bad ideas are filtered out of science and good ideas are replicated, we are less sanguine than the Smiths. Yes, many bad ideas that initially receive a lot of attention are eventually pushed out of scientific belief. But just as we cannot forget the value of great ideas, we should also be mindful of the potential costs of bad research. We must keep in mind two things. First, what happens in the intervening time between a false finding and correction can lead to huge misallocation of resources (e.g., in the case of the Mozart effect example, the governor of Georgia proposed spending state funds on classical music for infants). Second, the human suffering that can occur as a result of an ineffective or inefficient scientific filtering process is real (e.g., autism and vaccines, repressed memories) can be incredible and does not disappear when the scientific community subsequently realizes its mistake.

Some recent controversies appear to have been uncovered relatively quickly (e.g., Bohannon, 2015; Broockman, Kalla, & Aronow, 2015), in our opinion, as a result of some of these practices. Processes such as preregistration and the use of larger samples help researchers act as their own filters and may help prevent false findings from entering the *zeitgeist*. Furthermore, processes such as open data, replication, and meta-analysis serve as additional filters that prevent published falsehoods from becoming ingrained as "truth."

However, it is important to differentiate filtering flaws out of the current system with having clearly defined goals for an improved system. Throughout this book, authors have shared numerous such goals and strategies for achieving them. With this chapter we combine and synthesize many of their proposals into a uniform vision for a research culture that would create more accurate, trustworthy, and transparent research results.

ORIGIN STORY

In Chapter 1 of this volume, Vartanian makes a compelling case that scientific innovation is driven by researchers with access to high-quality theories. Without theory choice, conducting good science is substantially more difficult (perhaps impossible). Vartanian also makes a key observation when noting that, in the minds of most psychologists, accuracy and consistency are often more strongly tied to research quality than theoretical grounding, thus overlooking issues of scope, simplicity, and the extent to which the research yields new findings. As Vartanian argues, without further development of accurate, consistent, broad, and parsimonious theories, psychology's research quality will suffer. Individual researchers choosing good theories (when they are available, and beginning to develop them when they are not) must play a vital role in contributing to psychology emerging as a cumulative science.

The relative theory weakness of our field is likely a strong contributor to a false sense of accurate findings. Theory weakness can include a lack of theory in many research studies as well as the prevalence of undead theories (Ferguson & Heene, 2012). A theory is considered undead (a zombie) if it does not seem to die despite numerous, apparently fatal wounds that should lead researchers to seek alternative explanations. These zombies can survive by being so malleable that regardless of what the data reveal, the theory is supported, or not falsified, because the developers of the theory have established a mini-empire where they can serve as gatekeeper for what does and does not get published in the realm. A National Bureau of Economic Research working paper titled "Does Science Advance One Funeral at a Time?" (Azoulay, Graff Zivin, & Fons-Rosen, 2015) found evidence that, on the death of eminent researchers, the contributions of those who had been collaborators shrank and the contributions of researchers who had not previously been part of the eminent researcher's field increased their activity in that field and published research that went on to be highly cited. Moreover, the productivity of those who had previously collaborated with the eminent researcher declined substantially. They concluded that researchers are often reluctant to challenge the scholarship and theories of eminent researchers until they are no longer able to defend it. Such delay may seem polite deference to the eminent researcher, but it also prolongs the time in which the world fails to benefit from a superior theory and results.

Zombies aren't just limited to theories, which is worrying. There are zombie research practices too, some of which we ourselves have been guilty of practicing. For example, based on how they are portrayed throughout this book, one might think that null hypothesis testing and the reporting of *p* values would have died a death of a thousand cuts over the past 50 years of researchers pointing out their flaws (e.g., Bakan, 1966; Cohen, 1994; LeBel & Peters, 2011; Lykken, 1968; Rozeboom, 1960). But alas, *p* values continue to play a significant role in the field ($p < .05$).

One way many such zombie theories and practices are being identified is through an increased number of retractions. Since 2000, the number of retractions has increased over 1,300% (to more than 400 per year), whereas the total number of articles published has increased only about 44% (Van Noorden, 2011). Although formally retracting published work differentiates what is actually science from what may be science fiction, letting the findings be published in the first place can still cause real harm. Helping researchers identify the flaws in their own research and the research of others before publication would help the field avoid the harsh punishment of a retraction while also protecting society from the potentially harmful effects of basing policy or behavior change on flawed research findings.

As evidenced by zombie theories, science is not always as self-correcting as we'd like to believe (Ioannidis, 2012). Numerous relatively minor examples can be given (just ask any researcher if his or her work has ever been mis-cited or overlooked), but serious cases of fraudulent actions have led to major, negative consequences, such as thousands of people worldwide mistakenly associating vaccination with negative consequences that the data do not support.

Numerous authors have lamented the excessive focus on attaining statistically significant results for deeming a research project "successful" as well as the lack of statistical power in psychology research preventing much precision in results (see, e.g., Chapters 2 and 3, this volume). We believe that a greater emphasis should be placed on the role of successful problem finding in science because doing so can increase the probability of focusing on phenomena that are sufficiently important to warrant study. It is the research question and methodological approach to answering these questions that should be of the utmost importance. Moreover, researchers have also pointed out that most research study participants are WEIRD (Western, Educated, Industrialized, Rich, and Democratic; Henrich, Heine, & Norenzayan, 2010), thus potentially limiting the generalizability of the associated results or, at the least, overlooking the lives and experiences of non- (or less) WEIRD populations. We mention this because assessing non-WEIRD populations as a means of theory testing can help establish theory boundary conditions. A good theory need not be universal; if a theory is predictive of the behavior of only WEIRD samples, that need not be its death knell, but such limitations need to be made clear. There are often wide within-WEIRD sample differences in research findings and intervention effectiveness, and Ledgerwood and colleagues (Chapter 2) highlight the potential costs and benefits or relying on online samples.

FROM IDEA TO ACTION

Once you have developed your idea and research question, the next clear step in the research process is to develop the specific steps to answering your question. Numerous authors in this book emphasize the importance of laying the foundation for a strong study that occurs before any data are collected and provide suggestions that we believe would improve the accuracy, trustworthiness, and transparency of social science research.

An assumed infallibility on the part of a well-intentioned researcher is too similar to godlike status for most mere mortal researchers. This is especially true given the wealth of research on how poor we as humans and as researchers are at self-evaluation. Despite this deficiency, self-regulation of their actions is often left to researchers. We demand checks and balances in our government and lament when one branch is perceived as overreaching or growing too powerful. We believe many of the practices proposed in this book can help better serve the field as a more rigorous system of checks and balances.

The preregistration of predictions, methods, and analyses opens the door to transitioning science from a field that naively assumes honesty to a more realistic one that acknowledges that even scholars with the best of intentions have bias and can make mistakes. Preregistration helps alleviate many of the questionable research practices mentioned throughout this book, such as outcome reporting bias and p-hacking. The power of preregistration grows stronger when it is combined with the open policies described by Wicherts in Chapter 14 of this volume. Numerous third-party sites exist that allow researchers to preregister their projects (e.g., the Open Science Framework [https://osf.io] and https://aspredicted.org). Moreover, the use of such third-party sites can actually help researchers keep track of their own work, especially if they are collaborating with colleagues from other institutions.

The importance of confirmatory research is emphasized in several chapters herein (e.g., Chapters 2 and 3). Preregistration and open data need not completely remove all instances of exploratory research. Indeed, in the social sciences, between research planning, data collection, and analysis, many events can occur, and information be gained, that can rightly influence researcher behavior. The benefit of preregistration is that it creates a clear distinction between what is actually a confirmatory question and what is an exploratory question (or a question that is altered on the basis of an intervening event). Exploratory research questions can still happen, but preregistration serves as an independent reliability check so that we need not rely on researchers to accurately self-report what they had (and had not) planned to do. Such safeguards not only protect us from unscrupulous ill-doers who purposefully lie about what they had "predicted," often referred to as *hypothesizing after the results are known*, or *HARKing* (Kerr, 1998), but also safeguards us from honest mistakes by forcing researchers to articulate their specific plans and reasons for their decisions. Without such safeguards, it can be quite easy for researchers to have a vague idea of what they plan to do and find but then still have the flexibility to adapt later. Some call this *researcher degrees of freedom* (Simmons, Nelson, & Simonsohn, 2011) and others *a garden of forking paths* (Gelman & Loken, 2013).

Psychology is hardly innovating in this realm, given that preregistration is mandated for all clinical trials (for a complete list of data repositories, visit http://www.re3data.org/). Nevertheless, the use of such sites allows researchers to receive independent confirmation of their intended research projects while maintaining privacy until they are ready to share their findings. The existence of such sites makes it easier for researchers to show that they haven't HARKed or engaged in other questionable research practices.[1] Doing so alleviates concerns on the part of research consumers while creating a clear distinction between confirmatory and exploratory findings.

It is important to remember that a shift from a focus on *p* values to an emphasis on power, confidence intervals, and confirmatory research is not universally agreed on as the ultimate fix. There has been some vocal disagreement about the potency of power as well as how confidence intervals are interpreted and what they actually tell us (e.g., Hoekstra, Morey, Rouder, & Wagenmakers, 2014; Morey, Hoekstra, Rouder, Lee, & Wagenmakers, 2016; Wagenmakers, Verhagen, et al., 2015, but cf. Miller & Ulrich, 2016), not to mention some concern that a focus on confirmatory research could feel stifling to some research practices in which new data collection is not easy. This is always the caution of new practices: They appear better than current practices, but they also have their faults. Similarly, although this was not discussed in detail in any chapter, the use of Bayesian statistics in the social sciences is growing and can also be leveraged to address some of the statistical concerns pointed out in this book (e.g., Gelman, 2011; Wagenmakers, Morey, & Lee, 2016).

---

[1]Unless they are committing outright fraud by lying about when data were collected, but we think everyone agrees fraud transcends "questionable" and falls fully under "always unacceptable" (for a humorous perspective on this serious topic, see Neuroskeptic, 2012).

Another idea not discussed at length by chapter authors, but that helps incorporate many of their proposals, is to shift the publication process to more closely mirror the dissertation and grant application process. Under this model, researchers develop their question, predictions, and planned methods (including power analysis for estimated sample size) and then submit a draft of all these to a journal for review prior to collecting data. Thus, publishing is the step remaining after results are known (*PARKing*; Makel, 2014), in contrast to HARKing. Similar to the registered replication reports section that exists in some journals (e.g., *Psychological Science*), tentative acceptance is given before data collection, and as long as researchers follow the methods they proposed and write the manuscript in an appropriate manner, their manuscript will be published by the journal.

PARKing shifts the bulk of decision making not only for the researcher before data collection but also for reviewers and editors. We believe that a move to PARKing would place even greater power and importance on reviewers and journal editors, thus placing an even heavier burden on them to accomplish the goals Richler and Gauthier discuss in Chapter 6. Under a PARKing model, editors and reviewers not only determine what research gets published but also play a role in what data get collected. Given the existing gap between current and preferred editorial and review practices that Richler and Gauthier enumerate, it is unclear whether PARKing would fit best as part of the traditional peer review system or as part of the newer technical accuracy review system implemented by journals such as *Frontiers* or *PLOS*. By shifting the review phase earlier, the PARKing model requires reviewers and editors to make their decisions solely on the basis of the caliber of the research question and method and not on the "splash" the results may make.

We believe PARKing, when combined with the other proposed practices discussed above, would lead to more accurate, trustworthy, and transparent research findings while also "maximizing the informational value" of each study (Chapter 2). Such a shift would place clear emphasis on the fact that good science is based more on asking significant questions than on obtaining statistically significant results.

WORKING IN CONTEXT

You've got your plan, you have your measures and your sample, you know how many participants you want, and all other components of your project are in place. Now it's time to do the work. If your work is applied in any way, or requires data that will be collected outside the laboratory (which most researchers should do at some point to avoid focusing on only the aforementioned WEIRD participants), as described by Berends and Austin in Chapter 9, then partnerships with nonresearch individuals and organizations will be vital not only to conducting research but also to getting your findings applied so that they influence actual practice. As Berends and Austin also make clear, there is no single idealized path to forging and maintaining such relationships.

In the neurological and clinical research communities discussed by Shelton and D'Onofrio, Viken, and Hetrick in Chapters 10 and 11, respectively, the contextual challenges may have less to do with partnerships with nonresearch entities and more to do with competing interpretations and practices. Regardless of the vast differences in the type of work conducted in clinical psychology or neuroscience, the authors emphasize the need for the rigorous practices described in the other chapters of this book.

WRITING AND CITING

The phrase "Don't let the truth get in the way of a good story" is often attributed to Mark Twain. However, as scientists, we have to change this around to: "Don't let a good story get in the way of the truth." Maintaining an appropriate level of flexibility is important when revising your manuscript (see Chapter 6). But what constitutes "appropriate" will often depend on what is being requested. Editors and reviewers can often provide helpful guidance and direction regarding explanation, clarity, and putting research questions and results in the larger context. This can be exceedingly helpful. However, it is also not unheard of for editors and reviewers to make inappropriate requests, such as asking for the removal of some analyses (for the sake of telling a cleaner story). It is our hope that in instances such as this it is editors who will maintain flexibility and help authors tell the story of what they actually did and not attempt to transform the science into science fiction.

Gardner (Chapter 7) as well as Plucker and Silvia (Chapter 8) provide perspectives on the potential costs and benefits of writing nonempirical articles. Such work can reach far wider audiences and can be leveraged to gain greater attention to your research. However, as they caution, such alternative outlets can distract you from your actual research. Gardner also wisely advises researchers to consider whether they actually have something to say to nonresearchers and whether such work is something they enjoy. There is a high level of disagreement on the use of social media communication. Many individuals successfully use social media as a means of learning, rumination, collaboration, and dissemination. Others embarrass themselves repeatedly.

In Chapter 5, Lavigne and Good provide an excellent suggestion for all researchers to keep in mind:

> The reference list should include the most important publications that inform the author's research, help readers understand the contribution an author's study makes to a field of study, and alert readers to the extent to which the study replicates or contradicts prior research. (p. 99)

Also, as several authors noted, dissemination is always well served by conducting high-quality, rigorous research in the first place. Implementing the more rigorous methods and practices introduced in this book also provides the added benefit and value of giving your work a leg up on serving as the basis for—or at the very least, being cited in—future work. If this is the case, such benefits outweigh any added time or resources required by the use of more rigorous practices.

INDIVIDUAL RESEARCHER CHECKS AND BALANCES

To some, a gauntlet of obstacles may seem to entail an unnecessarily onerous battle before one can be published. But we view such obstacles as essential filters to reduce and remove as many problematic practices as possible so that as many published results as possible represent precise and accurate findings. The three chapters that constitute Part IV of this book, which focuses on reproducibility components of data reanalysis (Chapter 13), replication (Chapter 14), and meta-analysis (Chapter 15), help serve as an additional system of checks and balances for the studies that make it through the prepublication gauntlet. Although each of these practices provides a unique check on assessing published findings, they also share common benefits. Reanalysis, replication, and meta-analysis (should) all focus on findings that the research community finds important. If researchers adopt this perspective, they should be overjoyed when someone wants to use their work as the basis for any of these reproducibility components. Not only will it provide citation of their work, it will also provide a new platform to attract additional readers. Moreover, if practices such as preregistration, PARKing, and open data have already been implemented, then taking advantage of any of these reproducibility components should be relatively easy for both the original researchers as well as any new team seeking to use existing data or practices.

Even with the implementation of the aforementioned individual study practices and the reproducibility components, disagreements between researchers or theoretical perspectives can still remain. When this is the case, we suggest consideration of implementing preregistered adversarial or proponent–skeptic collaborations (e.g., Kahneman & Klein, 2009; Matzke et al.,

2015; Tetlock & Mitchell, 2009). We believe such collaborations have a strong capability to achieve McBee and Field's conceptualization of "rigor" of persuading skeptical individuals (see Chapter 3, this volume). What better way is there to persuade skeptics than to rely on methods that both you and they agree to a priori? Moreover, such collaborations could still allow researchers from each perspective to comment separately in the discussion section (e.g., Matzke et al., 2015). This way, much like in a U.S. Supreme Court decision, groups can still interpret the results differently (or, much like a concurring opinion, even interpret them differently despite essentially coming to the same conclusion).

VIEWING THE FIELD

Many existing problems with social science research may stem from a misalignment of incentives in that what is beneficial for the individual actor (i.e., publishing in a high-impact journal) does not always align with what is beneficial for the field (i.e., accurate and precise findings). Highly precise findings are good for the field but not necessarily for the individual researcher if those findings require far more time and resources to collect than imprecise findings. For the individual researcher, publishing in a high-impact-factor journal gets them attention, glory, and promotion. However, there appears to be little relation between statistical power and journal impact factor (Brembs, Button, & Munafò, 2013), or between a journal's impact factor and its actual impact (Chapter 5, this volume).

One relatively new action that aligns individual researcher and larger field incentives has been the use of a badge system (e.g., http://www.psychological science.org/index.php/publications/journals/psychological_science/badges) as a means of communicating to readers which articles made use of some of the newer (currently optional) processes such as preregistration, open data, open materials, or any number of other practices (e.g., https://osf.io/tvyxz/). Although the use of badges is new, initial analyses of them and other reporting practices appears to reveal that reporting effect sizes and confidence intervals increased substantially, as did materials and data sharing rates, in the journal *Psychological Science* (Tressoldi, Cumming, Fresc, & Giofré, 2016).

As Richler and Gauthier discuss in Chapter 6, new journals have their problems. Are they predatory or for real? If I submit to them, will my article be read (although, as Lavigne and Good point out in Chapter 5, this question easily extends to many traditional journals as well)?

Costs are tough as well. One potential benefit of the traditional publishing system is that it pushes costs onto institutions and away from individuals (assuming individuals are affiliated with an institution), who may not have the resource to pay hundreds or thousands of dollars to have their research published. Many new journals focus on the data. But we don't necessarily live in a world where we can or should trust data (see, e.g., Chapter 4).

One obvious check is to require open data (Chapter 13). Another is an increased reliance on external evaluation groups such as the What Works Clearinghouse and the Cochrane Collaboration. Such groups have their detractors, but they can help differentiate levels of credibility in what we do and do not know. Another similar, if slightly less external, level of assessment is the model used by the Association for Psychological Science's *Psychological Science in the Public Interest*, which invites teams of researchers to collaborate on evaluating the research of a particular domain. The journal has covered topics as disparate as assessing online dating to eyewitness testimony to the effectiveness of teams. Although perhaps less systematic and rigorous as an actual meta-analysis, this method gives authors a bit more freedom to provide greater context for and interpretation of existing knowledge.

Restoring regular and lively commentary sections in journals could also serve a similar, though less formal, function. Also, if journals view such commentaries as outside their scope, organizations such as the American Psychological Association could establish new journals whose primary focus is to publish commentaries and responses that focus solely on articles that have appeared in other journals published by the organization. The addition of postpublication commentary (e.g., Duncan, 2015) that allows reader comments to be associated with the online version of the published text would also benefit the field. This would allow readers to post and share their reactions and questions to the article as well as permit authors to reply. Attaching such conversations to an article would likely yield positive snowball effects in terms of readership and article impact. Another feature, shown in Duncan's (2015) example of what he wishes journal articles would include, is the ability of (online) readers to download an article's data set. Such open practices as sharing data, code, and other research materials allow researchers to assess whether statistical errors were made (e.g., Bakker, van Dijk, & Wicherts, 2012) as well as reanalyze and possibly use different statistical methods (e.g., Wagenmakers, Wetzels, Borsboom, & van der Maas, 2011) or include the study as part of a synthesis or meta-analysis. All of these practices increase the transparency of individual studies as well as the field as a whole.

CONCLUSION

In our careers, we have often found ourselves having to justify psychology's status as a science, and we are not alone (e.g., Ferguson, 2015; Lilienfeld, 2010, 2012). The fact that the content we study is often accessible to a lay audience is a blessing because it makes our ability to share findings with the world that much easier; we have fewer conceptual and comprehension barriers between our ideas and lay audiences than, for example, someone studying quantum physics.

However, ease of access can also act as a curse, or at the very least an added burden. Deferring to expertise (or even the acknowledgment of expertise) is less likely, and the confidence with which laypersons will misstate research findings can create huge hurdles to breaking down misinformation (Lewandowsky, Ecker, Seifert, Schwarz, & Cook, 2012). For example, people still think of themselves as being left-brain or right-brain thinkers despite this notion having no basis in research (and substantial research contradicting such classification). More dangerously, there is no empirical evidence that vaccinations are associated with autism or that giving fewer vaccines is safer, and yet people still hold such beliefs.[2] Without trust in the results that psychology produces, laypersons will continue to rely on their implicit beliefs (often called "common sense" but, in our experience, common sense is neither common nor sensible if it is not grounded in empirical findings). Alternatively, they may scoff at results that contradict their beliefs with such excuses as "figures lie and liars figure" or—and we have heard policymakers say this verbatim—"Researchers can make research say whatever they want it to say." Because the content of psychology and the other social sciences is so relevant to everyone's daily lives, people often do not believe they have to defer to expertise because of a belief that "it's all common sense." As such, it is important for the field of psychology to bring about trust in its findings.

As we have emphasized throughout this chapter, we view science as the filtering process through which ideas are assessed as to their quality. To borrow an analogy we have used previously, this filtering process serves as the kidney of the scientific process, and "without a properly functioning kidney, the organism will quickly wither and die. Waste products (i.e., false findings) will not be removed and will pollute the entire system" (Makel & Plucker, 2014, p. 29). Anything can be done poorly. But our goal with this book has been to point out areas where things are being done poorly and, in particular, to provide examples of how to move toward a more perfect psychology. Science is an aspirational endeavor in that scientists attempt to better understand how the world works. We aspire to a psychological

---

[2]Also, more to the point, vaccine manufacturing and administration have substantially changed because of the mistaken beliefs, and not in good ways. For example, mercury-based preservatives have been removed from many childhood vaccines because of parent concerns. However, mercury is no more dangerous in those compounds than chlorine is in table salt. Yet the preservative was critically important for vaccine storage in areas without ready access to refrigeration. One could argue that unnecessarily removing the mercury put children at risk with no positive benefit for anyone.

science in which researchers are able to make accurate predictions and solve real-world problems. We want psychology to be associated with how to treat illness effectively, improve academic performance, and overcome human difficulties.

After reading the chapters of this book, we are optimistic. Our sense is that the current era marks the beginning of a large and long-term change in how science is done. The perspectives communicated here are a snapshot in time and will likely evolve over time. Such is the nature of science. In addition to the many thoughtful observations and suggestions included in this book, a great many psychologists have been working diligently to develop ways to minimize, remove, work around, and avoid many of the problems that plague social science research. Such openness to looking for problems, developing methods for alleviating them, and helping the social sciences improve and evolve fills us with a new hope for an ever-increasing understanding of the human experience.

REFERENCES

Azoulay, P., Graff Zivin, J. S., & Fons-Rosen, C. (2015). *Does science advance one funeral at a time?* Working Paper No. 21788, National Bureau of Economic Research, Cambridge, MA.

Bakan, D. (1966). The test of significance in psychological research. *Psychological Bulletin, 66*, 423–437. http://dx.doi.org/10.1037/h0020412

Bakker, M., van Dijk, A., & Wicherts, J. M. (2012). The rules of the game called psychological science. *Perspectives on Psychological Science, 7*, 543–554. http://dx.doi.org/10.1177/1745691612459060

Bohannon, J. (2015). Science *retracts gay marriage paper without agreement of lead author LaCour.* http://dx.doi.org/10.1126/science.aac4659

Brembs, B., Button, K., & Munafò, M. (2013). Deep impact: Unintended consequences of journal rank. *Frontiers in Human Neuroscience, 7*, 291. http://dx.doi.org/10.3389/fnhum.2013.00291

Broockman, D., Kalla, J., & Aronow, P. (2015). *Irregularities in LaCour (2014).* Unpublished article, Stanford University. Retrieved from http://stanford.edu/~dbroock/broockman_kalla_aronow_lg_irregularities.pdf

Cohen, J. (1994). The Earth is round (*p* < .05). *American Psychologist, 49*, 997–1003. http://dx.doi.org/10.1037/0003-066X.49.12.997

Duncan, G. J. (2015). Toward an empirically robust science of human development. *Research in Human Development, 12*, 255–260. http://dx.doi.org/10.1080/15427609.2015.1068061

Ferguson, C. J. (2015). "Everybody knows psychology is not a real science": lic perceptions of psychology and how we can improve our relationsh policymakers, the scientific community, and the general public. *American Psychologist, 70,* 527–542. http://dx.doi.org/10.1037/a0039405

Ferguson, C. J., & Heene, M. (2012). A vast graveyard of undead theories: Publication bias and psychological science's aversion to the null. *Perspectives on Psychological Science, 7,* 555–561. http://dx.doi.org/10.1177/1745691612459059

Gelman, A. (2011). Induction and deduction in Bayesian data analysis. *Rationality, Markets and Morals, 2,* 67–78.

Gelman, A., & Loken, E. (2013). *The garden of forking paths: Why multiple comparisons can be a problem, even when there is no "fishing expedition" or "p-hacking" and the research hypothesis was posited ahead of time.* Unpublished article, Columbia University. Retrieved from http://www.stat.columbia.edu/~gelman/research/unpublished/p_hacking.pdf

Henrich, J., Heine, S. J., & Norenzayan, A. (2010). The weirdest people in the world? *Behavioral and Brain Sciences, 33,* 61–83. http://dx.doi.org/10.1017/S0140525X0999152X

Hoekstra, R., Morey, R. D., Rouder, J. N., & Wagenmakers, E. J. (2014). Robust misinterpretation of confidence intervals. *Psychonomic Bulletin & Review, 21,* 1157–1164. http://dx.doi.org/10.3758/s13423-013-0572-3

Ioannidis, J. P. A. (2012). Why science is not necessarily self-correcting. *Perspectives on Psychological Science, 7,* 645–654. http://dx.doi.org/10.1177/1745691612464056

Kahneman, D., & Klein, G. (2009). Conditions for intuitive expertise: A failure to disagree. *American Psychologist, 64,* 515–526. http://dx.doi.org/10.1037/a0016755

Kerr, N. L. (1998). HARKing: Hypothesizing after the results are known. *Personality and Social Psychology Review, 2,* 196–217. http://dx.doi.org/10.1207/s15327957pspr0203_4

LeBel, E. P., & Peters, K. R. (2011). Fearing the future of empirical psychology: Bem's (2011) evidence of psi as a case study of deficiencies in modal research practice. *Review of General Psychology, 15,* 371–379. http://dx.doi.org/10.1037/a0025172

Lewandowsky, S., Ecker, U. K. H., Seifert, C. M., Schwarz, N., & Cook, J. (2012). Misinformation and its correction: Continued influence and successful debiasing. *Psychological Science in the Public Interest, 13,* 106–131. http://dx.doi.org/10.1177/1529100612451018

Lilienfeld, S. O. (2010). Can psychology become a science? *Personality and Individual Differences, 49,* 281–288. http://dx.doi.org/10.1016/j.paid.2010.01.024

Lilienfeld, S. O. (2012). Public skepticism of psychology: Why many people perceive the study of human behavior as unscientific. *American Psychologist, 67,* 111–129. http://dx.doi.org/10.1037/a0023963

Lykken, D. T. (1968). Statistical significance in psychological research. *Psychological Bulletin, 70,* 151–159. http://dx.doi.org/10.1037/h0026141

Makel, M. C. (2014). The empirical march: Making science better at self-correction. *Psychology of Aesthetics, Creativity, and the Arts, 8,* 2–7. http://dx.doi.org/10.1037/a0035803

Makel, M. C., & Plucker, J. A. (2014). Creativity is more than novelty: Reconsidering replication as a creativity act. *Psychology of Aesthetics, Creativity, and the Arts, 8,* 27–29. http://dx.doi.org/10.1037/a0035811

Matzke, D., Nieuwenhuis, S., van Rijn, H., Slagter, H. A., van der Molen, M. W., & Wagenmakers, E. J. (2015). The effect of horizontal eye movements on free recall: A preregistered adversarial collaboration. *Journal of Experimental Psychology: General, 144,* e1–e15. http://dx.doi.org/10.1037/xge0000038

Miller, J., & Ulrich, R. (2016). Interpreting confidence intervals: A comment on Hoekstra, Morey, Rouder, and Wagenmakers (2014). *Psychonomic Bulletin & Review, 23,* 124–130. http://dx.doi.org/10.3758/s13423-015-0859-7

Morey, R. D., Hoekstra, R., Rouder, J. N., Lee, M. D., & Wagenmakers, E. J. (2016). The fallacy of placing confidence in confidence intervals. *Psychonomic Bulletin & Review, 23,* 103–123. http://dx.doi.org/10.3758/s13423-015-0947-8

Neuroskeptic. (2012). The nine circles of scientific hell. *Perspectives on Psychological Science, 7,* 643–644. http://dx.doi.org/10.1177/1745691612459519

Rozeboom, W. W. (1960). The fallacy of the null-hypothesis significance test. *Psychological Bulletin, 57,* 416–428. http://dx.doi.org/10.1037/h0042040

Simmons, J. P., Nelson, L. D., & Simonsohn, U. (2011). False-positive psychology: Undisclosed flexibility in data collection and analysis allows presenting anything as significant. *Psychological Science, 22,* 1359–1366. http://dx.doi.org/10.1177/0956797611417632

Tetlock, P., & Mitchell, G. (2009). Implicit bias and accountability systems: What must organizations do to prevent discrimination? *Research in Organizational Behavior, 29,* 3–38. http://dx.doi.org/10.1016/j.riob.2009.10.002

Tressoldi, P. E., Cumming, G., Fresc, L., & Giofré, D. (2016). *Effects of the* Psychological Science *new statistical, research disclosure statements and open practices submission guidelines from 2013 to 2015.* Retrieved from http://papers.ssrn.com/sol3/papers.cfm?abstract_id=2712603

Van Noorden, R. (2011). Science publishing: The trouble with retractions. *Nature, 478,* 26–28. http://dx.doi.org/10.1038/478026a

Wagenmakers, E. J., Morey, R. D., & Lee, M. D. (2016). Bayesian benefits for the pragmatic researcher. *Current Directions in Psychological Science, 25,* 169–176. http://dx.doi.org/10.1177/0963721416643289

Wagenmakers, E. J., Verhagen, J., Ly, A., Bakker, M., Lee, M. D., Matzke, D., . . . Morey, R. D. (2015). A power fallacy. *Behavior Research Methods, 47,* 913–917. http://dx.doi.org/10.3758/s13428-014-0517-4

Wagenmakers, E. J., Wetzels, R., Borsboom, D., & van der Maas, H. L. (2011). Why psychologists must change the way they analyze their data: The case of psi. Comment on Bem (2011). *Journal of Personality and Social Psychology, 100,* 426–432. http://dx.doi.org/10.1037/a0022790

INDEX

Baltimore City Health Department, 160
Baltimore City Public Schools, 160,
    163–165
Baltimore Education Research
    Consortium (BERC)
  common language for, 164–165
  cultivating trust in, 163–164
  described, 160
  long- and short-term priorities for,
    167
Banks, G. C., 85
Baselines, cognitive neuroscience,
    176–177
Basic science research, 193–194
Bayes factors, 65
BBC (British Broadcasting Corporation),
    132, 136
Behavioral designs, in cognitive
    neuroscience research, 174–176
Behaviorist paradigm, 20
Bem, D. J., 4
Bennett, Tony, 161, 163
BERC. See Baltimore Education
    Research Consortium
"Better ideas" approach
  collaboration in, 284
  described, 280–281
  effect of, 274
  improving validity of research with,
    283
  inventing understanding through,
    281–282
  limitations of, 290
  and quality vs. quantity of research
    studies, 283–284
Biases. See also Outcome reporting bias
    (ORB)
  in clinical psychology, 189, 193
  confirmation, 50
  and data sharing, 221–222
  gender citation, 102–103
  omitted-variable, 70
  and peer review, 121–122
  publication, 36, 81
  self-citation, 104
  of stakeholders in scientific field, 246
Big data, 178–180
Binswanger, M., 111
Blog posts, 143–145

Blood-oxygen-level-dependent
    functional magnetic resonance
    imaging (BOLD fMRI), 172, 177
Böckenholt, U., 38
Bodies of work, disseminating, 140–141
BOLD fMRI (blood-oxygen-level-
    dependent functional magnetic
    resonance imaging), 172, 177
Bonferroni correction method, 179
Books, dissemination via, 143, 144
Borsboom, D., 90, 228
Brain imaging. See also Cognitive
    neuroscience research
  behavioral designs for, 174–176
  interest in, 172
  research questions answered by,
    172–174
Braun, T., 99
British Broadcasting Corporation
    (BBC), 132, 136
Brown, Roger, 132, 136
Brus, H., 103
Bryk, A. S., 156
Business management, selective outcome
    reporting in, 85

Campbell, D. T., 190
Canada, D. D., 83
Career age, 24
Causal inference, 68–74
  in clinical psychology, 190
  and confounding variables, 68–69
  directed acyclic graphs in, 70–72
  propensity score matching in, 72–74
CCSR (Consortium on Chicago School
    Research), 155–159, 166
Center for Research on Educational
    Opportunity (CREO), 161–163
Cerebral cortex, imaging of, 173
Chan, A.-W., 84, 86
Chance results, investigating, 239
Charlton, K., 82
Citations, 97–111
  conscious decision-making about,
    109–110
  and data sharing, 223
  failure to use, 105–107
  function of, 98–99
  incentives related to, 284

Nosek, B. A., 234, 281, 282
No surprises policies, 163–164
Novel findings
    from data sharing, 222–224
    interest in, 282
    from theories, 21–22
NSC (National Student Clearinghouse), 156
Nuijten, Michèle, 225
Null hypothesis, 81, 85

Objectivity, in research–practice partnerships, 164
O'Boyle, E. H., Jr., 85
O'Brien–Fleming method, 41
Observation, value of a single, 236
Occam's razor, 20
Office of Secondary Education Services, 165
Olkin, I., 258
Omitted-variable bias, 70
One-stage analysis, 265–266
Online samples, 42–45
Op-eds, newspaper, 143
Open data, 227–228
Open Science Collaboration, 234–235
Open Science Framework, 89, 227, 234–235, 248, 275
Operationalizations, in conceptual replications, 50
Operational replications, 236
Opportunity costs, of writing, 145
Optional stopping, 248
ORB. See Outcome reporting bias
Osgood, C. E., 104
Outcome reporting bias (ORB)
    benefits of reducing, 92
    defined, 80–81
    prevalence of, 81–84
    remedies for, 87–91
Overciting, 101
Ownership, data sharing and, 218

Palmer, C. L., 100
Paradigms, 17–18, 20
Parapsychology, replications in, 248
PARKing (publishing after results are known), 295
Partial replications, 236
Participant selection, for replications, 239

Partnerships, research–practice. See Research–practice partnerships
Pashler, H., 274, 275
Patall, E. A., 258, 265
Peer-reviewed articles, dissemination via, 143, 144
Peer Reviewers' Openness Initiative, 120
Peer review process, 119–129
    author's role in, 124–126, 128
    editor's role in, 126
    and effect of harsh reviews, 127–128
    new models for, 119–121
    for research–practice partnership findings, 164
    reviewer's role in, 126–127
    traditional vs. new, 128–129
    value of traditional system of, 121–124
Peer reviews, postpublication, 121–122
Penuel, W. R., 162
Perspectives on Psychological Sciences, 249
Perugini, M., 37, 38
PET (positron emission tomography), 172, 173
Phantom scans, 179
Phrenology, 172–173
Pigott, T. D., 83
Pilot studies, 37
Pinker, Steve, 134
Plagiarism, 208–210
PLOS, 295
PLOS ONE, 120, 228
Plucker, J. A., 246
Polanin, J. R., 83
Popper, Karl, 14–15
Popularization, 134–137. *See also* Dissemination to public audience
Positive predictive value (PPV), 34–35
Positron emission tomography (PET), 172, 173
Postpublication peer reviews, 121–122
Postsecondary outcomes, 163–165
Power
    confirmatory, of replications, 238
    statistical. *See* Statistical power
Power analysis, 38–39, 177
PPV (positive predictive value), 34–35

p values
    comparison of, 243
    in confirmatory study design, 64–65
    impact of outcome reporting bias
        on, 91
    misleading, 65
    and recording of analysis plans, 46
    in Reproducibility Project, 235

QRPs. *See* Questionable research
    practices
Q statistic, 245
Qualitative narrative reviews, 257–258
Quantity
    of publications, 111
    of research studies, 283–284
Quasi-experiments, 61–63
Questionable research practices (QRPs),
    234
    parapsychology procedures to avoid,
        248
    replication to investigate, 240
    selective outcome reporting as,
        279–280
    and social practice of science, 245,
        246

Rabi, Isidor Isaac, 75
Radder, H., 236
Random field theory (RFT), 179
Randomization, 61–63, 69
Rapid response studies, 167–168
RAT (Remote Associates Test), 22
Raudenbush, S. W., 83
Reanalysis
    by readers of journal articles, 222
    reducing errors with, 220–221
    and research waste, 216
    verification vs. secondary analysis as
        motive for, 224–225
Reasoning Mind, 159
Reference lists, 98–99, 297
r effect sizes, 244
Reflection, on ethical issues, 211
"Reflections on Multiple Intelligences"
    (Gardner), 135
Regions of common support, 73–74
Registered Replication Reports, 248–249
Registry of International Development
    Impact Evaluations, 89

Regression models
    model building in, 65–66
    propensity score matching vs., 73–74
    Table 2 fallacy in, 69
Reis, H. T., 100
Rejection, in peer review system,
    122–123, 128
Reliability
    of data from online samples, 43
    and number of studies in
        meta-analysis, 260
    and replication, 275–276, 283
    scale, 39
    validity of research vs., 283
Remote Associates Test (RAT), 22
Renear, A. H., 100
Rennie, D., 87–88
Repeat papers, for reviewers, 127
Repetition procedures, 236
Replication(s), 233–249
    alternatives to, 51
    conditions for, 237–238
    data sharing for, 223
    defined, 236
    ethical issues in research related to,
        210–211
    functional approach to, 238–243
    implicit procedures, 246–247
    importance of, 235
    and meta-analysis, 263–264
    new incentives for, 248–249
    in psychology vs. educational
        research, 4, 5
    rate of, in psychology field, 234–235,
        275
    and reliability, 275–276, 283
    in reproducibility crisis, 275–278
    research synthesis for, 256–257
    resources needed for, 283
    in social practice of science, 245–246
    statistical analysis in, 243–245
    for studies with unconventional
        claims, 247–248
    and study design for maximum
        informational value, 49–51
    of systematic reviews, 264
    types of, 236–237
Replication diagonal, 243–244
Replication files, 219
Replication plane, 243–244

Repositories, open data, 227
Reproducibility crisis in psychology,
 273–285
 arguments over, 274
 and "better ideas" approach, 280–281
 and collaboration in research, 284
 and data sharing, 218
 defining, 274–275
 and failure to cite, 105
 hypothesizing after results are known
  in, 279
 journal editors' roles in, 284–285
 and quality vs. quantity of research
  studies, 283–284
 and recommendations for improving
  psychology, 285
 and reliability/validity in research,
  283
 replication in, 275–278
 selective outcome reporting in,
  279–280
 and understanding as purpose of
  research, 281–282
Reproducibility Project
 described, 234–235
 functional approach to replication
  for, 241–242
 and reproducibility crisis in
  psychology, 275–278
Research Domain Criteria, 192
Researcher degrees of freedom, 294
Researcher flexibility, 82–83
Researchers. *See also* Authors;
  Dissemination to academic
  scholars
 checks and balances for, 297–298
 as gatekeepers, 291
 ORB reduction recommendations
  for, 90
 outcome reporting bias surveys from,
  83–84
 self-regulation by, 293
 writing by, 133–134
Research–practice partnerships,
 153–168
 Baltimore Education Research
  Consortium, 160
 Center for Research on Educational
  Opportunity, 161–162
 common language in, 164–165

Consortium on Chicago School
  Research, 156–159
 cultivating trust in, 162–164
 history of, 154–156
 Houston Education Research
  Consortium, 159–160
 longitudinal data systems for,
  165–166
 Minority Student Achievement
  Network, 160–161
 research quality improvements
  related to, 295–296
 resources for establishing, 168
 stakeholder communication in,
  166–167
 timelines and reward structures in,
  167–168
Research protocols, for reducing ORBs,
 87–88, 91
Research quality improvement strategies,
 285, 289–301
 in "better ideas" approach, 280–281
 changing incentives for research,
  298–299
 and checks/balances system for
  individual researchers,
  297–298
 collaboration, 284
 conducting research in context,
  295–296
 current disagreement over, 289–291
 for journal editors, 284–285
 and quality vs. quantity of research
  studies, 283–284
 reliability/validity in, 283
 and science as filter in psychology,
  299–301
 in study design, 293–295
 in theory choice and problem finding,
  291–293
 understanding as purpose of research,
  281–282
 unintended consequences of, 5–6
 in writing and citing processes,
  296–297
Research synthesis. *See also* meta-analysis
 benefits of, 256–257
 defined, 256
 types of, 257–259
Research waste, 216

Resolution elements (resels), 179
Resources, for research–practice
    partnerships, 168
Rest, functional neuroimaging studies
    during, 174
Resubmissions, 128
Results reporting, in journal articles,
    219–220
Retractions, 201, 202, 219, 290, 292
Reviewers
    authors as, 123
    biases of, 121
    citation recommendations for,
        108–109
    of HERC's research, 159–160
    inappropriate requests from, 296
    ORB reduction recommendations
        for, 80, 88
    in PARKing model, 295
    in peer review process, 126–127
    suggesting, in cover letters, 125–126
Reviews. *See also* Peer review process
    empty, 260
    harsh, 127–128
    narrative, 257–258
    postpublication, 121–122
    qualitative narrative, 257–258
    systematic, 87, 258–260
Revisions, 128, 141
Reward structures, in research–practice
    partnerships, 167–168
RFT (random field theory), 179
Rigor
    adversarial collaborations to
        improve, 298
    of CCSR studies, 157–158
    of confirmatory studies, 61–64
    defined, 61
    and directed acyclic graphs, 71
    procedural vs. technical, 74–75
Risk factors, 192
Ritz, Glenda, 161–163
Robust approach to data analysis, 66–67
Robustness, of findings, 234, 256
Roderick, M., 154–155, 157, 158
Roediger, H. L., 126–127
Rosenthal, R., 85, 237, 243, 244

Safeguard power analysis, 38
Sagan, Carl, 134, 135

Sameness, in replication, 238
Samples, online, 42–45
Sample size
    in cognitive neuroscience research,
        177–178
    and effect size estimation, 37
    of online samples, 43–44
    and power analysis, 38–39
    prespecification of, 248
    for replications, 278
    in sequential analyses, 41
Sampling error. *See* Type I error
Scale reliability, 39
Schedule, writing, 142–143
Schmidt, S., 241, 263
Schneider, B., 156
Schneider, M., 91
Scholarly societies, 146
Scholarship, dissemination and, 134–135,
    141
Schönbrodt, F. D., 37
School choice, 163
Schubert, A., 99
Schwarzenegger, Arnold, 142
Science
    core norms of, 223
    cumulative, 13, 19–21
    discovery–justification distinction
        in, 14–15
    as filter in psychology, 299–301
    as framework for clinical psychology,
        188–192
    HARKing in practice of, 279
    normal, 17–18, 280
    in psychology field, 188, 299–301
    self-correcting mechanisms in, 292
    social practice of, 245–246
Science (journal), 275
Scientific Data, 223, 228
Scientific innovation, 13–27
    cumulative science for, 19–20
    and discovery–justification
        distinction, 14–17
    improving psychological science
        with, 27
    problem finding for, 23–27
    promoting research quality and, 17
    theory choice for, 17–23
Scope, of theories, 19
Sebring, P. B., 154–155

Study design for maximum informational value, 33–51
    exploratory vs. confirmatory research in, 45–49
    online samples in, 42–45
    power in, 34–42
    replication as consideration in, 49–51
Subgroup analyses, in IPD meta-analysis, 265
Submission to journals, 124–125, 146–147
Suciu, S., 265
Synthesis research. *See* Research synthesis
Systematic replications, 49–50, 220
Systematic research, 140–141, 158
Systematic reviews, 87, 258–260

Table 2 fallacy, 69
Tanner-Smith, E., 260–261
Tannock, I. F., 81
Technical rigor, 74
10-year rule, 24
Tenopir, C., 102
Theory(-ies)
    bad, 22–23
    defined, 18
    disconfirming, 22
    evaluation of, 20–23
    good, 17–22, 26–27
    hypothesis selection based on, 282
    interesting, 247–248
    undead, 23, 85, 291–292
Theory choice
    criteria for, 19
    evaluation of theories after, 20–23
    paradigms in, 17–18
    research quality improvement strategies for, 291–293
    for scientific innovation, 17–23
Theory weakness, 291
Thomas, Lewis, 134
Thresholds, cognitive neuroscience, 180
Time, for dissemination efforts, 134–135
Timelines, in research–practice partnerships, 167–168
"Toothbrush problem," 19
Traditional peer review process
    improving, 120–121

new vs., 128–129
    value of, 121–124
Training
    in clinical psychology, 188–190, 193–194
    clinical science model of, 194
    integration of applied work and research in, 188, 193–194
    in philosophy of science, 189, 190
    on research methods and data analysis, 63
    for writing, 142
Trainor, B. P., 84, 85
Translational research, 192–194
Transparency, 80
Triage decisions, in peer review system, 122–123
Trust, 102, 162–164
Truth, 282
t tests, 66–67
Twain, Mark, 296
Tweedie, R., 91
"Twelve Tips for Reviewers" (Roediger), 126–127
Two-stage approach to IPD meta-analysis, 265
Type I errors
    in adaptive design, 37–38
    controlling for, in replications, 239
    and recording of analysis plans, 46
    in sequential analyses, 41
    and statistical power, 34, 35
Type II errors, 34

Unconventional claims, 247–248
Undead theories, 23, 85, 291–292
Understanding, as purpose of research, 281–282
Unexpected results, 75
Uniformity of nature, principle of, 236
Universal laws, 25
University-based partnerships, 163, 167–168
University of Chicago Urban Education Institute, 156
University of Michigan, 89
University of Notre Dame, 161, 163
Unknown authors, 102
U.S. Constitution, 3
U.S. Department of Education, 154

Vaccinations, autism and, 201, 300
Valentine, J. C., 83
Validity, 283
    construct, 190
    external, 191. *See also* Generalizability
    internal, 191, 239–240
    statistical conclusion, 190–191
    threats to, 62
Van der Maas, H. L. J., 90
Van Noorden, R., 108
Variables. *See also* Covariates
    collider, 70
    confounding, 65–66, 68–69, 73
    context, 239
    control, 68, 70, 176–177
    dependent, 242
    nonsignificant, 66
    and omitted-variable bias, 70
Vedula, S. S., 85, 86
Verification
    and publication, 222
    requesting data for, 217–218
    secondary analyses vs., 224–225
    sharing data for, 220–221
Vohra, N., 101, 104
Voxels, 178–180

Wagenmakers, E.-J., 90
WEIRD (Western, Educated, Industrialized, Rich, and Democratic) study populations, 292–293
Welch's *t* tests, 66–67

Wetzels, R., 90
What Works Clearinghouse (WWC), 89, 154, 299
Whitehurst, Grover, 155
"Why Most Published Research Findings Are False" (Ioannidis), 4
Wicherts, J. M., 84–85, 223
Williams, R. T., 83
Williamson, P., 86–87, 91
Wilson, S. J., 260–261
Within-subject designs, 39
Women, citations of men vs., 102–103
Writing
    for dissemination to academic scholars, 141–143
    opportunity costs of, 145
    procrastination-by-, 144
    research quality improvement strategies in, 296–297
    training for, 142
WWC. *See* What Works Clearinghouse

Xhignesse, L. V., 104

Young, J. W., 283
Yow, W. Q., 278

Zeigarnik, Bela, 137
Zeigarnik effect, 137
Zombie research practices, 292
Zombie theories. *See* Undead theories
z scores, 244

ABOUT THE EDITORS

Matthew C. Makel, PhD, is the director of research for the Duke University Talent Identification Program. He received his master's in developmental psychology from Cornell University and his doctorate in educational psychology from Indiana University. His content-specific research focuses on how to identify academically talented students and how they experience the world. His methodological work explores the replicability of social science research findings. Dr. Makel also translates research findings into language that is both understandable and actionable for nonresearchers and has won multiple awards for Excellence in Research from the MENSA Foundation.

Jonathan A. Plucker, PhD, is the Julian C. Stanley Professor of Talent Development at Johns Hopkins University. He received his PhD in educational psychology from the University of Virginia. His research examines education policy and talent development, with over 200 publications to his credit. His books include *Exceptional Gaps in Education: Expanding Opportunities for Talented Students* with Scott Peters, *Critical Issues and Practices in Gifted Education: What the Research Says* with Carolyn Callahan, and *Intelligence 101* with Amber Esping. Dr. Plucker has worked on projects involving educators, schools, and students in all 50 states and several countries. He is a fellow of the American Psychological Association (APA) and American Association for the Advancement of Science. He is the recipient of the APA Arnheim Award for Outstanding Achievement and the Distinguished Scholar Award from the National Association for Gifted Children.